Please remember that this is a library book,
and that it belongs only temporarily to each
person who uses it. Be considerate. Do
not write in this, or any, library book.

LIKE PEOPLE YOU SEE IN A DREAM

Like People You See in a Dream

FIRST CONTACT IN SIX PAPUAN SOCIETIES

EDWARD L. SCHIEFFELIN AND

ROBERT CRITTENDEN

with contributions by Bryant Allen and Stephen Frankel,

Paul Sillitoe, Lisette Josephides and Marc Schiltz

Stanford University Press, Stanford, California

Stanford University Press,
Stanford, California
© 1991 by the Board of Trustees of the
Leland Stanford Junior University
Printed in the United States of America

CIP data appear at the end of the book

The leaf ornament is from
the sweet potato (*Ipomoea batatas*)
widely cultivated in Papua New Guinea.

TO VIRGINIA SCHIEFFELIN

AND THE MEMORY OF BAYARD SCHIEFFELIN

AND TO JANIS BAINES AND

JAMIE AND RACHEL CRITTENDEN

PREFACE

The idea for this book came to us one afternoon in 1984 while we were drinking beer on the veranda of Crittenden's house overlooking the Mendi Valley in the New Guinea highlands. We were discussing stories our Papuan friends had told us about the early years of European contact and pondering the ways in which the experience had affected them. Although the people we had each worked with lived in ecologically contrasting regions considerably distant from one another (Crittenden in the Nembi Valley, Schieffelin on the Papuan Plateau) and although their ways of life were culturally quite distinct, they had both experienced their first contact with Europeans from the same exploratory expedition: the ill-fated Strickland-Purari patrol of 1935. We ourselves had become interested in Papua New Guinea partly through reading the account of this expedition in a book written by one of the two Australian patrol officers who had led it, a man named Jack Hides. Hides's chronicle of his experience in uncontacted country intrigued that sense of curiosity and adventure—and the desire to visit outlandish places—that lies in the hearts of most ethnographers and that is part of both the allure of fieldwork and the motivation to understand another people's ways of life.

Now, some 50 years later, with a great deal of ethnographic work on the southern highlands available, we saw the opportunity to put together another account of the expedition, one that would incorporate the experience of the Papuan people whom the patrol encountered. We would then have a basis for understanding why things happened as they did—and perhaps gain some perspective on the perceptual and cosmological impact that these cultural first encounters had on these Papuans' views of

themselves, of outsiders, and of subsequent history. In the process, we surmised, we might gain some general insight into the politics and sociology
of the early period of contact.

Initially, we planned this book as a series of papers, each to be written independently by an ethnographer who had worked with one of the
groups of people who lived along each segment of the patrol route. All of
the ethnographers we approached responded enthusiastically, and through
a remarkable stroke of luck all were able to return to their field sites to
collect additional ethnographic and historical material especially for this
book.

As the papers arrived, however, it became apparent that the format
we had planned would not work. Although the pieces individually were
all fine accounts of first contact, what was missing was a sense of the
accumulation of experience as the patrol proceeded: of how the people
encountered during the later stages of the journey were affected by the experience the patrol had had with the people it had met at an earlier stage.
Likewise, certain decisions of the patrol officers, seemingly unimportant
at the time they were made, turned out to have serious consequences in the
weeks that followed. We felt that to do justice to the material, there was
no alternative but to rework the book into a series of chapters wherein the
day-by-day account of the patrol formed the central thread of the narrative
and whereby the effects of the changing situation of the expedition on the
nature of each new situation of contact could be clearly perceived.

Bringing the different contributors' particular issues, points of view,
styles of writing, and modes of presentation into alignment while elimi-
nating repetitions and sorting out inconsistencies between their accounts,
was no easy task. But we seem to have managed it—and kept everyone
on speaking terms. The result is, we believe, that a great deal has been
gained in the understanding of first contact as a cross-historical as well as
a cross-cultural encounter.

It is in the nature of field research that ethnographers become emotionally involved with the people they study, become their advocates, and
establish a certain moral solidarity with them. All of our first drafts contained overtones of outrage at the way "our people" had been handled in
the encounter, compassion for their injuries, and indignation at the patrol.
But as these sentiments accumulated from one chapter to the next and
their underlying romantic advocacy became apparent, we came to realize that they were more embarrassing than ennobling. At the same time
we found ourselves caught up in the excitement of discovery and admiration for the courage and humanity of the patrol officers and saw that
this tendency toward romanticism too bore watching. We have attempted
to restore a balance, but inevitably—and we think justifiably—a certain

admiration and sympathy for both the "discoverers" and the "discovered" comes through.

A number of people were helpful in reading part or all of this manuscript and in offering comments and suggestions. We would like especially to mention Bruce Knauft, Zachary Schieffelin, Deborah Gewertz, Barbara Powell, Steven Feld, Ray Kelly, Arjun Appadurai, Don Donham, Marilyn Strathern, Bradd Shore, Rena Lederman, Roy Wagner, Meg Sibley, Nancy Baxter, Hank Nelson, Amirah Inglis, Jeff Clark, and Janis Baines.

Financial support for parts of our efforts on this book was granted by the National Endowment for the Humanities, the National Science Foundation, the Wenner Gren Foundation, the American Philosophical Society, the Southern Highlands Rural Development Project, the University of Papua New Guinea, and the University of New England. We are grateful to them all. Staff of the National Archives of Papua New Guinea, in Port Moresby, and of the Commonwealth Archives, in Canberra, and the librarians of the New Guinea Collections at the University of Papua New Guinea and the National Library in Port Moresby helped us locate patrol reports and other government papers. Staff at the Mitchell Library in Sydney, especially Leanne Collins, Curator of the photographic collection, helped considerably in locating material relating to the Strickland-Purari patrol and Papua in the 1920's and 1930's. We would like to thank them all.

The maps in this book were drawn by Robert Crittenden and prepared for publication by Steve Clarke and Mike Roach of the Cartographic Unit in the Department of Geography and Planning at the University of New England and Australasian Cartographics Ltd.

Finally, we would like to thank James Sinclair for supplying us with important primary materials for our project.

E.L.S.
R.C.

CONTENTS

1. Colonial Papua and the Tradition of Exploration   13
Edward L. Schieffelin and Robert Crittenden

The social, historical, and political background of Australian colonial society in Papua to the mid-1930's. The development and values of the Papuan Service. The history of exploration in Papua and the origins of the Strickland-Purari patrol.

2. The Strickland-Purari Patrol: Starting Out   44
Edward L. Schieffelin and Robert Crittenden

Sketch of patrol officers Jack Hides and Jim O'Malley. Organization of the patrol. The expedition moves up the Fly and Strickland rivers by steam launch and then dugout canoe. After 650 km the patrol reaches the limits of navigation on the Rentoul River in unexplored country.

3. The Great Papuan Plateau   58
Edward L. Schieffelin

The culture of three plateau peoples—the Bosavi, the Etoro, and the Onabasulu—and their historical situation in 1935. The patrol destroys its canoes and proceeds across the northern portion of the Papuan Plateau on foot. They encounter the

Etoro and Onabasulu people. Caught in a dangerous situation, Hides makes a decision that has fateful consequences. The expedition moves toward the highland rim through difficult limestone country. Discipline among police and carriers is shaky.

Photo sections follow pp. 124, 146, and 224

MAPS

CONTRIBUTORS

EDWARD L. SCHIEFFELIN received his B.A. from Yale University in physics and philosophy and his M.A. and Ph.D. from the University of Chicago in anthropology. He has conducted field research in the Southern Highlands Province of Papua New Guinea since the late 1960's and has published extensively on the Kaluli people of the Mt. Bosavi region and other topics. He has taught at Fordham University, the University of Pennsylvania, and Emory University. He is currently lecturer at University College, London.

ROBERT CRITTENDEN carried out fieldwork in West Africa, Papua New Guinea, and Australia's Northern Territory. He has an M.A. from Oxford University in geography and an M.Sc. in agricultural economics from London University. Following fieldwork on the Nembi Plateau in the Southern Highlands Province of Papua New Guinea, he was awarded a Ph.D. in geography from the Australian National University in 1982. From 1982 to 1987 he lived in the Southern Highlands Province, employed by the Papua New Guinea government in the Department of Finance and Planning. He now teaches transport planning in the Department of Geography and Planning in the University of New England, Armidale, Australia.

BRYANT ALLEN has conducted research in Papua New Guinea since 1971 and has carried out extensive fieldwork in Tari since 1978. He has an M.A. from Massey University in New Zealand and a Ph.D. in geography from the Australian National University. He has taught at the University of Papua New Guinea and at the Australian National University, where he is currently Senior Research Fellow in the Department of Human Geography. In 1985 he was a Senior Fellow at the Institute of Applied Social and Economic Research in Papua New Guinea.

STEPHEN FRANKEL qualified as a medical practitioner in 1969 and spent a number of years as a health officer in Papua New Guinea. He completed a Ph.D. in anthropology (studying the medical system of the Huli people of the Southern Highlands) in 1981 at Cambridge University. He was awarded a Doctor of Medicine (DM) from Oxford University in 1983 and has continued extensive research in Papua New Guinea. Since 1985 he has been Senior Lecturer in the Department of Epidemiology and Community Medicine in the University of Wales College of Medicine at Cardiff.

LISETTE JOSEPHIDES has carried out fieldwork in the Kagua region of the Southern Highlands Province since 1979. She has a B.A. in philosophy and a Diploma in anthropology from London University. She was awarded a Ph.D. from London in 1981. She has taught at the universities of London and Papua New Guinea and is currently a Research Associate in the Department of Anthropology at the London School of Economics and Political Science.

MARC SCHILTZ has a Diploma and Ph.D. in anthropology from the University of London. He has carried out fieldwork with the Yoruba in Nigeria and the Kewa in Papua New Guinea. He has taught at the universities of London and Papua New Guinea and is currently teaching at Kings College, London.

PAUL SILLITOE, a graduate of the University of Manchester, started research in the Wola region of the Southern Highlands Province of Papua New Guinea in the early 1970's and was awarded a Ph.D. from Cambridge University in social anthropology in 1975. He has since worked and published extensively on the Wola. He has taught at the University of Melbourne and is currently a lecturer in the Department of Anthropology in Durham University.

ABBREVIATIONS

IQ   W. R. Humphries. 1935. Enquiry held at the request of Mr. J. G. Hides, ARM, into the circumstances surrounding the shooting of certain natives on the Tari Furoro and Waga Furari Plateaux during the Strickland-Purari patrol (with letter to Lieutenant Governor Murray and letter from Murray to the Minister for Territories, Canberra). Australian Archives, Canberra, CA 822. Territories, Prime Minister Dept. 1928–41. Correspondence files multi-number series 1928–56, Patrols and Patrol Reports PNG, 1935–37.

PR   J. G. Hides and J. O'Malley. 1935. The Strickland-Purari Patrol Report, 1934–35 and associated material. Typescripts. Commonwealth Archives, Canberra, Series A510 Item B251/3/1 pt. 2, Series C708-1 Item No. 5, and CSR A518 Item C251/3/1.

PW   J. G. Hides. 1936. *Papuan Wonderland*. London: Blackie and Son.

The abbreviation PR is used in text citations of other patrol reports, in the form "Kikori PR 13, 1921–22." For a listing of patrol reports cited, see the section "Patrol Reports and Annual Reports," pp. 307–8 of the References.

LIKE PEOPLE YOU SEE IN A DREAM

INTRODUCTION

EDWARD L. SCHIEFFELIN

The fundamental theme of this book is the encounter with the Other. The focus, however, is not so much the significance and meaning of such encounters for human life and thought (a subject that has stood in the background of a good deal of European social and political thinking already), but rather a more preliminary question: how do we understand the structure and process of the encounter itself? What is the nature of the experience of initial contact between peoples of utterly different worlds, and how do factors of social structure, cultural perception, and historical contingency affect it? How, in turn, does this experience affect the subsequent perceptions, relations, and actions of the people involved? We approach the subject by an ethnographic and ethnohistorical examination of a particular set of historically recent encounters between people of the Anglo-European tradition and the tribal peoples of the interior of New Guinea.

The exploration of the island of New Guinea came at the very end of the era of European world expansion—a movement that had begun in 1488 when the caravels of Bartholomeu Diaz rounded the Cape of Good Hope. As European seafarers, adventurers, and commercial and colonial enterprisers moved outwards around the world, their encounters with other peoples and civilizations deeply stimulated the European imagination (as well as filling its pocketbooks), challenging contemporary ideas about the nature of society and the possibilities of humankind. Debates about the nature and meaning of other ways of life contributed to a broadening of philosophical horizons in European social and political thought virtually to the eve of the Industrial Revolution. This was accompanied by a burgeoning of great wealth and a growing sense of superiority in the European nations as they gradually gained political dominion over much of the rest of the world. This period reached its culmination with the establishment of the British Empire, symbolized principally by the Raj in India and its many lesser imitations in other places—of which the Australian colonial community in Papua was one.

By the beginning of the twentieth century, however, the days of European expansion were drawing to a close. Few regions of the earth remained unknown to the West, and during the waning years of empire building, the process of exploration itself became a subject of romantic nostalgia and the literature of adventure. By 1935 the interior of the island of New Guinea—protected from penetration over the centuries by rugged and mountainous terrain, unruly rivers, and the bellicosity of its inhabitants—remained one of the few places outsiders had never seen. It was in Papua and the more northerly located Mandated Territory of New Guinea that the last major discoveries of peoples previously unknown to the outside world were made in this century.

This book focuses on one of the last modern-day experiences of first culture contact. The Strickland-Purari patrol was also one of the final great expeditions of tropical exploration in the Pacific. It was organized and dispatched by the Papuan colonial administration in 1935 to examine the vast, remote tract of unknown country between the Strickland and Purari rivers, now known as the Southern Highlands (see Map 2). Headed by two Australian patrol officers, Jack Hides and Jim O'Malley, the party consisted of 40 Papuan carriers and police. The expedition left Daru on the Gulf of Papua on January 1, 1935, and headed inland up the Fly and Strickland rivers by steam launch and canoe. Reaching the limits of navigation 650 km inland in the middle of February, they abandoned the canoes and proceeded on eastward through the tropical forest on foot. Some weeks later, crossing a remote mountain barrier, they emerged into the grassland valleys of the Papuan highlands. There they encountered a large and hitherto unsuspected population—peoples who had never seen Europeans before and who were still using a technology of stone. The first groups they encountered received them warily. As the patrol proceeded southeastward along the Waga Valley and the Nembi Plateau, the local people became increasingly unfriendly. The patrol ran out of supplies near the site of present-day Nipa, and the locals refused to sell them food. Shortly thereafter patrol officer Hides became seriously ill. Hungry and increasingly beleaguered by aggressive warriors, the expedition eventually had to resort to rifle fire to force its way through to the Erave River and the Samberigi Valley in order to get back to the Papuan coast. Following a native trade route, they emerged, exhausted and starving, at the government station at Kikori on June 18, 1935.

During the journey the patrol suffered tremendous hardship. Forced to fight for their survival, Hides and O'Malley reported that they and their police killed at least 32 men in skirmishes along the way. The patrol itself lost two carriers and a policeman to sickness and starvation. In the four months since they had left the Strickland, they had passed through more than 1,800 km of country unknown to Europeans and discovered extensive populations whose cultures were quite different from those of the peoples hitherto known in Papua.

Cultural First Encounters

Stories of the first encounters between Europeans and the indigenous peoples of Papua New Guinea have always had a particular fascination for both Europeans and Papua New Guineans alike. To the Western popular imagination these accounts are contained in stories of exploratory expeditions moving into unknown regions beyond the borders of "civilization." The explorers, after suffering hardship and danger, come upon hidden valleys which hold promise of containing valuable resources, and are populated by exotic peoples who have never seen Europeans before.

To the indigenous people of Papua, on the other hand, the arrival of the first outsiders is usually recalled as an exciting but deeply unsettling event of apparently cosmological import: Strange Beings broke into their world from outside its known horizons. Sometimes these Beings were thought to be mythical heroes coming back to the lands of their origin; sometimes they were thought to be the ancestral dead returning (Connolly and Anderson 1983; Wagner 1979a). The people were filled with astonishment, fear, and wonder at these creatures and sometimes feared that their arrival was the portent of dire world upheaval.

Part of the fascination of these encounters derives from their special nature. These were encounters not between individuals, but between cultural systems—embodied in culturally organized groups of people: first contact in Papua was always a matter of comparatively large, complexly structured expeditions encountering organized communities of people living in their normal region. This is a very different situation from that in which a single outsider (a shipwrecked sailor, for example) arrives in a place where people have never seen his kind before. In that case, regardless of what cultural wisdom he can bring to bear on the situation, to the local inhabitants he is merely an anomaly who acts in the capacity of an individual. He has no context to mediate his situation except that in which they place him. An expedition, on the other hand, brings along its own cultural context, embodied in its purposes and internal organization, and it is this that comes to bear on the encounter. The group provides a reference point and support system for its members and has a much greater

capacity to carry out its purposes in the face of opposition. Here, it is a
community which confronts a community.

These encounters, however dramatic, were in turn the outcome of particular historical conditions. The exploratory journeys of Australian patrol
officers into the interior of Papua during the 1920's and 1930's were motivated by the desire to locate undiscovered natural resources (such as gold
or petroleum), to open new regions to the sphere of Western political and
economic influence, and to bring Western civilization and the rule of law
to people generally regarded at the time as primitive savages. The cultural-
historical situations of the Papuan peoples they encountered varied according to the nature of their particular cultures and their local social and
political circumstances. Although many Papuans regarded the first patrols
as coming from outside the human realm, what they thought the encounter
meant and how they reacted to it was also conditioned by local alliances
and animosities as well as their general social and political state of affairs
at the time.

Thus, when Australians and Papuans met for the first time, their worlds
in effect did not, for they represented two very different cultural and historical contexts. Even the quality of Otherness each sensed in the other
was different. In a sense, each of these encounters represented two different events. It is remarkable that anthropologists, who have experienced
analogous situations in their own fieldwork and have devoted their careers
to the study of the Other, have rarely examined the situation of first contact. Yet this represents a particular—and inherently interesting—moment
of encounter.

Cultural first encounters may be said to have at least three significant
dimensions. The first is an existential one—the raw shock of Otherness—
a dimension of experience that is present to some extent in all encounters
with other people (Sartre 1966) but is especially poignant in first contact
situations. Here one is confronted with the paradoxical familiarity of the
alien: a being who appears human but is at the same time so radically
unfamiliar that one is thrown into doubt—or senses that the ordinary
categories for understanding human behavior may be inadequate to the
task of grasping the nature of this one. Such an encounter throws one's
own conception of humanity and hence of oneself into question. The full
impact of the experience is usually short-lived, since cultural categories
are quickly martialed to rationalize it, but in it we momentarily glimpse
the epistemological edges of our own social understanding, leaving us in
dread and fascination.*

* The impact of this experience is visible in the splendid photographs taken by Mick
Leahy of first encounters with men near the Wahgi Valley in 1933 (published in Connolly
and Anderson 1987).

The dread of the epistemological edge is made more poignant and problematic when it is accompanied by an awareness of inferiority and threat. We suggest that this dimension of first contact was less problematic for European explorers in Papua than for the Papuans they encountered, because Europeans were used to meeting new people and almost always had the upper hand over them both in armament and in the element of surprise. In addition, they had a well-prepared category—"natives"—in which to place those people they met for the first time, a category of social subordination that served to dissipate their depth of otherness. Such was not the case for Papuans. European explorers often appeared to them as a complete surprise—for whom they had no easy categories, who they sensed were immensely powerful and suspected were probably supernatural. For them, the confrontation with radical otherness was much more problematic, and their confusion and astonishment were often a source for European smugness and amusement. The Strickland-Purari patrol was unusual, as we will see, in that for the Europeans involved the radical otherness of the Papuans they encountered became a problematic issue.

The second dimension of cultural first encounters is social-cultural. The encounter is always shaped by the local social and political structures and framed in prevailing cultural values, categories, and understandings. The issues here are familiar territory for anthropologists. The first and simplest questions—what did each party to the encounter think was happening, and why did they react in the way that they did?—lead directly to deeper issues of cultural categories and social organization: the relatively stable system of values, beliefs, and modes of understanding through which human beings live their lives, and the structure of social and political relationships which these values shape and serve. How then were both of these mobilized in the particular encounter?

Finally, there is the historical dimension, which raises issues of contingency: how particular accidents of circumstance, structures of relationship, particular individual personalities, and differing agendas are involved in shaping a set of events at a particular time.

Cultural first encounters can best be understood by bringing these historical and ethnographic aspects of the experience together. For our present purposes, this is more than a matter of understanding the experiences of the Australians and Papuans in the events of encounter or of specifying the cultural orientation and particular circumstances that each party brought to the encounter. It was the complex interaction between differing cultural perceptions and alien historical contexts from the points of view of differently positioned people that made the events what they were. The concern here is with the process by which two peoples from radically different situations came to terms with each other, responding to each other's moves without knowing for sure what the other was thinking, intended to do, or was trying to say. Human Otherness is never Wholly Other; it always is a product of social, cultural and historical conditions (as well as common humanity) and conditioned by the structure of the encounter itself. It is through this level of ethnohistorical integration standing above the encounter itself that we will try to approach the structure of situations met in this book.

The Strickland-Purari patrol provides an interesting case for the study of first contact for a number of reasons. First, it passed through at least six different groups—the Etoro and Onabasulu peoples of the Papuan Plateau and the Huli, Wola, Nembi, and Kewa of the Papuan Highlands. The diverse cultural vantage points of each and their different particular sociohistorical circumstances affected how the patrol was received and treated. Second, despite an extensive amount of documentation and contemporary press coverage, the patrol still raises a number of intriguing questions of ethnographic, historical, and geographic interest more than 50 years after its completion. It was unusual for Papuan people to attack exploratory patrols on first contact, particularly patrols led by experienced officers. Yet Hides and O'Malley had to virtually fight their way through the countryside, making their journey one of the bloodiest in Papuan colonial history. Were the people they encountered unusually fierce? Did these experienced officers mishandle their relations with them? Or was there some other tragic ethnographic misunderstanding as yet unexplained?

Third, where exactly did the patrol go? Neither Hides nor O'Malley had any training in surveying and cartography, and after the patrol was completed, neither of them was able to say exactly where they had been. Fourth, despite excellent accounts given in the official reports and in Hides's own book, we still have less than half the story. Little has been known about the identities, cultures, and sociohistorical circumstances of the groups Hides and O'Malley encountered as they were in 1935, let alone what they thought the encounter meant, or what their reasons were for responding to it as they did.

Until recently there was no way to answer most of these questions. However, in the last few years a number of anthropologists and human geographers have engaged in ethnographic research among the peoples along Hides and O'Malley's route. It is now possible to speak with some confidence about the economic, ethnographic, and sociohistorical circumstances of these cultures at the time of first contact, and to reconstruct people's experience of that meeting and its aftermath on the basis of what those who were there can still remember.

The Papuan experience, however, is not the only untold part of this story. Hides and O'Malley were themselves heirs to the cultural and historical traditions of Australian colonial society in Papua of the 1920's and 1930's and, in a larger sense, to the British Empire of which it was a small reflection. If we are to fully understand the character of these men and why they conducted the patrol in the way that they did, we need to know more about the nature of colonial society in Papua and of the particular social and historical circumstances from which it arose. In this way, we may get some insight into the unspoken values and traditions that lay behind such exploratory expeditions as this and the attitudes that the patrol officers brought with them towards the Papuan people that they met.

Finally, we are concerned with the lasting effects of the encounter on the participants involved and their cultures, how it altered their perceptions of themselves and their worlds, how it foreshadowed or set the stage and direction for their relationships and interactions with each other for the future.

Methods and Voices

The story in this book is told in many voices, some loud, some small, some clear, some indistinct, others overlapping or repeated by others who overheard them. Jack Hides speaks through his patrol report and his book and through letters quoted by his biographer, James Sinclair. Patrol carriers and police speak through their depositions at the official inquiry that followed the patrol. The Papuan people who remember the patrol speak through the ethnographers who sought them out. The ethnographers themselves have a great deal to say about the context and historical conditions of (and from) which their informants speak. Finally, an editorial voice emerges in the overall way in which the book unfolds its account by weaving this material into the chapters of a story rather than a series of academic papers.

The sources closest to the events are government documents, principally the official patrol report of the Strickland-Purari patrol (a typescript written by Jack Hides and dated July 22, 1935) and the report of the inquiry held over the deaths caused by the patrol. Hides's report was written from a daily patrol diary he kept during the expedition, but which was privately held and not available to us. Other information about Hides himself is taken from his books and his biography. A voice conspicuously missing from this account is that of Hides's second in command, Jim O'Malley. We do not know if O'Malley kept a diary of his own, and we have only a few of his remarks reported by Hides himself, his testimony at the inquiry, and the transcript of an interview with James Sinclair. As a consequence,

O'Malley's figure appears rather in the background of this story, and his role in the expedition is much more muted than was probably actually the case.

Hides's book about the expedition, entitled *Papuan Wonderland*, was published in 1936. It was written directly from his patrol report but contains interesting changes, expansions, and deletions that reveal aspects of Hides's personality and his perspective on the expedition that was the central achievement of his life. Other important documents providing context for the expedition include the patrol reports of government officers who were first into the newly discovered regions after Hides and O'Malley, numerous secondary sources of history of colonial Papua during the 1930's, and the biographies and writings of its principal figures.

Our sources on the perspectives of the carriers and police are severely limited. All we have are their words as quoted by Hides in his patrol report (and book) and their words as recorded in the transcript of the government inquiry into the conduct of the patrol. Of this material, the most available (and revealing) information comes from the police, since Hides valued their opinion and recorded their remarks fairly frequently in his writings. The patrol carriers, however, aside from their depositions at the inquiry, are virtually mute. Hides had affection for his carriers but did not take their thoughts very seriously. His descriptions of their actions and quotations of their words portray them mainly as faithful servants, irksome troublemakers, and occasionally comic relief—all closely following colonial stereotypes. The only fairly full account from a carrier we were able to obtain, a narrative tape recorded in 1960, is given in Appendix B. Finally, it would have been nice to have a stronger representation from the voices of Papuan women; those we do have add much to the story.

The contributors to this book, who give the ethnographic and ethnohistorical background for the Papuan peoples encountered by the Strickland-Purari patrol, are all veterans of two to five years of field research among the people of whom they write. They collected their accounts in a variety of ways and from a variety of sources, and an account of this is given in the notes to the chapters. Not all of the events described in the patrol report could be equally well documented from informants' accounts. In some places, informants could not remember the events clearly or accurately after 50 years,* and sometimes there were no informants left at all. At other times, informants provided considerable information, including important material not recorded in the patrol report. In the course of

---

*One of the most common problems here was the tendency of informants to combine in memory two or more separate events. Typically, they would confuse or even combine events of the earliest patrol with those of a later patrol. What is, in effect, a case study of this process appears in Appendix A.

writing, most of us came across important places in the story where informant accounts were not available (or, in our judgment, not reliable), and
we have had to make ethnographically informed speculations as to what
happened; such places are duly noted in the text.

In this context it is worth discussing briefly some of the general problems of gathering ethnographic materials which have affected the making
of this book. It has long been acknowledged in anthropology that the
preferred ethnographic interview is one undertaken by a trained ethnographer fluent in the vernacular of the people he or she is investigating. For
numerous practical reasons, this exacting standard has not always been
achieved in our discipline. What must be acknowledged, however, is that
other methods also work very well. In this book some contributors used
the local vernacular; some used *tok pisin*, the widely understood "lingua
franca" of the New Guinea highlands to converse with their informants.
Interpreters were also used in some cases. Although this method may miss
some symbolic nuances provided by vernacular fluency, a well-practiced
and sensitive ethnographer/interpreter team can do very well with collecting descriptive information in an ethnographic context with which they
are both familiar.

Few of the writers in this book heard of people's experience with the
Strickland-Purari patrol from stories told spontaneously by informants in
everyday settings. Some had worked for a considerable time among their
groups before they learned the patrol had passed through the area. "Why
did you never tell us this story before?" Josephides and Schiltz asked their
Kewa informants. "You never asked," was the response. As a matter of
fact, it is our impression that stories of the patrol were not often told by
the people amongst themselves and were not particularly well known to
the younger generation.* Most of what informants have to say in this book
was gathered through interviews initiated by the ethnographer's request
for information. Given informants' enthusiasm for telling these stories
once they were requested, however, it seems unlikely they were being
deliberately withheld. Once started off, especially if there was an apprecia-
tive local audience, old men frequently told their stories in detail and with
dramatic style. The presence of a local village audience overcomes to some
degree the disadvantages of the formal interview situation because the informant tells his story to his own people naturally and in a way relevant
to their own interests and understandings of the events. Afterwards, the
performance serves as the basis for the ethnographer's further questions
(see Chapter 4) concerning facts and issues on his own agenda. The result

* The reasons for this are bound up with the way the people of the Southern Highlands
socially construct and distribute their historical knowledge, which is discussed in Chapter 11.

is a combined, annotated account that is as faithful as possible to Papuan categories while not opaque to Western understanding.

Informants have a great deal to say in this book, and their statements are frequently quoted. Ideally their stories would be taken from translated transcripts of tape-recorded interviews. This, however, as every fieldworker knows, is not always possible. Probably most "quotations" of informant's words in the literature of our discipline are taken from the somewhat paraphrased and abbreviated versions of their statements that anthropologists write down in their field notes. Moreover, even tape recorders do not always prove useful. As Paul Sillitoe points out in Chapter 6, when an informant gives a long, rambling, repetitious account that requires considerable cross-examination to clarify and a lot of editing to present coherently, then what emerges on the page may be a good statement of his meaning, but is hardly a quotation of his words. In the end, it is the ethnographer who constructs the literary/ethnographic context and presents the informants' words, not the informants who define their own context and speak entirely for themselves.

This situation does not necessarily represent an ethnographic failing. On the contrary, the agenda of disciplined ethnography is to describe the structure and clarify the meaning of one way of life (or cultural-historical situation) to readers from another. What informants say, if it is to be fully understood, inherently requires delineation of the symbolic concepts, historical background, and social context out of which it arises, and this is increasingly a collaborative effort between informants themselves and interested outsiders who wish to understand their lives. At the same time, we bear at least some responsibility to canons of historical accuracy, which require fieldworkers to evaluate as best they can the quality of what they are told. Informants, like everyone else, sometimes have poor memories, tell lies, or glorify the past (or their part in it), and a few present their stories framed in cultural ideas and images that differ from those we accept in the West. They also tell the unadorned truth. But it would be self-deception for an ethnographer to accept everything he is told completely at face value, or for an informant to think that a statement that seems perfectly straightforward to himself will make equally good sense to someone unfamiliar with his way of life. Ethnography is inherently of the nature of annotated translation and interpretation; there may be objective materials, but there are no objective facts.

This story contains many ironies—within itself and by reflection upon Western and Papuan cultural perceptions. However, its aim is to achieve a degree of sympathetic understanding, both of the Papuan cultures encountered by the Strickland-Purari patrol and of Hides and O'Malley and the men who traveled with them. The purpose is not primarily critical (until

Chapter 10) but rather to establish a picture of a historical situation with multifaceted ethnographic dimensions.

The narrative of this volume follows the journey of the Strickland-Purari patrol as it moved day by day from one region to another. Each chapter that chronicles the encounter with a different group of people is prefaced by an ethnographic section outlining the important features of that culture and its historical/political situation at the time (Chapter 5 covers the ethnography for Chapters 6 and 7). The footnotes accompanying the narrative serve as historical and ethnographic annotation to the text and should be read along with it.

Finally, while this volume is intended as a work of ethnographic and ethnohistorical scholarship, the nature of the material—an epic first journey of tropical exploration into unknown mountain valleys inhabited by exotic peoples—renders it a compelling drama. It is an ethnographic adventure story.

I. COLONIAL PAPUA AND THE TRADITION OF EXPLORATION

EDWARD L. SCHIEFFELIN AND ROBERT CRITTENDEN

> They were brought up on Kipling, *The Boy's Own Paper*, and
> the whole attitude of the supremacy of the white race and their
> duty to enlighten the savages. Whether they actually said it or
> not, they accepted the complete right of Europeans to sweep
> through the world and scoop up anything they happened to
> think would make some money for them. I don't say that
> everyone had that notion, but most had it in their background:
> they were so imbued with it that it never occurred to them to
> question it.
> Penelope Hope, planter's daughter, quoted in Nelson 1982: 13.

The Strickland-Purari patrol was a result of a longstanding policy of
government exploration and patrolling of the Papuan hinterland by government officers, dating back to the earliest days of the colonial administration. Patrols, consisting of one or two white officers, a number of
armed Papuan police, and a line of carriers, walking from village to village along an established route, were the chief means by which the native
peoples of Papua were governed between 1885 and the early 1970's. For
most Papuans, experience with patrols was the only basis they had for
understanding anything about the ways, let alone the institutions, of their
colonial masters. Government officers were responsible both for maintaining peace and order in their districts and for exploring their unknown
regions, contacting newly encountered tribal peoples, and bringing them
under administration influence. The manner in which such patrols were
to be carried out was expressly laid down in the "Circular Instructions," a
handbook of procedures that every patrol officer carried in the 1930's.* In
the final analysis, however, the conduct of a patrol depended on the character of the officers in charge. This consideration was so important that
Sir Hubert Murray, the lieutenant governor of Papua from 1908 to 1940,†
insisted on picking his "outside men" (as they were known) himself. Patrol
officers had to be experienced in bush craft, courageous, resourceful, and
able to endure considerable hardship in the tropical wilderness. They were

---

* The "Circular Instructions" (1931) was itself an update of an earlier publication, "Information for the Guidance of Newly Joined Patrol Officers" (1920), which spelled out the
policies and procedures Sir Hubert Murray had advocated for field officers since about 1908.

† John Hubert Plunkett Murray was appointed chief judicial officer in 1904 and acting
administrator in 1907. He was appointed lieutenant governor of Papua in November 1908
and served until his death in February 1940.

expected to exercise qualities of leadership and determination in carrying out their responsibilities in situations that were rarely easy and often quite dangerous. The unflinching and uncelebrated performance of these duties, without regard to privation or peril, epitomized the esprit de corps of this body of men, who formed the backbone of the Papuan Service.

In 1935 the conduct of patrols toward the indigenous people they encountered was (at least in principle) guided by a policy of peaceful engagement and restraint in the use of force. This policy—and the broader humane, if paternalistic, philosophy it represented—was itself a subject of ongoing dispute and debate within the Australian colonial community concerning the relationship between Papuans and whites.

Colonial Papuan Society

Papua was one of the last places on earth to be incorporated within the sphere of European colonial expansion. By the last quarter of the nineteenth century the western half of the island of New Guinea had been appropriated by the Dutch to protect the flank of their colonies in what is now Indonesia, while the northeast quadrant of the island was being colonized by the Germans, who were belatedly attempting imperial expansion into the Pacific. The southeast quadrant wasn't brought under European influence until 1884, when it was reluctantly declared a protectorate by the British in order to serve as a buffer between the Germans on the north coast and the Australian colonies to the south. It was administered by Britain for 22 years before being handed over, in 1906, into the care of the new Commonwealth of Australia, which had been federated in 1901.

The Australian Territory of Papua was a sleepy backwater of empire. In 1935, its dense tropical forests and the inhospitable interior mountain ranges still enclosed sizable regions that had never been seen by outsiders. The men who came to the territory were, from the beginning, a mixed lot. Some were lured by hope of wealth or a sense of adventure; others were fleeing difficulties or embarrassment at home. All looked forward to trying their luck at uncovering whatever riches might be hidden in the unknown wilderness and doing well for themselves (Nelson 1982: 12; Souter 1963: 3–29). In particular they hoped to find gold, but many settled for employment in the government or commercial spheres. And there were the missionaries, who came to save the heathen for Christ.

Most who migrated to Papua achieved only modest success. Papua was a poor country, difficult to exploit, and it never lived up to the hopes of its white settlers; many went away disappointed. The colonial administration of this unproductive territory received only minimal financial assistance from the mother country and had to make do on a pinch-penny budget up

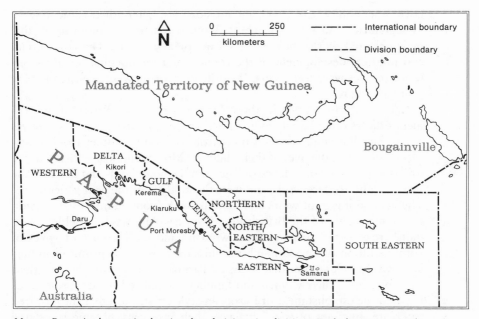

Map 1. Papua in the 1930's, showing the administrative divisions. Each district was in the charge of a Resident Magistrate (RM) or Assistant Resident Magistrate (ARM) who, with one or two patrol officers, a government clerk, and a detachment of Armed Constabulary, was responsible for the work of government in the district. Exploration and the extension of government control in that district were an integral part of this work. (Gash and Whittaker 1975; Inglis 1974; Papua Annual Report, various dates.)

until the outbreak of the Second World War. The government administration was chronically understaffed and underpaid—a situation made only more difficult in the 1930's by the hardships of the Great Depression.

The white Australian society in Papua at this time was extremely small in scale. Port Moresby, the capital and largest town in the territory, had a white population of only 66 in 1901; this increased to barely 700 by 1935, about half the total white population of Papua. By that time Port Moresby had grown to a dreary settlement of iron-roofed buildings: a few houses, offices, warehouses, and wharfs, and one paved street. After 50 years the seat of the government of Papua still contained no significant public building or monument (Stuart 1970: 17–20, 44). Another quarter of the white population inhabited the island of Samarai. The rest—adventurers, prospectors, planters, traders, missionaries, and patrol officers—were scattered about at plantations, remote police outposts, mining camps, and tiny mission settlements.

Women were among the white settlers from the earliest days as wives of government officers, planters, and missionaries. Later others came to serve as secretaries and school teachers. Women remained a minority in this male-oriented world, however (Nelson 1982: 99–101). The commercial and political development of the country and the opening up of the interior regions were seen as man's work, and women were expected to play a supporting role.

Life for white women in the colony was not easy. Wives of government officers often had to endure long periods of boredom and loneliness when their husbands were off on patrol. Malaria and other tropical diseases threatened the lives of their children. Most white women lived in the towns, especially Port Moresby. They ran the households and directed the servants, did welfare work, and were the mothers of the next generation.* The general image of women among the white community was a version of the memsahib of the British Raj. The prevailing wisdom held that remote areas were "no place for a woman" and the presence of wives of administration officers (though not missionaries) in the primitive hinterland was for a long time discouraged.† Part of the reason for this was that, for white men, their women and families symbolized the domestic security and the establishment of European-style civilization that they aspired to create. In times of social malaise, their insecurity became translated into fear for the safety (especially the sexual safety) of their women, and Papuans, who represented (in white imagination) the wild and ungovernable forces against which civilization had to struggle, were perceived as a particular underlying danger. It was partly because of this that white men didn't like the idea of white women entering "uncivilized areas," and passed extremely severe legislation against any Papuan men who might have sexual relations with them (Inglis 1974).‡

In Port Moresby, provincial colonial society was notable for its determined effort, despite its small size, to develop a social class system on the

* There were, of course, exceptions. According to Nelson (1982: 102) there were at least five women in the territory who ran plantations by themselves, and Papua from time to time hosted a number of important women scholars and intellectuals such as anthropologists Beatrice Blackwood, Hortense Powdermaker, and Margaret Mead, naturalist Evelyn Cheesman, and writer Beatrice Grimshaw. But the domestic and welfare contributions of white women in Papuan colonial society in the first quarter of the century were for the most part completely unsung.

† This did not prevent adventurous women from finding ways to accompany their husbands to remote patrol stations and sharing their lives there. Resident Magistrate C. A. W. Monckton described one woman married to a patrol officer in the Northern Division who refused to leave her husband even though Monckton had purposely assigned him to a remote and difficult post to separate him from her influence. Much to Monckton's irritation, she managed to circumvent him, trekked into her husband's post, and refused to come out (Monckton 1922: 90–96). But such women were the exception rather than the rule.

‡ The opposite but equivalent situation, severe penalties for white men sexually involved with Papuan women, was never suggested.

model of more sophisticated European capitals. An incipient elite made up of the more prominent government officials, businessmen, and planters was struggling to emerge at the top while people in less prestigious walks of life were relegated to lesser status below (Nelson 1982: 165–67; Inglis 1974: 1–24). The maintenance of this social system and the realization of its ambitions to develop the wealth of the country depended upon the availability and exploitation of Papuan labor. Thus, the treatment of the native inhabitants was a source of continuous bickering between the business community, the missions, and the administration.

Papuans and Whites

The principal use commercial interests had for the natives was as labor. The colonial administration, while interested in commercial development, was also concerned to protect Papuans from ill-treatment at the hands of their employers or from the loss of their lands to white speculators (Souter 1963: 96–97). This effort was supported by the missionaries, who, besides being concerned with fair treatment of Papuans on moral grounds, wanted to preserve stable populations in their village church communities. These differences in policy concerning Papuan labor regulations did not, however, reflect different views they held of the natives themselves. Australian colonial society was founded on the assumption, shared by both the most cultivated and humane individuals, as well as the worst scoundrels, "that the Papuans they ruled over, employed, taught, or converted were an inferior race to themselves" (Inglis 1974: ix).* All the debates over the provision of native labor and the disputes over the degree to which traditional ways could be disrupted by work or education were carried on in the light of this underlying conviction (Inglis 1974: ix).

The moral and physical inferiority of Papuan civilization seemed intuitively obvious to most whites from their observations of the primitive manner in which Papuans lived: their simple technology and material cul-

---

* This belief, by the way, was supported and validated by at least one prominent anthropologist of the day. Murray's government was sufficiently enlightened to employ a government anthropologist, F. E. Williams, to help with native affairs. Williams, an intrepid fieldworker, is well known today for his numerous important ethnographies of now destroyed coastal Papuan cultures. Less well known is the fact that Williams shared Murray's (and everyone else's) opinion of the racial inferiority of Papuans. In the opening chapter of one ethnography he wrote: "It will be the aim of the present book to describe [Keraki] life as it is lived and to show how the members of a primitive society, living under what may seem rather wretched conditions, contrive to make the most of them and get on well together" (1936: 12). This bemused and patronizing attitude towards the benighted (a tone that carries throughout the book) would be considered outrageous today, but it was right in line with Murray's paternalistic native policies. Williams also put time into editing a newspaper for English-speaking Papuans which was geared to making them recognize their lesser mental capacities and keep to their proper inferior station (Inglis 1974: 2).

ture and their slash-and-burn mode of cultivation, planting with a digging stick, seemed rudimentary by European standards. Whites found Papuans lazy, careless, and irresponsible as laborers and servants. Moreover, many customs of Papuan societies, such as polygamy or extensive female tattooing, were uncomfortably alien to Australian sensibilities or, as in the case of cannibalism and headhunting, completely abhorrent. In any event, most whites had only a narrow and superficial understanding of the social and political institutions of Papuan societies. Indeed, the fact of the matter is that, not only in the more obvious and visible aspects of social life but on the deepest levels of value and motivation, Papuan cultures could hardly have been more different from the culture of their Australian masters.

To make things worse, the indigenous population of the Territory of Papua was by no means a homogeneous cultural group. Rather, it was fragmented into small, autonomous, often mutually antagonistic communities, speaking many different languages and exhibiting a bewildering variety of customs and beliefs. Amidst this variety, however, there were a few common themes. Papuans were by and large subsistence cultivators of taro, bananas, and other crops. They lived in hamlets or villages (in some places, longhouse communities) practicing small-scale pig husbandry and supplementing the larder by hunting and fishing. Most Papuan societies were unstratified, though some were dominated by influential individuals. Social structure was based on various forms of kinship organization and marital alliance. People depended on their relatives and affines for support in pursuing their enterprises or avenging their injuries. Papuan societies lacked institutionalized processes of adjudication of any significant social range. Thus Papuans tended to turn rather quickly to armed confrontation, intimidation, and conflict to achieve redress for injuries or to press forward desired projects. This tendency to violence was frequently supported by or even enshrined within warlike cultural values or religious beliefs that led to the cultivation of qualities of forcefulness and bellicosity as desirable social traits. The point to be made is that, for many (though not all) Papuan societies, the extension of competitive claims and the settlement of disputes were regarded as matters for political maneuvering and armed confrontation quite unlike the methodical legal proceedings of the British tradition. To the Australians this gave Papuan life a disorderly and lawless appearance and led them to regard the Papuan people as bloodthirsty and violent.

Although violence and tribal warfare could be forcibly suppressed by the administration, it was much more difficult for Australians to deal with Papuan ideas and attitudes concerning work, productivity, and the value of wealth. As subsistence cultivators, Papuans were largely self-sufficient in terms of their day-to-day needs. Other items, tools, decorations, and shell valuables could be obtained through trade. Indeed, Papuans traditionally traded extensively up and down the coast, and along traditional trade routes that reached deep into the interior (see Chapter 5). But trade and ceremonial exchange played a much more important role in Papuan societies than merely providing extra necessities. Together with marriage they were major vehicles for cementing and maintaining political alliances and important social relationships, insuring the safety of individuals traveling outside their home areas, and maintaining peaceful relationships (or at least truce) between neighboring groups.

Economic productivity fostered social and political stability not by promoting accumulation of wealth but by providing the means for ceremonial feasting and prestation. Clever dealing in trade as well as hard-won productivity of gardens and pig husbandry enabled villagers to stage spectacular ceremonial feasts for their allies, affines, trading partners, and rivals. Such feasts celebrated many different kinds of occasions: marriages, death payments, religious festivals, rites of passage, or rituals promoting fertility and productivity. In the process, old relationships were renewed and new ones created as prestations were passed from one person to another. Ceremonial feasting challenged rivals and built political reputation, influence, and prestige both for individual participants and for the group. These ceremonial feasts represented the high points of display of Papuan oratory, cuisine, art, music, and dance, as well as dramatic distributions of wealth and demonstrations of group strength.

Papuans were capable of considerable industry, long-term planning, and organizational effort to bring off these spectacles. However, the motivation for hard work, productivity, and the accumulation of wealth for the purpose of staging prestations and ceremonial feasts was completely different from the orientation to accumulation of wealth that drove Australian colonial society. For Australians the object of productive work was defined by understandings and labor practice embedded in a capitalist economy. There the production of wealth provided workers with wages and businessmen with entrepreneurial profit. Accumulation of wealth enabled the individual to improve his personal life-style, enhance his social status, and finally to invest in further profitable production of wealth.

For Papuans, however, social prestige and political influence were gained not so much by the accumulation of wealth by individuals as through the strategy of giving it away to the right people and thereby creating ties of obligation or patronage. The wealth (whether in pigs, shell valuables, or garden produce) distributed at ceremonial feasts was given to settle outstanding political and social accounts or to open new ones, and to place friends and/or rivals in obligation to make return. In this way, feasts and ceremonies were the very stuff of Papuan social and political activity—the

counterpoint to warfare—the vehicle for obtaining influence and reputation and for stabilizing relationships with one's neighbors. This being the
case, Papuans were willing to work long and hard to accumulate wealth,
but only in relation to particular defined and usually dramatic ceremonial goals. Once the feast was held, the disbursement of wealth made, and
the goal achieved, extraordinary productive effort would taper off—until
galvanized again at a later date by another turn of the ceremonial cycle.
Without such a dramatic goal—or once such a goal had been temporarily
achieved—there seemed little point in most Papuan societies to make extra
efforts at production. Moreover, though Papuans were usually eager to
obtain wealth items, the nature of general reciprocity in their societies
mitigated against enterprising individuals accumulating wealth for themselves. Any enterprising individual who produced more than his needs in
the absence of a socially legitimate goal such as staging a feast, was likely
to be importuned to distribute it by needy relatives who would be difficult
to refuse. If he was smart, he might place his gifts in politically strategic ways and benefit thereby, but he could not easily accumulate wealth
only for himself. This kind of background to economic motivation could
hardly be more ill-suited to producing industrious workers for colonial
plantations. Colonial officials found it very difficult to interest Papuans
in schemes for their own economic development. White employers complained that they were indolent and unmotivated workers.

Missionaries and others who were familiar with Papuan feasts and ceremonies acknowledged the people's capacity for hard work and organization but found their spectacles wasteful and thoughtless in their lavish
distribution of food and wealth and the killing of herds of pigs. Why
Papuans should work so hard and sacrifice so long to accumulate a large
mass of food and wealth only to apparently throw it all away in a profligate
celebration aimed mainly at gaining social prestige seemed to practical
missionaries and planters to be simply foolish and extravagant—evidence
of a childlike mentality (Nelson 1982: 166; Inglis 1974: 2).

This colonial impatience with Papuan ways and motivations was made
more poignant by the frustration of those few well-meaning Australian
colonial officials, planters, and businessmen who over the years tried to
accomplish something more than merely their own self-interest and to
make a better way of life for Papuan peoples. The frustration of years
of such effort unrewarded tended to substantiate what white colonials
already believed: that Papuans were an inferior race.*

---

* Missionaries who had succeeded in making a fair number of converts were an exception
to this rule and often believed their efforts had been met with success.

Sir William MacGregor and the Early Administration

Until the Second World War the history of Papuan colonial society was dominated by two major figures: Sir William MacGregor and Sir Hubert Murray. Indeed, both men achieved the status of legends in their own time.

In 1888, when the British Protectorate of New Guinea was transformed into the crown colony of British New Guinea, Sir William MacGregor was appointed administrator; he was made lieutenant governor in 1895. The government he took over had been in existence only five years.[*] The vast territory and the population in his charge were almost completely unknown. MacGregor saw that the first task of his administration would be to explore the territory and try to bring the population under government control. The policy that all exploration should be undertaken by government officers (rather than private adventurers) had been established by an earlier administrator, Sir Peter Scratchly, and MacGregor strongly adhered to it. The job was enormous, considering the wild and difficult nature of the country and the independent-minded and warlike nature of its inhabitants. Moreover, MacGregor had only a minuscule budget to work with, and his government personnel never numbered more than twenty. With this tiny force he was expected to rule over about one million Papuans scattered over 90,000 square miles. MacGregor, however, was not a man to shrink from difficulty.

Born in 1846, the eighth child of a Scottish farm laborer, MacGregor had taken degrees at Glasgow and Edinburgh and a medical degree at Aberdeen (Joyce 1971: 3). He had then risen in the British Colonial Service through sheer ability.[†] He brought a stern Scottish moralism and an authoritarian self-confidence to his administration, tolerating no blasphemy or immorality among his subordinates and insisting on strict adherence to his instructions and standards of operation. A man of enormous energy, he set the example for his men by spending nearly 85 percent of his time as head of government on exploratory expeditions and tours of inspection

---

[*] MacGregor (1846–1919) had a number of predecessors. Sir Peter Scratchly (1835–85) was appointed the first Special Commissioner for New Guinea on November 22, 1884; he died of malaria in December 1885. His successor, Hugh Hastings Romilly (1856–92), served from December 1885 until February 1886 as Deputy Commissioner. Romilly was followed by Hon. John Douglas (1828–1904), who served as Special Commissioner until British sovereignty was proclaimed and he was succeeded by MacGregor in September 1888.

[†] MacGregor was a licentiate of the faculty of Physicians and Surgeons of Glasgow and of the Royal College of Physicians and Surgeons of Edinburgh as well as a Bachelor of Medicine from Aberdeen University. At the time of his appointment to British New Guinea he was chief medical officer on Sir Arthur Gordon's staff at Fiji. He had at various times been colonial secretary, and acting administrator as well.

in the Papuan hinterland. His manner of moving quickly and tirelessly in the bush, of forcefully disregarding difficulties and hardship, and of pushing determinedly through to places extremely difficult of access set the original standard for the corps of tough young officers he recruited to help tame the tropical wilderness. His style of leadership has been described thus:

One month he would take the government steam yacht *Merrie England* down to Sudest Island where 700 diggers were fossicking for gold, and the next he would land at Chad's Bay and lead a patrol inland to investigate the murder of Captain Ansell, a trader whose skull had been smashed by the Abioma people. . . .
    MacGregor chased cannibals up the Mambare River, punished the Merani people, who had managed to murder two prospectors despite the fact that the victims were wearing vests made of ships copper, and fought a pitched battle with a Tugeri armada which had paddled down from Dutch New Guinea to the mouth of the Fly in search of heads. (Souter 1963: 63–64)

In his time MacGregor twice crossed overland from Port Moresby to the Mombare River, and he ascended all the coastal rivers to their limits of navigation (see Map 2). In 1889 he climbed the highest peak of the Owen Stanley Range and named it Mt. Victoria.

Although MacGregor didn't like the use of force, he used it when he thought it was necessary. He believed that if the local Papuan people were to respect the government, no government officer could afford to back down in the face of force or violence. Thus, when patrols were met by warriors with drawn bows, officers had a tendency to fire first and ask questions later. The administration regarded villages that showed independence or were less than properly respectful or submissive towards British control as "cheeky" and in need of being taught a lesson. "These natives," MacGregor wrote, "—probably all natives in a certain stage of mental development are alike—respect first of all physical force" (MacGregor to Sir Arthur Gordon, February 6, 1889; quoted in Joyce 1971: 133). MacGregor dealt with raids and killings by Papuan people by dispatching punitive patrols. He or one of his officers would march into the appropriate village with a detachment of police and demand the culprits be handed over. If this was not forthcoming and further attempts at persuasion had no effect, the police would shoot a few people or burn down some houses as punishment for the unlawful action. C. A. W. Monckton, one of MacGregor's resident magistrates and a rather extreme advocate of this kind of retaliatory justice, explained his policy for ending tribal fighting in the Northern Division in the following way: "The only way you can stop these beggars hunting their neighbours with a club is to bang them with a club. Is it not better that a bloodthirsty cannibal should be hanged, or some of his crime-stained followers shot, than that a peaceful district of husbandmen should be raided, their houses burnt, and men, women and children slaughtered and eaten?" (Monckton 1921: 208–9).

No doubt such tactics were in part dictated by the difficulties of controlling such a large territory with such limited resources, but it was ironic that the administration's mode of meting out justice often seemed indistinguishable from the traditional system of revenge employed by the local inhabitants among themselves. Although Papuans could readily understand this policy of retaliation, it reflected an attitude unbecoming to the British tradition of law, and from a practical standpoint tended to place the administration in the same relationship of retributive violence with its subjects as they traditionally had with one another. A village might be intimidated or put in its place by a punitive action, but the underlying resentment at the loss of kinsmen and damage to property would simmer a long time and fuel a continued latent antagonism to the administration.

If MacGregor would brook little insubordination from Papuans, he nevertheless took a paternalistic responsibility for their welfare. He acted to protect Papuan people from the expropriation of their lands by white planters, from gross mistreatment by employers, and from "corruption by purveyors of liquor and guns" (Joyce 1971: 104–5, 182). Under his leadership and energetic example, the tradition of exploration of unknown areas by government officers and the government of controlled areas by patrol and inspection was firmly established. Indeed, by the time he left, MacGregor had single-handedly created the basic governmental structure for the colonial administration that was to endure in its essentials until national independence in 1975. The more directly violent and heavy-handed aspects of the administration, however, were to change.

Sir Hubert Murray and the Golden Age of Colonial Papua

MacGregor left British New Guinea in 1898 to become governor of Lagos. In 1901 Britain began efforts to transfer the territory, now renamed Papua, to the keeping of the new Commonwealth of Australia. The next six or seven years marked an awkward period of transition in which the Papuan colonial administration was left essentially on its own while the Australian government tried to make up its mind what to do with the territory.

After a series of crises in which one administrator resigned and another committed suicide,* the government was left in the hands of Capt. F. R.

---

* MacGregor's successor as lieutenant governor was George LeHunt who, like Monckton, supported the use of draconian measures for dealing with troublesome natives. This policy shortly resulted in a crisis that eventually led to the restructuring of the colonial administration. On Easter Sunday, April 1901, the much respected pioneer missionary Rev.

Barton, a weak man who was unable to prevail against the various factions in the government to provide effective leadership. By 1906 the Papuan government had become so divided in factional squabbling that a Royal Commission was set up to look into the administration of the colony. The key witness was Hubert Murray, the chief judicial officer of the colony, who provided testimony that led to Captain Barton being removed from his post and sent to a minor position in Zanzibar. Murray so impressed the Australian government that he was himself appointed administrator and in 1908 was made lieutenant governor of the territory.

The transition was not a smooth one. Murray inherited a social and political situation riddled with division, envy, and suspicion left over from the previous regime. The part he had played in the investigation by the Royal Commission did not help matters. He had enemies, rivals, and detractors to deal with from the very beginning. Some of these, like the politician Staniforth Smith, were to continue to oppose him for the next twenty years.

Murray introduced a new style of leadership into the Papuan government. He was Catholic, the son of a distinguished (but by then bankrupt) family of graziers and property owners from New South Wales. In appearance he was an imposing figure. Tall and solidly built, austere in his habits, he carried himself with the aloof, self-confident authority of the classical nineteenth-century empire builder. He had been educated at Oxford, where he had taken a double first in Classics, and he had twice won the English amateur heavyweight boxing championship. During the Boer War he had commanded a regiment in South Africa and won the DSO. He was over 40 when he came to Papua after an undistinguished career as a lawyer in New South Wales. A complicated personality, Murray had his admirers but, as one historian put it, "he was a cold, forbidding man . . . a cultivated Victorian of diverse talents who by accident found in Papua [the

---

James Chalmers and his assistant Oliver Tomkins were killed and eaten by the men of Goaribari Island off the mouth of the Kikori River. The Goaribaris had needed a victim for the ceremonial dedication of a newly constructed men's house. The wave of rage and outcry this killing provoked among the white community in Port Moresby motivated LeHunt to lead a punitive expedition which resulted in the slaughter of at least 100 Goaribari warriors (Souter 1963: 90–92). Some form of peace was made when Chalmers's skull was returned. Although the whole of Port Moresby society supported this expedition, LeHunt felt it had gotten out of hand and was rather shamefaced about it. He resigned in May 1903, and C. S. Robinson, the chief judicial officer of the colony, became acting administrator. Sentiment in Port Moresby was still high over the killing of the missionaries. Bowing to public pressure, Robinson led another punitive expedition against the Goaribari to recover the bones of Tomkins. About 60 more natives were killed, and the resulting furor in Australian press led to Robinson being asked to appear before an official inquiry in Melbourne. F. R. Barton was then appointed acting administrator. Robinson committed suicide rather than face the inquiry, and Barton remained in his post from 1904 to 1907.

career] for which he was temperamentally best suited"—the governance of a colony in a primitive land (Hastings 1969: 47).

Murray felt that his first priority in taking over the government was the consolidation of administration influence in the areas that had been contacted and explored since the days of MacGregor. Many of these regions had been roughly mapped, but their inhabitants were not yet under full control. Murray believed that further expansion of administrative influence into the Papuan interior had to be undertaken in a deliberate manner that would not outpace the government's ability to control new areas. He thought that this could be done most effectively, consistent with the protection of the local people, only within a framework of British law.

Partly for this reason, Murray disapproved of many of the heavy-handed methods of dealing with local Papuans that had been utilized since Mac-Gregor's time. In 1908 he published a directive (General Order, Armed Constabulary, no. 1 of 1908), which later became incorporated in handbooks for patrol officers:

Officers in command of armed constabulary are reminded that they can never, under any circumstances, be justified in firing upon natives by way of punishment. . . . It is the settled policy of the Government not to resort to force except in cases of necessity when all other means have failed, and that it by no means follows because an officer may have a good defense on a charge of manslaughter that his conduct, therefore, escapes censure. (Territory of Papua 1931 ["Circular Instructions"]: 15)

Crimes such as raiding and cannibalism or the murder of prospectors were to be dealt with by arresting the actual culprits and bringing them in for trial and punishment, not by mounting punitive reprisals against the culprits' people. Much to the disgust of old hands like Monckton, officers were directed never to fire unless they were first fired upon or otherwise found themselves in a situation of grave and immediate danger. In the case of intransigent people, persuasion or intimidation was to be attempted before resorting to any kind of force. The reception of this ruling by experienced bush officers was reflected in the sarcastic remark by one of them that, according to Murray, a man had to wait until he was killed before he could fire back at hostile warriors (Sinclair 1969: 49).

Murray justified his views on administrative rather than humanitarian grounds, pointing out that it was much more difficult to deal with people who had been treated with violence than with those who had not:

[It is easier, no doubt] to simply "deal it out" to the offending tribe, irrespective of individual responsibility, but there can be no doubt [what] is better as a matter of administration. The tribe that has once been visited by a punitive expedition— unless it has been so severely handled that its spirit is entirely broken, in which case it becomes useless for good or evil—will take years to pacify, and to the last will harbor a desire for revenge, whereas a tribe from which the guilty only are taken soon becomes friendly, especially when the prisoners return. (Murray 1912: 370)

Although couched in pragmatic terms these policies reflected a change in government attitude in the direction of more humane relations with tribal Papuans. Murray, like MacGregor, saw the administration's task in relation to the Papuan population as twofold: first, to protect Papuans from the undue exploitation by the white community and, second, to provide the conditions through regulation and incentive to "advance them in civilization." The administration proceeded on the assumption that social change—the "civilizing process"—was desirable in itself, and that Western legal processes and governmental institutions were both the right models to follow and the appropriate vehicles for accomplishing it.

The rule of law of which Murray spoke meant English law, of course, not Papuan notions of redress. Although most Papuans appreciated the peace and security that the administration brought to their lives, most of them regarded this as basically a matter of the power of the white man. If there was a dispute or injury amongst Papuans serious enough to come to the attention of the resident magistrate, he would deliver a judgment according to British-style law. Papuan customs were dismissed as a basis for legal settlement. This does not mean that magistrates were entirely insensitive to traditional customs, however. Papuan notions of justice and redress were frequently acknowledged as "mitigating circumstances" in a given case where it was recognized that the defendant had only acted according to the customs of his forefathers and in ignorance of the white man's law. This recognition could result in a more lenient sentence for the culprit from the administration's point of view, but didn't go very far in satisfying the villagers' own needs for redress. They soon discovered it was usually more satisfactory to try to settle things quietly among themselves if they could, without involving the government. The notion that administration procedures might be designed along the lines of, or in accordance with, traditional Papuan understandings of settling disputes simply never crossed anyone's mind.

In any case, few Papuans came to know anything about Western institutions and legal processes through example or instruction. For most of them, these forms were simply imposed by fiat of resident magistrates and patrol officers during their periodic tours of inspection through the villages. In practice, if not in principle, the word of the government officer was law. Government officers in their remote field stations had, in fact, virtually unlimited powers over their district populations. Within broadly defined limits, they could do almost anything they wished so long as it didn't upset someone in Port Moresby or detract from good order in their domains. Villagers in the 1930's were not necessarily expected to understand government directives or the principles upon which magistrates rendered judgment. They were simply expected (when handed a judgment or directive) to obey. This did not mean that Papuans were necessarily illtreated. Besides expecting them to keep their villages clean, obey the law, and occasionally do some work on the roads, the administration made few demands on them. But, given the potential in this system for abuse, Murray's conviction that moral character was the most important quality in a resident magistrate was pretty close to the mark.

Meanwhile, it would be a mistake to think that Papuans, for their part, were merely passive sufferers of an imposed order. Some, indeed, vigorously resisted the imposition of administration control over their domains during the period of early contact. Papuan societies had never been the static backward groups that the colonial Australians liked to believe. They had always existed amid the ebb and flow of population migrations, warfare, indigenous religious movements, and the changing distribution of trade routes and ceremonial exchange systems. As a result, they tended to respond actively to new historical situations.

The most visible effect of administration influence was pacification; Papuans could no longer use violence for settling scores and gaining political objectives. Less immediately visible were changes in local economic and political relations that followed upon the introduction of steel, labor recruiting, and a growing dependency on the colonial economy. However, Papuans quickly discovered that there were other, expanded opportunities for pursuing their traditional goals (and developing new ones) under the new regime. New sources of wealth became available, travel could be expanded, ceremonial exchange networks extended, and new directions explored for political and trade alliance. In many situations, the government presence even coincided quite satisfactorily with local Papuan desires, giving weakened groups relief from predation of their enemies, making rare trade goods locally plentiful, and putting nearby people at a trading advantage over their more distant neighbors. Papuans also found ways to "work" the system. They learned to avoid taking disputes to government officers unless they felt they could use his power for their own ends (Schwimmer 1987). Ambitious young men joined the constabulary, and canny village elders married their daughters to them. In these and various other ways Papuans levered the system to some degree for their own purposes.

However, despite the advantages they found to living under the Australian regime, Papuans also chafed under its inequities, especially their feeling of exclusion from the major benefits and privileges of the white man's world. The most dramatic kind of Papuan response to this took the form not of armed uprising or mass political movements (the latter were unfamiliar to their traditions) but of large-scale religious movements, or cargo cults, which attempted to redress their unbalanced relations to the white man by ritual means. These movements were usually quite irksome to the administration (not to mention the missions) and in the 1920's and 1930's government officers tended to arrest cult leaders, destroy their cult houses, and interdict further cult behavior by force (Worsley 1957; Lawrence 1964; Trompf 1977). As a rule Papuans could not prevail against such massive government response and found their most effective means of resistance in more subtle activity: pursuing their ends without making too many waves and so evading government scrutiny.

The Police

In his later years Murray was to take great pride in the claim that Papua was one of the few colonies in the British Empire where the native population had been brought under control without the use of military force. Instead, he used the police. Murray realized early on that if he wished to accomplish his goals, especially with the minimum use of force, he needed a highly trained, reliable, and disciplined native police force. An Armed Constabulary of Papuans had been established in the time of MacGregor. Murray now gave his personal attention to its expansion and development. Recruits were trained and drilled with military discipline. Murray saw to it that they understood the sense of duty and were indoctrinated with a sense of pride and mission. They represented the power of the government, he told them; theirs was the task of bringing an unruly territory under the order of law—and providing Papuan people with a better way of life. The Papuan policemen were awed by Murray and revered him deeply. They saw the power of his administration and their privilege to serve it as embodied in the blue laplap and jersey, red sash, and brown cartridge belt of their official uniforms, which they called "Judge Murray's clothes."

The police were crucial to the resident magistrate or patrol officer's ability to carry out his work. Whether they were organizing work details, arresting malefactors, putting a stop to tribal fighting, or encountering new people in uncontacted territory, government officers remarked again and again in their reports upon the indispensability of the Papuan police. When a patrol was on the move, the police would guard and rally the carrier line and see to the routine of breaking or setting up camp. Government officers depended upon their most experienced policemen to advise them about the whereabouts, dispositions, and probable intentions of local people, and delegated authority to the most reliable to carry out important tasks. The most experienced police knew nearly as much about running a patrol as the government officer himself, and newly appointed officers often looked to these Papuan veterans as mentors while they learned the ropes in the new situation (cf. Champion 1932: 218). In these circumstances the constabulary offered one of the few opportunities for the formation of personal relationships between Papuans and whites and represented the pinnacle of social advancement for Papuans in the colonial world.

Economic Development and Race Relations

Murray, like other administrators before him, believed the future of the Territory of Papua lay in economic development and the extraction of the rich resources that everyone believed were hidden in it. Businessmen, planters, traders, miners, and adventurers of all sorts were continually arriving in Papua to make their fortunes in the process, not all of them of the best character. Murray found himself quickly in the position of having to restrain and regulate the very commercial interests he wished to promote in order to protect the Papuan people from mistreatment and exploitation. Striking the right balance was not easy. Murray shared with his predecessors the view that Papuan ways of life must inevitably be changed by the march of progress and civilization. The question was how this could be effected without destroying the Papuans themselves, and also what part Papuans ought to play in the process. Murray realized that colonial contact, the cessation of warfare and the introduction of steel tools would have far-reaching effects on native society and morale:

If [a man] is suddenly told that he need never fight again, that his life is perfectly safe, and [if he] is presented with implements which will enable him to do as much in a day as he could do before in a week, but is told that he must never go on any more raids and never collect any more heads, he is likely to feel a void in his existence, for his chief occupations will be gone, and unless something is given to him which will fill the void, he and his descendants will suffer. This is the case with the Papuan; we have taken away his old ideals of war and bloodshed, and it is our duty to put a new ideal in its place. (Murray 1912: 361–64)

Although warfare and bloodshed were hardly the only traditional activities of Papuans, they struck just the right note of opprobrium and stereotype of native ways to give a positive cast to the "new ideal" Murray now proposed Papuans adopt: industrious labor. Quite apart from the colony's need for Papuan labor, Murray was a moralist at heart. He took the upper-middle-class attitude that, at least as far as the lower orders were concerned, idle hands were the devil's playthings and honest work built honest character. It was work, he thought, that was in the best interests of the Papuan. It was an ideal solution, serving the territory's economic needs while at the same time acting as an appropriate civilizing influence: "Labor is no doubt a curse, but the curse is not an unmitigated one; in the case of the Papuan the mitigation is that it will save him from the worse evil of despair. . . . [It should be our aim] to transform the tribe of disappointed warriors into a race of more or less industrious workmen" (Murray 1912: 361–64).

To promote this development Murray improved upon MacGregor's regulations aimed at preventing undue disruption of Papuan community stability and regulating the treatment of contract laborers.

This benevolent attitude was by no means shared by the rest of colonial society. The majority of businesspeople were there to make money and regarded themselves as doing most of the work of developing the country. They saw Murray's policies as impediments to more rapid economic advancement. They felt he was putting Papuan interests before their own, and increasingly they formed the local white opposition to his government (Nelson 1982: 18–21). This struggle between government administration and private enterprise continued throughout Murray's career, and he was continually exercised to keep his protective policies in place.

Murray's administration was a model of enlightenment for 1909, and he saw no need to alter it over the next 25 years. Ironically, however, as time went on, his policies began to undermine the possibility of a more liberal society of the sort that was appearing elsewhere in the colonial world in the first third of the twentieth century. Murray's rule has been characterized by present-day historians as classically paternalistic because, though it protected Papuans from mistreatment, it was founded on the belief that the white man knew what was best for them and gave them no choice but to accept it. Murray was careful not to allow them any room for development of political self-consciousness or even a public forum in which Papuans could make their complaints and desires known.

During the 1920's and 1930's, the white community in Papua experienced an increasing sense of insecurity. In large part this grew out of frustration that the colony did not prosper as it had been expected to. While the neighboring Mandated Territory of New Guinea flourished as a result of the discovery of gold at Bulolo and Edie Creek, Papuan mineral finds were disappointing. Plantations rose and fell with world commodity prices, and the administration continued to operate on a shoestring. People who had worked hard for years to make a successful life became disappointed or embittered. At the same time Papuans (at least those living around Port Moresby) were becoming more sophisticated in Western ways and aspired more and more to emulate their Australian masters. Hanuabada village near Port Moresby, for example, had itself electrified in 1911. These Papuans' increasing understanding of Western manners and motivations, their possession of money, and their growing social self-confidence implicitly challenged the assumptions of white superiority upon which the tiny Australian colonial society was based.* These developments increased the sense of social malaise and insecurity already growing in the white community and fueled the underlying racial antagonism towards Papuans. The response was an increase in racially discriminatory caste and curfew legislation.

Caste legislation had existed in Papua from the earliest days of Australian rule. Papuans were prohibited from drinking alcohol and from wearing clothes on the upper parts of their bodies.† Indentured laborers were required to be in their assigned quarters from 9 P.M. until daylight, or they could be jailed. Employers could slap, cuff, or kick (though not beat) laggard Papuan employees (Inglis 1974: 22). Papuans not on a work contract were not allowed within five miles of Port Moresby unless they could prove they could support themselves in town (Nelson 1982: 26).

In other legislation Papuans were not allowed to behave in a threatening, insulting, or disrespectful manner towards any white person in a public place. In the 1920's the penalty for rape or attempted rape of a white woman by a Papuan man was death. Papuans could not even attend European entertainments and had to get permission from senior government officers before they could indulge in any dancing, beating of drums, or other noisy celebrations of their own after 9 P.M. Curfew restrictions prohibited Papuans from even staying within the confines of Port Moresby after 7 P.M.

These ordinances were quietly but firmly enforced by the constabulary and served to reassure the white community that it still had the upper hand and that the dark-skinned population of Papua would keep its proper social place (Inglis 1974: 49). As a result there were no racial disturbances, native trade unions, or worrisome nationalist political activities while Murray was in charge. He became renowned among colonial administrators of his day for the peace and orderliness that reigned in Papua. Other commentators, less taken with these accomplishments, have characterized his regime as nothing more than a kind of benevolent police rule (Hastings 1969: 66).

---

* These racial barriers did not finally break down until the Second World War, when Papuans toiled alongside American and Australian soldiers to defeat the Japanese—and after the war the white community attempted to erect them again.

† The law that forbade Papuans to wear clothing on the upper part of their bodies was originally enacted (1906) for reasons of "health." The idea was to protect Papuans from the unhealthy effects of wearing dirty clothes, for Papuans seemed (to whites) to wear the most grimy tatters for clothing. This law, of course, also had the effect of keeping Papuans bare chested (and the women bare breasted) and so distinctly "native" and unsophisticated in appearance.

Meanwhile, in the mid-1930's, the bulk of the Australian colonial population, isolated and frustrated in Port Moresby, became increasingly encapsulated in a kind of siege mentality.

Exploration Under Murray

When Hubert Murray became lieutenant governor in 1908, more than half of Papua, despite the strenuous efforts of MacGregor and subsequent administrators, was still unexplored. Much of what had been explored was only nominally under government control. A year after he took office, Murray complained that it was a scandal that cannibalism was still practiced only 24 hours' journey from Port Moresby. Accordingly, he focused his first efforts as lieutenant governor on consolidating control of the regions surrounding areas of white settlement and enterprise. Most of these were strung out along the fringes of the south Papuan coast while the rest followed inland gold-bearing rivers.

The governmental organization Murray inherited partitioned Papua into six administrative divisions, each under a white resident magistrate who oversaw one or more assistant magistrates and a number of patrol officers (See Map 1). These men, who manned the distant outposts on the river estuaries, inland forests, and mountains, were the elite of the Papuan Service, the famed "outside men." With their small detachments of Papuan police, they formed the farthest reach of government presence and control into the interior. They were the key figures in the difficult and dangerous task of opening the Papuan frontier and consolidating control over the hinterland, and Murray handpicked most of them himself.

Murray continued MacGregor's policy of government by inspection and spent about half his time patrolling on foot and horseback with police and carriers through the villages up and down the coast and visiting remote stations in the inland mountains. His natural austerity and high principle and his tendency to carry only the barest minimum of equipment set a new and uncompromising standard of operation for his field officers.

The early years of Murray's administration were not marked by the dramatic expeditions of exploration into new territory characteristic of MacGregor's regime. The last great expedition in the MacGregor tradition had taken place in 1906, two years before Murray took office, when C. A. W. Monckton led an expedition from the headwaters of the Waria, across the central Papuan ranges and down the Lakekamu River to the south Papuan coast. Monckton originally set out under orders to explore a new route for British miners to a gold strike in the interior. But once he reached the headwaters of the Waria, the urge to explore (and the hope of fame) got the better of him, and he decided to keep moving towards the south coast rather than retrace his steps. "If I get through," he wrote in his diary, "it will be the biggest thing yet done in New Guinea. I've wriggled up about 4,000 feet and another six or seven should top the range; but the Lord only knows what's on the other side, or whether there is any food to be got" (Souter 1963: 85).

In the ensuing weeks his patrol encountered hostile tribesmen in the uncontacted Kunimaipa area, and Monckton was struck with an arrow in the stomach. Somehow he managed to keep walking, but in the following weeks a series of disasters took the lives of four carriers and nearly wrecked the expedition. Although the patrol was a remarkable effort, times were already changing, and upon his arrival in Port Moresby, Monckton was reprimanded for having exceeded his instructions and told to return on foot the way he had come. He did, but shortly afterwards he quit the Papuan Service in disgust.

Most of the patrols in the early part of Murray's administration were aimed at consolidation of government control in critical areas surrounding white settlements. The first major exploratory expedition was not carried out until after he had been in office nearly two years and was a result, not of Murray's administrative policies, but of the efforts of a political rival to unseat him from his post as lieutenant governor.

Staniforth Smith and the "Kikori-Strickland" Patrol

Miles Cater Staniforth Smith had been a senator in the first Commonwealth parliament in Australia when he became interested in developments in Papua during a visit there in 1903. In 1907 he went to Port Moresby to serve as Director of Agriculture and Mines and Commissioner for Lands. He quickly established himself as a force to be reckoned with in Papuan colonial politics and almost from the beginning became a rival of Hubert Murray for the post of lieutenant governor of the territory. When Murray was finally appointed to the position in 1908, Smith was given the secondary post of administrator. Disappointed, he aligned himself with the business and planter interests opposing Murray and maneuvered to undermine Murray so he could become lieutenant governor himself. His major opportunity arose in 1910 when Murray went on six months' leave of absence and, as administrator, Smith became acting head of the Papuan colonial government. He immediately set about establishing his own style of administration in the hopes of ingratiating local political support. Compared to Murray's austere, aloof, and understated style, Smith was flamboyant and outgoing. He held champagne suppers for friends and supporters at

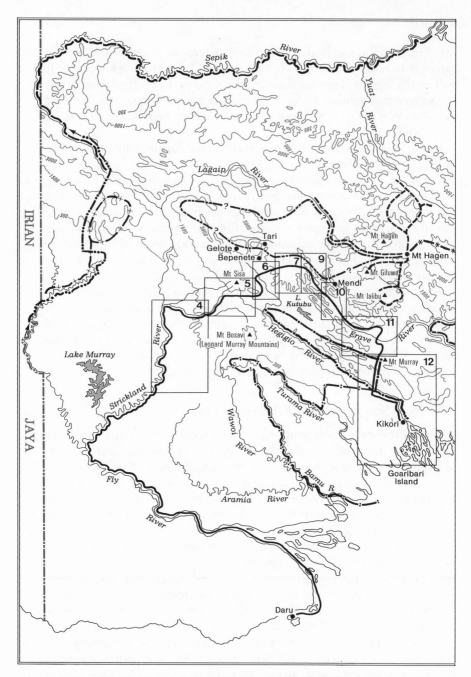

Map 2. Major exploratory patrols in Papua and New Guinea through 1935. (Sector maps of the Strickland-Purari patrol are shown and numbered as in the text.) (Gash and Whittaker 1975; Leahy 1936; New Guinea Annual Reports, various dates; Papua Annual Reports, various dates; Patrol Reports, various dates; Souter 1963.)

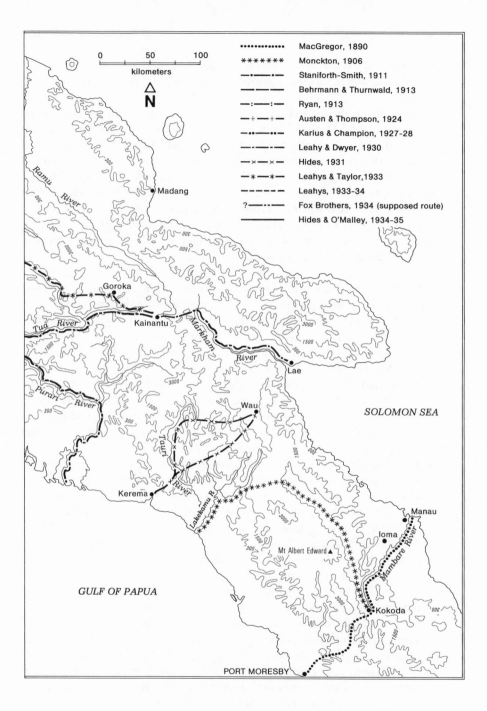

Government House and planned to undertake a glamorous exploratory expedition, which he clearly hoped would bring him renown and advance his ambitions.

Capitalizing on reports of coal deposits investigated by an Australian geologist named Donald MacKay, who had traveled up the Purari River and walked as far as the northern slopes of Mt. Murray three years before, Smith planned what he hoped would be one of the most dramatic and ambitious patrols of exploration to be undertaken in Papua. Smith intended to travel as far up the Kikori as he could by boat and then strike northwards to Mt. Murray. From there he planned to move west across the headwaters of the Kikori to the upper reaches of the Strickland River and then descend via the Strickland and the Fly to the coast. He expected to accomplish all this in six weeks.

On November 20, 1910, Smith left Goaribari Island and headed up the Kikori by steam launch with a party of 4 other white officials, 50 carriers, and 25 native police. The party's blue-ribbon membership included Smith himself, J. P. Hennely, Resident Magistrate of the Gulf Division, Leonard Murray, Acting Private Secretary, Leslie Bell, Chief Inspector for Native Affairs, and A. E. Pratt, a surveyor who had been on MacKay's expedition to Mt. Murray three years before (MacKay and Little 1911).

Smith had little experience of the Papuan bush and was ill-suited to lead such an ambitious expedition. One indication of this was his decision to minimize the staging of supplies along the route. He had decided to carry compressed foods: concentrated meat, meat lozenges, powdered soup, tea, Bovril, cocoa, and cartridges of emergency rations (Souter 1963: 104; Hope 1979: 20–42; Papua Annual Report 1911: 165–71). This mode of supply proved less than adequate, and food was already low two weeks later when they reached the foot of Mt. Murray. At this point, to conserve supplies, Smith sent the bulk of the patrol back to the coast with Hennely and Murray while he himself continued to push westward towards the Strickland with Bell and Pratt, taking eleven police and seventeen carriers.

At first things went well. Descending the mountains and heading northwest, the patrol discovered the well-populated Samberigi Valley, where they were able to purchase food and rest the exhausted carriers. Once past Samberigi, however, they came into difficult country. Trying to head west, Smith found himself continually forced northwards by rugged limestone ranges. Here the inadequacy of his supplies began to tell. His carriers, coastal men used to solid meals of sago and fish, fared badly on a diet of powdered soup and emergency rations. Exhausted and half-starved, they struggled under their loads with increasing difficulty, tying vines around their bellies to fight off hunger. Smith beat them with his walking stick to keep them moving (Souter 1963: 104). Following rivers, crossing ranges,

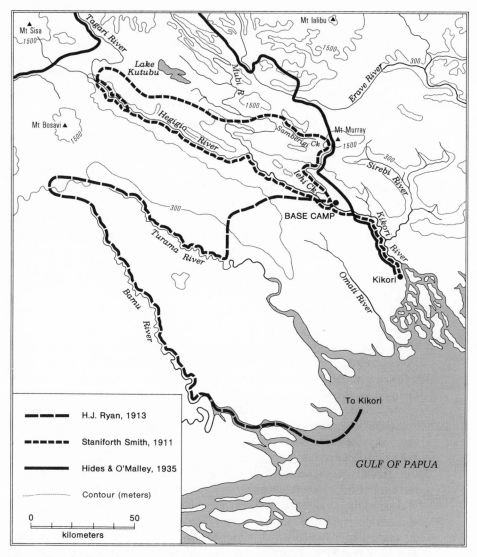

Map 3. Staniforth Smith's patrol of 1911, showing its relation to Henry Ryan's patrol of 1913 and the Strickland-Purari patrol. (Schieffelin and Kurita 1988; Papua Annual Report 1911, 1913.)

forced to move forward and backward by the difficulties of the terrain, Smith continued to travel in a generally northwesterly direction.

The deadline for the patrol's return passed. Smith's colleagues on the coast became alarmed at his prolonged absence and sent out three relief expeditions to try to find him. By late January, Smith was still moving northwest. Finally, following directions of local inhabitants, he emerged at the top of a small range to glimpse a large river flowing to the southeast. Convinced he had reached the Strickland at last, Smith was jubilant. After some trouble he managed to lower his party down the walls of the gorge with vines to a level spot near the water's edge. There they built rafts and set out on the water to float down to the coast. Shortly afterwards, however, they ran into heavy rapids; the rafts were overturned and dashed to pieces on rocks. Seven carriers, already weakened by hunger and exhaustion, were drowned. Virtually all of the patrol's equipment and supplies were lost, including all of Smith's notes and specimens. Smith and some of his party were washed up on the east bank of the river while Pratt, Bell, and the others were washed up on the west. They were left with a few rifles and ammunition, a single pack of matches and the clothes on their backs.

After cutting along the river for five days, Smith found a place to cross the river and join the others. Helpful natives gave them food and fire. The party then set off following the river to find their way back to the coast. The exhausted party had to trek for days through more than a hundred miles of tropical forest and difficult limestone terrain with hardly any food before they came to a place where they could safely put rafts into the water. During this time four more carriers died of hunger and exposure, bringing the count to eleven. Two days after they put rafts in the water, they were astonished to come across the canvas tents of a relief party sent out to find them. Far from having come down the Strickland, Smith was chagrined to learn he was still on the Kikori, in fact at precisely the place he had left it three months before—the patrol had traveled in a circle.

During the initial period of public relief that the party was safe, Smith was acclaimed for his courage and determination by the press and even awarded a medal by the Royal Geographical Society upon a visit to London later that year. However, the official inquiry into the conduct of the patrol and the deaths suffered by the carriers soon led history to take a less positive view of it. Not surprisingly, Hubert Murray had little sympathy for Smith when he returned to Port Moresby. "The loss of a third of the party is something quite unprecedented in Papuan exploration," he wrote in the Annual Report for 1911, "and the expedition cannot be looked on as other than disastrous." Murray made it clear that he thought Smith had brought the disaster upon himself by his own incompetence: "The most charitable and perhaps the true explanation of these regrettable incidents was that the party were hopelessly lost and were so worn out with despair and exhaustion as to be hardly responsible for their actions" (Souter 1963: 106). After the inquest into the carriers' deaths and Smith's handling of the patrol (and his concomitant neglect of administrative duties in Port Moresby), Smith was reprimanded by the Department of External Affairs.

Murray's opinion that Smith did not know where his patrol had been has become the accepted verdict on the matter. Certainly Smith's report, written from memory after the loss of his notes, is so confusing that it is impossible to gain a clear idea of what route he followed—or even to match it with the map, drawn by Pratt, that he provided. The dramatic fact that Smith had mistaken the Kikori for the Strickland confirmed for most people that he had bungled the expedition, and its accomplishments were largely discredited.

Until recently, the best estimates of where Smith actually went have placed the patrol's point of furthest penetration just north of the Mubi-Kikori junction, about 145 km from the coast. However, ethnohistorical fieldwork among the Fasu people west of Lake Kutubu make it clear that Smith's party passed up the Tegima Valley northwest of Lake Kutubu and put their rafts in the Kikori at the Hegigio Gorge, almost 300 km from the coast. They then met disaster in the rapids and whirlpools opposite the mouth of the Dibano River (Schieffelin and Kurita 1988). It is ironic that Smith's political disgrace destroyed any credibility that might otherwise have attached to his expedition, since he and companions were undoubt-edly the first outsiders to enter what is now the Southern Highlands.

The political reverberations of this patrol were a long time in dying down. Two years later, in 1913, Patrol Officer Henry Ryan undertook a similar, but less ambitious patrol. Traveling up the Kikori to where Smith had made his base camp, he struck westward through the rugged limestone forest country south of Mt. Bosavi. He was heading for the Strickland, but after several weeks of incredibly difficult going, he headed down the Aworra, a tributary of the Bamu. En route he had the misfortune to run into a group of Kasua or Kamula bachelors in the midst of an initiation program (cf. Wood 1983). Perhaps seeing an opportunity to meet the ritual requirement for taking human life, about 60 young warriors, with their hair worn in long ceremonial plaits to the middle of their backs, attacked the patrol as it was slowly crossing a log jam on the Wawe river. In the fight that followed, Ryan was struck twice with arrows when he refused to leave a disabled police corporal lying on the jam and barely escaped with his life. The initiates were eventually driven off by police gunfire, leaving behind ten dead.

When Ryan returned, his patrol became the focus of an attack on

Murray by his enemies. The *Papuan Courier*, an opposition newspaper in Port Moresby, implied that Ryan had sustained his injuries while robbing gardens or chasing native women. Staniforth Smith denigrated him for his well-known use of ear-withering profanity—and then, in a curious move perhaps intended to mitigate the appearance of his own previous performance, complained to one of his Australian supporters, "[This] alleged exploration will be quite useless as he [Ryan] knows nothing of surveying and cannot plot the natural features of the country" (Souter 1963: 108).

Murray, who had handpicked Ryan as a patrol officer, naturally took a different view and commended him for staying with the police corporal: "So courageous an action would, in regular warfare, have been awarded the Victoria Cross. But as it happened in an obscure Papuan patrol, Mr. Ryan must be satisfied with the consciousness that he formed a higher conception of his duty than most men would have done, and that he did that duty fearlessly and well" (Papua Annual Report 1913; Souter 1963: 108; see also Hope 1979: 45–50).

Explorations After the First World War

By 1913 the southern coast of Papua was under government influence, with a string of government stations from Daru to Samarai. Murray turned his attention to the exploration and consolidation of the interior. The outbreak of the First World War brought this program almost to a standstill when half the Papuan Service, including many of Murray's most experienced officers, enlisted in the army. Some of the best were killed in action, including Henry Ryan and Wilfred Beaver, who had led one of the relief parties searching for Staniforth Smith.

During the war the German colony established on the north coast of New Guinea was taken over by the Australian military. Following the armistice, this region, together with the Bismarck Archipelago and the German Solomon Islands became the Mandated Territory of New Guinea, administered under the articles of the League of Nations. Murray headed the commission that studied the proposals for the future government of this area, and it was a great disappointment to him not to be put in charge of a united Papua and New Guinea. In this case, however, lobbies for Australian commercial interests won out, promoting the idea of a separate administration—one that did not place the kind of restraints on enterprise that Murray did in Papua. The Mandated Territory turned out to be considerably more rewarding for business than Papua, not because of its administrative policies, but because of its greater natural resources, especially gold. Substantial finds of the yellow metal in the interior mountains at Wau and Bulolo in the early 1920's meant the Mandated Territory could afford to modernize its government services and had access to greater use of radio communication and aircraft than was possible in Papua.* It was inevitable that over the years there developed a certain rivalry between the Papuan Service and its equivalent government service in the Mandated Territory.

During the 1920's and early 1930's the white population of Papua became more closely knit as the second generation came of age. The sons of early government officers moved into positions of public importance, and children who had grown up in the territory linked the older families in marriage (Nelson 1982: 149). The Papuan Service gradually returned to strength after the First World War, now manned by a new generation of officers, many of whom had been born in Papua. However, it still remained small. In 1925 there were only 36 field officers to look after the entire territory. The work was still arduous, physically dangerous, and underpaid, but it was challenging and exciting to men with an adventurous spirit.

Throughout the 1920's and 1930's the work of exploration and consolidation continued. The strategy was for a patrol officer and a detachment of Papuan constabulary to move into a previously uncontacted area and establish a forward police camp. Using this as a base, over the succeeding months and years patrols would then move out exploring the surrounding regions, making (if possible) friendly contact with the people within it, and putting a stop to tribal fighting, cannibalism, and other outlawed practices. Other forward police camps built in neighboring regions would pursue the same objectives. When the patrols from adjacent posts were able to link up, the country was considered under control (Sinclair 1969: 24).

At this time the whole of the interior west-central area of Papua was still unknown from the upper reaches of the Purari River north to the boundary with the Mandated Territory and westward to the Strickland River— the very land that MacKay, Smith, and Ryan had sought to examine—an area of about 37,500 sq. km. In the 1920's a number of exploratory patrols were sent to probe the interior from patrol posts located at the estuaries around the Gulf of Papua. In 1922 Resident Magistrate Leo Flint and Patrol Officer H. M. Saunders revisited the Samberigi Valley for the first time since Wilfred Beaver had passed through looking for Staniforth Smith in 1911. A series of patrols in the following years established the trading links between the Samberigi Valley and three other populated valleys south of the Erave with people of the Kikori River.

In 1929 B. W. Faithorn and Claude Champion led a patrol north of Sam-

---

* This greater prosperity was reflected also in the differences of populations of Europeans in the two colonies. In 1921 the nonindigenous population of Port Moresby was 488 and of Samarai 293. However, in the Mandated Territory there were 1,350 in Rabaul, 356 in Kavieng, and 148 in Kieta (Hastings 1969: 40–61).

berigi that traced the course of the Erave River to the Purari and thence
south to the Gulf of Papua (Kikori PR 19, 1928–29). At its furthest point
north, the patrol crossed the Erave and sighted extensive grass valleys and
columns of smoke in the distance. However, they did not explore in that
direction but, adhering to instructions, turned southeast and followed the
Purari to the sea. In so doing they missed being the first Europeans to enter
the heavily populated valleys of the highlands. That was not to happen for
another six years, and then from a different direction.

Exploration also proceeded westward following the headwaters of the
Fly and Strickland rivers. In 1926 Leo Austen and W. H. Thompson, in
the culmination of a series of patrols probing to the headwaters of the
Fly, encountered rugged limestone country 1,000 km from the sea, part
of the immense limestone barrier that stretches east-west along the southern edges of the central cordillera of the island of New Guinea. No one
knew how wide it was or how far the mountains behind it stretched. But
somewhere beyond were the headwaters of the Sepik River, which wound
its way northwards to the coast of the Mandated Territory.* The final step
was now obviously to mount an expedition to cross the island itself between the headwaters of these two great rivers, by undertaking a journey
from the Gulf of Papua to the north coast of New Guinea.

This was an immense task, and Hubert Murray was determined that it
would be performed by officers of the Papuan Service.† When he failed to
interest the governments of the Mandated Territory and of the Commonwealth of Australia in participating in the expedition, he decided to undertake it anyway, using his own outside men. He chose Assistant Resident
Magistrate Charles Karius and Patrol Officer Ivan Champion, both seasoned veterans of the Papuan Service (Souter 1963: 161).

The expedition proved even more difficult than had been expected. In
the end it took two attempts over a period of thirteen months to penetrate
the mountain barriers.‡ On the second attempt, however, with the help of
guides from among the mountain Ok people, they managed with some
difficulty to get over the ranges to the Sepik losing only one carrier, who
died of exhaustion. It was an epic accomplishment. Hubert Murray, not a
man easily given to meting out praise, wrote that it "was the biggest piece
of exploration ever attempted in any part of New Guinea whether British,
German or Dutch. . . . [It is] unique in the history of exploration because

---

* German explorers Dr. R. Thurnwald and Dr. W. Behrman had explored the upper Sepik
headwaters from the New Guinea side in 1912–14, almost to the Strickland-Sepik divide.
  † Especially when he heard rumors a team of British explorers were going to attempt the
crossing.
  ‡ The first attempt left Daru on December 8, 1926, and returned to Port Moresby July 17,
1927. The second, successful, attempt left Port Moresby September 17, 1927, and made
rendezvous with the ship *Elevala* on the Sepik River on January 19, 1928.

of the scanty resources at the explorer's disposal" (quoted in Souter 1963: 158). The patrol had been accomplished, moreover, without a single shot being fired in anger or a single native warrior killed. It exemplified the highest standards of the Papuan Service.

In the few years following the success of this expedition, the focus of exploration and discovery shifted to the Mandated Territory of New Guinea. The existence of extensive grass valleys in the New Guinea highlands had been known to Lutheran missionaries and to a few prospectors who had been probing the area from the headwaters of the Ramu since the mid-1920's. These operations, however, had been undertaken very quietly, and the regions did not come to the attention of the wider world until after 1930 (Radford 1987: 40–77). In that year, two Australian prospectors, Mick Leahy and Michael Dwyer, led an expedition from the headwaters of the Ramu River across the island over the Bismarck Mountains and down the Purari River to the Papuan coast (see Willis 1969 for a reconstruction of this patrol). In the four years following this epic journey, Mick Leahy, together with his brothers* and government officer James Taylor, made a series of extensive explorations of the highlands west to the Wahgi valley and beyond as far as Wabag. It wasn't long before the significance of these highlands discoveries began to be known. The grass valleys hidden in the central cordillera held nearly half the population of the island of New Guinea—a fact completely unsuspected only a decade before.[†]

Meanwhile in Papua, after Champion and Karius's expedition, only the region between the Strickland River and the headwaters of the Purari remained unexplored. Once a patrol through that area had been completed —although there would still be pockets of uncontacted country for future patrol officers to investigate—all the major regions of the Territory of Papua would be known (Sinclair 1969: 118). The journey promised to be a difficult one, and in 1934 Murray cast about to find the right man to do the job. His choice fell upon a young patrol officer named Jack Hides.

---

[*] There were four Leahy brothers: Patrick, Michael, James, and Daniel. Patrick did not join his brothers' explorations, but managed their affairs on the coast.

[†] Excellent accounts of the opening of the highlands of the Mandated Territory are given in Radford (1987), *Highlanders and Foreigners in the Upper Ramu: The Kainantu Area 1919-1942*. Also see the film (1983) and the book (1987) by Connolly and Anderson, both titled *First Contact*.

2. THE STRICKLAND-PURARI PATROL: STARTING OUT

EDWARD L. SCHIEFFELIN AND ROBERT CRITTENDEN

> Something hidden. Go and find it.
>   Go and look behind the Ranges—
> Something lost behind the Ranges.
> Lost and waiting for you. Go!
>
>   Rudyard Kipling,
>   "The Explorer"

Hubert Murray believed that a man's character rather than his knowledge of the law or government was the most important consideration in picking his outside men. Moreover, he tended to give preference to young men who had been born and brought up in the territory and whose families he knew. Jack Hides was born in Port Moresby in 1906, the son of the warden of the jail. He grew up amid Papuan children and spoke fluent Motu before he spoke English.* Port Moresby was a rough-and-ready place at that time, already developing its own legends. Throughout his childhood, young Jack listened to tales of the exploits of such local heroes as Monckton, Beaver, and Ryan. He early established a reputation as a high-spirited, adventurous lad; at one time he ran away from home to live for a few days in a native village while his relatives searched frantically for him. As a young man, he was a dashing figure. Tall and good-looking, he bore a striking resemblance to the matinee idol Errol Flynn.[†]

Jack Hides and the Papuan Service

Jack Hides joined the Papuan Service in 1926 at the age of twenty, with the patronage of Hubert Murray. Seven years later he was a highly regarded officer who had risen through the ranks by outstanding achieve-

---

* This account of Jack Hides's background and personality relies heavily on James Sinclair's excellent biography *The Outside Man* (1969) and a portrayal of Hides in his biography of Ivan Champion (1988: 35–36, 118–25).

†As a matter of fact, Hides and Flynn knew each other at the time and once had a fight in a bar. Flynn had come to New Guinea to seek his fortune in plantations and gold mining. Failing at this, he made his fortune in Hollywood.

ment. Murray had already mentioned him in dispatches as "one of our best men in the bush."

From his boyhood Hides had developed a deep and enduring love for Papua and its people. Unlike many officers, he possessed a romantic imagination and a genuine love of exploring. As a fellow officer, Bill Adamson, once remarked, "To him the next ridge was not . . . just another few hours of hard slogging, it was something that might conceal a wonderful new river, a goldbearing creek, or an unsuspected pocket of population" (quoted in Sinclair 1969: 55). The miles of uncharted wilderness continually called to his imagination. Hides enjoyed the hard life of a bush officer, leading a line of carriers and police over difficult paths through the tropical forest or sleeping under a canvas fly in the midst of the Papuan Mountains. During one patrol he wrote these entries in his diary:

The sounds of the forest and the stream . . . died down, and as I sat outside my tent in the dying sunlight I felt once again that beautiful loneliness of the Papuan jungle. Carriers were near me filling tins of water for the evening meal of rice; some police formed an idle group just outside their tent and beside a small fire, while from the other side of the creek came the voice of a policeman lifted in song as he chopped wood for the fire that would blaze that night in the police tent. If you are a man who knows Papua and one who lives in its lonely places, the song of the Orokaiva policeman will make your blood surge.

I looked up at the roof of sago leaves with its occasional drips of water [and] thought of the cold, and the dry stick of sago I was eating. Since early morning we had been constantly wet and without food. . . . I thought of civilization, its warmth and comfort, bright lights and good food, and I suddenly wondered why I did this work. There was no answer to these thoughts; the jungle and its peoples just seemed to hold a fascination for me, one that provided a great interest in my life in which all hardship was soon forgotten. (Sinclair 1969: 52, 74)

Hides started his career as a cadet patrol officer working under Ivan Champion, already an experienced member of the Papuan Service. The two men had known each other throughout their boyhood in Port Moresby and had been both friends and rivals. They were posted to the remote police camp at Mondo in the Papuan Mountains among the Goilala, Kunimaipa, and Kambisi peoples. Almost as soon as they arrived, however, Champion was recalled to Port Moresby to join Charles Karius on the Fly-Sepik patrol. Hides, left behind to learn the ropes under Champion's replacement, was filled with envy and admiration—and a burning desire to do something as splendid.

At this time the administration was attempting to end the cycle of raids and revenge killings among the local groups around Mondo, particularly among the Kunimaipa. A cunning and (from the government perspective) intractable people, the Kunimaipa more than once ambushed patrols.

Hides learned the dangerous business of night raids to capture the tribal killers. The two patrol officers and a detachment of police would creep up on a village in the dead of night, take stations by the doors of each dwelling, and explain through an interpreter that the people should give up the culprits and that they meant them no harm. The people inside, terrified at this unexpected presence in the darkness, would bolt out the doors in a panic to be grabbed and handcuffed by the waiting officers and constables. The screams and shouts, the brandished clubs and axes, the snap of bowstrings, and the whiz of arrows made this kind of struggle in the darkness —and sometimes the pouring rain—extremely dicey business. Jack Hides loved it and soon proved to be a courageous and determined officer.

Like other government officers, Hides believed that the consolidation of administration authority over the Papuan cultures of the hinterland was inevitable, but he could not avoid a pang of romantic nostalgia at the thought of the passing of the "ancient Papuan way of life." * Once, when he was camped in the Kunimaipa Valley in pursuit of some tribal killers, he heard the inhabitants, who had fled to the ridges for fear of arrest, shout down at the patrol:

"What do you want? Why are you walking about here? We don't want you! Go away now!"
"Poor savages!" Hides remarked. "The patrol would not go away, and they were determined not to submit."
That night the people gathered and sang their war songs. Some hundreds of men were singing, and the sounds came across the valley quite clearly. The singing is wonderful, inspiring, and moves one in these lonely outposts. Some day the world will learn of the singing of these people and will want to hear them but until that day comes, it will remain with these people of the by-ways and back lanes of Papua, reserved for the patrol officer. (Sinclair 1969: 46)

Hides managed to combine this kind of sentiment with the belief in the law-bringing, civilizing mission that formed the rationalization for extension of administration control.

Around this time gold was discovered in the Tauri Valley near the Lakekamu River, and hopeful prospectors began moving up the creeks into the Papuan Mountains. Murray followed their progress closely hoping that the goldfield would prove to be a big one and help lift Papua out of its financial doldrums. As the miners moved deeper into the hills, they began to enter the country of a warlike group known at the time as the "Kukukuku".† Raids by these people into the lowland areas had made

* Rosaldo (1989) has called this "imperialist nostalgia," the tendency for colonialists to romanticize or mourn the passing of traditional societies they helped destroy. There is perhaps also something here of a mourning for Eden, as represented by the image of man in the state of nature.
† These people are known today as the Anga, the name they call themselves. "Kukukuku"

them widely feared by neighboring tribes, and their determined resistance to the penetration of their homeland by administration patrols had landed them a reputation among government officers of being "murderous" and "treacherous." In 1930 Murray sent Jack Hides, by then a seasoned officer, into the area to make friendly contact with these people and ensure that they did not molest the prospectors.

The Kukukuku met Hides's peaceful overtures and gifts by ambushing his patrols and harassing his camps with showers of arrows. Bolder warriors would creep up and lie in the undergrowth at the edge of the camp to try to pick off an unwary constable or carrier who might wander near. At the same time, Hides had to deal with other difficulties commonly met by patrol officers in the field: shortage of food, desertion of carriers, and unruly, disobedient police. When the going got rough, anxious or weary carriers tended to slip away in the night. To prevent desertions, some patrol officers would handcuff their carriers to a length of cable at night. Hides evidently did not do this, and his carriers tended to disappear one at a time when he entered the Kukukuku country. Another problem was that Papuan police, if not closely supervised by their patrol officers, would often "exceed orders" and ignore Murray's regulations against firing on native people.[*] Two of Hides's constables escorting a group of carriers in search of water killed a Kukukuku man who they claimed was drawing a bow on them. This killing and the resulting fury of the local tribesmen meant that weeks of attempts to establish peaceful contact with the natives had gone for naught.

Undaunted, Hides decided that if he could not, for the moment, make peaceful contact with nearby groups, he would try his luck with those farther away. He marched his patrol yet deeper into the bush. Still the Kukukuku did not approach him, but their long, drawn-out cries accompanied the patrol, warning others up the valley. Sometimes after a day or two of attacks, Hides met a friendly people who would give them food and hospitality, only to have the next group they met along the way shower them with arrows. Eventually one carrier was wounded, and the patrol was forced to return to base.

---

was actually the name applied to them by their enemies and raiding victims in neighboring areas, who first made them known to the administration.

[*]A typical example of this occurred during the patrol by Faithorn and Champion from Kikori to the Erave in 1929 (Kikori PR, 1928–29). On breaking camp one day, the patrol discovered that some axes and blankets had been stolen. A policeman sent back to recover them killed some of the local warriors. A few days later the same policeman and another killed more warriors while acting independently of the main body of the patrol. The officers relieved the two police of their rifles and put them under arrest. The first of these incidents took place at the edge of unexplored territory and may well have affected the reception that was given Hides and his patrol when they traversed the region nearly five years later.

Hides was determined to make one more attempt. Even though his carrier line was thinned by desertions, he set off again, planning to ascend the Tauri River, cross the divide at its headwaters, and come down the adjacent Tiveri Valley. He was accompanied by a small detachment of police and only nine carriers with the patrol equipment and three bags of rice, hardly enough to sustain them for such a journey. By the time they reached the headwaters of the Tauri, the food was almost gone. While searching vainly for a route to the Tiveri Valley, they heard the rumble of an aircraft motor in the distance to the north. Astonished and curious, Hides decided to investigate further. He abandoned his search for the Tiveri, and crossed the mountain range following the sound. He led his patrol down a long valley to emerge at the town of Wau in the Mandated Territory of New Guinea.

The unexpected arrival of a Papuan Patrol in the Mandated Territory caused rather a stir in the small gold-mining town.* It raised some eyebrows back in Port Moresby, too, since Hides had no business being over the border. When Hides requested permission to return to Port Moresby via Salamaua by coastal steamer, the response he received was similar to that given to Monckton after his unauthorized journey in 1906: "You walked over, you can bloody well walk back."

Hides took this as a challenge, purchased new supplies, and set off back into the mountains with his weary carriers and police. It was hard going. They were forced to cut their route through uninhabited and extremely rugged country. After a week and a half, they ran out of food. The next day, with incredible luck, they found a native garden. They helped themselves to some of the produce, and left a bush knife behind as compensation. A few days later a sick carrier died and was buried beside the track. Shortly afterwards they entered Kukukuku country again and once more had to be constantly on the alert for ambush. Despite precautions, one of the carriers was wounded by an arrow in the stomach. Finally, as they neared the limits of their endurance, they emerged safely at a mining camp. Hides's biographer James Sinclair, himself an experienced patrol officer, remarked that the party was lucky to have survived at all: "It had been a foolhardy venture, for Hides had not the men or equipment necessary for the walk he had undertaken. Courage, hardihood, luck and his carriers and police had brought them through" (Sinclair 1969: 67).

Such adventures revealed Hides to be a man who was impulsive as well as decisive, and bold almost to the point of recklessness. When faced with

* This was the year that Mick Leahy and Michael Dwyer had made their famous crossing from the Bismarck Mountains to the Gulf of Papua. It is quite possible that Hides intended his visit to Wau to serve as an unofficial response to their expedition, in the tradition of rivalry between the government officers of the two territories.

challenge, danger, or uncertainty, he tended to throw himself into the situation, whatever the difficulties, and trust to courage and luck to pull him through. These qualities, however, were tempered by his superb bush-craft and leadership. His ability to inspire his men was closely bound up with the fact that he did things with a certain panache. After he returned from Wau, Murray rebuked him, but could not forbear to congratulate him as well. In a comment on Hides's report he remarked: "I cannot think that the P.O. could have any real excuse for crossing into the other ter-ritory. Please remind him that his patrols should be confined to Papua, unless otherwise expressly instructed. . . . At the same time I think that the P.O. is to be congratulated upon the skill and pluck displayed by him, and thanks largely to his example, by his patrol" (Sinclair 1969: 68). Though not as spectacular as Champion and Karius's Fly-Sepik patrol, Hides's journey to Wau and back was still a remarkable achievement.*

Jack Hides and Jim O'Malley

In 1931 Hides met the man who was to be his companion on the Strickland-Purari patrol, Louis James O'Malley. O'Malley was born on January 22, 1912, and was Hides's junior by six years. Like Hides, he was a child of colonial Papua. His father, J. T. O'Malley, had been Resident Magistrate for the Central Division and worked as an administration offi-cer in Port Moresby a good part of his life. In 1933, when O'Malley was nineteen and had just joined the Papuan Service, he was posted with Hides as a cadet officer to the outpost at Kairuku: their task was to put an end to the tribal fighting that again had broken out in the area. On their ar-rival at Kairuku, Hides and O'Malley immediately departed for the bush with a patrol of 16 police and 68 carriers, to track down the leader of a confederacy of 12 Ivirupu villages who was responsible for a number of raids and killings as part of an attempt to extend his dominance over the whole Kunimaipa Valley. Hides carried out the task with his usual determination, pushing hard into the mountains to run down his quarry. At one time the patrol traveled without sleep for 36 hours. O'Malley had had little bush experience but nevertheless kept up with the experienced Hides. Through the forced marches and pre-dawn struggles to capture the men they were after, the two men became fast friends.

* Precisely because the successful completion of this difficult and dangerous journey was significant by the exacting standards of Murray's Papuan Service, it is important not to forget that it cost the life of one carrier and resulted in severe injury to another. In these patrols, as with a great many colonial achievements, the glory went to the leaders while a good part of the price was paid in the ranks who, willingly or unwillingly, made it possible. Patrol officers and police agreed to the risks of patrolling as part of their job, but carriers and local Papuans encountered by patrols did not always have a great deal of choice in the matter.

One night in the middle of this patrol, as Hides's biographer tells the tale, Hides and O'Malley were seated by the campfire discussing the events of the previous few days:

There came a long silence and Hides picked up a small-scale map of Papua and studied it for a few moments. He turned to O'Malley and pointed to the map.

"Jim," he said, "see that blank space between the Strickland and the Purari? You know that Ryan had a go at it from Kikori and also Staniforth Smith, but they didn't make it. I believe that if we went up the Strickland River and tackled it from that end we might get through. I wonder what is in there. . . . Wouldn't it be wonderful to see it and to find people and to be the first into unknown Papua?" His face glowing, Hides stared into the fire, lost in his thoughts. Then he turned again to O'Malley, "If I do this patrol, will you go with me?" Carried away by the spell of the night and the warmth of his companion's ardor, O'Malley told Hides that he would go. (Sinclair 1969: 97)

It was a pact of friendship that Hides would not forget. When the time came to embark on the Strickland-Purari patrol, a little more than a year later, Hides requested O'Malley as his second in command. It was a good choice. Sinclair remarks: "O'Malley was to prove a stalwart and competent companion. The two men were opposites, temperamentally and physically. Hides was strong but of wiry build; O'Malley was powerfully muscled. Hides was restless, impulsive, dashing; O'Malley tended to be quiet and retiring. He was also solid and methodical. He respected Hides immensely and remained fiercely loyal to him to the end of his life" (1969: 93).

Papuan Exploration and Colonial Romance

It was Hubert Murray's style to have Papua explored without fanfare or publicity, and officers of the Papuan Service generally did their work quietly out of the public gaze. However, the exotic nature of the island of New Guinea as one of the last undiscovered regions of the world seemed inevitably to exercise a romantic fascination on the public mind; it was the "Darkest Africa" of the South Pacific. When news of a major piece of exploration in Papua got out, such as Champion and Karius's Fly-Sepik patrol, it caught the public imagination as a kind of true-life *Lost Horizon* or *King Solomon's Mines*. Whatever the intentions of the explorers, it was difficult for most readers (and writers) of the media not to frame them within this genre of romantic adventure. Their real accounts and descriptions coexisted with such popular works as Buchan's *Prester John*, Rider Haggard's *She*, and countless adventure stories for boys.

Seen in social-historical perspective, this romanticized view was closely bound up with the historical processes of European expansion towards the end of the nineteenth century. While for indigenous people the establishment of colonialism meant subordination and exploitation, for Europeans new regions (whatever the nature of their inhabitants) were seen as marvelous opportunities for expansion and gain, where a man of mettle could really do something for himself—and "for England." They never questioned their right to establish dominion. What appears as greed and expropriation in critical historical perspective looked like the fulfillment of ambitious vision and pioneer effort to many colonialists of the time.

By the first quarter of the twentieth century, however, the heyday of European expansion was over. The more heavy-handed and buccaneering aspects of empire building lay largely in the past (where they could be safely ignored) while its adventurous surfaces and enjoyment of privilege became the subject of nostalgia and romance.

Within this context, during the 1920's and 1930's, New Guinea came to be seen as a last frontier. Its unexplored interior and exotic people exercised a powerful grip on the imagination of the reading public. It was almost the last place on earth where one could still go where no white man had gone before, establish something in new country, and escape the ordinary possibilities of conventional life.

This romance of empire was articulated in a growing number of books describing the work of patrol officers, written by admiring journalists and outsiders. The image of a white man leading his police and carriers through the jungle amidst danger and hardship to discover unknown regions and peoples became the empire-building version of the Quest of the Hero. Writers cast their accounts in explicitly heroic terms—one enthusiastic author even framed the subject in the aura of Arthurian legend: *Knights Errant of Papua* (Lett 1935). It is through this kind of literature that popular perception of Papua as a land of adventure and discovery must be understood. And it is how patrol officers of imagination like Jack Hides understood themselves and their jobs.

Government officers themselves also wrote about their lives and work in Papua. Straightforward accounts of true adventures and even descriptions of exotic geography were always well received. Austen, Beaver, and Monckton wrote articles, books, and yarns about their experiences in the bush—as indeed, in more sober vein, did William MacGregor and Hubert Murray. These writings were all eagerly read by the colonists themselves, as well as by others, and became one of the sources from which they constructed their image of themselves and their sense of historical tradition (cf. Hobsbawm and Ranger 1983).

In 1932, when Ivan Champion published *Across New Guinea from the Fly to the Sepik*, the account of the Fly-Sepik patrol, one of his readers was Jack Hides. Hides himself was a good storyteller and was much in demand for public lectures when he went south periodically on leave to Australia. Inspired by Champion, he decided that he too would write a book about his adventures as a patrol officer. *Through Wildest Papua* was written by lantern light during the long tropical nights at his isolated patrol station. Hides wrote well, with an appealing, evocative prose that revealed a sensitivity to people and place. He was just sending off the final draft to the publisher when he received the summons from Hubert Murray to lead the Strickland-Purari patrol.

The Strickland-Purari Patrol

For Hides the prospect of exploring the last major unknown region of Papua was the fulfillment of a lifetime dream. Upon receiving Murray's summons, he returned immediately to Port Moresby where he and O'Malley set about gathering supplies in preparation for the journey. In 1934 the government of Papua was still run on a shoestring, and patrol equipment kept in government stores was meager and often decrepit. Elsewhere in the world gentleman trekkers could carry lightweight tents of silk, but such tents were expensive, and patrol officers in Papua had to make do with heavy canvas. Portable radio transceivers were obtainable, but Papua could not afford them, and patrol officers had to make do with runners. In the Mandated Territory of New Guinea, flush with the profits of gold mining, aircraft were used routinely to scout proposed routes for exploration, and to drop supplies to patrols in the field. Papuan officers had no such luxuries. Murray's own abstemious style set the example for his outside men. They were proud of their reliance on their own resourcefulness and perseverance to carry out their tasks rather than having to depend on the quality of their equipment or adequate logistical support.

The expedition for which Hides and O'Malley were preparing represented the end of an era of exploration in Papua. It was the last major exploratory patrol to be carried out in nineteenth-century style, without benefit of prior aerial reconnaissance, without airdrops to replenish supplies, and without radio communications. Everything the patrol required had to be carried. It was to be the last patrol to push its way blindly into unknown country, slowly relaying its supplies forward day by day (Sinclair 1969: 118).

Hides's plan was not very different from the one he had outlined to O'Malley by the campfire a year before. They planned to ascend the Fly and Strickland rivers to the limits of navigation and then, proceeding by canoe, search for a tributary that they could follow eastwards. They would continue on foot across the headwaters of the Kikori until they found a major tributary of the Purari. Finally they would return to the coast either by traveling down the Purari River itself or by turning southward to link up with the established patrol route from the Samberigi Valley to the coast.

Hides and O'Malley knew very little of the region they were about to explore. What they did know from studying the reports of previous Papuan patrols that had encroached on the fringes of this area was that somewhere in that expanse they would encounter the difficult limestone country that had defeated the patrols of Henry Ryan and Staniforth Smith. They also knew, from the reports of James Taylor and the Leahy brothers in the Mandated Territory, that beyond the limestone barrier they were likely to encounter the large native populations characteristic of the highlands. Curiously, Hides never mentions this in his writings, but it seems to have entered his calculations ("Into Unknown Papua," *Pacific Islands Monthly*, Jan. 24, 1935). He was convinced that the patrol should limit its carriers to the smallest practical number in order to travel quickly (Sinclair 1969: 125), which meant it would be impossible to carry enough food for the whole journey. He and O'Malley were counting on meeting sufficient interior populations to be able to trade for food as well as being able part of the time to live off the land.*

This being the case, the particular items chosen for trade were crucial. For smaller items, they packed a variety of trinkets such as beads and small mirrors. For the more valuable items Hides chose steel axes and bush-knives, which from his experience were always popular with people in the bush. This proved to be a fateful decision. The people Hides and O'Malley were to meet in the distant highland valleys were unfamiliar with steel and preferred a far older commodity, the mother-of-pearl shell. Hides did not make his decision in complete ignorance of this. The reports of Taylor and Leahy in the Mandated Territory and of Leahy and Dwyer's expedition from the Ramu Valley down the Purari to the Papuan coast in 1930 clearly indicated how highly interior peoples prized pearlshell. That shell was highly valued in the nearer hinterland was also well known to Papuan officers, several of whom tried to trace the trade routes over which it moved into the interior (Austen, 1935). But in their experience steel was also a strongly coveted commodity everywhere in Papua. Murray's officers exploring new territory almost never entered a place where it was not

---

* Hides did plan to have enough food to carry him through the length of the unknown part of the country ahead. "I do not expect that we shall have any of our own food left by the time that we reach the Purari," he wrote a friend in Port Moresby. "In that area, however, I know what is ahead of us, and we shall be able to live, however uncomfortably, on the country" ("Approaching Mt. Hagen Area," *Pacific Islands Monthly*, May 21, 1935, pp. 44–45). On February 18, at the land base camp on the Rentoul River, Hides calculated that he had three months' stores left and that this was more than enough to get the patrol through the unknown part of the journey.

already known and desired.* Thus, while patrol reports of nearly every expedition into the Samberigi Valley from 1911 into the 1930's remarked upon the high value placed upon shell, they also emphasized the local desire for steel. Theft of steel implements there was a major problem in early expeditions—the locals desired it so avidly that they sometimes even grabbed the axes out of the carrier's belts (Papua Annual Report 1911). Thus, despite Leahy and Dwyer's reports of the highlander's desire for shell, Hides apparently based his decision on his experience that he had never encountered a Papuan man even in the remotest regions who did not covet steel (Sinclair 1969: 125). In this, as in many other ways, the people of the interior highlands were not to meet his expectations.

This would not be the only way in which Hides and O'Malley were ill-prepared for what they would find. One of the great hopes for this patrol was again that it might discover gold or some other mineral resource that would help Papua out of its poverty. But neither Hides nor O'Malley were experienced prospectors or had much knowledge of geology, although they planned to pan for gold in every stream they crossed. Neither was skilled in surveying or cartography: on their return they would not be able to make an accurate map of the route they traveled.

When Hides and O'Malley had all of their supplies and equipment together, they loaded everything on the government steam launch *Vailala* and headed for Daru at the mouth of the Fly River. They had chosen to limit equipment as well as food in order to keep their load as light as possible. They packed canvas tents for patrol officers and police, trade items, medical supplies, tinned meat and a few personal effects for the patrol officers, and five tons of brown rice. The *Vailala* stopped along the way to pick up carriers at Auma and at Goaribari Island (notorious for the killing and eating of Reverend Chalmers in 1901). A few days later, on January 1, 1935, the patrol set off up the Fly from Daru in the government launch—the 2 patrol officers, 10 Papuan police, and 30 carriers. The police were armed with single-shot, Martini lever-action Lee Enfield .303 carbines with twenty rounds of ammunition each. Hides carried a .303 rifle borrowed from a friend, and O'Malley had his own .45 caliber pistol. Behind the launch they towed four 45-foot dugout canoes.

They traveled by launch for ten days up the Fly and then the Strickland, covering more than 560 km from the coast by the time they reached the limits of motor navigation. Then they continued on in canoes, looking for the tributary that would take them east. Nineteen days later, on January 29, they found it—an unmapped river 65–70m wide, flowing slowly

* The fact that the appearance of steel tools always preceded the introduction of administration activity in remote regions prompted Murray to liken the movement of government influence into uncontacted areas to the spread of an oil stain (see Chapter 5).

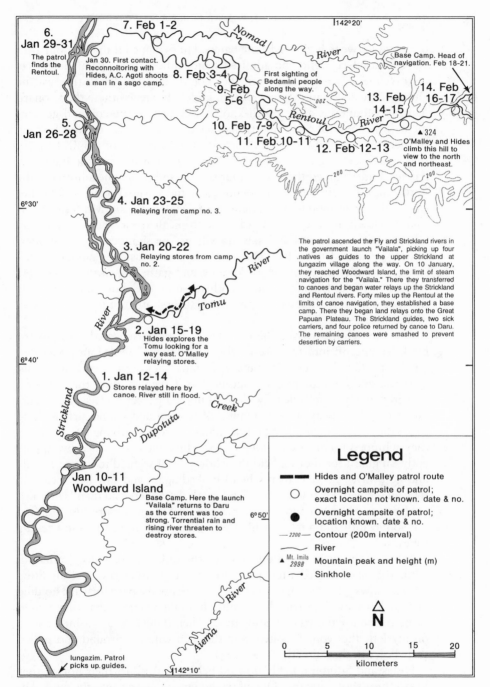

The patrol ascended the Fly and Strickland rivers in the government launch "Vailala", picking up four natives as guides to the upper Strickland at Iungazim village along the way. On 10 January, they reached Woodward Island, the limit of steam navigation for the "Vailala." There they transferred to canoes and began water relays up the Strickland and Rentoul rivers. Forty miles up the Rentoul at the limits of canoe navigation, they established a base camp. There they began land relays onto the Great Papuan Plateau. The Strickland guides, two sick carriers, and four police returned by canoe to Daru. The remaining canoes were smashed to prevent desertion by carriers.

6. Jan 29-31
The patrol finds the Rentoul.

7. Feb 1-2

Jan 30. First contact. Reconnoitering with Hides, A.C. Agoti shoots a man in a sago camp.

8. Feb 3-4

9. Feb 5-6

First sighting of Bedamini people along the way.

Base Camp. Head of navigation. Feb 18-21.

13. Feb 14-15

14. Feb 16-17

5. Jan 26-28

10. Feb 7-9

11. Feb 10-11

12. Feb 12-13

▲ 324
O'Malley and Hides climb this hill to view to the north and northeast.

4. Jan 23-25
Relaying from camp no. 3.

3. Jan 20-22
Relaying stores from camp no. 2.

2. Jan 15-19
Hides explores the Tomu looking for a way east. O'Malley relaying stores.

1. Jan 12-14
Stores relayed here by canoe. River still in flood.

Jan 10-11 Woodward Island
Base Camp. Here the launch "Vailala" returns to Daru as the current was too strong. Torrential rain and rising river threaten to destroy stores.

Iungazim. Patrol picks up guides.

Legend

▬▬ Hides and O'Malley patrol route

○ Overnight campsite of patrol; exact location not known. date & no.

● Overnight campsite of patrol; location known. date & no.

—2200— Contour (200m interval)

〜 River

▲ Mt. Imila 2998 Mountain peak and height (m)

⊶ Sinkhole

△
N

0 5 10 15 20
kilometers

Map 4. From Woodward Island to the limits of canoe navigation on the Rentoul River (January 10–February 21).

out from between high sandstone banks. Hides named it the Rentoul after Alex Rentoul, a friend and admired senior officer in the Papuan Service.

Traveling slowly up this river, they could make out far to the east the clustered peaks of an extinct volcano. Hides christened these the Leonard Murray Mountains after a well-known secretary of the colonial government (a nephew of Sir Hubert) and set them as a goal for the first leg of their journey. To the north, beyond a vast expanse of tropical forest, they could see range after range of mountains that marked the limestone barrier. Hides named these also after friends and people he admired—the northern mountain barrier he identified as the Karius Range, and farther east a cluster of mountains became the O'Malley Peaks (Mt. Sisa). Continuing slowly up the river amid thick tropical forest, they caught only glimpses of the natives and saw no villages or significant garden sites. Hides speculated the inhabitants of these parts must be "nomads" pursuing a wandering existence of hunting and gathering in the forest. He wished to make friendly contact with these people, but they kept their distance and were difficult to approach. His first attempt to do so was an ominous disaster.

One day while scouting the river bank, Hides discovered a well-worn track leading off into the forest, which he followed with four policemen and a Strickland River man named Situmu. They soon heard the sound of voices and the thumping of sago beaters. Creeping up to the edge of a clearing, as Hides tells it, they "looked upon a peaceful yet savage scene. Not thirty feet away were a number of women and young girls making sago; they were singing and talking, and occasionally giving tired sighs as they whipped the pith with long canes. Three men stood nearby, apparently on guard for they all held their bows. . . . I wanted to leave presents and go away, . . . (but) then when I looked again and saw how peaceful they all seemed, I wanted to be friends with them there and then" (PR: 13).

Hides stepped out into the clearing with Situmu before him holding out some cloth and a new bushknife to the natives and calling in friendly tones.

"One of the girls yelled and bolted; the older women stood amazed, while the men stepped a few paces towards us with arrows already fitted to their bows. . . . My hopes ran high. . . . I stepped a pace forward holding out my left hand in a friendly gesture. It seemed certain that they would come to me for the women still stood. Then there was a crashing sound on my left; the women bolted, and the men wheeled around and pulled their bows in that direction" (PR: 14).

Hides and Situmu quickly dodged behind a tree. To their horror they heard three shots ring out. One of the bowmen fell over into the mud. Apparently Constable Agoti, seeing Hides start to enter the clearing had tried to come out as well, but had sunk into the mud up to his knees, scaring the natives out of their amazement and putting himself in a helpless position at the same time. One of the bowmen had then advanced on him, releasing two arrows. Agoti dodged them but was unable to extricate himself from the mud. As the bowman came over to drive an arrow in at close range, Agoti had fired two shots above his head, and when the native did not stop was forced to kill him. Hides was understandably upset.

"Although I realize the awful position this constable had been in, I could not help expressing bitter resentment at his foolish eagerness. It was a most unfortunate happening, and one that I will always regret, I can see now that I should have left these people to approach me on their own time.

"I left a tomahawk, some cloth, and a knife all tied to a broken arrow beside the dead native. I still wonder if they understood afterwards that we meant them no harm" (PR: 14).

This incident was not a good omen for what was to come. Nevertheless, the patrol continued up the Rentoul in their canoes. About three weeks later, on February 18, they reached a series of impassable rapids that marked the limits of navigation on the Rentoul. Moving their equipment onto the riverbank, Hides and O'Malley prepared the patrol to begin staging its way by land. Hides climbed a tree to assess what route they should follow and discovered that they were about to enter upon a vast forested tableland which he named the Great Papuan Plateau.

3. THE GREAT PAPUAN PLATEAU

EDWARD L. SCHIEFFELIN

The country into which the patrol began to move on February 21 is a middle-altitude region of dense tropical forest stretching roughly from the Giwa (or Kiwa) River east to the Kikori (locally called Hegigio) and covering an area of roughly 1,709 sq. km. It is bounded to the north by the mountainous escarpment of the New Guinea highlands and to the south by the jumbled peaks of an extinct volcano, Mt. Bosavi. The latter formation, located about 45 km south of the highland rim, rises dramatically to 2,800 m from the midst of the forested plain, presenting an image of remote and lonely grandeur. The climate on the plateau is mild, the temperature averaging about 35°C (80°F) with occasional drops to 10°C (50°F) on cold nights. Rainfall is high, ranging from about 5,080 mm (200 inches) a year on the southern portion of the plateau to an estimated 6,680 mm (263 inches) a year near Mt. Sisa to the north (Kelly 1977: 32).

Within the forest the endless trees and the complexity of the vegetation create a bewildering and primeval aspect for an outsider. For Jack Hides it evoked the ancient past. "There is probably no other part of Papua so full of game as this huge tract of undulating forest lands," he wrote, "and it is on account of this fact, I suppose, that these primitive people are here, living today as they did before corn was discovered in Egypt. They are surely part of the oldest inhabitants of this great island" (*PW*: 133). Inside this immense forest, it is impossible to see far through the vegetation. An outsider without a compass or a river to guide him can easily get disoriented and lost in the vast anonymity of trees.

The Peoples of the Plateau

For the people who live there, however, the shapes of the ridges, the lines of the watercourses, the muddy, almost invisible tracks, the subtle changes in the vegetation all reveal a familiar and beloved world.* Footprints on the muddy tracks are read to monitor the domestic errands of friends and relatives or to reveal the arrival of visitors or, more ominously, the presence of strangers, perhaps enemies, bent on clandestine projects of conspiracy or violence. A bundle of thatching leaves or a net bag of planting shoots left by the path reveals a pause in the round of everyday activity. Stands of younger secondary forest or tangled plots of weeds and vines mark the former site of a garden or a longhouse.

Three groups of people inhabit this area, speaking mutually unintelligible languages but living broadly similar ways of life. On the southern portion of the plateau, just north of Mt. Bosavi, live the Bosavi people (Schieffelin 1976; Feld 1982), numbering perhaps 1,400 in 1935. To the north of them, between the Isawa (Rentoul) River and the highland rim east of the Sioa River are the Onabasulu, numbering about 900 in 1935. Finally, on the west banks of the Sioa along the steeply dissected flanks of Mt. Sisa live the Etoro people (Kelly 1974, 1977), numbering perhaps 780 in 1935.† In the 1930's all of these people lived in communal longhouses perched on ridges where they could command a strategic view of the surrounding countryside. These longhouses were substantial structures, being about 18 m long and 9 m wide with a humpbacked roof resembling the

---

* The ethnographic background for this chapter is drawn from five years of research by the author among the Kaluli-speaking Bosavi people of the southern portion of the Papuan Plateau and from the writings and personal communications of Thomas Ernst and Raymond Kelly, who worked among the Onabasulu and Etoro peoples of the northern part of the plateau. Material on the Strickland-Purari patrol itself was gathered during my field trips in 1975–77 and 1984–85 in the Bosavi area. All my interviews were held in vernacular Kaluli, including those with Onabasulu speakers. Most of my informants were Kaluli men whom I knew well and who had close connections with the Onabasulu people who encountered the patrol or who had seen it themselves.

† Estimates for pre-contact populations are difficult to establish. Kelly in 1967–69 carried out the most careful population studies undertaken on the plateau among the Etoro people and established through a number of lines of reasoning that the Etoro population in the 1960's (391) represented a decline of 50–55 percent from 1935. Ernst (1984), observing that 385 Onabasulu were presently living in 8 longhouses as opposed to 25–29 longhouses at the time that Hides passed through, estimated a 1935 Onabasulu population of about 1,250, assuming an average longhouse population of 50. Both Etoro and Bosavi pre-contact longhouse populations averaged around 35, so Ernst's estimates may be too high. If so, the 1935 Onabasulu population would have been more like 875–1,015. My own study of genealogies and longhouse movements among the Kaluli-speaking Bosavi suggests that the Bosavi population declined only a little from 1935 to 1966. Based on a 1966 population of about 1,200, I estimate there were about 1,400 in 1935.

carapace of a turtle. Built out on posts off the end of a spur, with the rear
veranda 12 m in the air, they made an imposing appearance. The location of the longhouse was chosen partly with an eye to defense against
attack, but at the same time it had to be located near a source of water and
convenient to gardening areas and sago resources. When these resources
became locally depleted, the community would move on and build in a
new location; over time these movements followed a garden fallow cycle
of about 25 years.

The people of these communities shared a way of life broadly resembling
that of the range of lowland Papuan cultures reaching from Mt. Karimui
to the Strickland River and south to the Gulf of Papua. Subsistence for the
Bosavi and Onabasulu people on the southern portion of the plateau centered around the staple of sago starch obtained from sago palms growing
in boggy areas around slow-moving brooks and streams. The Etoro to the
north, who lived on more precipitous terrain, relied more on sweet potatoes. These foods were supplemented by the produce of extensive swidden
gardens, including many varieties of bananas, pitpit, pandanus, bread-
fruit, and greens (Schieffelin 1975; Kelly 1977).* Meat was obtained by
hunting for small game in the forest, fishing, and keeping small numbers
of domestic pigs. Pigs, however, were usually killed only on ceremonial
occasions.

In 1935 a longhouse community consisted on the average of about 35
people, comprising five to eight domestic families, and was built on land
belonging to the patrilineage of some of its members. The inhabitants of
a given longhouse community participated together in making the major
communal garden, contributed to the bridewealth of its young men, provided mutual defense, and staged ceremonial events. However, aside from
observing these mutual obligations, they did not form a corporate or even
very unified group. This was in part because of the strongly individualistic character of the people themselves and partly because of conflicts of
allegiance inherent in their social system.

Society among the adult men of the Papuan Plateau was resolutely egalitarian. Individuals were expected to take the initiative and push forward
their own projects or enterprises, gathering whatever support they could
through their own networks of social connections. Every man had a core
group of relatives (usually his brothers and brothers-in-law) upon whom
he could rely for support and assistance and to whom he was obligated in
return if he wished to maintain their good will. Beyond these, he might
try to develop relationships with other more distant classificatory relatives

---

* Pitpit (*Setaria palmifolia*) and pandanus (*Pandanus conoidens*) are tropical vegetables
with no analogue in Western cuisine.

and affines* by exchanging prestations of pigs with them on ceremonial occasions. The result was that each individual in a longhouse had a different personal network of connections with people in other communities, and this created a basic divisive force in their own community. Thus, in times of trouble or dispute between longhouses, it was not unusual for some men to side with their affines or relatives in other communities against members of their own house group.

Communities could mitigate this situation by encouraging a number of marriages between the same longhouses, thus providing a number of overlapping individual affinal networks that could amount to a de facto alliance between the communities. From the point of view of the individual, however, who usually sought to maximize the number of nonconflicting ties around himself, the best solution was to arrange a marriage by sister-exchange. In this way the ties between siblings and between brothers-in-law paralleled and reinforced each other in a strongly solidary knot. Although difficult to arrange successfully in practice, sister-exchange was the ideal marriage for all the people of the Papuan Plateau. Indeed, for the Etoro, a longhouse community was ideally a cluster of close consanguineal kinsmen aggregated around two families linked by a sister-exchange marriage (Kelly 1977: 129–36). Onabasulu and Bosavi communities tended to organize more around groups of brothers or lineage-mates, but they suffered from the same conflicting social forces and recognized the advantages of similar social arrangements.

Marriage ties (and consequent relationships of matrilateral affiliation) stretched between adjacent longhouse communities from one side of the plateau to the other, forming a dense web of intercommunity relationships. Bosavi communities were intermarried with Onabasulu ones, and Onabasulu were intermarried with Etoro. Amidst these extensive networks, however, the plateau communities were not united by any overall political organization. Each longhouse community was essentially autonomous. A given house group had one or two men who, because of their forceful or influential personalities, were the acknowledged leaders of the community. Some of these men developed reputations and became known widely in other communities, but they had only limited influence outside their own group. None of them were on the level of "Big Men" who exercised regional influence in many places in the New Guinea highlands.

The social relations between longhouse communities were maintained by offering hospitality to relatives who came to visit and by exchanging

* The term "affine" refers to spouse's relatives or, in other words, relatives by marriage. The term is broad, however, and conveys a greater range of relatives by marriage than is normally assumed by the English term "in-law."

ceremonial prestations of pigs. The giving and sharing of food among the Etoro, Onabasulu, and Bosavi people was the major vehicle for expressing affection and good will. The offer of food and hospitality at a longhouse was the assurance that one was safe among relatives and friends and could sleep undisturbed. If one was not offered food while visiting a community, it was cause for alarm: one's hosts were acting like enemies, and one might well be in danger.

Prior to the government consolidation of the region in the early 1950's most of the communities of the Papuan Plateau lived in the shadow of violence. In part, this was a question of traditional enemies. Those communities living towards the eastern and western border areas were embroiled in endless conflicts with neighboring tribes. To the east, the Onabasulu fought with the "Namabolo" (Fasu) people from across the Hegigio (Kikori) River in a series of raids and reprisals that stretched as far back as anyone could remember. This conflict, in turn, drew in eastern Bosavi communities, who had allies on both sides, and thus frequently found themselves caught in the middle. To the west, the westernmost Bosavi communities traditionally fought with Bedamini people living on the western banks of the Giwa River and occasionally with the western Etoro communities to the north. Fighting of this sort took the form of raids in which the attacking party would surprise a small group of people working at an isolated sago camp or garden site, kill everyone—men, women, and children—and, if time permitted, butcher the bodies and carry them home for a cannibalistic celebration (Kelly 1977: 17; Schieffelin 1976). In an even worse, but less frequent, form of attack, a large force would surround a longhouse in the early hours of the morning and set it on fire— then dispatch all the inhabitants as they fled.

Besides external enemies the plateau people also fought amongst themselves. Disputes over stolen pigs, adultery or abduction of women, interference with marriage negotiations, and deaths caused by witchcraft provided them with plenty of reasons to grab bows and arrows. Of these, by far the most serious cause of violence was witchcraft.

Every death, whether from illness, accident, old age—even death in battle—was construed as resulting from witchcraft. Consequently any death was potentially an occasion for the seeking of vengeance. If the deceased was well loved and the identity of the witch could be determined, the aggrieved relatives might gather warriors and try to execute him.[*]

[*]A man was accused of being a witch on the basis of a number of divinatory procedures. For example, a side of a pandanus cob from the victim's garden and another from that of the suspected witch were cooked together with a hair from the victim's head. If the pandanus was still raw after a standard period of cooking, it confirmed the suspect as the witch. After a witch had been killed, his executioners would open his chest and examine his heart. A flabby

Among the Etoro, this was a relatively easy matter, since the accused witch was most often someone from the same longhouse as the deceased. Among the Onabasulu and Bosavi, however, it was usually someone from another community, and this entailed mounting a raid on the witch's longhouse to kill him. For people who were killed in an enemy raid, a witch was believed to have been responsible for "ripening" them for death. The deaths of people in a raid could then result in the aggrieved community executing one of its own members as the witch responsible rather than mounting a retaliatory expedition against the enemy.

The fear of witchcraft provided another important reason for people to tighten their personal networks and try to live amidst their closest kinsmen. Close kin were not supposed to use witchcraft against one another and were usually reliable supporters if one was oneself attacked as a witch.

Living amongst their kin, the people of the longhouse communities were a friendly, good-humored folk. But life was insecure, and it was necessary to be constantly vigilant. Men went armed with bows and arrows whenever they traveled in the forest, and in times of tension and uncertainty they escorted and stood guard over their wives and children at the gardens and sago camps. Illness, death, and witchcraft were frequent topics of conversation around the fireboxes in the longhouse at night, and the sorrow over loss of friends and relatives through death, together with rage for vengeance, were keenly felt.

Cosmological Geography

The larger world of the tropical forest in which the people of the longhouses live is one that includes the presence of spirit people and is scattered with relics of the mythological past. It is primarily by the sounds of the forest that people attune themselves to its hidden life. The gurgle of flowing water, the calls of the birds, the rasps and whines of insects, the rustling of the undergrowth or of the canopy—all convey the presence of life and activity to the attentive passerby. But it is primarily the voices of the birds calling from the canopy that alert people to the presence of the spirits, since spirit people often take the forms of birds and call with their voices (Feld 1982; Schieffelin 1976). Other spirits may roam the ground as pythons, wild pigs, or cassowaries. Particular spirits are usually associated with specific localities, and the reputations of some of them (particularly the fierce and dangerous ones) are quite widely known. If there is a spirit

---

quality to the heart and yellowish deposits around it were positive proof the individual was a witch. A firm, dark-colored heart indicated the individual was not a witch (but by then it was too late).

medium in the community, people may come to know the spirit person-
ages of their vicinity quite well through repeated seances, relishing their
personalities and even developing a certain affection for them.

For the most part the people of the forest simply coexist with the spirit
people of their localities. The Etoro, however, have a particular formal
relationship with some of their spirits. In the Etoro country, each lineage
territory is associated with several spirits known as *sigisato* (Kelly 1977:
89–92), and the local lineage community may be named after one of these
spirits. The *sigisato* live in specially planted palm trees located near the
longhouse site. They are not considered ancestral to the lineage members,
but they co-own the lineage land with them and on this basis act like
brothers toward them: warding off witches, advising in hunting, curing illness, and helping to locate lost pigs. They also advise the lineage (through
spirit mediums) on the appropriate conduct of warfare. Co-ownership
of the land ratifies the brotherlike relationship between an Etoro lineage
and its *sigisato* spirits, and, by the same token, the lineage relation to the
sigisato ratifies its relationship to the land. The land cannot be alienated
without alienating the spirit as well.

Besides the localities that mark the abodes of spirit people (whether
sigisato or other), the plateau forest is scattered with relics of the distant
mythological past. Thus, for example, in a streambed by the track from
Didesa to Wasu in Bosavi country, one can see a large boulder with a narrow hole pierced through it. Bosavi people chuckle when they see it for it
is the hole left by Newelesu, a clownish mythical figure who accidentally
plunged his penis through the rock while lunging after a young woman.
Three or four kilometers away, on the lands of clan Wabisi, is a curiously
shaped boulder called *kama hageo*, the remains of a runaway pig that
turned to stone long ago to avoid being captured by its master. The rock
is tabooed and must not be touched lest it precipitate a violent rainstorm.
Similarly, on the Wolu River near the longhouse at Sululib, there is a place
where the water divides and flows through a small cave or tunnel known
as *wefio alu* ("stunted hole/tunnel"). Long ago this cave was dug by tiny
"stunted men" no bigger than a finger joint. No one knows why they dug
the tunnel or where they went afterwards, but women and children are
kept away lest the children become stunted and stay small.

There are many such places, some with associated stories, some without,
scattered about on the lands of the Bosavi, Onabasulu, and Etoro people.
Some of them, like Newelesu's stone, are harmless curiosities; others, like
the *kama hageo*, carry varying amounts of residual magical danger associated with their anomalous qualities and origins. Many of these artifacts
are known only to the people of the localities in which they are found.
Others have a wider reputation, and a few are known widely over the

plateau. However, detailed knowledge of even the most important places is most likely to be held by people who live in or have their social connections with that locality. Indeed, information about some places was deliberately kept secret by the communities on whose lands they were located, lest some fearful cosmological disaster occur.

One of the most important of these places associated with the Origin Time was an area in Onabasulu country known as Malaiya. The Bosavi people on the southern portion of the plateau know only that there is a fire there that never goes out. The story behind Malaiya is known mainly among the Onabasulu people, especially those with connections to the Gunigiamo community, which owns the site.

Long ago, the story goes, a woman named Guni appeared with her husband at a place called Dobanifofa near the source of the Sioa River. They had many children, and some of them were light-skinned. However, these light-skinned ones turned out to be witches. They ate leeches, worms, and other things that people do not eat. So the others, the dark-skinned people, chased them away to the east in the direction of Lake Kutubu. These light-skinned people had possession of some marvelous things (now identified with axes, bush knives, matches, cloth, and other European goods), and when they were chased away, they took these things with them, leaving only their images engraved on a cliff at Dobanifofa and also at another (lesser) origin spot (also called "Malaiya") near the headwaters of the Kadi River among the eastern Onabasulu. A little later Guni followed her light-skinned children off to the east and left Onabasulu country. At this point all the people of the local world split up and went their separate ways. Those who went to the north became Huli people, those to the west became Etoro, and those to the south became Onabasulu and Bosavi. The light-skinned witch people who were chased away became the ancestors of the European people.

Some informants told me that this splitting up of Guni's children was the same as the time (in a Bosavi origin story) when everything split up into trees, birds, animals, fish, and spirit people—thus bringing into being the present world of the tropical forest. (For details of the Bosavi origin myth, see Schieffelin 1976; 1980: 506).

Now "Malaiya," Onabasulu people told me, was not a place but a fire that burns eternally by the water at Dobanifofa. Some say Guni lit and left it there, and it never went out. Others say that it was just there. In any case, it is important that it never go out—and that it never flare up. If the fire dies out, it is believed, so all the fires in the world will extinguish, together with the sun, and the world will die. On the other hand, if the fire ever flares out of control, it will roar out over the plateau and burn up the world. Older men at Sululib in the Bosavi area across the plateau recalled how in the old days one could look across the forest towards Malaiya and once in a while see a glow there in the distance as though the fire were burning high.

Bosavis on the southern portion of the plateau feared in particular that Malaiya would erupt and engulf the world in fire. The northern Onaba-sulu (who were Malaiya's custodians) were more afraid of the return of Guni and her light-skinned children from the east. If Guni returned, it was said, all the peoples and species that had gone their separate ways after her departure would also flow back to the origin point. That which was accomplished in the Origin Time would then be undone and the world would come to an end.

The World Periphery

As the inhabitants of the plateau regard certain locations on the pla-teau as centers of mysterious cosmological potency, so too did they regard the peripheries of their world as mysterious and unknown. Bosavi people asked me in 1967 if I had ever been to the place where the sky came together with the earth—the horizon, the visible boundary of the world —and if so, what was it like. The question was genuine. The people really didn't have any clear idea of what the edge of the world might be like; what they did know was all rather vague and fabulous. From the north, over the mountains of the highland rim, they occasionally received visits from Huli traders who came to exchange tobacco and home-manufactured vegetable salt for hornbill beaks and black-palm bows. The Huli are a bold and pushy people, and these traders coming to visit the plateau carried with them a certain "exotic foreigner mystique." Bosavis told stories of how Hulis could travel with unnatural speed from the highlands to the top of Mt. Bosavi, moving from tree to tree without touching the ground.

The Huli were known to live in a grassland area beyond the mountains, completely unlike the lowland tropical forest. Coincidentally, the Bosavi spirit world, as described by spirit mediums, is also a grassland area, which Bosavis explicitly compare to the Huli region. Thus, Huli-land (and its people) outside the periphery of the plateau forest is rather like the spirit world, at least to Bosavis.

Similarly in the west, beyond the regions inhabited by the Bedamini people, the major rivers of the plateau world are said to flow to the place "where the earth peters out" (hen mitiyowa). There, it is believed the waters converge in a huge whirlpool that drains away beneath the surface. Next to the pool sits a little man with a spear in his hand. It is his job to spear any big logs or tree trunks washed down the river and remove them before they block the whirlpool and cause the water to back up and flood the world. It is also downstream and westward along the rivers that the souls of the dead are thought to travel on their way to their final resting place.

To the south, below Mt. Bosavi in the rich hunting grounds at the headwaters of the Turama and Wawoi rivers, live the "Tulom" people, as they are known by Bosavis, the Kasua and Kamula. It is in "Tulom" country that many Bosavi people believe their souls, or spiritual counterparts, roam in the form of wild pigs. When Tulom people hunt wild pigs, it is believed, Bosavi people die.

The point to be made here is that the distant peripheries of the plateau forest have anomalous characteristics, not just because they have the unknown qualities of regions beyond, but because they have the unsettling features of cosmological unraveling. Places and people at the edges of the world are spoken of in ways that seem to mix aspects of both visible and spirit realms. These are categories that are supposed to have been separated once and for all in the Origin Time and that would threaten to bring the world to an end if they were brought together again.

What strikes a Westerner in all this (though the forest dwellers don't speak this way) is that the end of the world as it is projected in time (the rejoining of things that were originally set apart) has much in common with things as they are storied to be at the edge of space (where things that are normally separate seem to be mingled). Space and time become equivalent in terms of the unraveling of reality at the world-cosmological peripheries.

The Etoro, Onabasulu, and Bosavi people do not speculate much about these matters. To them the unraveling of the world was a remote possibility and could be ignored in getting on with everyday life. Nevertheless, this was the possibility that came to mind when things of the periphery began to move onto the plateau.

The Tropical Forest in 1935: The Social-Historical Context

Beginning in the early 1930's the first steel items began to appear on the plateau. One by one, axes and bushknives, battered and worn, but still serviceable, started to appear in the Bosavi area. They came along the trade route up the Turama River from the coast and then around the eastern flanks of Mt. Bosavi to the longhouse communities there. The Bosavi people eagerly traded for these tools, and by 1935 there may have been six or seven axes among the eastern communities, plus a number of bushknives. Despite their small number and poor quality, the use of these tools rapidly replaced the use of stone adzes. Oldtimers among the Bosavi recalled to me how, when people intended to build a garden, they would stretch their network ties to the utmost to borrow or inveigle the use of two or three axes. Then the entire workforce would trade off in using those axes to cut the trees over the garden rather than bothering to use stone tools.

In the Onabasulu area the response to steel was mixed. A few people in the eastern communities had obtained steel tools, but many others were deeply upset by them. "Truly they wept!" one Bosavi informant told me, chuckling. They suspected that these strange objects were things of Malaiya, the very same things that were depicted on the cliffs at Dobani-fofa, which had been taken by Guni's light-skinned witch-children when they were chased from the land in the Origin Time. They were things that should not be touched or used by mortal men. Now they were moving back toward their origin point, and many Onabasulu feared that their "owners," Guni's children, would soon follow.

The story of Guni's children, however, had been largely kept a secret by the Onabasulu from the other groups on the plateau. Bosavis, who knew little about this aspect of Malaiya, didn't take it too seriously. Since they themselves had come to no harm through the use of the tools, they continued to try to get them. The Onabasulu were right, however, in their assessment that steel was a portent of things to come.

In January or February 1935 a serious epidemic struck the southwestern communities of the Papuan Plateau and began to move slowly eastwards through the Bosavi communities. The symptoms were various, but a particularly horrible and well-remembered manifestation was that in some patients the throat and jaw became swollen bending their heads backwards and forcing their tongues to protrude from their mouths. At least 33 people died, and tension and suspicion of witchcraft added to the already high level of anxiety among the Bosavi communities.* To the north, the Onabasulu and Etoro apparently escaped the plague. One particularly hard-hit Bosavi community, Wosiso, lost nine members within a week. "It was terrible," one informant recalled. "They'd start wailing on one side of the house because someone had just died, and before people could gather to

* My estimate of the number of deaths is based on genealogies and informants' statements and is undoubtedly low. Even so it would represent about 2.4 percent of the Bosavi population of the time. The 1935 epidemic is well remembered, not only for the unsettling symptoms of the disease, but also because so many young adults died of it. Epidemics that mainly kill young children and very elderly people are not so well remembered. Such devastating epidemics have not been that unusual, at least since the 1930's (although the 1919 world pandemic of influenza also left its mark on the plateau). Another epidemic in the early 1950's, apparently was measles, was responsible for the reduction of the Etoro and Onabasulu populations to less than half their 1935 levels. In January 1969 Kelly recorded 22 deaths among the Etoro in one week of an influenza epidemic. This represented 71 percent of all the deaths he recorded among the Etoro during his fifteen-month period of fieldwork and meant the loss of 5.7 percent of the total Etoro population at that time (Kelly 1977: 28–31).

mourn, wailing would break out on the other side for another person. You looked out the door of the longhouse, and there were *kalu oido* [mortuary platforms] down both sides of the house yard. At one time we had four corpses hanging in the longhouse [for mourning]. The stink was awful." In the midst of this desperate situation a man in another community was identified as the witch responsible for one of the deaths. The Wosiso group gathered Onabasulu allies, ambushed him in his garden, and killed him.

Unfortunately this man, whose name was Sobolo, was an important local leader and had many powerful friends among the leaders in other communities. Though he was proved to be a witch by the traditionally accepted evidence, these friends were furious at his death. They accepted compensation but really wanted blood for this killing. Some of the young men of other communities began to harass the Wosiso community, forcing them to stay barricaded in their longhouse, damaging their property, killing their pigs, and wrecking their gardens. Finally the Wosiso people could take it no longer; the community split up, and everyone fled north to refuge among relatives in the eastern Onabasulu country until the heat died down. It was just about this time that Jack Hides and Jim O'Malley arrived on the plateau, about 16 km to the northwest.

The Progress of the Patrol

A month earlier, Hides and O'Malley had reached the limits of navigation of the Rentoul River. There they had destroyed their canoes, to prevent their carriers from deserting, and headed overland through the tropical forest on foot.

The patrol had more supplies than it could carry at once and so had to move them forward in stages. Hides, accompanied by two policemen, would lead off the carriers, who were loaded with about a quarter of the supplies, and cut a track through the forest to a new campsite. The supplies would be stashed under the protection of the constables, and Hides and the carriers would return to base to bring the next load of supplies forward the following day. When, after a few days all the supplies were relayed forward, Hides and O'Malley would lead off again to a new campsite.

For seventeen days, from February 22 to March 10, they traveled along northern forks of the Rentoul River, seeing few native tracks, gardens, or dwellings, and having only fleeting encounters with the local inhabitants (see Map 5; note that the camp numbers are those used by Hides in his journal). As they moved along, Hides wrote of the impressive mass of Mt. Leonard Murray (Bosavi), which loomed ever nearer to the southeast: "like a giant Fujiyama, [the peaks] drawing themselves together from the plateau to their 12,000 foot heights in the clouds" (*PW*: 46). He was in-

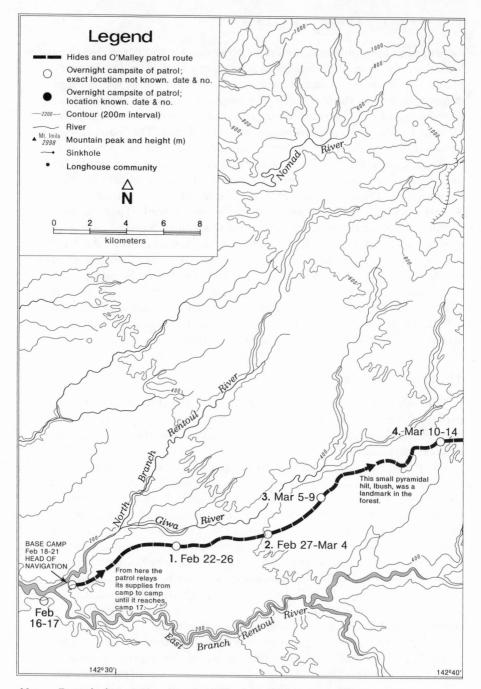

Nomad River

Rentoul River

North Branch

4. Mar 10-14

This small pyramidal hill, Ibush, was a landmark in the forest.

3. Mar 5-9

Giwa River

2. Feb 27-Mar 4

BASE CAMP Feb 18-21 HEAD OF NAVIGATION

1. Feb 22-26

From here the patrol relays its supplies from camp to camp until it reaches camp 17.

Feb 16-17

East Branch Rentoul River

142°30'

142°40'

Map 5. From the base camp on the Rentoul across the Great Papuan Plateau (February 18–April 6). Note: Hides numbered his land camps starting from this base camp.

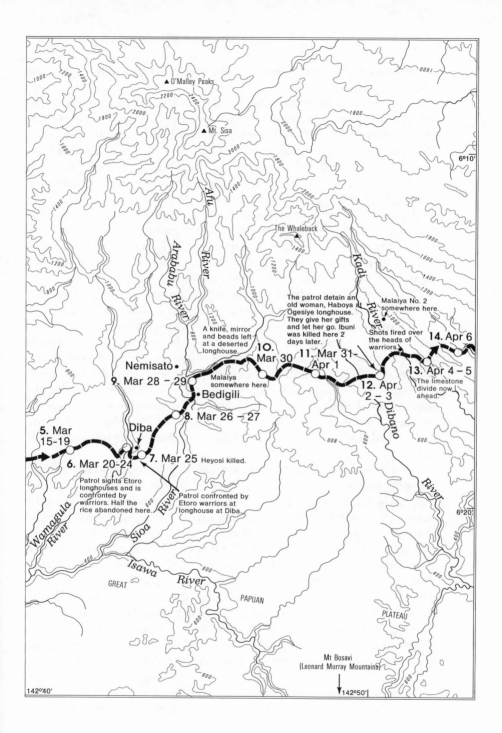

spired to see things larger than life: Mt. Bosavi is really only a little over 2,800 m (9,186 feet).

During this time the patrol established its routine of overland travel. The police, most of them experienced men handpicked by Hides, were responsible for keeping the day-to-day operation of the patrol running smoothly. They made sure the carriers were loaded when the patrol was ready to move in the morning and supervised the discipline of the line. They were supposed to see to it that carriers did not get too spread out along the track and did not steal from native gardens, damage local property, or kill local pigs, and they were responsible for the protection of the patrol in case of attack. When the patrol stopped in the afternoon, the police saw to it that the carriers set up the campsite properly, pitched tents, lit fires, and got their ration of food. The police also from time to time supplied the patrol with meat from wild game they hunted along the track.

The patrol officers supervised the police and made all the important day-to-day strategic decisions affecting the patrol: where to go, where to camp, how to respond to hostility or friendliness from the people encountered, whether—and for how much in trade—local food would be bought from the natives. The success or failure of the patrol in reaching its objectives was their responsibility. The officers carried special food—flour, tea, sugar, tins of meat, and other delicacies for themselves among the stores. They slept on canvas cots. Hides had a personal orderly among the police, Corporal Emesi, who did his laundry, saw that the officers' food was cooked, and made sure that Hides had hot bath water prepared at the end of each day.

The carriers did the manual labor, carrying loads, building shelters, chopping firewood.

By mid-March the canvas tents were rotting, and the flour had had to be thrown away. On March 20, following a native track, the patrol emerged at an old village site. The place afforded a grand view of the forested plateau. Across the valley Hides and O'Malley could see numerous cultivated areas, and perched on neighboring ridges were three longhouses. While clearing the brush for a campsite, they made a gruesome discovery: the remains of several large heaps of cooking stones were uncovered, with human skulls and cracked bones piled around them. Nearby there was a planting of fragrant flowering trees. The juxtaposition of flowers and the apparent remains of a cannibal feast evoked a paradoxical image of the primitive in Hides's imagination, followed by a vision of colonial salvation.

"In grim contrast to these beautiful plants," he wrote in his book, "was the presence of . . . heaps of broken human bones to tell their own story of the people's little ways. Yet notwithstanding their savage practices, primitive men have a mind for beauty. They love color, and they plant these sweet-scented flowers to add beauty to the landscape; their trend of thought seems always upward, and we can but lead them to higher levels. We give them axes, and we see them build bigger gardens and better houses, and so improve their living conditions. With protection and control they can stop killing and eating one another" (PW: 48).

The inhabitants of the nearby longhouses gave no sign that they noticed the patrol as it set up camp for the night, although it was in plain sight on the opposite ridge.

"Like People You See in a Dream": Encounter with the Etoro

Hides had emerged on the banks of the Wamagula River near its confluence with the Pugulei stream, right in the middle of Etoro country. There was no apparent response from the local people, and Hides spent the next two days staging his supplies. It wasn't until the afternoon of the third day that the Etoro showed any reaction. At that time a group of natives appeared on the ridge across the river from the camp. Hides called to them in a friendly manner, and they answered, but then they went away. Hides and O'Malley felt encouraged by this apparently friendly overture, but the situation was to change by the next day.

That evening Hides saw the light of torches in the distance near the longhouses. They moved backward and forward in lines as though people were dancing:

"We watched these lights interestedly for some time; then suddenly from across the valley there came to our ears the sounds of beautiful music. . . . Gradually it rose and rose in volume in delightful harmony. Then it slowly died away as though on the bass notes of some organ.

"I knew now [he later reflected] why these people had not shown any outward signs of [seeing us]. They had seen us all right, and probably their scouts had watched us at close quarters, but they were afraid. This singing and dancing was a call to strength, something to steel themselves against the strange and unearthly invaders.

"We sat there that evening until a late hour listening to these glorious bursts of song" (PW: 49).

Hides was perceptive. According to an Etoro man who had been a small boy at the time and learned the story from eyewitnesses, the patrol had emerged out of the forest virtually without any warning. "We jumped [with surprise]," he said. "No one had seen anything like this before or knew what it was. When they saw the clothes on the sowelo [the Europeans] and the others, they thought they were like people you see in a dream; 'these must be spirit people (*kesame*) coming openly, in plain sight.' "

The patrol was far enough away from the longhouse not to panic the inhabitants into fleeing into the forest. On the contrary, after a few days of consternation, the Etoro gathered in force to consult their *sigisato* spirits in a seance (Kelly 1974: 25) and inquire what to do—this was the singing Hides had heard. On the evidence available (Kelly 1974: 13), it appears that the *sigisato* advised that the community should have nothing to do with the patrol, and that they should drive them off or resist their further advance into their territory.*

The following morning, after the police and carriers had left to stage supplies, Hides, who together with O'Malley and five police had remained in camp, saw someone in the grass on the opposite ridge. He called out in a friendly manner, and all at once, with a loud burst of song, 50 or more warriors armed with bows emerged from hiding in the high grass across the ravine.† They pranced whooping up and down the ridge in what seemed to Hides a clearly hostile display. He wondered what had happened to change their apparently peaceful attitude of the day before and realized that to make his way towards or through them would be to invite attack. Suddenly, according to Hides, "I noticed an extraordinary figure among them. Watching through glasses I saw this tall, very thin, and very black figure start to harangue the crowd. He was mounted on the shoulders of another native, and although we could not hear his speech, I could see him using a lot of gesture and pointing to the camp. He appeared to be urging them to attack: the high priest ordering death for the devils."

From the description, this was undoubtedly a man named Aibali, a noted spirit medium and local leader who had held the seance that Hides had heard the night before. "When he had finished his speech," continues

---

*Getting a detailed account of Hides's encounter with the Etoro was difficult. Neither Kelly nor I was able to find any Etoro informants who remembered the details of specific incidents. Although several Etoro people could tell me with precision where Hides appeared and where he went as he subsequently traveled through Etoro and Onabasulu country, I could not find anyone who could give me any details of what happened that night or the following day from the Etoro point of view. The places where these events occurred were well remembered, while the events themselves were not. I was able to learn the details of Hides's route through the area from a Bosavi man, Susu of Sibalema village, who had had fairly close ties with the Etoro in pre-contact times. He had seen some of Hides's campsites and heard the story from several people. He also provided the identity of Aibali the spirit medium, who was a prominent man at the time and fit Hides's description. I have had to reconstruct the confrontation between the patrol and the Etoro people at the Sarodo community longhouse near Diba from Hides's account and ethnographically informed speculation.

† If the average size and composition of Etoro longhouse communities was the same in 1935 as in 1970, this group would have represented the combined fighting men of about four communities (see Kelly 1974: 138–39).

Hides, "[he took] up a drum . . . and still mounted on the shoulders of the other native, he began beating it . . . waving his body in a backward and forward motion."

This strange, wildly excited, but dead-serious pantomime struck O'Malley with amusement. On an impulse he put two fingers in his mouth and whistled shrilly. "The effect was electric," reports Hides: "the ceremony stopped and they stood still for a second: then the crowd broke and scattered for the shelter of the bush" (PW: 51).

To people all over the plateau a low whistle in the dark of night is the sound of the approach of a witch. While the medium was trying to muster the courage of the excited and frightened group of warriors, the uncanny noise of O'Malley's whistle, the only sound from the apparitions across the valley, completely unnerved them. "The high priest was dropped in the most undignified manner," says Hides, "and must have been one of the first out of sight" (PW: 51).

The natives did not reappear that day, and by the afternoon the carriers had brought up the last of the stores. In view of the natives' unfriendly display, Hides and O'Malley felt the need to be cautious. On the following day they mustered the entire patrol and, leaving the bulk of the rice stores unguarded at the campsite, set off in close order, keeping a careful watch out for ambush. According to Etoro informants, the local inhabitants had by now scattered to hide at small camps hidden in the forest. This was a conventional response to an overwhelmingly dangerous situation, and some men may have sent their families into the forest for safety, but this is not the whole story.

As the patrol moved off, Hides and O'Malley led their men upstream along the Wamagula River, over a convenient crossing place and then toiled up the slope on the opposite side. The country is very precipitous here, and the carriers had a rough time of it. When they emerged at the clearing near the top, Hides and O'Malley found themselves directly below a longhouse they hadn't seen before, which stood straddling the rise above them, thrust out over the edge on long stiltlike posts. On the overlooking veranda and along the sides of the house was a sizable body of men armed with bows and arrows, waiting.

Hides was in an awkward position. He was facing the longhouse in its most defensible position, the patrol struggling up the hill behind him. There was no room for maneuver or retreat. At the same time he wished to make friendly contact with the people. However, as he moved to approach, the men began whooping and shouting. Hides showed them a steel axe, but they threw out their arms indicating they wanted none of it and that the patrol was to turn back. Hides realized that if the patrol continued forward, the warriors would either bolt or attack. So he signaled his men to halt and, covered by O'Malley and the police, slowly advanced alone making friendly gestures.

According to comments of Onabasulu and Etoro informants to whom I told this story, the defenders at the longhouse didn't know what to do. Hides was not making their standard gesture of peaceful intentions: an offer of food or recognizable wealth objects (they had never seen steel). But they could not have accepted anything even if he had, because they feared that accepting these gifts would establish a direct and obligated social link with the unknown, perhaps the spirit world, bringing together realms that should at all costs remain separate, lest the world become unmade and everybody die. Yet this Being was advancing toward them in an unmistakably friendly manner.

At this critical juncture, two teenage youths came up with an imaginative solution. They began cautiously to make their way down toward Hides holding out a gift of their own: a dance headdress of cockatoo feathers. If Hides accepted the offer, a friendly gesture would have been established, but the Etoro would have accepted nothing from the spirit realm. A dance headdress was an appropriate item to offer a spirit being because spirits were associated with ceremonial song and dance. Hides was delighted at the gesture and felt that the establishment of friendly contact was assured. But, at that moment Aibali, the spirit medium, appeared again. "He shrieked at the two youths, [telling] them to come back and have nothing to do with us: he beat his drum and gesticulated wildly, and seemed to be urging the others to fight" (PW: 53). The youths silently drew back, leaving the headdress on the ground for Hides.

"The old sorcerer was like a madman," Hides wrote, "he danced and shrieked and beat his drum. 'Ua! Ua!' and then a flow of deep voluble sounds came from his mouth." Hides was hearing the mediumistic voice of the *sigisato* spirit. All the armed men began to advance on the patrol with drawn bows. As the first arrows were released, Hides gave the signal to O'Malley and the police fired a rifle volley over the natives' heads. In an instant the longhouse and ridge were cleared as the warriors fled into the forest. Hides entered the longhouse where he saw two human arms hanging from the eaves. He left a peace sign for the inhabitants along with presents of an axe, a knife, beads, a mirror, and some red cloth.

The patrol passed by, crossed the Bugulei (or Bubulei) brook, and climbed to establish camp on the opposite ridge. However, their troubles were not over. No sooner had the first carriers put down their loads than Hides heard a rifle shot from one of the police at the rear of the line. He rushed back to see what had happened. Passing the rear guard and running a little farther down the track he ran into two armed natives. He had just time to see one of them release an arrow at him before instinctively firing his rifle. At the same moment his orderly who was close behind fired his. One of the natives threw up his bow and arrow and fell dead into the brush. The other fled into the forest.

Hides was shaken. "I deeply regret the shooting of this native," he said in his report, "for I was prepared to risk a lot to save these people from their fear. Had I known that only two men were in ambush, I should probably never have shot this man; but everything happened so fast" (PR: 35).

Later he reflected: "In nine years of patroling, and from most of the hostile corners of Papua, I had captured nearly 150 convicted murderers; and this was the second man I had shot. A rifle against a bow and arrow; it did not seem fair to me. Yet the position might easily have been reversed; it could easily have been me now lying on the ground with an arrow in my chest" (PW: 56). For Jack Hides personally this patrol was to be a struggle with the end of innocence.

The dead man, Heyosi of Ingiribisato lineage, and a companion had evidently been shadowing the patrol to see what it was up to. Whether they had actually been trying to pick off a straggler as the police later claimed or the policeman had simply fired a shot over their heads when he felt they got too close will never be known. Two men were unlikely to be trying to ambush a patrol of 40. However, given the hostile display at the longhouse earlier that afternoon, Hides had reason to suppose that an ambush might be attempted. Nevertheless, in rushing back precipitously the way he did, he was asking for trouble. It seems likely that Heyosi and his companion were as surprised at his sudden appearance as he was at theirs and fired just as instinctively. Heyosi missed; Hides didn't.

Fear was not a word used by officers in the Papuan Service. Nevertheless, things were now at a very difficult pass. Having killed a man, Hides expected that his relatives would soon be gathering forces to seek vengeance, and his anxieties concerning ambush in the depths of the forest considerably intensified. The idea of carrying wounded carriers or police without adequate medical attention over a hundred miles of unexplored Papuan wilderness was not one he wanted to contemplate. The patrol camped under police guard that night and returned to the previous camp the next day by cutting a new track that avoided the longhouse. In one trip they brought back 28 bags of rice. Thereafter, Hides decided, they would make one relay every day with the stores they now had in order to move as quickly as possible away from the area. This decision hid a more fateful one: by making only one relay Hides abandoned more than half his supplies of food at the camp on the Wamagula. He now carried only enough food for about a month at full ration and they had three months to go.* This was undoubtedly one of the major factors in the incredible hardship that the patrol was to suffer later on. Hides, however, counted on being able to purchase food from local populations as they went along.

Two days later, traveling eastward over steeply dissected country, Hides and O'Malley remained uncomfortably aware that they were being shadowed at every point by native warriors they could not see. On March 28, they crossed the Sioa River and camped near a place called Bedigili in Onabasulu country. The patrol had spent eight days in the Etoro country, and when it left, the Etoro still had no idea who or what it was. The patrol was an event entirely outside their experience—"like people you see in a dream." Their best information about it came from their *sigisato* spirits, who counseled them to have nothing to do with it. The strange quality of the event was expressed in the elaborations that attached themselves to the story of Heyosi's death as it passed from community to community until it eventually reached the western Bosavi people. Heyosi's body was found, it was said, to have been *alu*, that is, tightly flexed in a fetal posture and nailed together with long spikes. While this was untrue, the image was a weird and frightening one, matching the quality of the event for those who tried to understand it.

Encounter with the Onabasulu

Having crossed the Sioa, Hides and O'Malley were now staging their supplies through the Onabasulu country. Some of the western Onabasulu communities had heard of Heyosi's death and knew of the approach of the patrol. According to some informants, spirit mediums warned them to avoid it. In any case, when the patrol arrived in the area, all the western longhouses of the Onabasulu were deserted, and their doors were closed with taboo signs. Nevertheless, Hides could tell, from the footprints on the track that the natives were still uncomfortably nearby.

* Hides does not mention this in *PW* or *PR*, but indicates in an article in *Pacific Islands Monthly* (Aug. 22, 1935) that he abandoned half his stores somewhere. Hubert Murray also refers to this in his introduction to *PW*. Careful comparison of the number of relays made from camp 5 to camp 6 and from 6 to 7 leaves no doubt the stores were left in the Etoro country. (Etoro and Onabasulu informants also confirmed that the patrol abandoned several bags of "sand" by the Wamagula.) It had taken Hides's carriers four days (from March 20 to March 23) to move his supplies from camp 5 in Bedamini country to camp 6 on the Wamagula River. If they made one trip a day, as Hides describes, that would have meant 4 × 28 = 112 loads, 103 of which were rice (9 were tents and other patrol supplies [*PR*: 44]). Moving from camp 6 to camp 7 beyond the longhouse, they made two trips (on March 24 and 25) or 56 loads, thus leaving more than half their supplies behind. The patrol was consuming about 1.4 bags of rice a day, which meant they now carried enough food for about 33 days at full ration. When the patrol arrived at the Wamagula it had enough food to advance about 35 camps. After abandoning half their food, and taking into account the necessity for relays, they had enough to advance them about 23 camps.

The Onabasulu, for their part, were carefully examining the footprints of the patrol. What they saw unnerved them. The footprints from the officers' boots seemed to indicate a being that had had its toes cut off. Moreover, the corrugations printed from the boot soles suggested the marks of a skeletal foot—a creature that walked along on exposed bones. For people who were used to reading footprints on the track for the nature of friend or foe, these footprints seemed to indicate a wholly unfamiliar kind of being. The impression was confirmed by the fact that at times the patrol's march cross-cut normal walking tracks, traveling across the grain of the country by an odd route that Onabasulu would never have taken (T. Ernst, personal communication). Continuing onward, the patrol unwittingly passed within less than half a kilometer of the site of Malaiya, the major Onabasulu world-origin place. The Onabasulu, however, do not seem to have connected the patrol's movements particularly with that spot (at least not at first). This was possibly because the patrol was coming from the west, not the direction of Lake Kutubu from where Guni and her light-skinned children of the Origin Time were expected to return (Ernst, personal communication). The Onabasulu in this area, like the Etoro, thought the patrol were probably spirit beings (*ane mama*), not beings from the Origin Time.

As they continued east along the side of the Sioa Valley, Hides and O'Malley began to see people working in the gardens across the valley who would pause and watch them as they passed. Their spirits lifted. The sight of these men peacefully engaged in their tasks was a refreshing change from the sense of being shadowed by hostile warriors that Hides had felt ever since leaving the Wamagula. Some of the locals even approached and tried to speak with the carriers. The patrol passed three longhouses, all of them deserted. Hides left presents of knives and beads along with a broken arrow at some of these dwellings as they passed.

When the Sioa River turned northward into the mountains of the highlands, Hides struck east in the direction of the Hegigio/Kikori. In so doing, he missed the major trade route across the limestone barrier to the highlands, which heads northeast, and set himself and his men on the road to greater hardships. Four days later, the patrol crossed the Dibano River into the watershed of the Hegigio/Kikori. News of their coming had preceded them; the path was blocked with a taboo mark: a cleft stick holding a bit of pork and a broken human bone. Hides read the message as: "If you come any further we will kill you and eat you."

A little farther down the track they arrived at a clearing with two large longhouses. The sound of voices indicated that these, at least, were not deserted:

"We approached to within fifty yards," Hides wrote. "A small girl came out to investigate, and bolted back when she saw us; then some armed men came out, while I noticed others with heavily laden women running away at the back with their belongings.

"Nothing could stay them, they were all terrified, men as well as women and children; so I decided to take a risk and catch one of them. Not far from me was an old woman hurrying away with heavy bundles. . . . I ordered A. C. [Armed Constable] Koriki to detain her. He did so, without any fuss, and she was led gently back to the house. At first she would not look at O'Malley and myself, nor would she accept our presents; but later, when her fears had calmed somewhat, and she realized we meant her no harm, she took the strings of beads and manifested an interest in what we were attempting to explain. I showed her an [axe], demonstrated its use in comparison with a stone adze that was brought me from one of the houses, gave it to her, and then indicated that we had more to give for food. Finally I lifted her heavy bundles and walked slowly up the garden with her, every now and then forced to halt while she dug a sweet potato for me with her long fingers. At last I left her, and she went slowly into the forest to the waiting men, who had never ceased calling for her.

We retraced our steps down the spur about two hundred yards and camped, hoping for the best" (PR: 39–40).

The next morning came with a spectacular sunrise. As the two officers overlooked the forest below their camp, a vision of the domestication and advancement of this wild region rose in Hides's imagination, the burgeoning of Australian colonial civilization: "We stood to watch the clouds rise from a thousand square miles of forested plains. This plateau must someday be put to its proper use. As I looked on it I tried to imagine that a few score years had passed; and in place of the forest I saw great fields of maize and millet, and a hundred cotton and coffee plantations; while everywhere was a place for all industrious Papuans" (PW: 66).

The natives did not return to their village that day.

In fact, the people of the Ogesiye community hiding in the forest nearby had been interrupted in the midst of playing out a desperate drama. They had heard of the killing of Heyosi ten days before and knew that the Beings that had killed him were coming their way. More important, these Beings were carrying axes and bushknives. The Ogesiye community was the custodian of the second Origin Spot (Malaiya #2) at the headwaters of the Kadi, and they had been especially involved in the controversy that accompanied the first appearance of axes and bushknives in the area. The approach of Hides and O'Malley now confirmed what they had feared: these objects were the very ones depicted on the cliffs, and now, as some had predicted, their "owners" were returning from the Origin Time.

Many people believed that with the arrival of the patrol the world was going to turn over. In the anxious discussion during the days preceding the patrol's arrival, one of the leaders of the Ogesiye community, a man named Fauwa, proposed a course of action. "Axes and bushknives are their children," he said; "they are coming to reclaim them." He told all those who owned these implements to bring them to Ogesiye where they could be gathered and returned to the Beings when they arrived. Then perhaps they would go away quickly, and disaster would be averted. Otherwise they would search for them. "Do not try to hide these things in the forest," he warned, "for they will cry out, and their parents will hear them and come after them. Gather and return them all at the same time." As the patrol drew nearer, even people who had ignored or scoffed at the idea these objects were related to the Origin Time brought their axes and bushknives in from the surrounding communities and, under Fauwa's direction, laid them out in the main hall of the longhouse. Fauwa killed two pigs to feed the assembly, and they were in the process of preparing them when Hides and O'Malley appeared outside. Wobowe of clan Keibi, who was about eighteen at the time, recalls seeing Hides from the Ogesiye veranda just as the patrol emerged from the forest. He was motioning for people to sit down and not run away. But everyone was panic-stricken. The light-colored man they saw was wearing a dark shirt, and they thought it was part of his skin. "If he had been wearing a loincloth, it would have been all right, we wouldn't have feared," Wobowe declared. "But when we saw his clothes, we didn't know what it was. Was this a spirit person or what?" The people of Ogesiye fled off the verandas, down the houseposts, and into the forest.

It was during this flight that Hides captured the old woman, Haboya, and after calming her, presented her with cloth, beads, and an axe as gifts to her people. Not surprisingly, when she brought them to the people hiding in the forest, they were thrown into even greater consternation. The specter of the world collapsing to its origin point loomed over the discussion that Wobowe remembered: "These are the taboo things, not for human beings to touch! If you take them, will their 'owners' not follow them? Give them back so they will go away!" The gifts were sent back and left where the patrol would find them. The Onabasulu added to them a packet of Job's tears,* used to make bracelets for ceremonial dancers, in a gesture akin to the Etoro offer of the dance headdress: to avoid obligation or giving offense and to defuse the hostility of these strange Beings. The paths to all the gardens were then blocked with taboo signs.

---

* Job's tears are the white seeds of a grass (*Coix lachryma jobi*), which are used as beads in Papua New Guinea.

Hides, hopeful of making contact, and anxious not to frighten the people further, did not enter the longhouse, but withdrew the patrol from the village to await developments. He never saw the axes and bushknives laid out for him or the two partially butchered pigs.

The following day, as the patrol passed through the village, Hides discovered his presents to the old woman lying on the path, returned. "A leaf packet of Job's tears lay beside the strings of beads," Hides wrote, "telling us, I presumed, that the inhabitants had beads of their own and did not require ours. They wished to have nothing to do with us. This was our last experience with these timid people" (PW: 65).

On this note of disappointment and compassion, Hides completed his account of the plateau people in *Papuan Wonderland*. His patrol report, however, records a further, rather different set of interactions with these "timid people." Later that same day as the patrol was negotiating the steep descent to the Kadi River, the report states: "Four men came to attack the rear of the party, and we were forced to fire a shot over their heads to scare them from their purpose." Hides was angry. "They are certainly a disappointing people," he wrote. "No garden or house of theirs was been disturbed, no pig or dog harmed, our actions are all frank and friendly, and the old woman, when she left us two days ago, was without fear and plainly understood our friendly intentions" (PR: 41).

The next day, while staging the balance of the rice forward from the former camp, "again the inhabitants came to attack the party, this time firing an arrow, and again we had to resort to rifle fire." *

Meanwhile, not all the Onabasulu were bent on harassing the patrol. Among those of the same community who had fled the longhouse at Hides's arrival was an unmarried youth named Ibuni (or Ubini, Ernst 1984: 52).† According to Wobowe, when Ibuni heard that Haboya, the old woman, had received a present from the Beings passing through, he decided, despite the warnings and fears of others, that he would go out, meet them and perhaps get something for himself. On the day after the patrol

---

* The incident is well remembered among the Onabasulu in the story of a man named Auwabe, who was one of the bowmen involved. After releasing an arrow, he ducked behind a rock. There was a loud explosion from the patrol, and the rock shattered in front of him. Auwabe threw away his bow and fled into the forest.

†One of my Bosavi informants, a man named Kiliye of clan Wabisi, was a close relative of Ilahido, who was with Ibuni at the time he was killed. Kiliye remembered the story vividly because Ilahido had recounted it to him the day after it had happened. I also interviewed Onabasulu informants Weyama, Ilabu, Faliga (Ibuni's younger brother), Wana, and Wobowe (who saw Hides and O'Malley at Ogesiye longhouse) at a big gathering at Waragu village for a baptism in 1976 and could then feel confident that I had the story of Ibuni correctly. Deba of Wosiso, who was also at Ogesiye when Hides arrived, provided details about Fauwa and the gathering of the axes.

had left the longhouse and the carriers and police were in the process of staging their rice to the new campsite, Ibuni, his companion Ilahido, and a visiting Huli trader named Digibi went to wait in a garden on the route the carriers would have to take to collect their last supplies. They were cooking sweet potatoes by a little fire when suddenly they heard a click. As Ibuni looked up, there was a loud explosion from the edge of the forest, and Ibuni went sprawling on the ground. Ilahido and Digibi fled, and as they did, they heard laughter coming from the forest edge. At no time did they see anyone. People returned after nightfall to see what had happened to Ibuni and to bear his body away. He had a hole in one side of his head and a bigger hole out the other side. His manner of death was particularly distressing because he had been killed while preparing food. No one in after years could come up with a reason for it. Indeed, they did not think he was killed by a Being of this world.*

It is difficult to reconcile these three accounts: Hides's book (which doesn't mention the Onabasulu harassment of the patrol), his patrol report (which mentions harassment but not the death of Ibuni), and the Onabasulu story. Assuming the outlines of the latter two accounts to be closest to the truth, a possible sequence of events would run as follows. Armed Onabasulu warriors twice harassed the patrol, once on the day it left the longhouse and again on the following day when they were staging supplies. Meanwhile Ibuni, who had scattered with his family to another hiding place in the forest and didn't know of this, decided to come out and meet the patrol. If the usual procedure was followed, Hides and O'Malley would have stayed at the forward camp and sent the carriers back to stage the last load under police escort. Two days of harassment and fear of ambush had left everybody edgy, anxious, and frustrated, so that when the police with the staging party saw Ibuni in the garden, they simply shot him out of spite. It is unlikely that Hides himself was involved in the shooting, and it is quite possible he may never have known of it (his report is, however, sketchy on this point). Nevertheless, it reveals a level of tension and a shaky condition of police discipline that did not bode well for the future. Meanwhile, the patrol was already pushing on. Hides recorded in his report, "It seems we have left these miserable people behind us, for all signs of a track are lost. The next population, I hope, will treat us more kindly" (PR: 42).

---

*As with Heyosi's death, apocryphal elements later crept into the story. Ibuni's body was said to have been found in a peculiar position: stretched out straight on his back between two cut poles, with his head resting on another pole. Such stories were ridiculed by eyewitnesses.

Aftermath

As the patrol moved away, the Onabasulu, like the Etoro, had no idea what it was or why (or even how) Ibuni had been killed.* The prevailing idea remained that Hides and O'Malley were probably spirit people (a fairly common reaction to first contact among the peoples of Papua and New Guinea). However, whereas peoples in other parts of Papua and New Guinea often welcomed explorers as returning ancestors or ghosts of the dead, the people of the plateau forest feared their return would lead to the unmaking of the world. Their hostile display and harassment of the patrol was both an attempt to hurry them on their way and a test to see what these beings were made of. The Onabasulu, like other peoples of the region, enjoyed playing with such dangerous edges.

When the patrol had passed and the Etoro and Western Onabasulu returned to their longhouses, they were dismayed to discover the beads, axes, and bushknives that Hides had left there as gifts hanging from the house posts. Fearing to touch them, at a loss what to do with them, they simply left them hanging where they were. The outcome of one such situation was related to me with great glee by a Bosavi informant: Umi, a man of Yuesa community, showed up at the Onabasulu longhouse of Gunigiamo above the Sioa River. There were an axe, a bushknife, and two pieces of red cloth hanging in the eaves where they had been for well over a week. "What are those?" he asked. He was told they were left by the strange beings who had passed through.

"Why don't you take them down?"

"We are afraid," the Gunigiamo people told him. "Who knows where these things are from. Perhaps they are from the Origin Time." Umi, who had seen axes and bushknives coming in over the southern trade routes and knew how rare and valuable they were, replied: "Since you are afraid of them, I'll take them off your hands." The Onabasulu gratefully allowed him to do so, and Umi gleefully took the treasures away. Similar tales are told about the artifacts Hides left in other Onabasulu and Etoro communities.

A final note: in the weeks following Ibuni's death his relatives man-

---

* The murder of Ibuni was sufficiently puzzling for Onabasulu and Bosavi people who did not know the story very well to attempt to remodel it according to more understandable typifications. One (Bosavi) version said that Ibuni was shot because he pressed an attack on Hides, who was signaling him to sit down in peace. Another (Onabasulu) version speculated that he was shot in retaliation for Heyosi's attack on Hides. Finally, a widespread version holds that he was killed because the patrol thought that he was part of an attempt to take revenge for Heyosi's death. It was a familiar trick, my informant told me, to have one man visible on the path and apparently vulnerable while an armed body of warriors hid nearby to ambush the enemy should they be tempted to attack him.

aged to divine the witch responsible for "ripening him" for the kill. They mounted a raid upon his longhouse and killed him in revenge.

As the events of the patrol receded into the past and nothing terrible happened, more pressing local issues reclaimed the attention of the long-house communities. The resentment and social unrest among the Bosavis as a result of the killing of Sobolo were beginning to be felt in the Onaba-sulu country. When the people of Wosiso sought refuge from harassment by fleeing to their Onabasulu relatives near Ogesiye (where some of them saw the tents of the patrol and heard the shot when Ibuni was killed), Sobolo's friends and relatives sought another target for vengeance. In life, Sobolo was bald and had customarily worn a makeshift wig. After his death, the wig was given as a memento to a relative, a young man named Yabeolo from a neighboring community. Yabeolo took this wig on a visit to relatives among the eastern Bosavi communities near the Hegigio/Kikori River. Both he and these relatives (and Sobolo too, be-fore his death) had connections among the neighboring Namabolo people, traditional enemies of the Onabasulu.

When the Namabolo saw the wig, they were furious and decided to raid the Onabasulu to pay them back for their participation in the attack against Sobolo. So, about the time Hides and his men were moving along the Sioa Valley, a Namabolo party descended upon an Onabasulu sago camp a few kilometers to the south, killed seven people, and carried their bodies off to eat. The Onabasulu communities of the area mobilized and went off in pursuit, but the raiders got safely away across the Hegigio/ Kikori River. While they were tracking them, however, the Onabasulu found strong evidence that the Namabolo had been assisted by Yabeolo's eastern Bosavi relatives. The longhouse of these relatives, however, was strongly defended, so the Onabasulu drew back to bide their time. Mean-while a young boy who had managed to escape being killed in the raid by hiding under a log reported that he had recognized Yabeolo's voice among the raiders, and Onabasulu suspicions turned in his direction.

The Strickland-Purari patrol had probably passed out of the region by the time Onabasulu divination revealed that a certain man named Dagawo, a member of the same community as those killed in the raid, was responsible, through witchcraft, for "ripening them" for their deaths. They planned his execution. Hearing of this, Yabeolo, who was look-ing for a way to clear his name with the Onabasulu, volunteered to grab the victim and hold him for execution. This was accepted, the raid was made, and the witch dispatched. Yabeolo returned to the good graces of his Onabasulu neighbors. Nevertheless, the latter later mounted a raid on Yabeolo's eastern Bosavi relatives and massacred about ten of them at a sago camp.

The Limestone

After leaving the Onabasulu country, on April 4 the patrol entered a difficult region of limestone: a geologically complex area of thrust faults tipped on edge with massive limestone blocks piled up on each other, intercalated with volcanic materials. Here there were no paths; the Onabasulu had wisely left the area uninhabited. This was the roughest country Hides had ever encountered: "It is . . . a desolate silent land where only bandicoots and pythons can find a home. The rock is honeycombed and stands on end; it forms fissures and craters, large and small, and every step has to be watched as the limestone edges are as sharp as broken glass. There are no running streams, no water, for the rain seeped immediately through the limestone. The fissures and cylindrical stone pits of this country sometimes seem bottomless to the eye. A stunted and tangled growth covers it all, the goru palm predominating. . . .

"We found it impossible to cut a straight course, for in dodging the impassable craters we were turned in all directions. From a distance every timbered elevation looked like a spur of some divide; but at close quarters we found them to be only the rims of more craters. Always finding a way northward, we walked up narrow and silent corridors of rock, sometimes with the rumble of an underground river far below in our ears" (*PW*: 67).

Hides's present goal, a big river to the east, was less than 20 km away, but the country—with its sinkholes and chaotic topography—was so formidable that the patrol struggled through it for nearly two weeks.

The strain was not long in telling. Within a few days, several carriers and police had been disabled with cut feet and gashed legs. Seven carriers stole rations and deserted, only to be tracked down and brought back by the police. Hides had great difficulty finding a way through this region, for low cloud cover prevented him from getting a look at it. In four very difficult days they were able to make less than 13 km. After six days there were only twenty bags of rice left. It was no longer necessary to relay, but Hides put everyone on half rations, for he did not know how long it would take to get out of this area. On top of all this, carriers and police began to show the swollen joints and bleeding gums of the onset of beriberi. The months of living on a diet of rice were taking their toll. Morale among the carriers was low. Undaunted, Hides pushed on, as he had in situations of similar hardship before. On April 16 they broke out of the limestone fault country and arrived at the banks of the Hegigio/Kikori. A few days later they breasted the highland rim into the richly cultivated valleys of what is today the Mananda census division.

The fertile valleys and large populations of this area were to be Hides's greatest discovery, for which he became famous. For the patrol, however, it was the beginning of their greatest trials. What might have been a difficult passage through the highlands under any circumstances was given heroic proportions by the exhausted condition of the patrol, which had been traveling through the tropical forest for nearly three months.

4. ACROSS THE TARI FURORO

BRYANT ALLEN AND STEPHEN FRANKEL

Hides and O'Malley got their first glimpse of the highlands on April 16 when the patrol passed out of the limestone country to a spot overlooking the Hegigio/Kikori River.* Climbing a tree, Hides saw stretches of rolling country and cultivation far ahead up the valley. After weeks of grinding hardship, it was a glimpse of the promised land—human population and food lay ahead. The morale of the tired carriers picked up immediately, despite the effects of half rations and festering limestone cuts and leech bites. For four more days the patrol picked its way down through the forest toward the distant valley. Then, on April 20, they came to an opening in the trees.

Hides and O'Malley stared spellbound at the scene before them: "Below us . . . reaching as far as the eye could see, lay the rolling timbered slopes of a huge valley system. On every slope were cultivated squares, while little columns of smoke rising in the still air revealed to us the homes of the people of this land" (*PW*: 77).

None of them had seen anything like this in Papua before. Below in

The authors would like to acknowledge the following organizations and individuals who have assisted in the preparation of this chapter: the Tari Local Government Council and District Management Committee; the Southern Highlands Provincial Government Research Committee; the Research School of Pacific Studies, Australian National University; the University of Papua New Guinea Library; the National Archives of Papua New Guinea; the Commonwealth Archives, Mitchell ACT; Helen Pickering, Ben Probert, Gilbert Rose, and Robert Crittenden; Steven Badya, Francis Bape, Henry Talu, Urufu Ibai, and Hiru Olabe, who interpreted; Raymond Lipe, pastor at St. James Enda Komo for hospitality; and numerous other men and women for guidance, forbearance, and companionship. This chapter is dedicated to the pupils of Tari and Koroba High Schools, for their great interest in Huli history and their deep concern for the future.

* Hides dubbed this river the Ryan after the prewar patrol officer Henry Ryan. He was right, however, in suspecting that it was the upper reaches of the Kikori.

the valley the cultivations were divided and orderly, reminding Hides of European plantations or Asian rice paddies.

"As I looked on those green cultivated squares of such mathematical exactness, I thought of wheatfields, or the industrious areas of a colony of Chinese. Here was a population such as I had dreamed of finding. . . .

" 'My mother,' said Sergeant Orai. 'People like the sand. They have plantations! What people are they?' . . .

"One of the carriers spoke up anxiously: 'What if they are bad-tempered?'

" 'Well what?' Corporal Dekadua replied with the greatest assurance: 'We are ten' " (PW: 77–78).

The Land of the Hulis

The patrol was looking up the Wada, Dagia, and Benaria valleys at the cultivations and homesteads of the Huli people.* Today the Huli are popularly recognizable by their large wigs decorated with daisies and appear in photographs on travel posters and coffee-table books about Papua New Guinea. Among anthropologists they are known for their social organization, which is said to stress patriliny less than other highlands groups (Glasse 1968).

The country of the Huli consists of a series of montane valleys and basins set within the central New Guinea cordillera at the headwaters of the Kikori (locally called Tagari) River. To the south the region is bordered by the limestone country the patrol had just passed through. From where Hides and O'Malley were standing, however, the central and largest portion of the region, now known as the Tari Basin, was out of sight behind

* Information for this chapter was obtained by interviewing Huli men who had witnessed the passing of the Strickland-Purari patrol or whose parents had been involved in some way. Individual interviews were carried out beginning around 1975 as an adjunct to other research. In 1985 Allen, using notes and names collected by Frankel in 1982, attempted to follow Hides's track from the Mananda Basin across the Tagari River. He discovered that many of the areas through which Hides and O'Malley passed are now unoccupied and the tracks overgrown. It proved impossible to visit Yubaye, where the patrol made first contact with the Huli, both for this reason and because Telenge, the one surviving witness of that event, was too frail to make the journey. Hides and O'Malley crossed the Tagari about 4 km downstream of the present cane suspension bridge. Of the men identified by Frankel who had seen the patrol, only Telenge Yenape and Ayakali Yambilida were still alive in 1985. Word has since been received that Ayakali died early in 1986.

Allen interviewed informants through a pidgin/Huli-speaking interpreter in the presence of a number of interested men, women, and children. The interpreter first explained to the old men the purpose of the interview. Allen then asked them to give a free account of the events they had witnessed. He next asked questions about the events based on the patrol report and material obtained from other informants but left out of this particular account. Finally he showed them the photographs in PW, and these were discussed. Both Telenge and Ayakali, to everyone's excitement, were able to identify themselves (and most of the other people) in the photographs.

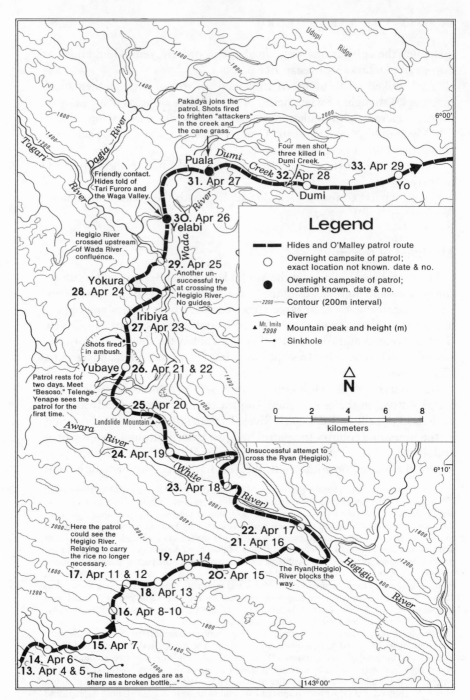

Map 6. Across the limestone barrier to the "Tari Furoro" area (April 4–29). Crossing the limestone barrier, the patrol encounters the Huli people of the "Tari Furoro" and hears of the "Waga Furari" to the east.

the low Udupi Ridge. This basin consists of a series of shallow valleys 25 to 38 km across, divided by extinct volcanoes, limestone ridges, rivers, and swamps. It was there, rather than in the country directly in front of Hides, that the majority of the Huli people lived. The climate is an agreeable 27°C (80°F) most of the year with moderate rainfall of 2,280–2,540 mm (90–100 in.) (Glasse 1968). The country varies in altitude from 1,500 to 2,000 m and slopes to the south, drained by the Tagari River, which curves first east and then south before passing out of the highlands through the Hegigio Gorge (where Staniforth Smith had met disaster). Below the gorge, it becomes the Kikori/Hegigio and flows to the Gulf of Papua.

The inhabitants of this region represent a formidable population, compared to the tribes Hides and his men were familiar with in the Papuan lowlands and the coast. The Huli probably numbered more than 30,000 in the 1930's with density of settlement ranging from about 15 per square km in peripheral areas to 50 or so to the square km in the Tari Basin.* They possess a highly productive subsistence economy based not on sago and bananas as in the lowlands, but on the cultivation of sweet potato. About 90 percent of Huli garden land is given to sweet potato, though taro, pitpit, beans, pandanus, sugarcane, and other crops are also grown. The soils of the region have a good structure derived from their content of volcanic ash, and the Huli are sophisticated farmers, skilled in techniques of mulching, composting, and drainage. The "mathematically exact squares" Hides saw in their gardens represent an ingenious method of planting special to parts of the highlands of New Guinea, where sweet potatoes are grown in mounds of earth turned with ashes or green compost. These are interspersed with drainage ditches and fenced against the depredations of pigs. Although there were areas of forest in the Huli region, hunting and fishing played a negligible part in the subsistence economy. Nearly all animal protein in the diet came from domesticated pigs, which Hulis kept (and still keep) in large numbers.

Pigs to the Huli are more than just a supply of protein. They are also the standard of wealth and the major currency of social transactions. It is partly through pigs that people demonstrate their worth, and it is through pigs that they fulfill their social obligations and further their relationships with others. Transactions and exchanges of pigs, whether for bridewealth, payments of compensation, sacrifices to the ancestors, or supportive gifts to friends, are always matters of great import. Though men dominate most transactions with pigs, caring for pigs is the central concern of the whole family. Pigs are the major productive capital and the stuff of dreams. They are the subject of endless calculations and machinations throughout

* Glasse (1968: 18–19) gives a population for the Huli of about 41,067 based on the 1960 Tari and Koroba census divisions, with density of 25 per square km in the Central and North Basin census divisions—then the most heavily populated.

Huli life, and few sights will gladden the heart of a man more than a presentation of fat pigs (Glasse 1959: 276).

Given the Huli obsession with pigs, it is interesting to note that, unlike other peoples of the highlands, they do not have a system of ceremonial exchange such as the Enga *te* (Meggitt 1974), the Melpa *moka* (Strathern 1971a) or the Mendi *mok ink* (Ryan 1961) in which Big Men make extensive gifts of pigs and shells to each other to build prestige and further their political influence. The closest equivalent to these large-scale ceremonial exchanges among the Huli were the *tege* ceremonies, now discontinued, which aimed to appease the ancestors and placate the *dama* spirits through gifts and sacrifices of pigs. In these ceremonies men became prominent through their ritual knowledge and not through exchange of pigs (Glasse 1968; Frankel 1981). Social and political influence was (and is) also gained through helping a wide range of others with bridewealth and compensation payments by making them loans and gifts of pigs.

Despite the large Huli populations and in contrast to the Papuan lowlands, there are no villages or longhouses in the Huli area at all. Rather, each man prefers to live in his own small homestead built in the midst of his gardens, while his wife and female relatives live in another small house or group of houses some distance away. These establishments and their nearby gardens are surrounded by ramparts, fences, and deep ditches, and traditionally the entrances were set in an arch of sharpened stakes. These precautions not only are aimed at discouraging the depredations of pigs, but also serve to prevent trespass and impede armed attack. The effect is far from welcoming, and indeed Huli generally regard casual visitors who are not good friends or close relatives with suspicion (Frankel 1981: 63).

The people of these scattered homesteads, however, acknowledge membership in larger territorial groupings known as *hameigini*, a word that means "sons of the father" (Frankel 1981: 57) and represents a locale believed originally to have been occupied and cleared from forest by a distant clan ancestor.* The *hameigini* is felt to belong principally to this ancestor's patrilineal descendants who still reside there and perform the ancestral rituals. However, although some descendants of the founder do reside on this land and are its proprietors, they usually make up only a small proportion of the actual resident population. The majority of residents are simply people who can trace some connection or other to the founding clan, and some have lived there for generations.

Huli men can in theory reside in any *hameigini* where they can establish ties and are willing to support local compensation payments and rituals. Given the unsettled and conflictual nature of traditional Huli society, many found it advantageous to establish homesteads and gardens in a number

* Following Glasse (1968), this unit has been called a "parish" by highlands social anthropologists.

of *hameigini*, both to expand their networks of personal connections over a wider area and to provide alternative places of refuge in the event of warfare or dispute with neighbors at another residence.

Like Huli farmsteads, the territory of *hameigini* usually had strongly marked boundaries, of which the most striking were extensive systems of deep ditches. In overlooking the country for the first time, Hides remarked upon the network of drainage ditches which crisscrossed the countryside and suggested to him a high order of agricultural advancement. These great ditches, often 5 m deep and 2–3 m wide, served not only as drains, but more importantly as sunken roadways interlacing the valleys and as paths for channeling pigs to foraging areas while keeping them out of the gardens. They also provided an ingenious network of hidden passages through which parties of warriors could make their way unseen from one section or territory to another, enabling reinforcements (or enemies) to suddenly materialize on the battlefield or allowing a fleeing group to escape. For this reason early patrol officers dubbed them "fighting ditches."

These sorts of Huli social and residential arrangements reflected both the cantankerous individualism widely characteristic of Huli social personality and the contingencies of a social fabric continually being torn by armed conflict. Warfare was endemic in traditional Huli society, and all Huli men were warriors. They could be unconscionably arrogant, quick to provoke and quick to take offense, and they fought amongst themselves frequently. Men quarreled over personal insults, adultery, damage to gardens, theft of pigs, failure to meet compensation payments, and homicide. Fighting frequently broke out in the midst of argument, for men were always armed with bows and arrows. If the fight could not be settled quickly, it would escalate to war (Glasse 1968: 88).

The aim of fighting was not only to even the score against a man with whom one had a grievance, but to exact as much injury and humiliation upon him as possible. When Hulis fought, houses were burnt, gardens despoiled, trees cut down, pigs killed, and men, women, and children slaughtered without mercy (Glasse 1959: 273–89). While they did not eschew the usual Papuan tactics of raid and ambush, Hulis also fought large-scale set-piece battles in open garden land, fielding as many as 500 warriors on each side. Such wars might continue on and off for four or five months, result in 50 or more casualties, and not come to an end until the warring parties ran out of food (Glasse 1959; 1965; 1968). Boldness and aggressiveness in battle were highly admired, and men often gained influence through their performance on the battlefield.

The individuals who initiated the war were held responsible for compensating their allies and enemies for any deaths and injuries they had suffered. Since an appropriate compensation for a man's death could be as much as 150 pigs, this was no easy task. Even with the generous assistance of kinsmen, payment of compensation to those aggrieved could be delayed for years, leading to more disputes, shifting of supporters, and more fighting. At the same time, even when compensation was appropriately paid to all those concerned after a war, it did not mean the dispute was necessarily settled. Rather it might simply be in abeyance until such a time as it surfaced again in another context and the cycle of fighting continued.

Cosmological Geography

The Huli region when Hides saw it was dotted with groves of hoop and klinki pines (*Araucaria* sp.), each of which marked the *kebanda*, or sacred site, of a particular *hameigini*. Hidden in these groves, which were carefully protected by taboos, was the shrine of the *hameigini* ancestral spirit, usually built near the place where he was thought to have emerged from the ground. These spirits were believed to be benevolently inclined toward their land and its inhabitants and to encourage their prosperity, so long as the shrines were kept in good repair and periodic sacrifices of pork were made. Huli tended to these matters mostly at times of illness amongst the people (or pigs), of poor crop yields, or of other misfortunes.

Other *kebanda* were dedicated to *dama*, powerful nonhuman spirits (Glasse terms them deities [1965: 33]) from the Origin Time. These spirits were generally indifferent to the plight of human beings and were regarded as predatory and treacherous. Huli propitiated them from time to time to keep them from causing trouble, or if an individual was willing to risk forming a pact with one, he would make sacrifices of pigs to the *dama* to persuade it to attack his enemies.

Finally, there were certain especially important *kebanda* located at sacred places roughly in a line from south to north, from Mt. Haliago (Sisa) to Mt. Ambua, which marked junctures along the "root of the earth," a cosmological feature of major importance to the Huli (see below).

Looking outwards from their lands, the Huli saw themselves at the center of a world occupied by five groups of people, all of whom were descended from a common ancestor, the *dama* spirit Hela (Frankel 1986). To their north were the "Obena" people (comprising the Enga, Ipili, and Paiela tribes). To the south and west in the lowland forests were the "Duguba" people (Bosavi, Etoro, Onabasulu, and Bedamini). On the southeast around Lake Kutubu lived the "Hewa" (Foi and Fasu), while to the immediate west were the "Duna." These peoples did not share the Huli view of common ancestry, but they were familiar with Huli men who traveled long distances along well-defined routes to trade with them. For the Huli these groups defined the points of the social compass beyond the periphery of their world, and they maintained important trade and/or ritual relationships with all of them.

The most important trade flowed between north and south. From the Obena people Huli obtained stone adze and axe blades and salt, manufactured from the Enga brine pools. From the Duguba they received black palm bows, together with hornbill beaks, bird feathers, and tree oil used for ceremonial decoration. From Lake Kutubu to the southeast they obtained small amounts of cowrie shell. Although Huli of the upper Waga Valley lived at the upper end of a major trade route to the coast, they received little from that direction. They were not particularly interested in the mother-of-pearl shell that was such an obsession for other highlands peoples to the south and east, and in 1935 they had not yet heard of steel.

Beyond trade, however, these people outside the peripheries of the Huli world had important cosmological and ritual significance for the Huli, particularly the Duguba people of the lowland forests to the south.* The Huli regarded the Duguba with a certain fascination and dread. In part this was because the Huli were repelled by the plateau people's practice of eating human flesh (the Huli were not cannibals), and also they feared the Dugubas' reputation for witchcraft and sorcery.† Moreover, Huli believed, hidden down in the dense forests of the Duguba country was the entrance to *humbirini andaga*, the Huli land of the dead.‡ But aside from fearing these disconcerting aspects of the lowland forest, the Huli also believed that the key to their own moral and physical well-being lay somewhere down in the Duguba country.

The Huli world view contains a strong sense of decline, of the deterioration of the physical earth and the decay of their culture into anarchy and immorality (Frankel 1986). This is reflected in recent times, they believe, in the decline in soil fertility and the falling of crop yields, in thin and sickly pigs, in promiscuity among young people, and in sons who no

---

*As a matter of detail, the term "Duguba" did not refer uniformly to the people of the Papuan Plateau for all Huli groups. To the more central and northern Hulis, the term tended to be used to refer to those groups to the south of themselves who were still Hulis but were beyond the periphery of their own regular social experience. Thus, as we shall see, the *dindi gamu* ceremonies were always supposed to originate among the "Duguba" people to the south of one's own territory and be passed through one's own sacred spots and then on to the next group to the north. Nevertheless, for the southern Huli, the people we are concerned with here, the "true Duguba" were believed to reside in the lowland forests of the Papuan Plateau (Frankel 1986).

† Hulis frequently purchased techniques of homicidal magic from the lowland Duguba. One of their favorite techniques, "*hambu* sorcery" (Glasse 1959: 273–89; Frankel 1986: 144–47), is simply a form of the most commonly used homicidal magic (*fofa*) of the Bosavi and Onabasulu people of the Papuan Plateau.

‡ Warriors or others killed in battle go to a somewhat more pleasant but equally vaguely conceived place called *Dalugeli* in the sky (Glasse 1965: 30), occasionally returning to take revenge on the living. Some people interpreted the Fox brothers (see below) as such vengeful returning spirits.

longer obey their fathers. Things have not always been so, according the Huli elders, and with proper ritual care there is hope that the wholesomeness of former times might be restored. According to Huli elders, many generations ago, during a time of similar decline, a great dark cloud came over the sky blocking out the sun and spreading darkness (*mbingi*) over the land. People fled into their houses as earth or sand began to fall from the sky. When the cloud had passed and people ventured outside again, they found this unknown material had covered their houses and gardens and indeed the whole countryside so that everything looked different.* After a brief period of shortage and hardship due to the smothering of the gardens, the Huli replanted and presently found themselves greeted with truly astonishing harvests. There followed a period of garden abundance and proliferation of pigs such as they had never seen before, and a time of peace and prosperity is said to have spread throughout the land.

Over time, however, the effects of *mbingi* began to diminish. Harvests became smaller, and the Huli people believe they have returned to another period of steady moral and physical decline. There is thus a periodic concern among them, when things look particularly bleak and unpromising, to try to bring back *mbingi* and with it the prosperity and harmony it is thought to have brought them before.

The principal means for bringing about the return of *mbingi* is thought to be the proper performance of a ritual cycle called *dindi gamu* (literally, "earth ritual" or "earth magic"). The Huli believe this stimulates a flow of magical power from south to north across the Tari Basin from the Duguba country of the Papuan Plateau to the Obena country of the central highlands. Although the details of *dindi gamu* knowledge are secret and known only to ritual specialists, knowledgeable Huli know the power passes through a series of sacred sites along a conduit called "the root of the earth," which is thought to have the form of a thick underground liana cane entwined by a python. Through this conduit flows water or (during performance of *dindi gamu*) smoke. Active points along this pathway are marked by spots where there is a cave or opening in the ground through which running water can be heard underground. The most important *kabanda* of Huli land are located at these spots, and it is here

---

* This description of *mbingi* almost certainly refers to a widespread fall of tephra, or ash, from a distant volcanic eruption. Geological and vulcanological evidence collected by Blong (1982) in the Tari Basin and elsewhere in the highlands indicates that the *mbingi* incident probably took place in the mid-seventeenth century and resulted from the catastrophic Krakatoa-like explosion of Long Island in the Bismarck Sea off the northern coast of New Guinea at a distance of more than 650 km from Tari. This ash fall dropped a layer of gritty gray-green sand approximately 1 cm thick over the Huli houses and gardens (Allen and Wood 1980). Stories of "a time of darkness" resulting from the Long Island explosion are widespread throughout the highlands and extend even down onto the Papuan Plateau, where the incident is remembered as "the time that sand fell out of the sky." No particular benefits are attributed to this event by the plateau people, however.

that the root of the earth can be ritually manipulated (Frankel 1986). According to Huli ritual experts, however, the source of the power of *dindi gamu* lies beyond the periphery of Huli land among the Duguba down on the Papuan Plateau. Moreover, because the Duguba control the source, only they can initiate *dindi gamu*. The cycle is supposed to begin when the Duguba perform rituals at a vaguely conceived location known as "Malia" or "Malea" in the Etoro or Onabasulu country (probably the Onabasulu origin spot "Malaiya" discussed in Chapter 3).* No Huli has actually seen these rituals performed, but it is believed that when they are, smoke passes along the root of the earth, under Mt. Haliago (Sisa), and emerges from the ground at a sacred spot called Hari Hibira in Huli country. When the smoke appears, Huli ritual experts know that the cycle has begun and commence its Huli segments. The *dindi gamu* rites are then supposed to be performed from one sacred site to the next and from one Huli group to another across the Tari Basin until handed on for completion to the Obena people. If this entire ritual cycle is performed properly, Hulis believe that *mbingi* will return.

Ironically, given the politically fragmented nature of traditional Huli society with its continual outbreaks of dispute and armed conflict, it is very likely that Hulis have never been able to organize themselves on a large enough scale to actually bring off the full rites of *dindi gamu*, and the full cycle has probably never been performed. The "Duguba" people, for their part, know little or nothing of the importance of *mbingi*, the rites of *dindi gamu*, or the immense significance Hulis put upon their (Duguba) ritual activities. The reputation for ritual power they enjoy in Huli imagination results largely from the fact that they are people beyond the periphery of the Huli country, who thus have the magically potent qualities that those who live beyond the edge of the world are often said to possess.

First Contact: The Fox Brothers' Expedition

The Huli people had encountered their first Europeans only five months before Jack Hides and Jim O'Malley arrived. In November 1934 two gold miners, Tom and Jack Fox, and their sixteen carriers crossed the Tari Basin.† The Fox brothers had come from Mt. Hagen in the Mandated Territory and were engaged on an unauthorized prospecting expedition.

* The Duguba rite that is supposed to initiate *dindi gamu* was described to Frankel by one Huli ritual expert (who had not, however, observed it). It involved certain features that suggest he was referring to the final ceremonies for a *bau a* ceremonial hunting lodge, a plateau ritual complex that from the point of view of its performers does not have anything to do with *dindi gamu* (for details of the *bau a*, see Schieffelin 1982).

† Though Hides and O'Malley are usually credited with being the first to contact the Huli people, the Fox brothers actually preceded them by about five months; their route lay some distance to the north.

They were tough, hard-bitten characters, veterans of nine years in the gold-fields of the Mandated Territory. They had left Mt. Hagen on August 23, 1934, and traveled west via the Lai Valley, accompanied by carriers loaded mostly with trade items (including shell and cloth) packed in old kerosene tins. Their aim was to prospect the headwaters of all the rivers to the border of Dutch New Guinea. They returned on December 15, thin and worn, but with their party intact. "We've been clear to the foot of the rainbow, and there's not a pot of gold anywhere," Jack Fox told Mick Leahy. "It's limestone country mostly, rich soil in the valleys and plenty of natives, all of them full of beans and ready to fight, but there is not enough gold in the lot to fill a tooth" (Souter 1963: 188).

While they claimed to have traveled all the way to the border of Dutch New Guinea, the Fox brothers never made a proper map, and it is difficult to reconstruct their journey from their diaries and the records of journalistic interviews taken in later years. Gold rather than an accurate description of the geography and local populations was the aim of their journey. In a radio interview in 1973 an aging Jack Fox was asked, "Did you have an awareness that you were breaking new ground, discovering new people?"

"Well no, not in that way," he answered. "We were looking for gold, you see, and the idea is we were going over new country looking for another Edie Creek [a lucrative goldfield in the Mandated Territory], and we didn't find one. The natives were before us, we knew, but . . . We weren't really interested in the natives. They were just there because they were there" (Australian Broadcasting Commission 1973).

In a handwritten account, apparently set down after their return to Mt. Hagen (Ms. Diary, UPNG) they described their journey.* Without going into detail, it is probable they reached not the Dutch border but the eastern bank of the Strickland River, traveled downstream for some distance and then turned east through Duna country south of Lake Kopiago and approached the Tari Basin from the west. On November 6, 1934, they describe entering an area inhabited by men wearing half-moon shaped "hats" made of human hair and decorated with flowers, where they had to travel on "sunken roads" (fighting ditches), where pigs were plentiful and the natives "were inclined to be cheeky." Distinctive landmarks are described, including the Hiwai Falls on the Tagari near Pureni, which leave little doubt that they went directly through the center of Huli territory, passing unknowingly within a kilometer of Gelote, the most important Huli sacred site, and then very close to Bepenete, the second most important *kabanda*, critical to *dindi gamu* ritual (see Map 2).

The diary contains no reference to clashes with the Huli, and both men

* Editors' note. See also *Pacific Islands Monthly*, Feb. 21, 1936: 41–44.

vigorously denied causing any deaths or violence during their explorations. The Hulis, however, tell a different story: "They came, killing men
as they came," Panguma Lomoko of Piango *hameigini* told Allen in 1986.
He described how the two Europeans and their black-skinned companions
(who were dressed differently from the police who came in later years)
appeared from the west, traversed the South Basin from west to east and
crossed the Tagari-Waga divide through what is now known as the Tari
Gap, about 2 km north of where Hides and O'Malley were later to cross.
Panguma claimed that over two days of repeated clashes, they killed more
than ten Huli warriors, including Panguma's brother-in-law. One can trace
the route of the expedition described by Panguma as far west as Koroba,
a path strewn with accounts of shootings, deaths, and near misses. The
Fox party apparently traveled much of its way across the valley through
the network of fighting ditches.

Looking for his brother-in-law after a clash in one of these trenches,
Panguma found him leaning as though exhausted with his face against the
trench wall. He touched his shoulder, and his brother-in-law collapsed
to the ground, his chest blown away, dead. The Fox brothers apparently
referred to such violent contacts with the Huli through veiled remarks
in their diary like: "the natives were frisky today." The detailed descriptions of bullet wounds, visits to the sites where the fights took place,
and confirmation of the names of most of those said to have been killed
by independent informants leave little doubt of the veracity of the Huli
accounts.

Once past the Tari Gap, the Fox brothers apparently proceeded due
east, passing just north of the present Margarima airstrip and then southeast to cross the Mendi Valley from where they returned to Mt. Hagen.
Thereafter, they spoke little of their expedition, and it received little public
notice. Their reticence may have been related to the fact that they had been
traveling through uncontrolled country without proper permission and
had crossed illegally from the Mandated Territory into Papua. Moreover,
at the time the Fox brothers returned, two other prospectors at Kainantu
had been threatened with suspension of their entry permit for shooting
local New Guineans, and another, a German named Ludwig Schmidt, was
being held under arrest in Rabaul for the same crime. While prospecting
along the Karawari River earlier in the year, Schmidt had shot so many
people that the government brought charges against him. He was eventually hanged in 1936, the only white man ever to suffer such a fate in the
Mandated Territory or Papua (Souter 1969: 186–87).* The Fox brothers
certainly did not want to draw attention to themselves at this time.

* This was the turbulent time of early exploration when prospectors, government officers,
and missionaries were fanning out into the highlands valleys of the Mandated Territory.
Two missionaries were killed in the Chimbu district just prior to the Fox brothers' return

Hides and O'Malley had left Daru for the Strickland only fifteen days after the Fox brothers returned to Mt. Hagen, without, as far as we know, having any knowledge of their journey.

The Arrival of the Patrol

Hides and O'Malley emerged from the forest on the southern borders of Huli country on April 21, 1935. When they had recovered somewhat from their sense of wonder at the vista before them, Hides wrote: "The whole floor of the . . . canyon was under cultivation. . . . Some of the inhabitants were in the fields below, and on calling out to them, a number of short, stockily built men all carrying bows and arrows appeared not more than a hundred . . . yards away. They looked at us queerly, with their heads to one side, and appeared to be whispering excitedly amongst themselves; then they started to call in pretty yodeling tones, and soon we saw women and children hurrying away across the fields towards the top of the canyon. The men stayed, however, and for about an hour we endeavored to induce them in, but they appeared afraid" (PW: 78–79).

Eventually they signaled that Hides and O'Malley could take what food they wanted from the gardens but continued to keep their distance: "Towards evening three men approached us to within a hundred yards, and waving their arms to us several times, indicated we must go back whence we came. When I showed them a bright steel tomahawk, called in friendly tones and indicated they come up to us, they shook their heads vigorously" (PW: 80).

Hides watched them leave and decided that he would stay for a day or so to establish friendly relations because "in view of the population ahead on our path, it is vital to us that these people, the first, should be friendly" (PR: 50). Later in his book he reflected: "But what did the people in the little farmhouses think of us? I pictured the males gathering in certain of the houses below; I saw them eating and talking excitedly, and asking one another what was to be done with the strange devils above. Should they fight or should they leave us well alone? They would fear us, for we were something they could not understand" (PW: 80).

If these were really Hides's thoughts at the time, they convey not only his excitement and curiosity at emerging in the highlands but also the romanticism that lay behind his outgoing approach toward the new people

---

to Mt. Hagen. This, together with continual trouble between prospectors and natives in the region, led to the amendment of the Uncontrolled Areas Ordinance in 1936 so that the administrator could declare any area "uncontrolled" and restrict the entry of persons into it (Radford 1987: 134–46).

he met—and that led him to feel betrayed when they did not fulfill his expectations. The next few days were to be filled with misunderstandings.

Telenge Yenape

The patrol had emerged at a place known to the Huli as Yubaye, located about 6 km southeast of present-day Komo Station.* One of the Huli who saw it was a youth named Telenge Yenape.

In 1986 Telenge Yenape was a frail old man living alone in a house hidden among tall cane grass behind high walls, at a place called Enda. In 1935 he was about 18 years old and lived at Yubaya. On the afternoon of April 21, 1935, he was weeding his garden. Glancing up he saw a group of strange "men" standing at the edge of the bush about 150 m away. Most of them had dark skins, but their bodies were partly covered with unknown material. A number of them held what appeared to be wooden staves. Others carried regularly shaped burdens, some on their shoulders and others slung on poles, which they placed on the ground when they halted. The most frightening feature of the group was the two creatures who stood in front. Their skins were so pale they seemed to glow, and their feet and their lower legs were covered with something. The only creatures Telenge knew of who were said to have pale skins were ghosts or powerful spirits. These creatures then must be *dama*, a conclusion also reached by other men who gazed in amazement from other parts of the garden.

Telenge was so frightened by the apparitions that had appeared at the garden's edge that he took his bow and arrows, which Huli men carried at all times, and hid them in some long grass. *Dama* should not be provoked. He peered from behind a felled tree. Two of the strangers, little more than boys, came up to the edge of the garden and called out in Huli for him to come out of hiding and not be afraid. After some discussion, Telenge and the men took the axes offered to them and helped cut poles for the tent frames.

"We cut the posts," Telenge told us, "and stood them up and pulled the tent canvas over them. We made two houses, one for the police and the carriers and one for the Europeans. They gave axes to some of us. They gave me one to cut the poles for the house. When I was finished, I gave it back. It was the first time, and we were very frightened. We didn't know what this stuff was then [tapping his own steel axe blade].

---

* This area is now unoccupied, having been abandoned some years ago after a landslide that devastated houses and gardens. Although no one was killed, people believed it was a bad omen and moved elsewhere.

"I thought the axe came from a *dama* and was afraid. They must have dropped a small spade in the long grass and left it behind. I found it later in the garden and it was made from the same strange material. I asked myself, 'What is this stuff?' I didn't like it and was frightened of it, so I threw the spade into the river, and it disappeared. They also left a bush-knife in the garden at their next camp, Iribiya. A man took it and traded it for pigs.

"When the houses were ready, they wanted to sleep. I dug up some sweet potato, pitpit, abika [*Abelmoschus manihot*], and yams [*Dioscorea* sp.] and gave to them. I said to them, 'You sleep.' I went to my house and slept and came back in the morning."

These two apparently straightforward descriptions of the first meeting between the patrol and the Huli reveal significant differences that are unlikely ever to be resolved. (This is, of course, typical of remembered accounts of events long in the past.) Telenge insists that two young men who could speak Huli accompanied the patrol, whereas Hides makes no mention of interpreters or guides. As for Huli assistance in erecting his camp, Hides says the Hulis would not even come near on the first day. It seems unlikely that Hides would have forgotten something as important as guides or interpreters.* It is also possible that Telenge is confusing incidents from the Strickland-Purari patrol with those of later patrols into the area. Be that as it may, there is no doubt Telenge met Hides, for he appears in one of the photographs in *Papuan Wonderland* (this photo is included in the photo section following p. 124).

A Highlands Big Man

The next morning, April 22, about twenty men assembled near the camp: "Their cheekbones were high, but their features, more especially of nose and lip, were finely molded. They were all graciously friendly, cutting us bunches of bananas and indicating that we eat to our heart's content. I kept showing them steel, beads, and cloth; but they always waived [sic] them away from them, and indicated that there was *tomo* [food] everywhere" (*PR*: 51).

Hides was "suddenly conscious of a new figure making his presence felt. He was rather a splendid figure of a man, with a black, pointed beard, a cassowary quill through his nose, and a carefully coiffured and flower-decked mop of hair. He came up to where O'Malley and myself stood in

---

* Many of the people living on the northern borders of the Papuan Plateau could speak some Huli as a result of the frequency of trade, so it is not impossible a Huli speaker or two could have attached themselves to the patrol. But Hides does not mention any, and he surely would have, because their presence would have been most useful.

front of a huge pile of food the natives had collected in camp" (*PR*: 51).

This man was Puya Indane, also known later in life as Indawi Indane, a leading man, or *agali haguane*, of the time. He is portrayed in a plate in *Papuan Wonderland*, where he is referred to as "Besoso," a Motuan word meaning "big beard" (and see photo section following p. 124). Puya's arrival in the camp and the drama he set into motion give us a fascinating picture of the forces in play between the Huli and the patrol at this moment of contact. Puya struck everyone as an extraordinary figure the moment he appeared: "As he strode in before us," Hides related, "the younger natives made way for him." The patrol police were evidently unsettled by his instinctive air of authority, for they immediately began to belittle him—to Hides's naive amusement:

" 'This is what?' asked Sergeant Orai jokingly.

" 'It must be the village policeman,' said Dekadua. 'True he has no clothes, but his woman is washing them.'

" 'Look at his beard!' came from another constable. And afterwards they always referred to this imperial figure as 'Besoso,' meaning big beard" (*PW*: 82).

Dekadua and the others were painting Puya as a pretentious village constable (a local villager appointed by the administration to be its representative in communities under its control). These officials were well known to put on airs with their borrowed authority, and they were regarded with contemptuous amusement by patrol police who (with their rifles) carried the real force of the government. "Besoso," they mockingly implied, couldn't even meet the patrol in proper dress because his uniform was in the laundry. Puya, however, was so impressive that Hides was initially quite taken with him.

"Besoso appeared a very serious person, and when he came to a halt before O'Malley and me like a military officer, he looked us both up and down very critically. He jerked his head to me questioningly. I thought he was asking where we had come from, so I pointed southwestwards over the limestone barrier . . . [and thus, unknowingly, directly toward *humbirini andaga*, the Huli land of the dead]."

At this point Puya launched into remarkable speech:

"With his pantomime language and [gesturing with] the jawbone of a pig one could really understand most of his subject," Hides wrote.

"He appeared to be telling us that north, east, and west people were in thousands—like the sands of the soil he picked up and let fall through his fingers. We were in a land of plenty. They did not want our steel. . . . They had their own stone axes which gave them all they wanted.

" 'What a man!' [mocked] one of the police as Besoso dramatically concluded his words. 'He is like a Hanuabada man talking for money' " (*PW*: 82–83).*

Hides, however, was so affected by what he thought was "Besoso's" generous manner in this speech that he placed his hand on the man's shoulder in a friendly gesture. But Puya's arrogant demeanor in response—the natural manner of a Huli leader—quickly put Hides off. So he too decided a speech of his own was in order and delivered a harangue in Motu with appropriate gestures, telling Puya that the patrol had come from the southwest on a mission of friendship and would not molest people or property as it proceeded through their territory. Puya interrupted him: "Where are you going?" he wanted to know. Hides pointed northward across the canyon. Puya nodded but suddenly became thoughtful (*PW*: 83).

Hides continued pointing to the axes, beads, and cloth, all of which had been refused, and declaring his unhappiness at not being able to give them something in return for their hospitality. Puya cut in again: "With lofty disdain, he indicated that I should put back all these axes and knives; and after telling us . . . that everywhere we went there would be plenty of food, he pointed to the northeast and said something that we didn't understand. With that, he went off, every native in camp going with him, and we were alone again" (*PW*: 83–84).

The police again had remarks to make about "Besoso," which influenced Hides's thinking—this time they implied Puya was treacherous and a coward: "The police, with keen intuition, distrusted this man. I could hear them saying that one of so many words, who was so unafraid now after sending young men in to meet us [first], was to be watched. And they watched him all right, as will be seen" (*PW*: 84). Their "intuition," however, seems to have been uncomfortably bound up with threatened amour propre at the arrogance Puya showed toward them.

By now all the Hulis who had visited the strangers on the southern edge of Yubaya were convinced that they were spirits. Quite apart from Hides's gesture toward *humbirini andaga* as where the patrol had come from, Puya believed he recognized his dead brother Barina among the police. One of the reasons he had left the camp was to kill a pig for him.

He returned in the afternoon and presented the gift of freshly butchered pork to Hides. Then he touched a tiny string of cowries and gestured (Hides believed) to ask if there were any in Hides's tent. Hides tried to explain that he had none, picking up a handful of dirt to show that where he came from these things were as common as dirt. Some men "gasped with astonishment" though what they actually took as Hides's meaning is

---

* Hanuabada was the Motuan village of partly acculturated Papuans located close to Port Moresby.

anyone's guess. In the meantime, Puya had gone around to the tents to see for himself. There he found no cowries, but in the police tent he spotted some hornbill beaks sticking out of Dekadua's bag. Next to the shells he wanted those things. Hides gave some to him, promising Dekadua he would compensate him for them when they returned to the coast (*PW*: 84). This particular gesture of good will, however, is likely to have been considerably resented by the police. During this time, Hides had had some knives and beads brought out again, for he still wanted these people to accept his trade goods, but they continued to refuse them. Finally he gave one man a looking glass. The man examined it with increasing fascination. Then Puya saw this.

"[He] called the man to bring this interesting thing, and when the native did so Besoso jumped back from seeing his face. He was bidden [by others] to hold it at such and such a length. Now it must be right in front; now on the ground; now ten feet away. I was beginning to think vanity would overcome fear; but suddenly, Besoso, like a big bully, said something in an authoritative tone, and the unfortunate native, who had no fear and would dearly have loved to keep the glass, came and handed it back to me" (*PW*: 85).

Puya had been uneasy about the unfamiliar objects the "spirits" were offering them. He had warned the other men that they should not keep any of the steel tools in case they proved harmful to humans. The shock he received at seeing his own face in the mirror evidently clinched his conviction on this matter and he ordered it returned. Telenge recounts, "The mirror was small and round. They gave it to Tebele.* . . . He wanted to keep it, but we were afraid of it. It was the first time we had seen anything like it. So Puya made him give it back. Now I think they are quite useful for adjusting the flowers in my wig or painting my face."

Hides was furious at "Besoso's" interference with his attempts to form peaceful trade relations with the other people and stung by his contemptuous manner: "The people, it seemed, could do nothing without the sanction of this arrogant old sorcerer—who now appeared to think we feared him" (*PW*: 85).

In the late afternoon Puya took Hides by the arm to convey a message he had apparently been pondering since the morning. Pointing north across Yubaya and shaking his head vigorously he said "*Na bopi! Na bopi!*"

---

* Editors' note. Tebele was not a Huli but a visitor from the Lake Kutubu region, possibly an in-law or other relative of someone in the Yubaya area. Telenge says that Tebele had gained permission from Puya before taking Hides's trade goods for examination. It may be that Puya felt he was an appropriate guinea pig on which to test the possible danger of these strange items: being from another area, if he was harmed or died it would have few local repercussions.

[You cannot go that way.] Then he waved his arm to the eastward. Hides understood very well that he "meant that our road lay in that direction and that we were not to cross the canyon." According to Telenge: "Puya wanted them to go towards Kerewa [the large volcano to the east]. He wanted to stop them going further north where there were many people and gardens. He thought the *dama* would affect the gardens badly or kill women and children. So he showed them a place with no roads and no people." *

"Treachery"

On the morning of April 23, having rested for two days at Yubaya, Hides and O'Malley led the patrol north, noting that "a child could see that such a route [to the east recommended by Puya] was impossible" (PR: 53). As they moved down the valley, the Hulis in the line of their route were thrown into consternation: "The natives . . . started to wave us back and to yodel and rush to and fro; when we arrived in this area we found twenty of them to meet us, all armed" (PR: 53). Now, however, they affected a friendly eagerness for the patrol to be on its way across the canyon. Hides was initially gratified to see that "Besoso" was not with them, but became alert when he noticed the warriors did not attempt to lead the way but rather followed at a little distance. Looking ahead he saw that a deeply incised creek lay across the track, a perfect site for an ambush if there were armed men on both banks. He halted the patrol for a few minutes at the bank to see what would happen. Behind them the warriors following betrayed a nervous impatience to have them continue on their way. Ahead O'Malley spotted armed men moving in concealment in the grass on the opposite side. To prevent the situation from developing any further Hides had the police fire a shot over the men lying in ambush, and they made off "with surprising speed." He then had the warriors behind them disarmed and broke one of their bows as a sign he did not want to fight. He herded them ahead and made them cross the ravine in front of the patrol.

The patrol then followed across and moved on through an area of houses and gardens. The people there seemed somewhat friendlier, and one man

* Editors' note. It is legitimate to wonder whether Puya may have heard something of the bloody passage of the Fox brothers across the Tari Basin five months before, since that would be additional reason for him not to wish Hides and O'Malley to cross the cultivations of his own people's *hameigini*. The Fox brothers' route lay to the north of Yubaya three or four days' walk across the intervening territories of numerous other, often conflicting, *hameigini*. Nevertheless, it would have been possible for the news to have covered that distance, and Frankel thinks it likely Puya had heard of it. Telenge Yenape, however, told Allen that he had heard nothing of other patrols before Hides and O'Malley appeared.

offered to guide the patrol out of the canyon. Hides tried to explain to him the reason for the shot and that the patrol had come in peace. "He nodded," Hides recorded, "in perfect understanding" (*PR*: 54). Moving on Hides suddenly found himself facing "Besoso" by a knoll at the side of the track, accompanied by about 50 armed warriors. Hides suspected that he had just run from the ambush site at the ravine. "I fancied I could see his chest still heaving from the exertion of his run . . . to this solicitous retreat. His arrogant manner was gone. Now he waved a friendly arm and said a meek 'augwa fobei' [*agua pobe*—Go that way] to the good road we were following" (*PR*: 54).

However, Hides was so angered at what he saw as the man's treachery that he ordered the police to chase him away:

"Dekadua and Borege stepped closely to him, only too pleased to carry out the duty. Together they addressed him in Motu. 'You think Judge Murray's police are schoolboys. Ah?' . . .

"Besoso did not understand Motu and did not give an answer; so without more ado the two constables picked up handfuls of gravel and pelted him out of sight in a most undignified manner. Besoso's people realized what it was for; they stood by and laughed, and the guide led us on" (*PW*: 87).

When Telenge watched the patrol set off across Yubaya that morning, he was unaware of any concerted plan to ambush it, but he was aware that some men wanted to kill the spirits.

"They left Yubaya and moved to Iribiya and camped there. On the way they wanted people to move away from their path. They said, 'Move back from the stream.' It was then that they fired the gun.

"We all carried bows and arrows in those times. There was no 'law' then. We fought incessantly in those days. When we saw the *dama* moving towards the north, we wanted to kill them. We waited there to try and shoot at them, but they fired the gun. Some ran away. Some just fell down, we couldn't work out where the sound had come from. They fired over our heads at the rocks. We had no understanding at all of what sort of men these were. We were frightened of them so we thought of killing them."

Telenge was one of those who fled at the shot and joined Puya and the larger group of men further down the track. But now they were terrified. "They [the police] broke our bows and arrows, and they threw stones at us and chased us away," Telenge told Allen. No further attempt was made to prevent the patrol from following its own course, and they went on their way.

It is worth remarking on this curious incident, since it reveals something about Hides that was already evident in his encounters with people on the

Papuan Plateau and was to continue to affect his conduct of the patrol. Puya's response to what he thought was happening seems understandable, but Hides's manner of dealing with Puya is less so. Although by his own account Hides knew the Huli were frightened and confused, he seems to have been unable to take the attitude of circumspection and restraint this insight might have suggested and spend more effort in calming their fears.

Instead, his general liking for Papuans, his outgoing manner, and his eagerness to establish friendly relations as soon as possible seem to have led him to assume that a tentatively friendly response on the part of the local people he met meant a more unequivocal acceptance of him and his men than it did. If these same people later threatened or attacked the patrol, he took it as treachery, as though he thought a person toward whom he had extended affection and friendship had turned on him or let him down. Thus, he sometimes switches from sounding effusive and friendly at one moment to injured and vengeful at another. It seems to be this sense of injury that led him to have the police humiliate Puya.

Hides's vocabulary for characterizing his feelings about those he met on his journey strikes a theme throughout his writings. Those he liked or found cause to admire he viewed as noble savages, picturing them as "gentlemen" or comparing them to figures of ancient civilizations. Those he disliked or didn't trust he characterized as "cunning," "treacherous," "arrogant," "old sorcerers." In contrast to Hides's tendency to extend himself warmly to the people he met, his armed police trusted nobody and were always ready to teach uppity locals a lesson.

Across the Tagari

Leaving the knoll where Puya was pelted with gravel, the patrol moved north seeking a route down to the Ryan/Tagari River. The river here flows wildly through a steep-sided gorge 25–30 m wide. Ivan Champion later described the river at this point as "a snarling monster waiting to get you in its grip" (Lake Kutubu PR 1, 1937–38). The walls of the gorge are steep and dissected. The slopes above are covered with dense stands of thin-stemmed trees, extremely difficult to move through without a track and affording few breaks from which to gain a view of the surrounding countryside. The patrol had no guides to show them the way and spent the whole of the next day hacking their way around in this thick brush unable to find a crossing place. Setting camp that afternoon, Hides and O'Malley looked across the gorge, once again captivated by the beauty of the Huli farmsteads:

"It is hard to describe the beauty of these neat squarely cultivated areas: the park-like farms with hedges of croton and poplar; the yellow of the fallowing areas; the rich green of harvest, the chocolate brown of the newly tilled ground. One must picture pretty little farming areas of Australia—scores of them, in a setting of great rolling timbered plains. This wonderland belongs to Papua" (PR: 55).

The sight encouraged Hides and O'Malley to make another attempt to cross the river the next day, this time successfully. It was a difficult task but cleverly executed. Telenge who, with some companions, had been shadowing the patrol at a safe distance describes how it was done:

"They went down to the Tagari near the junction with the Toro stream, opposite the Wada River [about 2 km upstream from the mouth of the Benaria River]. They made a bridge.

"They cut a very tall, thin arienge tree, a really long one. They pushed this up through the branches of a tree on this side, to catch the branches of a large tree on the other side which was growing out over the water. They tied a hook onto the other side of this pole so that it would catch in the tree on the other side. They tried to do it two or three times before they succeeded. A policeman climbed up into the branches of the big tree and tied the pole on. Then they lashed a hipi tree on top of the pole with cane. They made a hand rail. They used nails to do this. Then they all went across. Where they went over there, I don't know."

"Broke camp as usual without a meal," Hides recorded as they started off the next day, April 26 (PR: 56). He continued to be concerned about his men. "The carriers are weak and worn with 120 days of incessant toil," he wrote, "one is crippled with an abscess on the knee caused by a limestone cut; while all of them, and the police, are haggard of face and form. Both officers, too, have not escaped the effects of short rations and hardship" (PR: 55). They had not been able to purchase local food for two or three days.

Following a large track up the Wada Valley, they entered an area of cultivations where they were confronted by a group of armed men. Reassured by the peaceful manner of the patrol's approach, however, these warriors laid aside their arms, sat the visitors down in a cultivation, and cooked them all a welcome meal of sweet potatoes.

"It was not long before hundreds of curious men were around the party," Hides remarked. "All unarmed except for their bone daggers, and a few of them with stone adzes. . . .

"After a while there came a nice old man . . . his cheeks adorned with fluffy side-whiskers. He had the appearance of a gentleman and in civilization might have been a squire, a country doctor, or a sedate lawyer entrusted with the family fortune, so naturally affable was he. A string of beads and he gave me a draw on his bamboo pipe; a looking glass and in great glee he affectionately tugged my beard and was in a mind to give

O'Malley and myself the whole valley. 'Aija! Aija!' [exclamations of as-
tonishment] he kept exclaiming; and sometimes he would take hold of our
arms and look into our eyes in wonder. Then pointing to our clothes, to
the knives and axes, he pointed to the sky, indicating to the crowd around
us that we had come from above; the police and carriers were the same as
themselves he appeared to tell them" (PR: 56).

Hides questioned him about the country and thought the old man told
him the name of the valley was the "Tari furoro" (probably *Tagari porago*,
"the Tagari runs [there]"). When Hides pointed to the east, the old man
said "Wagi, Wagi furoro" (PR: 57), evidently speaking of the Waga River
several days' march to the east, but Hides in great excitement believed
he was hearing about his goal, the Purari. (Hides uses the spelling "Waga
Furari" in his book [PW: 91], following the pronunciation of speakers of
the dialect nearer the Waga headwaters.)

Moving up the valley, Hides and O'Malley continued to marvel at the
carefully squared gardens, wood-slab fences, and deep contour drains. It
was hard for them to believe these marks of civilization were indigenous
to these primitive people:

"It made one wonder who had taught these people their excellent methods of husbandry. To us who were conversant with the rather lackadaisical
farming methods of the average Papuan, it was an amazing sight to see this
primitive race of people employing a procedure of husbandry that is only
of comparatively recent introduction in civilized countries. These people
were not Papuans as we knew them" (PW: 93).

At least not of the sort that any of the patrol were familiar with. That
evening they got their first glimpse of tension between *hameigini*. Sitting
in camp that afternoon with their guide, they were approached by three
men carrying bows. When these three saw the guide, they moved on, indicating that the patrol should follow them. "When they had left, our guide
informed us . . . that they would attack us; and slinging his net bag across
his shoulder, he also waved us good-bye and disappeared quickly in the
opposite direction" (PR: 57).

The next day, a couple of the police near the end of the carrier line
were harassed by bowmen and had to fire over their heads. Later, as the
patrol climbed toward the head of the valley, a mass of yodeling warriors
appeared and began to surround them in a determined manner. To avoid
what looked like a developing attack, Hides had the police fire a volley
over their heads. The yodeling ceased immediately, and the warriors stood
petrified with amazement.

Hides cannily shouted "Augwa fobei!" at them several times (words
meaning "go that way," which he had picked up from Puya Indane four
days before) and indicated he was moving east. The grammar wasn't quite

right for exactly what he wanted to say, but it was clear enough what he meant. The warriors continued to follow the patrol for a while—but no longer in a threatening manner.

Shortly afterwards the patrol camped at a place called Puala. Looking back over the route they had come, Hides was taken by reflection on the future of this land and its people:

"As I gazed over this fertile valley, this wonderland where practically every crop will grow, the question of the future of these people occurred strongly to me, and I wondered whether the introduction to civilization would make them any happier than they appeared to be when we first came in contact with them" (PW: 94).

"One reads of missionaries coming from various parts of the world to be first among our newly discovered races as soon as they are controlled; but is it not possible that civilization for these people does not begin with just spiritual enlightenment? They have a religion of their own, and they seem to tell me they would become real farmers, growing better foods in maize and millet, and that we could teach them to build roads and breed cattle. We will have to give them a lot if they are not to be disillusioned; for if industry cannot be brought to them by the wealth of their land, then I do not see how we are going to give it to them. The population of this valley may possibly have been brought about by their intense methods of agriculture; and if this is so then the plough and cereal foods would create an even greater population—provided they were given them in a manner that did not break up their social system" (PR: 59).

The Huli people who gathered around the camp at Puala seemed nervous, but apparently friendly. "Among the men collected on this spot was a curious native who called himself Kamburu. He appeared to be a sort of chief and was always accompanied by a funny-faced 'secretary' who consistently reiterated the ends of the chief's speeches. They made a cunning pair" (PR: 59). Like Puya and other Huli leaders, Kamburu subjected Hides to a pantomimed speech and interrogation intimating that he knew they came from the sky. Hides went along with it but was tired and wary. He thought he detected a false friendliness, an insincerity, about this man and didn't trust him. At the same time, he was unable to purchase food from the people. Despite many requests, all he was offered was a small bag of very poor quality sweet potatoes. To his repeated requests for more food, the people replied, "*Nahai! Nahai!*" [there is none], while all around them Hides saw sweet potato fields and pig pens. This treatment was all the more alarming because of Hides's knowledge of Papuan custom:

"With the savage, hospitality is generally one of their principal virtues; but if he despises you, he will give you no pig, and the potatoes shall be measly and fit only for animal consumption. The treatment meted out to us [here] is the worst I have ever been subjected to; for they have not acted in this way from fear of us or through a shortage of food" (*PR*: 62).

Despite their hunger and frustration (for Hides believed the Huli knew they were hungry and should have offered them food) he forbade any theft from the gardens because the attitude of the Hulis hanging about the camp led him to believe they were only looking for an excuse to justify an attack. At the same time he did not want to use what little rice was left lest he endanger the party later by having no food when they had to cross the limestone barrier again. Most of the patrol went to bed hungry that night.

Ayakali Yambilida and the "Attack" at Dumi Creek

In 1935 Ayakali Yambilida was a young man living near the present site of Benaria government station, 10 km from Puala. He was unmarried and spent much of his time with four other youths. As the patrol approached, he reported:

"Word reached us that two white-skinned men and some strange black-skinned men had appeared at Puala. We heard that many men had gone there to see them and that they had covering on their bodies and white skins, and red and other colored body decorations. We [he and his four companions] decided to go have a look too. We heard they had made a house at Puala, not a normal house, but a canvas house. So the five of us went to the place where they had made this house.

"Kambu Kuapa [possibly the man Hides calls Kamburu], my maternal cousin, was there. He gave them sweet potato, and they gave him an axe. He pointed to the trees, and told them, these are my trees, cut them down if you want to.

"They gave us matches and a knife. When they had given us these, they told us to go and kill a pig. We had no pig so they told us to find one somewhere, to ask other men for one, but again we told them it was not possible for us to give them a pig. They gave another man an axe and a kina shell and asked him to get a pig. There was plenty of food at that time, but we didn't have any sweet potato to give since we came from elsewhere. These were not our gardens. Other people were frightened and brought them rubbishy sweet potato that were fit only for pigs. They didn't have a suitable pig to give, and they became frightened when they [members of the patrol] kept asking for one. They got some sweet potato, but they wanted a pig."

Ayakali's account contains some confusions. We know, for example, Hides did not carry any kina shell. It seems likely that Ayakali has mixed this element into the story from his experience with some later patrol (possibly Ivan Champion's in 1938; Lake Kutubu PR 1, 1938–39). But if Ayakali is confused on this point, all his other observations, and above all his photograph in Hides's book, confirm he is describing the Strickland-Purari patrol.

Ayakali and his companions came from 10 km away. We know that men contacting later patrols through the area came from far and wide, so we can surmise that a good many of the crowd gathered about Hides's camp came from similar distances. If so, then there might have been few people present who actually owned the land or had rights to the pigs and vegetables that Hides so desperately wanted to buy. The problem may have been not that the people refused to sell it, but that there was no one there who was actually entitled to sell it to him.

The next morning, April 27, "hundreds of men were at the camp very early, while scores of others, concealing their arms, stood at a distance to watch us" (PR: 60). After another frustrating and unsuccessful attempt to trade for some sweet potatoes, Hides was confronted by Kamburu, who indicated (so Hides thought) that there was no food available and that the patrol should be on its way. Hides was immediately wary. A tense atmosphere pervaded the camp, and he was sure the local inhabitants had prepared some kind of ambush. There was nothing for it, however, but to move on.

At this point, given the uncertain situation with the local people and the debilitated state of his men, Hides decided to turn eastward and move straight toward the Purari rather than spend time investigating areas farther to the north. In so doing, he missed entering the Tari Basin, a more truly magnificent piece of country than anything described in *Papuan Wonderland*.*

The campsite at Puala is on a spur overlooking the Wada. A track cuts around the side of the spur into the valley of Dumi Creek. On either side of the valley are high, rugged, bush-covered spurs. On the northern side the forest comes down to the stream, but on the southern side enclosed fields and fallows run halfway up the valley side. Upstream the valley rises steeply to the higher slopes of Mt. Kerewa. The stream has incised itself into landslide deposits in the center of the valley. On each bank is a narrow boulder-covered terrace along which a small track runs. To progress up the stream it is necessary to cross repeatedly from one low terrace to the other. About 10 m above on each bank is a higher terrace now (1986) covered in low secondary forest. In 1935 these higher terraces were being cultivated, and vestiges of old ditches can still be seen beneath the trees.

---

*As noted above, "Tari" is not a Huli word but a mistaken hearing of the name of the Tagari River (Tari furoro—*Tagari porago*), and it is likely that the present-day name of the whole Tari area has its origin in Hides's misunderstanding.

Kamburu had indicated to Hides a track that ran up the spur from Puala towards the forest, but as the patrol moved off in that direction a young man who had been in the camp came up and, tugging at Hides's arm, insisting that the patrol should go with him instead. Hides at first did not know what to do, but eventually, trusting the forthright and sincere demeanor of this young man, decided to go with him and they headed down into the Dumi Valley. He came to call the youth "Mambu," the Huli word for friend, and later believed that by following him he had avoided walking into a trap.

Mambu's real name was Pakadya Magada, and he was the leader of Ayakali's small band of companions. The path Kamburu had shown Hides led straight up the spur. It seems likely that Kamburu, like Puya, was attempting to direct the *dama* back into the bush whence they had come and keep them away from human gardens and habitations. The track he had indicated leads only into the forest and is used mainly by hunters and foraging pigs. Mambu, on the other hand, wanted Hides to cut around the spur to the north and then move east up the Dumi Valley. There was almost certainly no concerted plan to ambush the patrol on the ridge as Hides believed. But the route Mambu was showing them led directly through a populated area.

They descended from the campsite with Mambu and about twenty others in front. Hides describes what happened: "A hundred men were behind us, while scores of others followed [parallel] tracks below and above us. Yodeling commenced: Mambu urged us to hurry. We advanced across three farms, then went down to a little stream that flowed west into the Orai [named after Sergeant Orai?] creek. Now Mambu and four others were guiding us; the others had disappeared, as had those behind and on both sides of us. The situation was developing quickly" (*PW*: 98).

It is difficult from this distance to get a clear picture of what was happening. It seems clear that the Huli were greatly upset when young Pakadya/ "Mambu" began leading the *dama* into the midst of their farmsteads and cultivations. They were frightened and confused about what these creatures might do and uncertain about how to react. Arming themselves as they went along, they shadowed the patrol on both sides, moving in and out of the brush, yodeling and calling back and forth. Some undoubtedly wanted to attack strangers, but as a group they were not organized enough to do so. They were acting as agitated warriors often do in such a situation: by being intimidating and provocative toward their adversaries. To Hides, worried about his food supplies and the safety of his men, this behavior was ominous and threatening. He had believed all morning (almost certainly incorrectly) that the people were planning an ambush, and it now seemed about to materialize. Everyone in the patrol was tired and hungry, and there was a lot of tension in the air. The situation was set for trouble.

"As we rested in a cultivation," Hides wrote, "we saw scores of armed men on both sides of the creek and ahead of us, while I saw one armed man with an arrow fitted to his bow, come up to a hibiscus hedge not fifteen yards from where O'Malley and myself were standing, and then disappear. We had to wait for these people to close in on us; they could come as close as they liked; they could do almost anything to us; but we were not going to let them murder us. The suspense was exasperating" (PR: 60–61).

Certain that the warriors were preparing to attack, Hides decided to keep moving. He closed up the carrier line and proceeded in close order with armed police at the front and rear. He himself marched at the front of the line with five police and O'Malley a little distance behind him. As they passed along, O'Malley saw (as he later reported) a large crowd of men openly receiving their bows from women not 60 yards distant from him (PR: 62). Seeing that Hides and the five police had already passed out of sight ahead on the track, O'Malley fell back past the carriers to warn the police at the rear where he thought the attack would take place.

Shortly afterward Hides heard three shots in rapid succession. He halted the patrol. There were no more shots or calls, so he waited for O'Malley to come up. Quickly scanning the situation, he noted that there were now only two youths guiding him, Mambu and one other. He looked at Mambu, wondering if he had anything to do with this, but saw no signs of treachery in his face. He asked him by signs if he knew what the explosions meant, and Mambu indicated with snaps of his fingers the firing of arrows. Then he mimed that it was no concern of his, that the attackers were people different from himself and that they had not given the patrol food (PW: 99).

O'Malley came running up greatly excited, shouting that they had tried to kill him and had nearly got Dekadua. Later, at the official inquiry, he explained what had happened at the rear of the line. Having warned the police about the men he saw being armed, O'Malley had continued on ahead up the creek. He could hear them laughing and talking behind him as he walked:

"I had not gone more than 100 yards when three shots rang out. I turned around and saw armed men retreating into the bush; I fired one shot myself but did not shoot anybody.

"A.C. [Armed Constable] Dekadua of the party came up and showed me an arrow that had passed through his jumper, but had not injured him. The Sergeant [Orai] came up to me and reported that the natives who had

been following us had attacked with bows and arrows and that he had
ordered the police to fire at the attackers and two men had been killed*
(*IQ*, O'Malley's testimony).

This was the first time the junior officer had felt he experienced a really
close call, and he was highly agitated when he reported to Hides. When he
saw Mambu sitting nearby on the ground, such a "wild Irish look" came
into his face that Hides hastily stood up and made it clear that Mambu
was a friend. "This was O'Malley's first contact with primitive treachery,"
he later wrote; "he had come out of a dangerous position only by a very
narrow margin" (*PW*: 99–100).

Ayakali Yambilida had a different recollection of the attack. He, together with Pakadya/"Mambu" had accompanied the patrol down to the
stream.

"They said: 'Seeing as there is no pig, you can carry some of our cargo.'
So we went with them. The five of us accompanied the two white men. But
some other men stayed back. They believed they were *dama*. They had
bows and arrows, and they followed us at some distance along the edge of
the bush. They kept calling to us that they would kill us if we guided the
dama to their territory. They said they would kill the *dama*, and if we did
not want to be killed too, we should get away from them.

"We followed the small stream, Dumi. We came to a place where there
was a large boulder on one side of the stream. A man named Haiapela
was sitting on this stone. We passed by. One European went first and the
other came last, and we were in the middle. One European with police
went ahead, and the other came behind with some police. We were in the
middle carrying things. The European and the police coming behind told
us to hurry up. They were afraid. Afraid the other men [warriors] would
come.

---

* The evidence about this incident given by Hides, O'Malley, and the police at the inquiry held in Kikori after the patrol was over contains many inconsistencies, but Resident
Magistrate W. R. Humphries did not cross-question them. A.C. Dekadua, who had been
hand-picked by Hides stated: "One [warrior] fired at me and the arrow went through my
jumper. The Sergeant [Orai] shot that man. I fired twice. We fired twice, me one, Sergeant
one. I shot one man, Sergeant shot one man. Alright, that fight finish" (*IQ*, Dekadua's
testimony).

Hides heard three shots "in rapid succession." O'Malley heard three shots and fired one
himself, which makes four. Dekadua says he fired twice, but corrects himself to say he fired
once. The latter is probably correct. The police rifles were single-shot, Martini lever-action
Lee Enfield .303 carbines (Sinclair 1969: 124–25). After a shot is discharged, the user must
open the breech with a lever (which ejects the spent casing), insert a new cartridge by hand,
and close the breech again. This takes considerably longer than firing, reloading, and firing
a bolt-action rifle with a magazine. It is unlikely Dekadua had time to fire twice. It is also
unlikely that riflemen caught in an all-out attack from concealed ambush positions would
have survived a reloading unscathed. It is likely that two of those killed were hit by the same
bullet.

"Haiapela was a big man but he was sitting down. On the boulder. They shot him, and he fell face first into the water. He was just sitting there, he wasn't going to attack them. Labe was there too. He had an arrow in his hand and was rubbing it through his beard. That is how we clean arrows so they fly straight. He may have wanted to shoot the arrow at them, but he didn't have it fitted to his bow when they shot him too. The bullet hit him on the point of the left shoulder, went diagonally through his chest and came out under his right arm. He was hit but he ran back a short distance before he fell dead. Kayako was with the others. He must have called out or something. He was hit right in the center of the chest and knocked over backwards into the undergrowth."

Another man, Nokope, was standing behind Kayako. He was narrowly missed by the bullet that passed through Kayako and was spattered with his blood. As he instinctively ducked away, he tripped over a boulder and fell face down in the undergrowth. Kayako fell dead on top of him. From that day until his death a few years ago, Nokope held audiences of young Huli spellbound with this tale. His son recounted it to Allen at the place of the shootings.

Ayakali was near Hides at the head of the carrier line farther up the stream and did not actually see what happened, but he and Nokope's son (born after 1935) both strenuously deny that any of the men killed shot an arrow at the patrol. Perhaps so, but someone fired the arrow that went through Dekadua's jumper.

After O'Malley had run back to warn the rear guard police to be alert for trouble, someone probably shot an arrow at the last man in the patrol as they disappeared around a bend in the stream. It may have been Labe or some unidentified person on the terrace above. (The description of Labe's wound suggests he was standing side-on, the way a right-handed bowman who had just released an arrow would have been standing.) According to a reenactment staged by informants at the site, the police, including Sergeant Orai and Constable Dekadua, turned and ran back down the stream about 10 m and fired three shots in quick succession at four men on the opposite side, one of whom was possibly sitting on a boulder. Three were killed (though the police thought they only hit two).

If an arrow was released, it may be seen as a harassment or a test of nerve, but a single arrow was not the rush of a full attack. Orai and Dekadua, however, seem to have used it as an excuse, in the anxiety and uncertainty of the moment and with the apparent (if unstated) support of their officers, to retaliate against the Huli for giving them a hard time. This response was precisely what Hubert Murray's policy of maximum self-restraint for constabulary and patrol officers was designed to avoid.

After the shooting, Ayakali recalls:

"We hurried up the stream as fast as we could. We climbed out of the stream. Some men there called to the five of us [Ayakali and his four companions]: 'These creatures are *dama* or Hewa cannibals. You had better not stay with them. Trick them and run away from them quickly!' That's what they said.

"They shot a pig there. When the people watching saw the pig shot, they fled into the bush, and we took the pig. We carried it on to Dumi [where the patrol camped] and made a house [tent]. They told us to put the pig down. We put down the pig, all the cargo, and everything at Dumi. The police went about stealing sweet potato and bringing it back to camp. They divided it up. Some they kept for themselves, and some they gave to us.

"Then we boiled water and washed the pig. All the bristles came out. We cut it up and gave it to the white-skinned ones and the police and kept some for ourselves. The people [who had run away] began calling to us again. They told us three men had been killed in the stream. We should run away because they were going to kill the strangers. But we stayed. We cooked our parts of the pig in a ground oven, but they cut theirs up into small pieces and put it into a saucepan.*

"They had a rope around the camp.† They said to us, 'You cannot go outside this rope. You can stay in the camp.' So when night came, we stayed with them. Those outside kept calling to us to come away. We called back to them to bring more sweet potatoes, and some did. The white skins gave them salt and mirrors. When they saw these things, they stayed with us. We stayed with them for a whole day.

"By now many people had gathered at the *duguanda* [a mourning house] to cry and mourn the deaths of the men below. Talk came that these strange people were Dugubas or Hewas, who are cannibals, and we should get away from them. This was the third time they tried to get us away. In the middle of the morning we packed up the camp. The five of us talked together. I told the others I was becoming frightened and wanted to leave. So we pretended we were going down into the stream for a drink. One

---

* The "ground" or "earth" oven is a common method of cooking used in the New Guinea highlands. Pork and vegetables are steamed with hot stones in a covered pit in the ground. The preparation of the pig, by removing the bristles with boiling water, was novel to Ayakali.

† The stringing of a rope around the patrol camp was a practice commonly used in the highland areas of the Mandated Territory during the 1930's. The rope marked a boundary across which the local people were not permitted to pass. This enabled the patrol personnel to control the number of inquisitive (or threatening) visitors in the camp space, keep them away from areas where room to work was needed, help prevent theft, and give the officers some degree of privacy from interested touching, poking, and prying of curious people. Hides may have used such a method from time to time, though evidently not always, since he also sometimes complains of the large numbers of curious natives in the camp.

of us went one way and another another. Three of us ran away and two [including Pakadya] stayed."

Hides's account of the aftermath of the shooting varies from Ayakali's. He does not mention the shooting of a pig—or the theft of sweet potatoes by the police—although it is possible they occurred without his knowledge. Instead, according to his report, as soon as the patrol had made camp, Mambu presented them with a pig and then brought them all the food they could eat. While people from the opposite hills were shouting to Ayakali and his companions that the strangers had killed people and that he and his companions should flee them, Hides found the camp a peaceful respite and the local people outgoing and friendly. Many of them were apparently relatives of Pakaya.

As the patrol sat around for the afternoon, an old man suffering from severe asthma was brought to Hides. Giving Hides a packet of specially cooked spinach, he entreated him to cure his affliction. Hides was touched and to please him gave him some sugar dampened with a few drops of kerosene (an Australian folk remedy). "After he had taken it," Hides remarked, "the look on his face told me he was cured already" (PR: 63). This bold approach and request for medical help on the part of the old man seems a little surprising. But as one of Frankel's informants explained: "We thought that we squander so many pigs to give to *dama*, but we had never seen the face of one. Now a real *dama* had come amongst us. We thought it would be good to take this sick man to ask the *dama* to remove his illness. . . . The sick man was delighted with the cure. We wanted to give more pork but the *kiap* [patrol officer] didn't understand, so we left it at that" (Frankel 1986: 14).

Toward nightfall Pakadya came to the door of Hides's tent to pay a little visit. Hides was once again struck by his apparent genuineness, and his heart went out to him: "He was a real friend, with a real smile. He sat down on the ground in front of us as we rested on our canvas beds, and [made] a little cigarette with his tobacco rolled in a dried leaf. . . . He patted his abdomen and asked if we had eaten enough. And he smiled when we nodded our heads." Later Hides asked himself: "What fairies and magic did he believe in? What did he think of O'Malley and myself? I wondered, and I still wonder. The more I see of Papuans, and the more I learn about them, the more I realize the little that I really know" (PW: 101). This problem would continue to plague him about all of the people he was to encounter on the journey.

While we cannot be sure why Pakadya went out of his way to befriend the patrol, he was at the time an ambitious young man. He may have hoped that by offering food and hospitality to these powerful and mysterious beings, he could forge some kind of relationship that would bring him benefits in magical influence, prestige, or other political capital through which he could further his career. The personal warmth and human fellow feeling that Hides thought he perceived are unlikely to have been the only basis for his behavior.

Pakadya had nothing to lose. By contrast, older leaders like Puya and Kamburu, whose influence was well established in the local area, feared the patrol posed a danger to their *hameigini*. Thus they tried to steer the patrol away from populated areas and opposed it when it tried to enter them.

Landscapes and Populations: A Digression

To arrive at Dumi the patrol had been traveling slowly from the gorge of the Tagari River toward the mountain pass marking the divide between the Tagari and Waga watersheds. In all it was to travel from 980 m above sea level to 2,700 m, covering 35 km.* For the first three days, the patrol traveled in the valley of the Wada River, which cuts its way out of the Tari Basin in a deep gorge.

Hides's report and his book even more so create the impression that the Wada and Tagari valleys were heavily populated and intensely cultivated. He describes from time to time "hundreds of men around the party" and "scores of farm areas . . . the people of this valley system are to be counted in the thousands" (PR: 57). At Puala, looking down the Tagari Valley, he remarked there were "cultivated areas on practically every slope. The population is astounding" (PR: 58–59).

The view from this site today is of secondary forest, patches of grass, and a few scattered areas of garden, all of which are well away from the Tagari Valley. Population densities today are below 15 persons per square kilometer—compared to 80 to 100 persons in the Tari Basin. If these areas were heavily populated in 1935, what has happened to the people who formerly occupied them? Has there been a substantial depopulation in the area, or were there not really as many people living there at the time as Hides's report implies? The available evidence does not provide a simple answer.

In the years after Hides passed through, this area became a major route for patrols moving up from Lake Kutubu patrol post (opened in 1936) to explore the Tari Basin. In August 1937 just over two years after Hides

---

* This amounts to an average of about 5 km a day over fairly easy country. This slow progress (compared to later patrols in the 1930's) may have been in part a result of the debilitated condition of the patrol members, but it was actually about the same rate they had been traveling since emerging onto the Papuan Plateau.

crossed the Wada Valley, Claude Champion and F. W. G. Andersen followed the Wada River to the Tagari Valley, moving down from the north (Daru PR 4, 1937–38). They crossed Hides's easterly track between his camps 30 (at Yelabi) and 31 (at Puala). There had apparently already been some changes in settlement by then, due to extensive fighting. Champion reported traveling through successive patches of scrub and grass, past "burnt houses" and "wrecked gardens" and walked all one day in "scrub country." He did not comment upon the numbers of people in the area. In 1938 Champion's brother Ivan camped to the south on the edge of the Tagari Gorge at a place called Maribu. Looking northward up the valley, he remarked: "Further up could be seen gardens, but there seemed little population" (Lake Kutubu PR 1, 1937–38). Champion was aware (as Hides had not been) that many of the people who visited his camp did not live locally: "Of the hundred men and boys we saw . . . the greater number came from villages many miles away." Later, traveling a little to the north, close to Hides's camps 29 and 30 (Tagari and Yelabi), he wrote: "This country is sparsely populated. From Maribu to Heora there is not a single habitation, and from Heora to Bakai, another five miles, not one" (Lake Kutubu PR 6, 1939–40).

In assessing this situation, it does appear as though there has been a change in settlement patterns in this area. People have moved away from the lower parts of the valley above the gorge and also from the higher parts of the valley. On the other hand, it also appears that Hides exaggerated the size of the population he saw.

Dumi Creek to the Waga Divide

After spending the night at Dumi, according to Ayakali:

"The strangers carried on to Yo in Nene *hameigini*. There the child of Butakoma was killed. I cannot remember the name of the child, and today there are no people living up there to ask about it. They are all dead. They say the police met the mother and child while they were searching for wild pandanus and killed the child, but I did not hear the details.

"From Yo they went between [Mt.] Ne and [Mt.] Kerewa. I had met them at Puala [Hides's camp 31]. They camped at Yelabi [30], Puala, Dumi [32], and Yo [33], then at Pandupu [34], Tolonima [35], and Andidame [36]. From there they went into the Waga Valley and we heard no more of them.

"Pakadya later became a leading man on the eastern side of the Tagari River. He had just married at the time of the visit of the white-skins. He was killed in a fight later and the others who were with us those two days are also dead. I am the only survivor."

For Hides the few days after leaving Dumi Creek were happy ones. Although the health of the patrol members still left a lot to be desired, they were well fed and traveled among friendly people. No mention is made of the killing of a child. Pakadya's friendship towards the patrol influenced the reception they received from other people along the route.

In his book Hides recalled: "The children seemed to treat him as a great favorite . . . and when they saw how familiar he was with us, the little boys would come to hold our fingers as we walked along the roads, or to crack us gatora nuts between their teeth when we sat down for a rest. These little chaps were as likable as they were numerous."

This fond reflection led to another worthy of Jean-Jacques Rousseau: "How free and happy they always seemed. They had all the food they wanted and all the clothing they required. As I watched them, it made me think of the slum children of many of the big cities I had seen. . . . I tried to compare their lives with these primitive Papuan boys, and I am afraid the comparison was very much in favor of the little dark-skins" (PW: 102).

The patrol report, however, preserves more of the demanding than the engaging qualities of these youngsters, which Hides had to endure among other stresses of the journey: "All along the track today a youth pestered O'Malley and myself to give him a steel adze if he brought us a small pig. I have a headache each night from continually humoring the new people we meet each day, lending a willing eye and ear to always try and understand what everyone wishes to tell me. There are so many of them. It is always a relief when night has fallen" (PR: 65).

On the morning of April 30 Pakadya indicated that he could travel no farther with the patrol. He had first met the patrol at Puala, one day's walk from his home, and had traveled with it for three days through what appears to have been at least three *hameigini*. The evening before he had exercised considerable caution in approaching the people upon whose land they camped for the night and now felt he had reached the limits beyond which he could not safely travel. He bid Hides farewell, a new guide was assigned, and the patrol carried on. Hides had been much impressed with Pakaya's friendship and generosity and had developed a certain affection for him: "To the last his thoughts had been of our welfare," he wrote in his report. "I shall never forget this pretty, youthful savage, or his smart, hawk-faced 'secretary' " (PR: 64).

Over the next couple of days, the patrol was received in a friendly manner and supplied with plenty of food by the people they met.* The sick were also brought for Hides's ministrations—two cases of fever on one

---

* Today all of the areas above 2,000 m are unoccupied. People are now settled near to the dirt track that links Benaria government station to Tari at about 1,300 m above sea level.

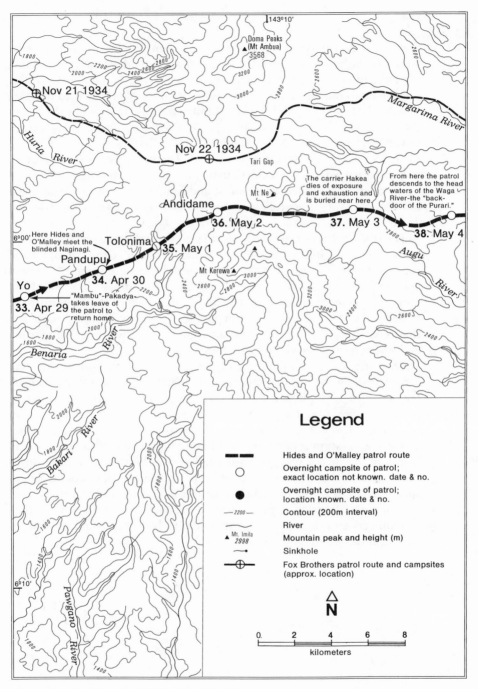

Map 7. To the "Waga Furari" (April 29–May 4).

night, and at Pandupu a youth who had been blinded in both eyes by an arrow in battle was brought in to be cured. Hides could do nothing for him, of course, but this man, whose name was Naginagi Polowabe, survived into old age and became one of our informants; he died in 1980.

At 8 A.M. on May 1 Hides and O'Malley were bid farewell by the last of their Huli guides, and the patrol proceeded alone up a well-defined track toward the peaks of "Mt. Champion" (Mt. Kerewa), which "towered easily five or six thousand feet above us." The patrol camped at 2,600 m and experienced intense cold that night. The next day they continued on through uninhabited moss forest and camped at 2,790 m, near some old shelters. They were following one of the major trade routes from the Tagari headwaters to the headwaters of the Waga.

The track emerges from the forest to pass through large patches of short grasses near the highest point of crossing. On May 3 the patrol passed through the narrow gap between Mt. Ne and Mt. Kerewa and "dropped gently eastwards still through trees and tree fern country" (PR: 67). Here they unknowingly almost converged with the route of the Fox brothers. Hides and O'Malley were to travel parallel to the Fox brothers' route less than 5 km away for the next four days until they moved past Margarima and began to descend the Waga Valley.

That afternoon, at an altitude of around 3,000 m, cold wind and rain forced Hides and O'Malley to head for a patch of low forest, in the shelter of which they pitched camp. Everyone was exhausted and suffering from exposure. About 4:30 P.M. a policeman came in to report that one of the carriers had collapsed on the track. Despite Hides's orders, the other carriers were so miserable with cold and fatigue they refused to go and help him. By then it was getting dark. So Hides himself went back down the track and, with the assistance of his personal orderly, Corporal Emesi, succeeded in dragging the delirious carrier into camp. But it was too late. Five minutes after they put him by the fire, Hakea, an Orokolo man, died. The officers and their men slept the night as best they could next to his corpse in the windy, frigid rain.

"Port Moresby, the Harbour Town of Papua." (Photo: Hides, 1935, *Through Wildest Papua*, facing p. 78)

Members of the Papua Legislative Council in 1909, including Sir Hubert Murray (far left) and M. C. Staniforth Smith (center foreground). (Photo: Small Picture Library, Australian School of Pacific Administration Donated Collection, Mitchell Library, Sydney; FM2/614-621, Sheet 7, No. AO, ACC no. 20)

"Dressed in Judge Murray's Clothes": Papuan Armed Constabulary at headquarters, Port Moresby. (Photo: Hides, 1935, *Through Wildest Papua*, facing p. 102)

"Patrol Officer Hides and Some of His Police." These men with single-shot, Martini lever-action Lee Enfield .303 carbines are typical of the Armed Constables who accompanied patrol officers on their exploration and administration of Papua before World War II. (Photo: Hides, 1935, *Through Wildest Papua*, facing p. 6)

"Our Carriers—Taken at the Base Camp on the Rentoul." Tent flies are visible in the background. (Photo: Hides, in *PW*, facing p. 48)

"Sergeant Orai." (Photo: O'Malley, in *PW*, facing p. 16)

Longhouse on the Papuan Plateau, similar to the Etoro longhouse where Hides was confronted by armed men on March 25, 1935. (Photo: Schieffelin, 1966)

(*Facing*) Canoe men on the Kikori River. Men and canoes such as these were recruited from Kikori and towed by the government launch *Vailala* to the Strickland River. (Photo: Mrs. G. Allen-Innes Collection, Mitchell Library; File A2118)

Huli sweet potato garden. These large circular mounds are typical of Huli gardens in the Tari region. Spindly cordyline plants (*tanget*) mark boundaries between plots. (Photo: Crittenden, 1980)

The Tagari River, about 4 km upstream of where the patrol crossed in 1935. Ivan Champion later described the river as "a snarling monster waiting to get you in its grip." (Photo: Allen, 1985)

A typical house of the Huli people. Huli houses are scattered among their sweet potato gardens. (Photo: Hides, in *Illustrated London News*, August 24, 1935)

"Not a very welcoming appearance"—the fortified gateway to a Huli homestead. (Photo: Crittenden, 1980)

"The First of the Light-skinned Men Met with Just After Crossing the Limestone,"
on April 21, 1935. According to Telenge Yenape, the man sitting on the left is Po-
Horeye; third from the left is Alupago; second from the right is Takame, Telenge's
younger brother; and third from the right is Telenge himself. (Photo: Hides, in
PW, facing p. 78)

Puya Indane, "Besoso," in his
flowered wig. The police keep a wary
eye in the background while Puya
stares at the camera with an expression of arrogance, perplexity, and
fear. (Photo: Hides, in *PW*, facing
p. 82)

Ayakali Yambilida, indicating himself in Hides's photograph. Ayakali also recognized Puya Indane's photograph in *PW*, although Puya lived on the western side of the Tagari, two days walk away. This is evidence of the unusual range of movement Hulis enjoyed before contact. (Photo: Allen, 1985)

"O'Malley and Some of the Light-skinned Natives," taken by Hides on April 29, 1935, in a garden between Dumi and Yo. The six young Huli men are (standing, left to right) Murapu, Pakadya Magada ("Mambu"), and (sitting, left to right) Adiki Kayu, Kurapu Pake (obscured), Peya, and Ayakali Yambilida. (Photo: Hides, in *PW*, facing p. 102)

An armed constable marches above Huli gardens. Hides thought these orderly rounded mounds, typical of this area of the highlands, were evidence of a more advanced "civilisation" among the people of the "Tari Furoro." In the foreground are stands of *marita* pandanus (*Pandanus conoideus*). (Photo: Hides, in *Illustrated London News*, August 24, 1935)

Blind Naginagi. One of several people who asked Hides to cure them during the course of the patrol, he had lost his sight when both eyes were shot out by a single arrow during a fight. (Photo: Allen, 1979)

5 · THE BACK DOOR TO THE PURARI

ROBERT CRITTENDEN AND EDWARD L. SCHIEFFELIN

The morning dawned clear and freezingly cold. After burying Hakea, the dead carrier, at the campsite, the patrol set off, wet, weary, and demoralized. They traveled all day over practically uninhabited grass tablelands and camped for the night in the pouring rain. The following day, before they had gone very far, they emerged at the head of a large valley draining to the southeast. Below them Hides and O'Malley could see miles of grasslands, shining streams, and cultivations dotted with numerous scattered hamlets. To Hides it presented "a beauty of country that is unsurpassed by anything I have seen in Papua" (PW: 111). They were standing at the head of the valley system of the Waga and Nembi rivers.

The region they were about to enter forms the upper end of a series of parallel valleys and basins running northwest to southeast, separated by rugged limestone ranges. This is the eastern extension of the same formidable karst barrier that the patrol had already crossed before entering Huli country and that reaches from the Strickland River to Mt. Karimui. The soils of these limestone regions with their pinnacles and sinkholes are usually thin and infertile. But they are conducive to human settlement where they have developed upon a stable base of volcanic ash that can sustain crop yields (albeit low ones) for long periods without fallow. Below where the patrol was standing was just such an agricultural area. The valleys appeared broad and fertile and heavily populated. Today the overall view is of a vast sea of grass with hamlets, scattered gardens, and parklike ceremonial grounds standing out as islands, while the whole is bounded by the steep forested slopes of the limestone ranges. This area makes up the southwestern limits of habitation of the New Guinea highlands.

Much of the information in this chapter is drawn from Crittenden 1982: ch. 5.

Hides was convinced that he and his men had at last passed out of the Kikori watershed and were standing at the headwaters of the westernmost tributary of the Purari. He was almost right. The Waga River does flow to the southeast, in the direction of the Purari, but farther down the valley, out of sight of where the patrol was standing, it makes an abrupt loop to the southwest, cuts directly across the limestone ranges, and flows through the Kutubu lowlands to the Mubi. It is beyond this loop of the Waga that the true westernmost tributary of the Purari, the Nembi River, flows in.

The World of the Wola and the Nembi

In the 1930's (and still today) the people of this valley system recognized three roughly differentiated groups among themselves. At the very head of the valley, where Hides and O'Malley were standing, lived the last fringe Hulis (and a few Enga speakers). A little to the south, and reaching to beyond the loop of the Waga, lived the Wola. In the distance, in the lower part of the valley system, were the Nembi. All these peoples spoke languages that were partially intelligible to each other, and most people could tell where visitors from other parts of the region came from by their speech.

While the scattered farmsteads and neatly tended gardens of the Wola and the Nembi were reminiscent of those the patrol had passed through in the Huli country in the previous week, the societies of those peoples were organized quite differently. In the 1930's the Wola and Nembi hamlets, nestled among their cultivations, were not the homesteads of single individuals as among the Huli, but usually consisted of a men's house inhabited by a set of brothers (or male agnates). Their wives, children, and female relatives lived in other small dwellings nearby. The people of these hamlets, in turn, were arranged in territorial groupings conceived of as patrilineal clans and associated with one or more *hauma*, or ceremonial grounds. The ceremonial grounds were grassy parklike areas, carefully cleared and leveled, their borders planted with casuarina trees and decorative shrubs. There the people staged their ceremonial exchanges, the dramas of feasting, dancing, and prestation of pigs that were the driving engines of social and political activity for Wola and Nembi society (Sillitoe 1979a; Crittenden 1982; Nihill 1987).

Relationships within and between clans were extremely complex. Although the people spoke as though patrilineal descent and clan brotherhood was the basis for social solidarity, membership in clans was actually based on the ability to establish rights to clan lands according to whatever kinship links one could muster and through cooperation in exchanges and other local affairs. As a result, the actual composition of Wola and Nembi clans was a good deal less than purely patrilineal. Most men were assimilated as fictive "brothers" within each locality group that identified itself as a clan. In practice, these groups defined themselves as those who shared in collecting bridewealth to help pay for a wife for one of their men or in receiving bridewealth for one of their women. For various reasons the accumulation of marriage ties between clans often resulted in the formation of named pairs of clans linked by the especially high density of marriage ties between them. Marriage and exchange provided the basis for the formation of numerous defensive alliances among Wola and Nembi clans.

The flexibility in recruitment to clan membership in the local group was matched by flexibility in the formation of network ties between men in different groups. Every man had a wide range of possible kinship ties by marriage, matrifiliation, or descent with people in other clans; but only those relationships he personally chose to activate by developing them into exchange partnerships became important and viable links in his personal network. These individual networks of exchange partners, especially those of ambitious individuals, could (and did) range widely up and down the valley system, and many men could travel back and forth fairly freely, even between groups which were nominally at war.

The entire system of clan alliances and individual networks was maintained by frequent ceremonial exchanges of pigs between affines and exchange partners staged on the focal *hauma* ceremonial grounds. The size and frequency of these ceremonial exchanges not only maintained network ties in good repair but also added to the prestige of the individuals and clans sponsoring them. Indeed, ceremonial exchanges were the major means (apart from warfare) of gaining regional renown and political ascendancy over other clans and alliances in the valleys. The result was a situation of constant competition and fierce rivalry among the clans that often left the Waga and Nembi valleys simmering with antagonism, suspicion, and violence. In this atmosphere, an accusation of sorcery or even ordinary misconduct quickly led to armed combat, and, as among the Huli, fighting was endemic in the region.

In the midst of this situation, ambitious men with wide-ranging network ties were often able directly and indirectly to manipulate the passage of pork and pigs through the exchanges of others. In this way, they gradually came to control wider and wider parts of the exchange system itself until they emerged as Big Men, the hallmark of highland New Guinea society. These Big Men, who added their own rivalries to the already seething rivalries of surrounding clan alliances, were the instigators of the largest of the ceremonial exchanges, organizing the efforts of a number of clans, to display and distribute perhaps as many as 1,500 pigs, and gain the edge in prestige over their rivals.

Complex highlands social systems grounded in such ceremonial exchange usually had their economic roots in a sophisticated system of intensive agricultural production based on the sweet potato. Sweet potato production was used to support large herds of domestic pigs, which were needed for participation in the exchange system. The exchange system in turn continued to increase the demand for pigs. Indeed this dynamic interaction between garden production, pigs, and ceremonial exchange in highlands societies is believed to be partly responsible for the intensification and spread of highlands agricultural systems following the introduction of the sweet potato, sometime after the seventeenth century (Brookfield 1972, 1973; Brookfield and White 1968; Watson 1977). The movement of ceremonial exchange systems is thought to have proceeded outwards from those highlands centers most favorable to sweet potato and pig production, crossing language and cultural barriers, promoting agricultural development and population growth among adjacent peoples, and eventually reaching even the people of the distant highland fringe (Brookfield 1973; Strathern 1979).

The Wola and the Nembi in their karst valleys at the edge of the highlands inhabited such a fringe area. Though their land was relatively fertile, the arable areas were small and scattered in pockets amongst the limestone ridges and pinnacles of the region. Consequently, compared to the rest of the highlands, the region was marginally productive: sufficient for subsistence but not for the foddering of a pig herd on the scale of more central areas like Wabag or the Mendi Valley. Even so, the people of the Waga Valley, and even more the Nembi plateau, were relatively well-off and able to develop nearly as elaborate exchanges as those of their neighbors (and exchange partners) in the nearby Lai and Mendi valleys. The Wola and Nembi were able to hold their own primarily because they inhabited a strategic position along the inner reaches of the major network of trade routes that stretches from the highland interior to the far distant Papuan coast (see Map 8). The interaction of the trade passing along these routes and the ceremonial exchange system profoundly affected both societies.

Trade Routes

Because of the nature of the terrain, entry to the highlands grass valleys from the lowland and intermediate tropical forest areas of this part of Papua is limited to a few points. The most important routes are those which follow up the major river systems of the Purari-Erave-Nembi and the Mubi-Kikori, which zigzag across the limestone ranges to the coast.

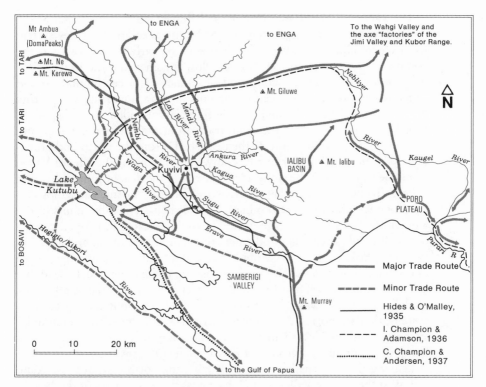

Map 8. Traditional highlands trade routes and major patrols of 1935–37.

Up the major routes, before European penetration into the area, moved coastal mother-of-pearl shells, which were traded into the highlands for use as personal adornment and items of wealth in ceremonial exchange. Up other, lesser, trade routes from the forested lowlands of the Lake Kutubu area moved *tigaso* oil (also used for body decoration), which was produced by the Foi people (Williams 1940). In return, down from the highlands, men carried pigs, salt, and (before the appearance of steel) fine stone ceremonial axe blades and working blades for adzes.

Trade goods moved in two ways: either passing between exchange partners and allies over short distances from one ceremonial ground to another (Strathern 1971b: 255–65; 1978: 253–64) or carried by enterprising men who regularly took long (and often quite dangerous) journeys to distant peoples to seek the items they desired (Langlas 1974: 177).*

* Early patrol officers noted meeting many individuals on such long-distance trade expeditions. Traders from the Samberigi Valley traveled to Bara along a trade route that scaled the uninhabited slopes of Mt. Murray. In 1936 Ivan Champion met Huli traders on the Papuan Plateau who had traveled to the headwaters of the Turama to trade tobacco for shells (1940:

The valleys of the Waga, Nembi, and Erave rivers were central to the upper part of this trading system. At the far lower end of the valley system from where Hides and his patrol were standing early in May of 1935, the Nembi, Lai, Kagua, and Mendi rivers flow together into the Erave. Near this confluence, among a collection of hamlets, is a ceremonial ground called Kuvivi, which was a central trading junction, a meeting and parting of the ways for all of the major trade routes (Crittenden 1982: 194–255). From the southeast came the main track from the Samberigi Valley and the Gulf of Papua, the route of the pearlshell. From the north and northeast, skirting the shoulder of Mt. Giluwe and following the Mendi Valley came the routes from the stone adze quarries of the distant Jimi and Wahgi valleys. To the southwest lay the track to Lake Kutubu and the Mubi Valley along which came *tigaso* oil and cowrie shells. The inhabitants of the Kuvivi area, the Nembi people, were favorably located to take advantage of this flow of goods. As middlemen, they dominated the interchange between the Foi people of the Mubi Valley/Lake Kutubu area and the people of the highlands valleys. This critical position made them widely desirable as exchange partners, and they had connections with people at all points of the compass. It was this, rather than a highly productive agricultural system, that supported their intense networks of competitive ceremonial exchange and enabled them to overcome many of the disadvantages of living in a marginal environment (Crittenden 1982: 195–209).

Leaving the interchange point of Kuvivi, the northwestern trade route followed the Nembi Valley and Plateau past the headwaters of the Nembi River into the upper Waga Valley. Here among the Wola people was another (though lesser) trading junction through which pearlshell from Kuvivi and cowrie and *tigaso* oil from the Kutubu lowlands made their way to Wabag to the northeast and the Tari Basin to the northwest (Meggitt 1956). In return, the Wola obtained packets of salt from the Enga of Wabag, which they then passed back down to the Nembi and the Foi.* Salt was valuable enough in these regions to be used as bridewealth (Crittenden 1982; Sillitoe 1978), and the Wola near the head of the Waga Valley

200), and a few weeks later he met traders from the grassland valleys at Lake Kutubu (1940: 201–5). In 1938 Champion met traders at Usa in the Kagua Valley just south of the Nembi Plateau who had come all the way fro Samberigi (Papua Annual Report 1939–40: 28–30). Kurita's Fasu informants claimed regular visits in pre-contact times by trade partners from Baina near the Mubi-Kikori junction, over 100 km away (Schieffelin and Kurita 1988). A detailed discussion of this trade is found in Hughes 1977: 42–45.

* Most of the salt in the Wola-Nembi region came from the salt wells of the Enga country to the northeast (Meggitt 1958). Much smaller amounts came up from the Samberigi Valley to the south (Saunders 1924: 31) or from wells on the slopes of Mt. Giluwe to the east. This salt was manufactured from potassium salt deposits and vegetable materials and was brown in color. Wrapped in round packets of pandanus leaves, it was traded as far as Lake Kutubu (Williams 1939).

were an important link in the salt trade with their neighbors farther down. The Wola also traded the nuts from the high-altitude pandanus trees (*Pandanus julianettii*) to people in the southern, lower-lying areas; orchards of pandanus set high up on hillsides are still a distinctive feature of the upper Waga Valley today.

Five-Toed Pigs and Pearlshells

Despite the limited agricultural potential of their lands, the Nembi reputation for trade depended importantly on the production of pigs. In particular they were known for an unusual variety of pig prized for having five toes instead of the usual four (Crittenden 1982: 210–13). These especially large pigs represented the single commodity the Nembi produced themselves for which the Foi and Fasu people of the lowlands around Lake Kutubu and further south were willing to trade (although they also collected bird of paradise plumes from the forested ridges to the west).[*] This trade followed a well-recognized pattern (Leroy 1979), in which pigs from the more intensive agricultural areas of the highlands are traded to the less intensive lowland systems in return for shell.

While Nembi pig production could not match that of Wabag or the Mendi Valley, it was more intensive than that of the Foi and Fasu (Langlas 1974: 29). The lowland method of raising pigs involves allowing the animals largely to forage for themselves in the forest; their owners feed them periodically so that they don't become completely wild. Males are castrated, and sows breed only with feral pigs in the bush. As a result of these methods, a large number of the young pigs born die before they are weaned, and productivity is low. Thus it was, and still is, necessary for Foi to import shoats (young hogs) from the "Augu" (Wola) to their northeast and from the Kewa and Nembi to the east. Langlas (1974: 29) estimated that over half the pigs in the Mubi Valley were imported from the Nembi Plateau, and Williams remarked in 1939 on the long distances that "sucklings were carried" in a string bag under the arm "to be exchanged for a string of cowries" (1939: 46–47). The cowries, called *bari* by the Foi, came through the "Bari" people (Bara village) south of the Mubi/Kikori junction along a trade route up the Kikori, and the people of the Kutubu area were the main source of cowries (as well as *tigaso* oil) to the Nembi.

Besides pigs, the major items of ceremonial exchange in the highlands areas, of course, were pearlshells. The Wola and Nembi needed pearlshell

---

[*] Pigs originating on the Nembi plateau were traded over considerable distances. Early explorers found five-toed pigs, probably originating from the Nembi/Wola, as far south as the Delta division (Kikori PR 22, 1928–29) during the 1920's and also along the Turama River (see Crittenden 1982: 210–19).

both for purchasing pigs to use in ceremonial exchange and as items of ceremonial exchange in their own right. Moreover, their strategic position on the pearlshell trade route was the principal advantage they had over the interior pig-rich groups of the Lai and Mendi valleys. Consequently trade in pearlshells became something of a Wola and Nembi obsession, and they became well known as extremely canny traders and hard bargainers.

The trade in pearlshell along the Samberigi and Erave valley routes was probably quite ancient. The Nembi and the Wola possessed pearlshells (*Pinctada maxima Jameson*), cowrie shells (*Cypraea* sp.), tambu (*Nassa* sp.) and bailer shells (*Melo* sp.) well before the arrival of Europeans. However, the particularly large quantities of pearlshells that moved up the trade routes to the highlands exchange systems probably dates only from the last half of the nineteenth century and was likely an artifact of European activity. European pearl fishers used coastal Papuan divers to obtain pearlshell in the Torres Straits, and quantities of this shell made their way into the Papuan hinterland well before 1880 (Hughes 1977: 45, 193; Beckett 1977; Joyce 1971: 199–200). This source of shell, however, was interrupted in 1910 when the shallower beds became exhausted and Papuans were no longer employed by the pearling industry (Joyce 1971: 199–200; Papua Annual Report 1911: 65, 1912: 69–70).

In consequence, the movement of pearlshell up the trade routes into the Papuan interior began to slow down and even to reverse.* More importantly, as the quantity of pearlshells began to diminish, the value began to rise, strengthening the position of those, like the Nembi, at the key points on the trade routes and intensifying the struggle to possess it.

Stone Axes and Steel Axes

Another ancient item of trade for which the Nembi acted as middlemen were stone axe blades. A few axe blades came from the Enga by way of the Wola (Sillitoe 1978), but most of the axes on the Nembi Plateau originated from the quarries of Abiamp and the Wahgi and Jimi valleys (Hughes, personal communication, 1981) and were traded all the way to the Papuan coast along the Erave River and the Samberigi Valley.†

* In the late 1920's and the 1930's the people to the south and southwest of Lake Kutubu distinguished between pearlshells that were traded in from the coast along the Kikori River and those moving down from inland via the Nembi Plateau (Williams 1940: 147–48). The Foi, unaware that the latter were actually traded in to the Nembi from the coast via the Samberigi Valley and then down to them, believed these shells derived from a mythical cache hidden somewhere in the highlands (Austen 1935: 22). As the quantity of pearlshells began to diminish, it appeared to people living along the smaller branch routes in the Kutubu lowlands that the "inland" source was drying up.

†Axes of this provenance were collected in the gulf lowlands by Hurley and McCulloch in 1923 (Hughes 1977: 20–40), but the trade was much older than that. Jukes mentioned

The Nembi and the Wola tended to trade the inferior-quality axe blades to the lowland Foi, keeping the finer ones for themselves and for trading southward into the Samberigi Valley. Wilfred Beaver, who entered the Samberigi area in 1911, found these stone axes to be of impressive quality, "apparently of jade or greenstone, splendidly beveled" (Papua Annual Report 1911: 179).

In the early 1930's the trade in stone axes began to decline, first in the Wola region (Sillitoe 1978) and then on the Nembi Plateau—as steel was introduced in the distant valleys where they were made, the quarries gradually ceased production (Hughes 1978: 308–18; Crittenden 1982: 242). Paradoxically, while this slowed their movement along the trade routes to a snail's pace, it did not destroy their value. On the contrary, even after the introduction of steel to the Nembi and Samberigi valleys, the best stone axes were retained and treasured as ceremonial objects and heirlooms (Sillitoe 1978: 266). As early as 1922, patrol officer H. M. Saunders was unable to purchase one in Samberigi (Papua Annual Report 1922–23: 147), and on the Nembi Plateau their value has further increased in the last 30 years since no new ones are available.

The movement of steel into the highlands, starting from the Gulf of Papua, did not begin in earnest until the last decades of the nineteenth century. Before that, the scarcity of metal, obtained from passing ships and from wrecks (Hughes 1977: 26, 33, 38) confined it mostly to the coastal region. Only with the establishment of government stations and missions in the gulf did steel begin to be available in sufficient quantities to begin following the pearlshell up the trade routes north.[*]

By 1911 Wilfred Beaver had found that steel was fairly well established in the Samberigi Valley and to the west as far as the lower reaches of the Mubi (Papua Annual Report 1911: 165). Steel axes probably did not arrive in the highlands by this route before 1925. In 1936 Ivan Champion saw many old, blunt steel tomahawks around Lake Kutubu and in the upper Mendi Valley (1940: 206, 246). The influx of steel northward from the gulf was later met by a counterflow from the Wahgi Valley to the northeast, originating from patrol posts established there 130 km away (Chinnery 1934: 409–10; Leahy 1936: 251; Hughes 1977: 56). This accentuated the north-south flow of trade and again further strengthened the domination of Nembi clans over trade with the Foi to the southwest.

---

such axes in the Turama River estuary as early as the 1840's (1847: 265–77), and the 1892–93 *Annual Report for British New Guinea* reports the use of these stone axes among the inhabitants of the lower reaches of the Vailala River (p. 27).

[*] Thursday Island government station was established in 1889 and Daru in 1893 (Hope 1979: 10, 43). The London Missionary Society opened stations at Orokolo and Kiwai Island in 1892. Government stations were opened at Kerema and Kikori in 1906 and 1911. All traded with steel (see Hughes 1977: 25–56).

Steel axes, however, were more than new items of trade; they were har-bingers of the outside world. In 1929 Sir Hubert Murray had likened the exploration of Papua to the spread of an oil stain (Papua Annual Report 1929–30: 8). The first percolation of government influence into uncon-tacted areas was through the spread of trade goods, principally steel, into the hinterland. This was followed eventually by the first exploratory ex-peditions, and then in due course by extended patrolling, administrative consolidation, and the establishment of control. Thus, steel and rumors of strangers or spirit people usually preceded the arrival of the government itself, and government officers moving into the Delta division from the coast frequently followed the trade routes. Indeed, as government patrols began to explore the Samberigi Valley in the 1920's, rumors of powerful strangers filtered inland far beyond the limits of actual contact.

Along the periphery of government control, those newly contacted, and their uncontacted friends and trade partners further inland, regarded the patrols with considerable ambivalence. At first it was the very presence of powerful outsiders in their domain that made people uneasy. They could not control where the patrols went on their territory or what they did, and they feared the power of these strangers. Later the imposition of govern-ment prohibitions on warfare (and headhunting and cannibalism where practiced) made it difficult for people to continue to obtain meaningful redress of injuries or to further political objectives by force and violence (although it did not stop them entirely from doing so). Just as irksome were government demands that latrines be dug, houses kept in good repair, patrol tracks maintained, food supplied, and the dead buried (rather than left to decay on traditional mortuary structures above ground). However, even worse in the long run was that regular patrolling by the government and the establishment of government stations along the trade routes short-circuited the traditional process of trade. The Samberigi people seem to have caught on to this quite early, and in 1924 they declared that not only did they not understand why the government had visited them three times, but they wanted it to stop coming and upsetting their business (Kikori PR 17, 1923–24).* When government patrols carried pearlshells and steel into the hinterland, they were bypassing and competing with traditional networks. Moreover, the *pax Australiana* allowed Papuan traders to travel farther along the trade routes themselves than previously without fear

---

* It was not uncommon for early patrols to be greeted with lies and dissimulation aimed at preventing their further penetration inland. When Flint and Saunders reached the Erave River north of Samberigi in 1922 and asked whether anyone lived on the other side, the Kerabi exclaimed the river was impossible to cross (Kikori PR 13, 1921–22). Other patrols met with denials that anyone lived on the other side at all (Kikori PR 15, 1922–23; 17, 1923–24; 14, 1924–25).

for their lives. They too bypassed traditional middlemen and neutralized traditional strategic trade positions.

This happened early in the 1920's to the people of Bara/Bari village, who had served as traditional middlemen between the Samberigi Valley and the Kikori delta. When patrols made the track to Samberigi safe for anyone to travel, Samberigi traders began traveling down to Kikori station, bypassing Bara entirely (Kikori PR 17, 1923–24). The Bara people's strategic trade position became peripheral, and thereafter they faded from the economic scene.[*]

During the 1920's and early 1930's, however, the Waga Valley and Nembi Plateau were still far inland from the deepest probes by government patrols. Only rumors of light-skinned strangers filtered north, while pigs and pearlshells, salt and *tigaso* oil moved in their usual manner up and down the trade routes. By the early 1930's steel axes began to arrive in the lower Nembi area.

The World Periphery

Commodities were not the only things that passed along the trade routes. Religious and fertility cults also followed them inland. For example, the Timp, a fertility cult,[†] with its characteristic conical-roofed ceremonial houses, apparently moved from Samberigi to the Mendi Valley sometime in the first quarter of the twentieth century. By the 1930's the cult had become common throughout the portion of the southern highlands valleys south of a line drawn between Mendi and Nipa.

Malaria, too, apparently moved up from the lowlands via the trade routes in the second quarter of this century. Highlanders believed it was caused by sorcery, and its appearance in the Erave Valley in the 1930's and 1940's was a source of an upsurge of revenge killings and tribal fighting that lasted well into the 1950's (Crittenden 1987).[‡]

[*] The people of Bara also acted as guides and interpreters for early government patrols. Flint and Saunders in 1922 made great efforts to secure help from Bara before visiting the Samberigi Valley (Kikori PR 13, 1921–22).

[†] Ryan (1961: 16) describes the Timp cult in the Mendi Valley and attributes its origin to the south. Flint and Saunders mention it in the Samberigi Valley in 1922 (Papua Annual Report 1922–23: 30); the Samberigi said they themselves had obtained it from the south. Hides mentions it on the Nembi Plateau (*PW*: 152), and Ivan Champion describes it in the Kagua Valley in 1939 (Papua Annual Report 1939–40: 30). Later patrols, especially after the Second World War, described the characteristic Timp spirit houses in the southern regions of the Southern Highlands. Champion interpreted possession of the Timp cult as distinguishing the people of the southern grasslands as a single cultural group (Mendi PR 4, 1952–53), thus indicating its widespread distribution in the region.

[‡] The Kewa people immediately to the south of the Nembi Plateau call malaria *pole yanya*, "a sickness from Erave" (Franklin and Franklin 1978: 7) Nembis called it *weli-yanya*.

The Nembi and Wola had always regarded the lowlands with uneasiness. The enclosing expanses of rain forest and malarial climate made it seem a mysterious and dangerous place, rather off the edge of the world. Moreover, the cannibalistic practices of lowland people evoked horror in Wola and Nembi alike, who, like the Huli and other highlanders, regarded this custom as revolting and unnatural (Sillitoe 1979b; Crittenden 1987). The prevalence of malaria in the region contributed to the belief that the lowland inhabitants were masterful sorcerers who could invoke the ghosts of the dead to devour the vital organs of their enemies and cause them to die (Sillitoe 1979b). As a result, the Nembi and Wola treated lowlanders with caution when visiting them to trade, and this attitude prevailed even among those Nembi and Wola who had close links with lowlanders, visited them frequently, or believed their own ancestors originated there. However, Wola and Nembi were not averse to putting lowland sorcery to use for their own purposes, and on occasion would hire sorcerers from Lake Kutubu to operate against their enemies or would purchase lowland sorcery techniques to use themseselves.

Forests, in any case, were places of supernatural danger for Nembi and Wola people. The malevolent ghosts of the recently dead were believed to live in the caves and sinkholes of uninhabited stretches of jumbled limestone forest that bordered or interspersed regions of cultivation and habitation throughout the Waga Valley and the Nembi Plateau. From these caves and dark places the shades would keep baleful watch upon the affairs of men and bring misfortune down upon them.

The malevolence of the ghosts was believed to be the major cause of illness and death and could be appeased only through the *kaebal* ritual sacrifice of pigs. The sacrificial act was embodied in the spilling of pig blood over magic stones and the leaves of edible ferns, which were then cooked with the meat in earth ovens. It was thought the ghosts would smell the blood and pork and be pleased. Failing to offer blood and pork to the ghosts from time to time risked incurring their wrath, and they would return to plague those who had not done so or to gnaw the vitals of people who had not repaid debts to them when they were alive. It was no wonder then, that a man who became ill would often search his memory to see if he had forgotten to repay debts of pork to exchange partners now dead. If he made recompense to the dead man's kin, they in turn would kill the pigs that would appease the ghost. All deaths were related in one way or another to the activities of ghosts, and Wola and Nembi believed that the power of lowland sorcerers resided in their ability to magically incite these ghosts to attack a chosen victim.

Patrolling and early trading brought malaria to the highlands (Black 1954; Peters et al. 1958; Meggitt 1981; see also Crittenden 1987: 343–47).

Sorcerers were feared, but there were a few ways that they, and even the ghosts, could be discomfited. One of these was bound up with the Nembi and Wola belief, held in common with the Huli and many other highlands peoples, that women, while vital to subsistence, to alliance, and to the continuation of the clan, were also dangerously polluting and inimical to the vitality and special powers of men. This danger was especially embodied in the female genitalia and its secretions and was doubly dangerous at the time of menstruation or at the birth of children. Nembi and Wola men had to keep away from their women at these times or risk becoming debilitated and ill. Similarly, food became contaminated if a woman stepped over it, as did bows and arrows, men's instruments of hunting and war. It is not surprising then that men felt a wary ambivalence, and sometimes hostility, towards women and their sexual parts.

For a woman to expose her genitals to a man was (for the man) deeply shocking and unsettling, not because it was sexually arousing, but because, on the contrary, it was a powerful blow to his vitality and strength. This dangerous power of women, however, could also be useful. If a woman exposed herself to a sorcerer or ghost approaching on a nefarious errand, the act might stop or turn them back and sap their magical strength.

The people of the Waga Valley and the Nembi Plateau shared not only a fear of the inimical powers of women but also a widespread body of myths and stories of dramatic local happenings, of the deeds of ancestors and of mythical figures far in the past. One story, like the Huli account of *mbingi*, told of a time of darkness when the sky fell down, the earth quaked, forests burned, and the hills slid into the valleys (unlike the Hulis, however, they did not consider this a beneficial event). Another story told of two mythical brothers, one with light skin and one with dark, who quarreled over a meal of sweet potatoes. Angered, the light-skinned brother took up his net bag and departed down a sinkhole, but promised he would return some day. Other stories told of the being *Sabkabyin* and his wife *Sabyabkintin* who lived in the sky. They were quasimythical beings who had little to do with humans but were the makers of rain and thunder and the protectors of migratory birds, especially the cassowary. The birds were believed to go to these beings in the sky when they periodically disappeared from the region. Although these stories and the beings they were about did not play an important part in Wola or Nembi everyday life, they were a part of the richly textured world in which these people lived. They were, like the cannibal sorcerers of the lowland forests, beings who lived just beyond the peripheries. As such they were part of the available knowledge Wola and Nembi could bring to bear when that periphery began to break in on them.

In sum, as pigs and valuables moved up and down the trade routes,

men facilitated their trade relationships by forming exchange relationships in the local (and extra-local) systems of competitive ceremonial exchange. The two systems thus played upon and intensified each other,
increasing the stakes in each. It is not surprising that the Wola—and
even more so the Nembi—developed the reputation for being extremely
tough, hard-bargaining, and tightfisted traders. Competitive exchange, as
we have mentioned, together with the manipulations by Big Men, provided
much of the energy and rivalry that underlay political relations within
and between different clan alliances. This rivalry was further intensified
by accusations of sorcery and warfare.

Sorcery was, of course, a perfectly legitimate means used by Big Men
(and others) to discomfit or eliminate political competitors and advance
their own careers. Illness and death were incorporated directly into the
political process because they were interpreted as the sorcery attacks of
rivals. Vengeance for sorcery attack was the most important motivation
for fighting (together with the usual pig theft and adultery) and fear of
sorcery generated the interclan distrust and hostility that kept the various alliances of the valleys fragmented in multiple enmities. The result
was a situation in which suspicion was the better part of wisdom, and
contentiousness, intimidation, and belligerence were the best demonstration of strength. Both Wola and Nembi preferred to obtain vengeance and
(through it) relative political advantage by cutting down the enemy directly
in battle rather than fooling around with magical sorcery retaliation. Consequently, warfare was endemic among the Wola and extremely fierce on
the Nembi Plateau. These peoples' reputation for fighting amongst themselves was to endure among later government officers until well after the
Second World War. All of these qualities were to play an important part in
their reception of the Strickland-Purari patrol as it began to move down
into their country.

Into the Upper Waga Valley

It was about midmorning when Hides and his men emerged at the head
of the Waga Valley (see Map 9). Gazing at this great populated land, Hides
later wrote in his book, "I imagined what those other officers, Woodward,
Saunders, Rentoul, and Flint would have given to see this sight. . . . Here
was something that surely went beyond all their expectations. I did not
forget that it was through them, and the other 'outside men' of the Papuan
Service, that this remarkable discovery had been made possible for us"
(PW: 112).

Moving down from the timber, the patrol came upon a small farmstead.
Entering the enclosure, they surprised a native man just coming out of

the dwelling. "He received a terrible fright," Hides wrote, "but seemed to understand [our] friendly greeting . . . for he did not run away." Indeed, the man was very likely petrified with fear and astonishment at this unexpected encounter. When Hides indicated that his men were hungry and wanted some food the man returned to his house, brought out a few handfuls of potatoes and motioned the patrol hurriedly to be gone. "He was an unfriendly kind of native," Hides commented, "and wanted to be rid of our company quickly." The man pointed to a track down the grass slope, and as soon as they set off, he began to yodel loudly from the height behind them.

As this alarm echoed out across the valley, it was taken up from all the little hamlets and farmsteads around, and soon scores of men armed with bows and arrows came running from all directions. In a short time the patrol was surrounded by a hundred or more warriors. In this area of the valley, the people Hides was facing were a mixed transitional group of Hulis and Wolas. Hides and O'Malley halted the patrol in a cultivated area to see what they would do. Eventually several men laid down their arms and approached in a friendly manner to offer them sugarcane.* Two of them indicated that, if the patrol would move to the other side of a nearby creek, they would bring them some pig. As Hides started moving his men, the armed warriors who stood in the background once again began yodeling. At this point Hides perceived a large body of armed men hidden in the high grass to one side of the track. It is difficult to know in the absence of informants just what these warriors' intentions were, but Hides clearly believed it was an ambush. He told his police to keep a careful watch. Crossing the creek, he and O'Malley stood guard while the rest of the patrol passed over. Seeing this, the man who was acting as their guide stood up in view of the warriors, and (Hides thought) signaled to them not to come down. "He knew we had seen the trap," Hides commented; "I was amused to note his discomfiture." Bringing up the rear of the line, the police found themselves almost surrounded by armed and truculent men, "but not one of them flinched. They held their ground cool and undismayed though they knew as well as I that there was treachery all around us" (PR: 70).

Meanwhile the warriors were apparently at a loss as to how to deal with these mysterious strangers. They changed their tactics. "After we had pitched camp," Hides wrote, "our would-be murderers arrived in scores,

---

* Sugarcane and bananas have ritual significance throughout the highlands (Feil 1988: 35). One or both are typically offered in hospitality and refreshment to important visitors when they arrive at a homestead or ceremonial ground. Sugarcane is often seen as a "cooling" food, which may be offered to sorcerers or spirits to weaken their powers and spells (Lindenbaum 1976: 39). It is used in a number of highlands rituals and in some places is grown only by men—or men can only eat cane that has been grown by men.

all without their weapons and with cunning smiles on their faces." They brought about 40 women with them—which, at first contact, was usually a sign that the local people no longer feared the patrol and wanted to be friendly. The intent here, however, was quite different. The women arranged themselves in rows seated on the ground in front of the camp. Hides gave out beads among them as a gesture of goodwill. Suddenly the women all pulled aside their pubic coverings and flashed their vulvas at him. Hides was quite taken aback and mystified at this surprising act. He did not know they were treating him as a malevolent supernatural being and were trying to defuse his power and chase him away.

Despite what Hides took to be earlier promises, no one appeared to offer them pork or any other food that evening. He and O'Malley were becoming worried. There was not much rice left, and everyone in the patrol was hungry and weak. Although there appeared to be plenty of food in the local gardens, they wanted to establish friendly contact with the local people and so forbade the carriers and police to steal from them. The following morning they proceeded onwards down the valley and pitched camp in the early afternoon in the rain at a place known as Laeng. They were now in Wola country proper. Rain continued the next day, and Hides decided to remain where they were and rest. As the weather cleared, crowds of curious people, including women and children, gathered to look at them, some bringing small amounts of food. The atmosphere was completely different from the day before: "Dozens of old men [came] to whistle and clap their hands in astonishment at the door of our [tent] fly. Our white skin, our boots, clothes and matches seemed to take a great hold on their interest. . . . The people were all very friendly, the women personally handing us food and tobacco and indicating we dig for the potatoes we required" (PR: 71).

In the mimed communication Hides learned that the parklike area in which he was camped was a ceremonial ground where people met for festivals—and, he imagined, for cannibal feasts. Communication was clearly difficult: Hides also believed he was told that the cassowary bone "daggers" every man carried in his belt were weapons fashioned from human bone.* He was delighted when he was presented with one of these exotic items.

The following day, May 8, the patrol was on the move at dawn and soon passed out of the lands of this friendly people. Still moving along the edge of the valley above the Waga River, they could see the smoke rising

---

* These "knives," widely used in the highlands and Papuan Plateau, are usually fashioned from the femur of the cassowary, which bears a superficial resemblance to a human bone. They are used principally for scooping the pith out of lowland pandanus fruit in preparation for cooking. They are also used as a minor item of trade.

from scores upon scores of farms extending far down the valley. Local inhabitants pointed out the track to them as they went along but timidly kept their distance.

That afternoon, they were well into the territory of the Wola, and a change in the demeanor of new people was perceptible. As the patrol rested at the river bank, four large groups, totaling (in Hides's estimation) about 800 warriors, appeared. "The atmosphere was tense," he later wrote, "as we stood watching them silently closing in on us. They seemed, however, uncertain what to do." Presently, a leading man signaled the warriors to put down their weapons and with a companion, approached the patrol unarmed. Hides's relief was palpable. With buoyant feeling, he pictured these men as noble figures from ancient civilizations:

"I was struck with their Biblical type of face. The first could have been a black Pharaoh; while the other had the appearance of an old Hindoo brahman. . . . [The first] came up to me and grasped both my arms. 'Ei Kaimare,' he said in a deep guttural tone and tugged my beard affectionately. He had lovely eyes, bright and expressive of genuine friendliness. He was a fine-looking man, wearing a long, striking beard, cut flat at the bottom and [wore] a wig of closely woven human hair shaped not unlike the hat of a cossack. . . . They both made us sit down; then with their beautiful axes of green stone cut us huge bundles of sugar-cane."

Later that afternoon, having made their camp at a ceremonial ground (Songura), the patrol became acquainted with the Wola love of pearlshell. Hides wrote in his report: "Hundreds of men, women, and children were with us until darkness set in. They all wanted pearl and cowrie shell, though I could see little of this among them. They held up little broken pieces of shell and with a questioning look asked if we had any. I had to tell them we had not, but their searching eyes discovered the pearl buttons on our (shirts and trousers), and before night had fallen [O'Malley and myself] had no buttons left" (PW: 112–14).

In contrast, Hides and O'Malley had difficulty persuading the Wola to accept steel axes as payment for food. Axes had not yet arrived in the region, and the Wola may not have known what they were. The crowds of friendly, curious people were so thick that afternoon that Hides and his men could hardly move around the camp. Hides had to bathe in his shorts because of the numbers of people, men and women, who followed him around to see what he was doing. It was impossible to write his patrol notes or work on the map due to the press and touching of curious onlookers.

The next day the track was lined with more crowds of curious people who greeted them as they passed and gestured, "Where are you going?" Hides in answer would point towards the lower end of the valley. The people were particularly fascinated by the two officers' hats, and Hides and O'Malley had to continually raise them to satisfy their curiosity as they went along.

In the late afternoon Hides became aware that they had crossed a boundary into the territory of another group. They camped at another ceremonial ground (at Pinjweshuwt) where the main track crosses the Waga as it begins its sweep westward to cut through the mountains. The friendly crowds of the morning were now left behind, and amidst this new group of people Hides sensed something was not right: "I did not like the shifty looks of some of the men," he wrote. "None of them would answer our appeals for food, and the forced friendliness of [their] scoundrelly old chief, who thought we had concealed pearl shell in [our] tin box of medicines, could not be mistaken" (*PW:* 115).

This particular interest in the medicine box as a suspected container of pearlshells was to be repeated at several places down the valley system. It is possible, though we have no evidence to support it, that the local people had some knowledge of the passage of the Fox brothers' patrol five months before (see Chapter 3). Although the Fox brothers did not penetrate any farther down the Waga Valley than the *hauma* at Laeng, they did carry shell—in square tin boxes. If they had done any trading with shell in the upper Waga Valley, this news would have very likely been passed down the valley, together with any interesting particulars (such as square metal containers) that contributed to the interest of the story.

There were about 200 men milling around in the ceremonial ground as the patrol tried to make camp. Again, as we have no informants from this area, we do not know what they were thinking. However, since the previous people had not escorted the patrol into this territory, and since the people here seemed unwelcoming, it is probable that the two groups were not on friendly terms. Caught between dread of the unknown strangers and an unbearable eagerness to discover whether the strangers were carrying pearlshell, these Wola held back, remaining tentative and standoffish, while at the same time watching the patrol closely.

Hides and his men were tired and hungry. With neither food nor a clearly warm reception forthcoming and outnumbered five to one at the campsite, they had reason to feel uneasy. It was a situation fraught with ambiguities. The nervousness of the Wola and the uncertainty of their intentions communicated itself to Hides, and he went on the alert. He thought he detected them whispering "cunningly" among themselves; when he thought a group was quietly trying to surround the police, he became convinced they planned to massacre the patrol. The Wola, in fact, were not carrying any bows and arrows (or at least Hides doesn't mention any), but many of them fidgeted nervously with stone axes in their belts.

These implements are normally considered (and used) as working tools by Wola, not weapons. However, in the tension of the situation, Hides saw their utility as "battle axes" (PW: 115). Taking no chances, he deployed the police defensively and posted a strong guard over the camp that night, thus, he believed, averting a murderous attack.

An Incident

The patrol departed immediately at daybreak, without eating breakfast, to cross the Waga and get away from these people. Hides and O'Malley hoped to find more friendly folk on the other side of the valley. Hooting and yodeling erupted from behind them as soon as the Wola discovered they were on the move and sounded the alarm. The bridge across the Waga, suspended by vines, was rotten and dangerous. It took two hours for the members of the patrol to pick their way across. While they were thus engaged, a crowd of warriors gathered to jeer on the opposite bank and hoot at them as they crossed, and a group of women flashed their genitals at them. The noise and numbers and the intimidating manner of the people were unnerving. As Hides stood guard over his men crossing the bridge, he became increasingly angry.

"My rifle was loaded, and I would have shot the first native that made an attempt to murder one of my weak and gallant carriers. These despicable people! We had not touched a house or garden, nor harmed a dog or man. Why did they treat us like this? . . .

"I suppose it was because they saw in our weak and ragged condition a small band of meek foreigners who were unarmed and thus easy prey. Our rifles to them were just so many wooden clubs, for not a shot had yet been fired in their country" (PW: 117).

But nothing happened. Easy prey though Hides thought he and his men must appear, the scores of nervous warriors around them were apparently more interested in being noisy and provocative to see what the patrol might do than in attacking it. Hides followed the last of his carriers up the track on the opposite bank and found O'Malley with the rest of the party resting on a ceremonial ground. This was a place known locally as Huwguwn. Facing the patrol about 200 men sat on the ground, watching them.* Hides noted these men were bigger and darker than the ones they met the day before and wore large pompoms of cassowary feathers on top of their wigs. From the expressions of their faces Hides judged they were unfriendly. Nevertheless he appealed to them for food, offering an axe if they would allow the patrol to dig some sweet potatoes from the nearby

* The figure of 200 is from PR (74). In PW (117) Hides expands this number to 400.

gardens. The men refused, waving their arms for the patrol to be gone. Hides was frustrated. To him it seemed that all around were acres of sweet potato gardens. He could not understand why these people would not give his starving and weakened party something to eat. At the same time he was still determined not to take the food by force.

In the absence of informants who remember this incident, it is difficult to know what this new group of Wola were thinking. The fact that they remained seated and apparently unarmed argues against an attitude of active hostility.* On the other hand, it also seems clear that they did not want these beings to stop there. What Hides saw as silent hostility could just as well have been an embarrassed paralysis of uncertainty and fear. Hungry and exhausted, it was difficult for Hides and O'Malley to appreciate that this might be an understandable response if the Wola, like the Huli, thought they were visitors from another world. Even if they understood Hides's appeal for food, they apparently wanted nothing to do with him: the sooner he went away from their land the better.

As the two patrol officers sat on the grass pondering what to do, a young man whom they had seen in company with the "scoundrelly chief" of the day before approached in what Hides believed was an insolent manner and opened a small bag containing seven sweet potatoes. To Hides, on the defensive, the implication was clear.

"The self-assurance, the smirking insolent smile on this man's face gave me a sick feeling in the stomach. He had not come to trade, but to mock and belittle us in the eyes of this new section of people.

"He took the potatoes out with his hand, and placing them on the ground, demanded an ax. All the police were watching intently, as were the people of this new section."

Faced with what seemed clearly a test of dominance in the situation and still rankling from the jeering abuse heaped upon the patrol at the crossing, Hides nevertheless tried to act with restraint. After the man had placed the sweet potatoes on the ground, Hides handed him a string of beads.

"He took them, but also smilingly started to take back four of the measly potatoes. . . . I indicated he must place all the potatoes on the ground, and when I thought he would not do so, I made him by force. . . . He stood back and flung the beads violently in my face, [then] turning his back on me, walked over to where all of his fellow men were sitting down. He calmly sat down with them . . . making a gesture which obviously [meant]: 'That's the way to treat these people' " (PW: 118–19).

* Nowhere does Hides mention that these seated men carried any arms, and mention of whether men were armed is usually a distinctive feature of his narrative.

Hides was incensed. He was sure that if he allowed the patrol to be abused in this way with impunity, it would tempt the Wola to more dangerous actions later. To many patrol officers it would have been unthinkable that a Papuan should be permitted to treat a white man this way. "We had stood [for] more than I thought possible," he wrote. He grabbed the native by the hair and pulled him to his feet, then he ordered Constable Dekadua to kick him out of the ceremonial ground.

"Dekadua did it well. He went up to the native. 'Who child are you?' he asked insolently in Motu. And when the native did not answer him, Dekadua . . . kicked him good and hard right out of the park.

"I then explained my action to the assembled crowd. Their faces never moved; they all remained silent and sitting" (PW: 119).*

What the warriors thought of this we do not know. Their silence and inaction suggests that they were afraid and did not know what to do. Hides, however, had his own troubles. As the patrol moved on, he pictured their plight:

"Like a small band of outcasts, we went on without guides, but with as much dignity as our weak and stumbling legs would allow. Hooting and yodeling followed our departure. We passed the last cultivation in sight and entered timber; we were leaving the Waga Valley system behind and approaching a new watershed" (PR: 70).

The patrol was entering the northern end of the Nembi Plateau overlooking the Nipa Basin. They passed by a number of houses and cultivations and camped at the ceremonial ground at Boiya. They were now on the lands of a new group of people, and the yodeling warriors of the previous group had been left behind. After a time five unarmed men came into camp. Again the patrol was confronted with the now familiar tightfistedness of the Wola.

"We asked them for food and indicated we would pay them well; but a small bag of potatoes and a demand for an axe was the only response. Another hungry night; yet we are in a land of plenty. The police were complaining bitterly in their tent. I am quite sure they are inclined to believe that I am afraid of all these people" (PR: 75).

Things were at a critical pass. The changing reception they had met from the natives—from effusive friendliness to jeering hostility—as they moved from one group to the next down the valley was nerve-racking and disconcerting. They never knew what to expect in moving from one area to another. Hides's comparatively gentle response to the many provocations they had endured now raised the ugly possibility that he might

* In his testimony at the inquiry (IQ: 2), Hides says he himself grabbed the native by the hair and pulled him to his feet; in his book, he says Dekadua did this (PW: 119).

lose the confidence and respect of his police and hence the precision of his command over them. Now more than ever success in getting through depended on maintaining discipline in the patrol. Aggravating all of this was the problem of the food supply.

The patrol had been on severely reduced rations since passing the Tari Gap. There was very little rice left, and Hides knew he had to save it for when the patrol had to cross the uninhabited limestone barrier again. According to informant accounts and occasional statements by Hides himself (PR: 60, 88–89, 96), it seems that he and O'Malley allotted themselves a meager ration of rice each day as they went along, but they could no longer afford to feed the carriers and police on precious rice. They had planned to feed their men on food purchased from the local people— but inexplicably, this was not forthcoming. Consequently, the carriers and police had eaten hardly anything in the previous two days.*

Up to now Hides had been determined to make friendly contact with the people, and following the procedures of the Papuan Service, he had told his carriers and police not to take anything from local gardens (although they had already been doing so without his knowledge). The time had come to make a decision: "If we do not meet with a friendly section tomorrow," he wrote in his patrol report, "I shall be forced to take the food and defend my party" (PR: 75).

The following day, the patrol continued deeper into the Wola country. Hides and O'Malley, preoccupied with their own worries, had little idea of the anxiety and consternation that was preceding them down the valley.

---

* Throughout his report and subsequent book Hides makes it clear that the carriers in particular suffered from hunger and often described them as being on the verge of collapse. The officers and police, on the other hand, are usually described only as showing "signs of hardship." This contrast raises questions about how the available food was distributed among members of the patrol. The matter is not easy to resolve, as Hides is not forthcoming about it. Nevertheless, judging from what little is available in his account, the situation was probably somewhat as follows. Hides and O'Malley always seem to have had a little rice for themselves. The police and carriers had to share whatever local native foods could be obtained (which sometimes was very little). The 28 carriers remaining by this time had little to carry, the bulk of the stores having been consumed or abandoned in crossing the Papuan Plateau, but in those first three months of very hard labor, they had exhausted their reserves of strength. The police, on the other hand, all tough, handpicked men, accustomed to the hardships of this kind of expedition, had had to carry only their rifles. They may also have fared better than the carriers because they were more experienced in foraging locally (legally or illegally) for something to eat for themselves.

The Waga Valley today as seen from a point near where Hides first overlooked it. Here the homesteads are associated with ceremonial grounds (*hauma*). (Photo: Crittenden, 1980)

Cultivated landscape in the upper Waga Valley. Here dense populations are sustained by sweet potato grown in a marginal environment. (Photo: R. Pullen, CSIRO Division of Land Research, 1961)

"Hides Making Friends with Natives of Waga Furari"—probably at Laeng on May 6 or 7. (Photo: O'Malley, in *PW*, facing p. 124)

"Black 'Pharoahs' of Papua." These friendly men in their headdresses near Songura in the upper Waga Valley reminded Hides of ancient Egyptians. (Photo: Hides, in *PW*, facing p. 112)

Friendly natives of the Waga Valley following the patrol, probably along the track between Laeng and Songura, on May 8. (Photo: Hides, in *PW*, facing p. 116)

Cane bridge across the Waga River near where the patrol crossed between Pinjweshuwt and Huwguwn. Hides's carriers had to cross a similar structure one by one and fully laden while warriors hooted and yodeled from either side. (Photo: Crittenden, 1981)

The "Wen" valley and Korpe defile, looking southeast towards the Nipa Basin and Nembi Valley. The patrol passed down into the Korpe defile (cleft descending on lower left of the picture) where the shootout occurred and then out onto the relatively open grassland of the "Wen" valley beyond. (Photo: Sillitoe)

Kal Naway points to the scar of the wound he received at Korpe defile. (Photo: Sillitoe, 1984)

The Patrol rests and cooks at Shobera after the "attack by the Injigale" at the defile. Boxes and packs are scattered around on the ground. Hides sits on the right with a feather in his hat. (Photo: O'Malley, in *PW*, frontispiece)

Yort Haelaim indicates the bullet wound on her arm inflicted by the police at the pig house. (Photo: Sillitoe, 1984)

Tape recording Maenget Tensgay's reminiscences of the patrol as, with a dramatic chop of the hand, he relates the shooting. (Photo: Sillitoe, 1984)

Wol Enjap recounts the names of the casualties; each stick represents one of those he remembers as shot. (Photo: Sillitoe, 1984)

"One of those white men grabbed Waelembow's father by the beard, like this," relates Wol Ongat. (Photo: Sillitoe, 1984)

6. FROM THE WAGA FURARI TO THE WEN

PAUL SILLITOE

" 'Oh, there's something coming, something very strange approaching from over there. They say that it is ancestor spirits arrived to eat us.' That's the kind of thing we said when we heard about those first whites. Some of us fled in fear into the forest, while others said they would go and have a look at them." *

As Hides and O'Malley moved down the Waga Valley on May 11, warning of their approach was shouted or yodeled from hilltop to hilltop or carried by travelers moving between local groups. The news, preceding the patrol by only a day or a few hours, threw the Wola into a turmoil of fear and excitement.

* I am grateful to a number of men and women, all in their late teens and twenties at the time of the patrol, for telling me about their experience. They wished to tell me their side of the story because they think they were, to say the least, treated badly. In September 1984 I recorded over four hours of their recollections which, freely translated and presented as a pastiche, form the bulk of this chapter. To present their comments as literally recorded would be to give a long-winded, repetitive, digressive, and sometimes incomprehensible account, since the Wola narrative style jumps back and forth and assumes a considerable amount of local and circumstantial knowledge on the part of the audience. I believe, however, that my edited and reordered presentation of what they told me faithfully conveys their recollections of this momentous and frightening event. Specifically, I wish to extend thanks to Huwlael Hunmol and Laerop Minina, who lived at Huwguwn on the territory of Silol *sem* (editors' note: a social grouping very roughly analogous to the Huli *hameigini*); Hoboga Lem, Hoboga Makwes, and Wol Ongat, who lived at Ungubiy (Hoboga *sem* territory); to Kal Naway, Kal Pabol, Yort Haelaim, and Kal Waeb, who lived at Korpe on Kalol *sem* territory; to Maenget Tensgay and Konjiyp Obiyn, who lived at Haelaelinja (Aenda *sem* territory); to Mak Naenk at Segerep (Kalol *sem* territory, near the entrance to the Korpe defile); to Wol Enjap living at Payaway (just above Sezinda, Kalol *sem* territory); and to Haenda Leda at Hombila and Kolomb Kabiyn at Kaenda (just northeast of the ridge comprising the Korpe defile on Kalol *sem* land). The places named are where these people were living at the time of the patrol in 1935.

Wola Recollections of the Patrol

People learned about the patrol in different ways. Some recalled that there had been signs a few months earlier that something strange was afoot. According to Naway, "Before [the patrol] arrived, someone, whose mother came from up Margarima way, returned from that . . . region with a piece of tatty cloth and showed it to us. 'Where did that come from?' we asked. He said it came from some white spirit. Also before they came, someone up there heard something strange which he thought was an *ogimp* wasp, but it was a plane he saw—something to do with those whites, just before they arrived." *

Once the patrol had entered the valley, word of its approach spread rapidly. Makwes recalled, "We had gone off over towards Wola way [southeast towards the Nembi region]. The pandanus were bearing ripe nuts at the time. We were cooking some at Shonguwt. We had them in the earth oven when this woman arrived—Kal Walow's mother it was. She pulled her skirt to one side and revealed herself to us completely. 'Ahh, look at that,' she said. 'Some ghosts have come!' † We decided that we should go and have a look. We ate the nuts first and then set off." Naway continued: "What's-his-name's father was so shaken up he fetched along a pig and was going to kill it. 'Ghosts are coming. Quick, let's kill our pigs,' he said. But Walow's father, Kal Sholomb, said, 'No don't.' " ‡

* The piece of cloth and the aircraft were undoubtedly associated with the passage of the Fox brothers' expedition to the north near Margarima six months before. The Fox brothers were using cloth, among other things, for trade (see Chapter 4). The aircraft was a Fox Moth piloted by Bob Gurney and chartered in December 1934 by Mick Leahy to search for the Fox brothers after they were overdue returning to Mt. Hagen. (The search found nothing, but the Fox brothers walked into Mt. Hagen the next day.) Some informants contested Naway's account, saying the aircraft was heard after the patrol had passed through. However, they were undoubtedly referring to later aircraft that the Wola heard themselves. Naway was speaking of an aircraft that was heard in the Margarima area to the northwest, too far away to be audible to the Wola.

   Editors' note. At least four series of flights passed over the Southern Highlands area prior to 1937. The first was the search for the Fox brothers in 1934. The second comprised two flights (on February 1 and 2, 1936) out of Mt. Hagen undertaken by Ivan Champion, Jack Hides, Jim O'Malley, F. E. Williams, Lewis Lett, and James Taylor to determine more accurately the route of the Strickland-Purari patrol (see Chapter 10). The third (in March 1936) was also undertaken by Ivan Champion, scouting the route of his planned Bamu-Purari patrol (see Chapter 10). Finally, Stanley Middleton, Ronald Speedie, Lett, and Leslie Ross (pilot) flew over the area on December 15 and 16, 1936, searching for the Bamu-Purari patrol when it was overdue.

   † This was a most extraordinary act, given highland taboos on exposing female genitalia. It was a dramatic flourish to signify the momentous nature of the news she brought (Sillitoe 1979b).

   ‡ Whether this man thought it was the end of the world and decided he might as well eat his pig first or whether he intended the pig as an offering to placate the spirits (the patrol) is not clear.

Ongat recalled, "They said: 'There are things coming, making houses and then taking them down again as they come. They are coming along the path now. They're white-skinned, with their bodies covered, and there are black men with them too!' We were frightened that they were going to come over this way to molest us. We hid ourselves at Haeretaegoiya, waiting for them. But they never came this way."

Some happened upon the patrol unexpectedly. Obiyn recalled, "I don't know where they had slept or come from. But we were going up that way [in the direction of Margarima] when we saw them at Imish. They put their houses up in that vicinity. We turned around and hurried back, with the patrol coming behind us."

Tensgay continued: "Waebis (and Obiyn) were going up there when suddenly everyone started to yell, 'There are bush spirits coming!' Waebis came back then, and everyone sat in his house. 'They'll do something,' he said. 'I'm going to have a look at them.' They came down the path from Huwguwn. That was the very first time white people came. 'Bush spirits are coming, my sons,' Waebis informed us."

According to Makwes, "We said: 'Those ghosts are wearing houses, they've put on *baen* arrow-sheaths.* They're different from us.' But we could see they had bodies. When we heard about them coming, we didn't know what to think. We had a great surprise when we saw them."

Waeb continued, "We said, 'Here comes something we've never seen before, come to see us and go.' Had we seen the like before? No, we'd seen nothing like it. Who was there to tell us who they were or where they'd come from?"† And Naway went on, "That white person wasn't like Paul [Sillitoe], he was tall. I saw only one of them. There were two, eh? The other must have gone on ahead. How should we know where they came from? I didn't think anything about them. Terror, that was all that occupied my mind, and I fled."

Few believed that the patrol were actually human beings. Their minds turned more readily to spirit explanations. Some people thought they were the returned spirits of deceased ancestors. Lem caricatured them, calling out in a high-pitched, mock-frightened voice: "'Ancestor spirits are

---

*A *baen* is a sword-grass leaf sheath put over the point of a carved, bone-tipped arrow to protect it. This passage probably refers to the clothes, or sleeves, worn by Hides and O'Malley.

† Few Wola had extensive knowledge of the patrol's route outside their own locality. Putting together several accounts, the following route emerges (see Map 9): the patrol appeared at Maesa-*hauma*, near Kapaenda, then camped at Laeng. They came on to Songura, where they slept, then on to Weshuwt, Pinjweshuwt. They crossed the Waga River by the Shobka bridge and went to Huwguwn, then slept at Boiya. Next they went to Sezinda (near Korpayaenda), where they shot many men and pigs and spent the night at Shobera. They next slept at Mungtay, then went on down to Merut.

coming, there are ghosts coming!' Then they shot up two communities. Where they went then, I don't know."

Naenk continued the story: "We considered them ghosts come to eat us. We ran off in fear. We said they were ancestor spirits, and were frightened, weren't we? 'They've come to kill us,' and we went in fear. When we heard about them, when we saw them, we were terrified." *

Some people even thought they recognized their dead relatives. Lem said: "You know, we said it was Kenay Hond's spirit come back. He was light-skinned, like those first whites. We thought it was him or his father, come back to demand a ceremonial exchange payment owed them. We said they were ancestral ghosts come back to eat us."

Other people, seeing the blackened teeth of the carriers and police (the result of chewing betel nut) thought they were confronted with malevolent forest spirits: grotesque walking heaps of vegetation, with human-like limbs and features, that lurk in dark regions of the forest to kill and eat the unwary: "We said 'There are bush spirits coming! Their teeth are black like *piyt* berries. Bush spirits are coming, their teeth like *pong* fruits. Black, real black, like *piyt* fruits, they're coming.' † Man-eating things, we said they were. We'd seen nothing like it before. Our fathers, our ancestors, hadn't told us about anything like that. 'Sabkabyin [see Chapter 5] is coming!' some said. 'He is crazy and seeking for a path, a way out.' Lost they were, just wandering around. 'They're white-skinned spirits,' that's what we said. We went in terror. Where they came from we had no idea. 'A spirit something is coming.' We fled in fear. Rotten terrified, we all fled when we went to see them. 'Don't go!' some said, but I went. I saw them at Shobera."

Not everyone felt the strangers were evil and dangerous. Kal Aegol had come running in excitement, yelling: "They're coming, they're coming! It's Sabkabyin dropped from the sky and bringing many pearlshells to share out among us!"

Minina thought it was another mythical personage: "We said, 'Look, it's the descendants of that fair-skinned brother who lived here long ago but left by jumping down a sinkhole after arguing with his do-nothing black-skinned brother over an earth-oven of sweet potatoes [see Chapter 5]. Look, its spirits coming back.' We thought they were long-lost brothers and would have treated them so. They had the same faces and bodies and everything, though they wore laplap cloth. We were excited to

---

*As mentioned in Chapter 5, Wola believe that their ancestral spirits and other spirits are malevolent, attacking them and causing illness and death. Wola refer to these ghostly attacks as "eating" them, the ghosts being pictured as gnawing at vital organs in order to kill.

†*Piyt* is a maroon- and green-leafed Cordyline cultivar with dark berries; *pong* is another Cordyline.

think that it was that fair-skinned brother from the sinkhole come back. It was that white brother who had told the black one to stay and that he'd be back some day. 'It was him come back,' we said."

Waeb and Pabol recalled that men egged each other on to go and see the patrol: "Others came for us. . . . They even persuaded us to leave some pandanus nuts in the earth-oven and come. . . . A brother of mine came that night, and we decided to follow them. We met them at the path fork to Segerep, coming from Boiya." Tensgay added, "Four or five of us went over there together to see them. There was me, Kal Laebon, Tomind Gamonk, and Yunaib. Us four. Before we arrived at the path, people started yelling that bush spirits were coming. We didn't go close. We kept our distance —watched from [the cover of] the cane grass . . . to see what they were doing. We didn't walk across where they were camped. Just up to the edge to have a look and then away again. When they moved, they were between those whose lands they had passed over and those whose lands they were approaching. We just looked from our side, not crossing to the other. They separated us. They were in the middle, where they camped."

The Wola had reason to keep their distance. The police and other Papuan members of the patrol, hungry, exhausted, and under the constant stress of vigilance against a feared attack, were evidently edgy to the point of violence.

Kabiyn explained: "They had killed a man called Hul Korhae. They killed him at Ugaim. He was barricading a path with branches to hide it from the patrol and protect his wife and children, so the patrol wouldn't see it and find them. The path was to his wife's house and gardens, where she and the children were hiding. It was not on the main path followed by the patrol but off it. One of the black men in the patrol saw him as he passed and cleaved him with an axe. Just like that, for nothing. [Others surmised the patrol member might have thought he intended to impede their passage.] They only killed the one man there; Hul Korhae. No pigs. I didn't see it. I only heard about it. I was hiding in the forest."

If this story is true, it would have been a random murder, committed by an anonymous Papuan constable or carrier on the march, somewhere in the middle stretch of the carrier line. Hides, who was in the lead, does not mention it in his report and seems not to have known that it happened. If so, this was at least the second time that a member of the patrol had covertly killed an innocent bystander, and it was not to be the last. Nevertheless, some bold Wola did approach the patrol as it went along, although their reception was often puzzling. Ongat remembered: "One of those white men grabbed hold of someone, Waelaembow's father it was, who had gone to see them. Grabbed him by the beard, like this, and said something to him. We supposed he was telling him not to molest them.

He also took two blades of sword grass and tied them together and gave them to him. I think he was trying to tell him something, like 'Our fathers have never fought.' "

Enjap expanded: "We were returning from the forest, after collecting and cooking pandanus nuts, when we met with those whites. One of them took a blade of sword grass and held it up to someone's nose. A *showep* taboo gesture, eh? 'Hands off!' " *

According to Naenk: "They didn't say anything to us. Who could have understood what they said anyway? We went in terror, I tell you. They didn't communicate with us. One of the whites had his compass which he kept looking at, and the patrol followed its own path. It was the first time we had seen them [white people], and we went in fear. At Huwguwn they indicated to us that they wanted us to show them the path, with their arms —waving them—no words. We showed them, but we were frightened. And then they killed us. After that we were terrified and ran off in fear."

As mentioned in Chapter 5, the members of the patrol had eaten very little in recent days, and the carriers and police were nearly at the end of their tether. By the time they reached Boiya, they had been covering hardly more than 2–3 km a day. From Hides's point of view, their desperate plight resulted largely from the refusal of the local people to give or sell them any food. When the patrol had arrived at Huwguwn, Hides reported that the crowd of natives had simply responded "*Nahai*" (*Nae hae* in Wola: "There is none") to his entreaties and waved their arms for him to be gone. In response to questions about whether there might have been a *taim hungri*, a period of food shortage, throughout the Wola region at this time, all my informants said that not only was there plenty of food in the gardens at the time, but that the pandanus was in season as well, and its nutritious nuts were in abundance.

Enjap's comments were typical: "It was a time when we had sweet potato. It was not a time of hunger. We had pandanus too." Hunmol said: "We had gone off to collect *pebet* [pandanus] nuts when [the patrol arrived]. . . . There was no hunger. If they [Hides and O'Malley] said so, they were lying to their masters to excuse their wrongdoings, eh?"

In this event it seems probable that those who said "*Nahai*" to Hides and O'Malley were simply trying to hasten the patrol on its way out of their area by saying that whatever they had been searching for was not to be found there. At the same time the patrol was severely disadvantaged by not having brought along the one thing that the Wola would readily have accepted in trade: pearlshell. Many people assumed these light-skinned

---

*A *showep* taboo sign consists of a bunch of leaves or other vegetation placed on something to stake ownership. For example, if someone finds an immature wild fruit, he will mark it, indicating his intention to return and collect it when it is ripe.

beings must be carrying shell, and Hides was twice forced to open all his boxes to show that there was none.

The people around Huwguwn and Shobera did not realize that the patrol had anything to offer for trade at all.* Only at Laeng, shortly after the patrol entered the north end of the Waga Valley, were they said to have offered anything: "At Laeng they tied an axe and a large knife to a *maenget* [genus *Dillenia*] tree to pay for the bags of sweet potato they had dug up for themselves. They never did that at Huwguwn [where Hides had offered the insolent young man a string of beads for seven poor quality sweet potatoes].† They stole food from there."

Tensgay elaborated: "They stole and ate everything: taro, bananas, sugar cane, harvesting it for themselves. We feared them killing us. Even pigs, they did for them with their guns."

Ongat added: "Who were they going to buy food from? They went in anger. They erected their houses, ate, slept, and then left."

Lem continued: "They didn't give us anything like that [axes, beads, and so on]. We didn't see those things. They didn't buy their sweet potato. After they shot all those men, then perhaps they gave things for food? We don't know, we ran off in terror. They didn't have anything—like pearlshells, axes, and beads. Those things the later whites brought with them."

Despite this, some people did offer the patrol food. Obiyn was one: "People picked and gave them *momoniyl* berries.‡ They had heard that others had done this before along their route, and so did it. They gave them sweet potatoes and things too. They never gave anything in return."

"And when they established camp," Naenk continued, "they put up their house and ate and slept. They took food without paying and then left. Then we gave them bananas and other food, they didn't give us laplap cloth or any of those other things of yours. We just threw down sweet potatoes, bananas, and firewood, and then cleared off in fear. We didn't know what to expect, it being the first time we had seen them."

Thinking of what he saw as his kinsmen's generosity, Minina asked: "Why did they do it [attack]? When they were at Huwguwn and Boiya, we gave them pandanus nuts and sweet potato and bananas. I went and dug some up myself for them. They were wild things. We gave it to them for nothing. They just took it. We were frightened of them and didn't

* Later patrols, knowing of the highlanders' desire for pearlshells, had few problems securing food.

† No one in the area could remember this episode related by Hides (see Chapter 5). The young man, however, showed surprising boldness in his behavior, given the terror all informants say they felt at the time.

‡ *Rubus rosifolius*, a small, strawberry-like fruit, with a dry, bland taste.

demand anything. If they had been true men, they would have left some payment. We just threw the food down and scuttled off."

Other people thought the patrol was carrying its own food. Hunmol explained, "When we went to see them, they had packed up their house and had it in their bags, ready to leave. They had something white, some of which they left behind. Someone picked up some of it. It was like sago starch [flour?]."

It was not until after the patrol had left Boiya, however, that Hides reports telling his men to take food from gardens. This followed one of the most terrible events of the journey.

The Battle at Korpe Defile

On the morning of May 11, Hides and his men got under way from Boiya, hungry and dispirited. Three Wola guides carrying unstrung bows led the way. Hides had asked them for food, but they indicated that the patrol could get it farther on. Hides immediately became suspicious that they were up to something but felt there was nothing he could do but follow along. As had happened in the other places, the advent of the patrol had caused a sensation in the countryside, and men came from miles around to see it, forming crowds that followed behind or flanked the patrol on parallel pathways. Many were calling out and yodeling with excitement as they went.

After a mile or so Hides and O'Malley and their men began moving out of the territory of the Silol people around Boiya and into that of their neighbors, the Kalol.* There were no significant tensions between these people at the time, and most of the crowd of followers simply continued across the boundaries. Presently they approached a pair of limestone pinnacles. Through the gap Hides could see another cultivated valley. In response to his questions about it (which they did not understand), his Wola guides replied: "*Wen, wen*" ("Soon, soon"; in effect, "be patient"), and Hides concluded the valley beyond the pinnacles was known as the "Wen."

The crowd following the patrol was by now becoming substantial. Although Wola informants insist nowadays that they accompanied the patrol unarmed and without hostile intent, that is not the way it appeared to Jack Hides:

"A large crowd of men now began to appear at our rear. Some of them trailed their bows behind them. Whenever they saw us look back, they

* The neighborhoods or territories of the principal *sem* mentioned in the text from west to east are as follows: Boiya and Huwguwn are in Silol *sem* territory; Sezinda, Shonguwt, and Korpe are all in Kalol *sem* territory; and Shobera is in Yaerol *sem* territory. (These are all at the *semonda* not *seng*ˀnk level [see Sillitoe 1979a].)

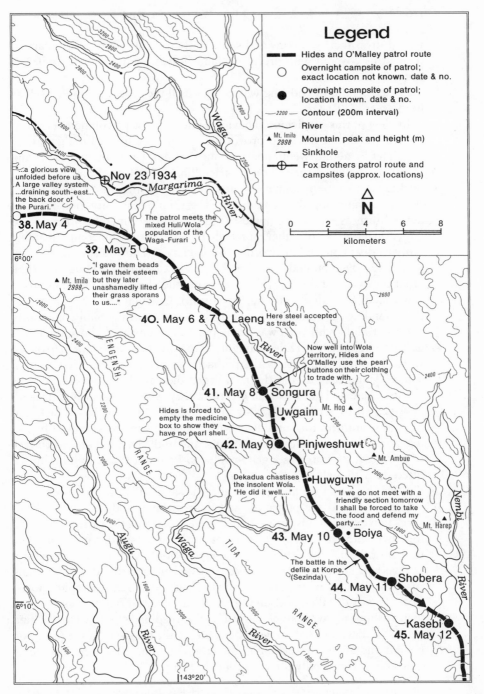

Legend

▬ ▬ Hides and O'Malley patrol route

○ Overnight campsite of patrol; exact location not known. date & no.

● Overnight campsite of patrol; location known. date & no.

—2200— Contour (200m interval)

⌇ River

▲ Mt. Imila 2998 Mountain peak and height (m)

•⌒• Sinkhole

⊕—⊕ Fox Brothers patrol route and campsites (approx. locations)

△
N

0 2 4 6 8
kilometers

"...a glorious view unfolded before us. A large valley system ...draining south-east... the back door of the Purari."

⊕ Nov 23 1934
Margarima

38. May 4

39. May 5 ○

The patrol meets the mixed Huli/Wola population of the Waga-Furari

"I gave them beads to win their esteem but they later unashamedly lifted their grass sporans to us...."

▲ Mt. Imila 2998

40. May 6 & 7 ○ Laeng Here steel accepted as trade.

E N G E N S H

R A N G E

Now well into Wola territory, Hides and O'Malley use the pearl buttons on their clothing to trade with.

41. May 8 ● Songura

Uwgaim Mt. Hog ▲

Hides is forced to empty the medicine box to show they have no pearl shell.

42. May 9 ● Pinjweshuwt

▲ Mt. Ambue

Dekadua chastises the insolent Wola. "He did it well...."

● Huwguwn

T I D A

"If we do not meet with a friendly section tomorrow I shall be forced to take the food and defend my party...."

▲ Mt. Harep

43. May 10 ● Boiya

The battle in the defile at Korpe. ○ (Sezinda)

44. May 11 ● Shobera

R A N G E

Kasebi ●
45. May 12

Map 9. From the Upper Waga Valley to the Nembi Plateau (May 4–12).

would drop their weapons and stand with arms akimbo. Others carried their arms covered with green pandanus leaves, or hidden in bundles of sugar-cane.

"A terrific din of yodeling was going on all the time, in front as well as in the rear" (PR: 120).

In view of this suspicious behavior, Hides had the patrol members keep careful watch but made no provocation. Climbing toward the gap, they were met by about twenty unarmed men. Hides, keyed up and expecting treachery, believed their show of friendliness was forced and overdone. Striking a posture of toughness, he tried to show that he "neither feared them, nor anything they could do." The grimly tense situation took an absurd turn as Hides attempted to explain to these men his intention to pass down the "Wen" valley. Somewhere in the natives' uncomprehending reply he distinguished the words: "*Inj kal bay?*" (Did you say no?) "*Paengael bay?*" (Do you understand me?) "They . . . told me," Hides asserted, "that they were of the *Injagale* people, and the place where we now stood was called '*Bangalbe*" (Sillitoe 1979a: 16n). In actual fact, the patrol was then standing at the border between the territory of the Silol community and the Kalol. While this was going on, a man appeared above them and gestured impatiently, Hides thought, to the others to move the patrol onwards into the defile below the pinnacles (a place locally called Korpe). The yodeling ceased, and the men urged the patrol onwards—this time without guides. Hides was now certain they were going to be attacked.

"I turned to Sergeant Orai standing by me. His beard was black and fuzzy, his uniform torn and dirty with a hundred and fifty days of breaking across as many miles of mountains, and in the haggard and worn face of this great Papuan was a grim coolness. I did not speak to him, but he uttered my thoughts.

" 'It is here that we find it, Taubada,' he said," (PW: 121).

Hides ordered the police to load their carbines and allowed them to carry two extra rounds between their fingers. Keeping the carriers bunched together, with police deployed in front and behind, they descended into the timber of the narrow defile. Events then developed with blinding rapidity:

"We had not gone two hundred yards when a terrific din of yodeling rose on all sides of us, and shots rang out at the rear in rapid succession. Then O'Malley and myself were attacked. I fired at a number of men rushing me with stone axes; I also turned and fired at men behind me. O'Malley, too, had to defend his life; while the shots of the police on my left and an arrow sticking in the ground told me they were also being attacked. It lasted only fifteen seconds" (PR: 77).*

---

* The confusion of that moment extends into Hides's various accounts of it, for in *PW* he says he was rushed by men with short stabbing spears, not, as in his patrol report, stone

"The natives were so close to us and so mixed with us [O'Malley later testified] that the carriers as they ran towards me [he was firing his pistol] cried out: 'We are the carriers, we are the carriers'" (*IQ*: 12).

"Terror galvanized the carriers into action, and they yelled and threw their tomahawks at the attacking natives. The attack lasted only a few seconds, and the yodeling then ceased and the people disappeared" (*PW*: 122).

Hides ran back down the line to see if the rest of the police were all right. The first constable he met was Borege, who had a broken arrow sticking through his leather pouch (*PR*: 77). Close behind was Sergeant Orai, who had been at the rear of the line as the patrol descended into the timber of the defile. A large crowd of bowmen had followed close behind them. Orai said he saw a man fit an arrow to his bow and fire, and his recollection of the battle after that has a curious slow-motion quality:

"Two arrows came first, one caught Borege, one caught the ground. Another came at me, and I stepped or twisted aside, and it went by close up. I turned around then and fired at the man who had fired at me. He wanted to fire at me again, and that is why I fired at him. He fell down, and another man take his place. Dekadua shot him. He dead. Then another man came down and pulled his bow at me, and Borege shot him.

"They no fright. Borege shoot, and they came at us again. I said, 'If this goes on, Borege, we are done.' Then another man came and pulled his bow at me, and I shot him. I shot this man, but the other no run away. I said to Dekadua, 'Like this and we shall all be dead.' I said, 'Shoot that man there.' Dekadua shot him, and I said, 'Come on, let us go, we stop here and we die.' Taubada was in front. We got there and found that they too had been fight . . . and they shoot too . . .

"All right, Taubada go on, and I came behind. I saw where Mr. Hides police shot the man. I saw four bodies. We went on, and at a potato garden two men blocked the road, and Mr. Hides and Agoti fired. I looked up and saw the track was filled with men. They were armed with shields and bows and arrows. I behind, Mr. Hides in front. Mr. Hides and his men went on and fired at the men in front. They fired, and I hear. I was behind. The men fled and left their shields. I went up and saw two dead men. I went on and saw the two shields" (*IQ*: 16).

"The thunder of the rifles had brought silence in the country around us," Hides wrote, "and we walked out of the timber into cultivations again" (*PW*: 122). He counted nine dead bodies scattered in the scrub around them.

---

axes. In addition, in his book he conveys the close quarters of the battle by weaving in an account of an event that didn't actually occur (according to the patrol report) until several days later (see *PW*: 122, *PR*: 81, and discussion in Chapter 10).

As they climbed out of the defile, they arrived at a cluster of houses a few hundred yards away, at a place called Sezinda.* There a number of natives came up to present them with bunches of bananas. Hides was not in the mood for (as he saw it) appeasement for treachery. "I threw the bunches back at them," he wrote, "indicating that we did not take presents from people who tried to murder us; and further that when we were ready for the food we would take it" (PW: 122).

After rejecting this peace offering, and after traveling another half a kilometer† from the site of the battle, they arrived at another settlement at a place called Shobera. They were met by a group of elderly men carrying gifts of sugarcane, who explained with elaborate care that they were not from the group that had attacked them. Although this may have been true (Shobera was in the territory of the Yaerol people), Hides did not believe them, but without making an issue of it simply instructed his men to take whatever food they required from the locality.

"We killed two pigs in a pen nearby, dug what potatoes we wanted, and then handed the old men axes, which they all smilingly accepted. Then with large fires going, and food cooking, we gorged ourselves to contentment." Within an hour, as they cooked and ate, more than a hundred men gathered around them,‡ sitting, talking and laughing in apparently genuine friendliness. Hides was sure these were the very men who had attacked his patrol shortly before, and he was intrigued by their present good-humored conviviality. It struck him as somehow sporting of them that they should be sitting down like this with their enemies after a fierce battle. "They seemed to treat a fight like a football match," he wrote. "I could not help liking them, even though they had tried to murder us. They were treacherous, but they could also be gentlemen" (PW: 123).§

The Wola Version

Hides credited the courage and fast reflexes of the officers and police for their escape from what he was convinced was a treacherous ambush. The Wola, however, recollect these events quite differently. The confusion and terror of that moment and the numbed bewilderment of its aftermath

---

* Sezinda is the nearest grassed *hauma* ceremonial ground to the defile where the battle took place and consequently is the place name most well-known to those not familiar with the locale. Thus it is extended in usage to include the defile, of which the actual name is Korpe.

† Hides records this as "two kilometers" (PR: 77) but the actual distance is much smaller.

‡ In his book, Hides expands this to "fully three hundred men" (PW: 123).

§ Although Shobera was the territory of the Yaerol, given the lack of local hostilities and the comparative freedom of movement for those who had relatives in Yaerol at this time, a number of Kalol or even Silol people may indeed have been present.

come through in the recollections of Waeb, one of those who went down into the defile that day to meet the patrol. More than 40 years afterward, his account still has a confused and breathless quality.

"They came down this way from Boiya, and we proceeded together into that narrow place, where they killed us. Down there in that defile where the rock face runs along, they followed that path. When they arrived we were cooking pandanus nuts. We left them, shutting up our house. They went along there, where the rock face closed them in. There were four of us; they shot two of us with their 'arrows.'* People say that Aez Saendaep and Haerep Saziy carried bows down there at the time we were watching them, and they shot us, down there in that narrow path. They didn't kill over there or over there, just down in that defile. Nobody fired any arrows or anything. Not Aez Saendaep, even if he was carrying his bow. They just suddenly fired: *Tuw-tuw*!† No one, not even Aez Saendaep drew a bow, not even playfully. When they fired, I fled in terror. I ran up there, to Shonguwt, to the top of the hill. We left the pandanus nuts. I had nothing to eat. They shot us all at once, together. We couldn't have retaliated with our bows, even if we had had them. We couldn't fight against that. Their 'bows' and ours weren't the same. They didn't shoot one by one, slowly, but all together: *Tuw-tuw*!"

Pabol, who was wounded in the neck during the skirmish, said, "They went down into the defile by that *pay* [oak] tree. They were traveling laterally. I stood there watching where Ndikiy's father had tied up some sugarcane. I didn't follow them down there. The two whites and the patrol traveled along, and I traversed the slope higher up until I reached Paziy's house. When I arrived there—wah! something made a loud *tuw-tuw*! noise. Someone shouted that there was a landslide, that the cliff was falling down. Again and again there was this *tuw-tuw*! sound.‡ I turned my back to it. Lol's father and Hiyt Duwaeb came tearing up screaming they were spirits come to kill and eat us. They hit many of my brothers. Lol's father had been carrying his axe, and they had hit its stone head and shattered it to pieces! I was hit in the neck here."

Naway, who was wounded through the shoulder, described the battle this way: "They put up their houses and slept at Boiya. We followed on behind them. They came to the Korpe. We did nothing down there. They

---

* These were possibly the two men with shields Orai mentions that Hides shot as they climbed out of the defile. Hides doesn't specifically mention these men in either his report or his book.

† *Tuw-tuw!* is the Wola expression for the sound of gunshots, equivalent to our "pow-pow!" or "bang-bang!"

‡ The confined space and rock wall must have magnified and echoed the rifle fire considerably, giving a fearsome impression.

shot to the front first, and then *tuw-tuw*! behind and all around. I was hit. I had blood pouring out. I wasn't knocked off my feet. I didn't fall down. I just fled—Oh, terror!"

Makwes gave a more thoughtful account—perhaps because he wasn't there and therefore not so emotionally involved. "From what I hear about those Kalol men [the group living around Sezinda], they surrounded the patrol to look at them and blocked the path. They were like a garden fence all around them, and the strangers became worried and feared an attack. They opened fire with their guns and shot many men. All those men running hither and thither, pushing and shoving, breaking down undergrowth noisily frightened those whites. They thought it was an attack. There they were in the middle of all this rumpus, thinking that we intended to wrong them. *Tuw-tuw*! They opened fire on us. We thought that their guns were man-eating things, belonging to ghosts, and that they were seeking men to eat. Some say a Yaerol man did something. I never saw it with my eyes. They say he had a bow and drew it, pulling it in fun and not intending to loose off an arrow. The whites and their carriers saw it, I suppose. People say it was Aez Saendaep. What was in his mind—who knows? He was the only person carrying a bow. He came from the other side of Sezinda [in the direction which the patrol was heading] to meet the patrol, along with a crowd. He had a bow, which the whites thought signified we were up to something. He and his relatives have always strongly denied it. There has been some dispute over the business. Those who lost relatives in the attack have demanded *ol komb* reparation payments from Aez Saendaep and his relatives as the *saendtay* [basic] cause of the misfortune. They've always denied any responsibility and have never paid over anything, maintaining that the demands are empty, nothing. The patrol killed them for no reason. They were so close to them, too. The path was narrow, hemmed in by a cliff on one side, a steep forested slope on the other. In this confined space, with all of us milling around, they became frightened and—*tuw-tuw*!—opened fire. For no reason. They did wrong. They should have been friendly with us, not assaulted us like that. We gave them no grounds. We were all coming along the path together. Aez Saendaep, I suppose, was waiting up ahead for the patrol. When they saw him, that was it, they opened fire on everyone."

Tensgay, who was also not present at the shooting, concurred. "When they went down into that defile, the Kalol men were leading the patrol, and the others were following behind. At Korpe they entered that short narrow pass, hemmed in with trees and tall cane grass. There some of those Kalol men said something and turned around. The whites found themselves caught in the middle and thought they were going to be attacked. Then *tuw-tuw*! with their guns!"

Ongat picked up the story: "Wah! it was like thunder—*tuw-tuw*! They shot many men. They shot one man, it is said, and the bullet went clean through his shoulder and into someone else. Everyone fled in terror."

These stories clearly conflict with Hides's report on a number of points, and they do not explain the arrows sticking in the ground or in Borege's pouch, but it seems clear that the Wola remember themselves as accompanying the patrol in great excitement and curiosity, to see what it would do, but unarmed and without treacherous intention. Considering the number shot in the short space of the fighting, quite a few of them must have been very close in on the patrol. Wola believe the patrol opened fire on them without provocation. All informants vehemently denied that they or anyone else they saw were carrying weapons when they went to look at the strange arrivals.

According to Lem, "We all went empty-handed. We carried nothing. We said that they were ancestor spirits come, so what do you think we would be doing going off to fight them? Come on! We didn't carry axes or bows. I had my string bag, that was all. We just went to look at them. What were they up to, we wondered?"

Hides's description of the Wola manner of fighting is also confusing. In his patrol report he describes them as carrying stone "battle axes" (*PR*: 77) and in his book "short stabbing spears" (*PW*: 122). Few Wola possess or fight with spears; their favored weapon is the bow and arrow. I have never seen or heard of a short stabbing spear. The few spears known to me have been six or more feet long, which men insist they hurled in fighting, never advancing to stab their enemies with them. They also told me they never used the spear in ambushes, where they employed only bows —the one weapon Hides does *not* mention was used in this "ambush." One thing that particularly bothered Hides was the yodeling of the Wola, which he interpreted as their "kill call." According to Makwes, "We did hoot and dance a bit before they shot us. But not a sound did we make afterwards. We just fled in terror." Tensgay continued, "Those of us who were following the patrol, we didn't hoot. It was those leading in front who did that [to warn those ahead of the patrol's approach]." There was nothing aggressive in this, Pabol explained: "Who were we going to fight? Anyway, we went empty-handed. What would we be doing with a bow? We just went to look. No *warlike* shouting or hooting."

In view of their belief that the patrol's attack was unprovoked, the Wola have subsequently tried to figure out for themselves why it occurred. Enjap said, "Those Silol men told us not to fear because those spirits had 'sat quietly' with them at Boiya, and they assured us that they would do the same with us. Why did they kill us?"

Several have taken up the Aez Saendaep rumor, blaming him for carrying a bow, even stringing it, and so inciting the patrol to open fire on them. Others, present at the massacre, dismiss this as nonsense. Comparison with Hides's account isn't particularly helpful since the Wola maintain that Aez Saendaep approached the patrol from the front, whereas Hides and Orai say the first arrow was loosed at the police guarding the rear. Perhaps many Wola were unarmed and had no intention of harming the patrol, but some apparently did carry bows, and it wouldn't be the first time the patrol had encountered people who loosed an arrow or two at them to see what might happen. Judging from the experience of later patrols in the area, it is likely some of the younger warriors did this to stir up the action (cf. Lake Kutubu PR 9, 1938–39). At the same time, it is worth noting that two of the police at the end of the line were the same Sergeant Orai and A. C. Dekadua who had shot the three Hulis at Dumi Creek under questionable circumstances a week or so before.

Whatever precipitated the unfortunate shooting at Korpe, the result was a number of killed and wounded and the panic-stricken flight of the Wola into hiding. Naenk described it: "We scattered into the forest in fear, where we cooked pandanus nuts. We fled terrified after the shooting. Before that we watched them nervously, and as some came to see, others left."

Pabol, with his hand on his gashed neck said, "We fled in terror up the side of the garden there, towards Sezinda. Some entered Perol's house nearby. They all piled in and huddled there in fear. Women, too, they cowered in their houses, with doors fastened. I hurried on to Sezinda proper [the ceremonial ground]. I tore open the door of Pawiyn's father's house. There was a woman in there who shrieked, 'Who's that coming into my house?' Scared us both. I told her what happened."

I asked Pabol if he thought of taking revenge for the killings. He looked at me in amazement. "What! Oh, no, we were all terrified. Who could have taken revenge against that?" Lem agreed: "Aaah, no, no. We couldn't fight back. Terrified, we ran off to hide. Who would even go look at them after that? Panic-stricken, everyone fled away. We hid ourselves in the forest, under rock faces, curled up in balls like this. We feared those strangers would come back and eat us." *

The death toll at the defile and the number of seriously wounded were considerable. In a few moments the patrol had wreaked greater carnage

---

* In earlier investigations into this incident (Sillitoe 1979a: 16), I placed too much credence in Hides's account and, thinking that the Wola had made repeated attacks on his party, misunderstood their comments, erroneously imputing to them a wish to revenge the deaths of relatives killed by the patrol as prompting their "attacks." In hindsight, I fear that I might have even suggested these reasons to them, when they understandably gave me none themselves for attacking the patrol. Or they may have been commenting on attacks I told them others had made on the party.

than the Wola could have achieved after weeks of fighting amongst themselves or even in the course of an entire war. The list of casualties given
by different informants varies; each forgot some fatalities; some included
only those killed instantly, others those who died subsequently of wounds,
and all tended to recall only those related to or known to them personally
when alive.

Hides reported finding nine dead after the shoot-out. According to
Lem, "They killed Sol, Obil, Moromol, Wenja Taiz, Haenda Wabuw,
Henep Pes's brother Henep Obaynol, Hwimb Kem, his brother Hwimb
Olnay. That's two Hwimb men, the Henep one makes three, Aeron makes
four, five. Let me list them again: there was Sol, Obil, Moromol, Wenja
Taiz, Haenda Wabuw, Obaynol, Penj's brother-in-law—that's seven—and
Ezom, Eborol's father (he's the one whose head was blown to pieces),
and Hwimb Olnay. That's ten. They killed this many men," and Lem held
up all his fingers. "Many died. Those wounded who survived were Hiyt
Duwaeb, Kal Hobor, Periyen's husband, Naway, Waediyaem, Hoboga
Waeniym, a woman—who's-it—Haelaim, Hwimb Hiyp, and Waendor.
That's another ten. That's twenty altogether. Ten killed and ten wounded
who didn't die."

Naway listed six names for those killed, and Enjap named eleven. If one
counts all of the *different* names given, the dead total fifteen.

When Hides presented some of the senior villagers with axes at Shobera
and let the patrol forage what food they wanted from the local gardens,
it was perhaps an understandably stern action. It was also, unfortunately,
not the whole story. The police, who went off to get the pigs, descended on
a small women's pig-keeping house near Sezinda where—with or without
the knowledge of their Australian officers—they took the animals with a
barbaric vengeance.

All the women and children of the area had been kept away from the
strange spirits to protect them and were in hiding in their houses or the
forest. According to Tensgay, "We said, 'They've come to eat us.' And so
only men remained behind. Women and children we sent off to places to
hide." In the pig-keeping house near the top of the rise where the patrol
emerged from the defile, Haelaim was hidden with several other women
and children.

"We were sitting indoors with the door fastened when they came. Huwlael Tila had told us to go inside and stay there, to close the door securely
and stay there. 'Don't open the door; don't run off in fear,' he told us. 'Stay
and look after the pigs and the children.' So we were indoors when they
came and forced an entry. All the men ran off in terror. They had killed all
those Kalol men. We had stayed indoors all the time. We heard the *tuw-
tuw*! of them shooting our men. We hadn't any idea what it was. 'Has

the rock face fallen?' we asked ourselves. 'Has there been an avalanche of stones?'

"We were terrified. After they had killed our men, they came to kill our pigs, and us women and children. They tore open the door of our house and demanded everything. Puliym's mother released the pigs one at a time and drove them out of the door to them waiting outside. They were black-skinned men, policemen. The whites were in the clearing over there. The laplap cloth I saw was black with red—like policemen wore. I saw it around their legs. We didn't see their faces. I didn't get a good look at what they were wearing. When they arrived we were sitting inside with our door securely fastened. They tore the front off the house, attacked it with axes and bushknives. They ripped off the pandanus bark lining and some of the wall stakes, besides pulling out all the door slats. Then they stood there signaling us to give them the pigs. I was cowering with the children. It was Puliym's mother who released the pigs and put them out.

"They took the pigs one at a time and shot them outside. After they killed them, they singed off the bristles over a fire made from wood torn off our house. They broke up our house for wood to singe the pigs. Then they butchered them ready to carry off, ready to cook in an earth oven. They lashed the pork on poles with their belts to carry it. After they had killed and prepared the pigs to carry off, they turned on us. They attacked us women. We didn't see well what was going on. We were cowering inside, terrified. They returned and stood there [within 3 m] and fired their guns into our house. They shot Hiyt Ibiziym, Bat Maemuw, my sister, Ndin, Maeniy, and me. That's six of us. Also my son Maesaep and my daughter Perliyn. We were all hiding inside that house. They came right up to the house to shoot into it. And they fired on us. We sat indoors petrified. We didn't cry or anything like that. We just sat. When they were taking and killing our pigs, one of them stood at the door preventing us from going out. Sitting inside, we couldn't really see what was going on outside. All we could see were their feet and legs.

"After they had shot us up, they carried off the butchered pigs to Shobera. We remained huddled indoors terrified. All the men had fled. What was to become of us? We didn't do anything. We were so frightened that we were all dizzy and faint. We slumped into a sort of stupefied state. When we went outside we couldn't walk, but trembled and kept falling over. We couldn't go and join the men where they were cooking pandanus nuts [in the forest]. Who was there to bandage our wounds with moss and leaves? No one bandaged them. We had all been shot and wounded, so there was no one present fit enough to bandage us up, we just slumped indoors. We didn't think anything. All we felt was terror and dizziness. I was sort of senseless.

"The pigs they killed, one was Injil's, that girl what's-her-name's in-laws, that's another. Those other in-laws, one and two. Then there was my grandparents'. And Wezim's. And three belonging to my deceased brother. They killed them all. Nine pigs. And they were all big ones too. Like this [she indicated the height], no small ones."

Hides, of course, does not mention any of this in his report; he may have been ignorant of it. The police waited until they had finished butchering the pigs before they shot the women up, giving the rest of the patrol a chance to pass on up the track to Shobera. Fortunately, no one was killed.

After discussing the attack on the women's house, Tensgay remarked with some irony: "Well, they didn't rape any women. That was done by later patrols, when they not only stole our pigs but our women too, and broke into our houses and smashed up our possessions, like our bows and things. They even excreted in our fireplaces."

One of the wounded women—the one who released the pigs—became a celebrity years later when, as Tensgay related, "That Puliym's mother, she received a bullet here in the temple [and survived]. A bit of it came out of her head by itself years later."

Some of the wounds the men received in the defile were gruesomely described. Leda recalled, "They shot my cross-cousin Huruwmb, and I went to see him. You could see his liver exposed. They kept sending me to fetch water for him to drink because he was thirsty. Back and forth, I kept going to fetch water for him. He lived in agony for three days. On the fourth day he died. They laid him to rest at a rock face [an exposure burial]."

Tensgay related: "Kal Aenknais had his thighs and lower torso smashed. Completely pulverized here and here [pointing to the position of the wounds]. He kept groaning 'Oh, ah.' I saw him. He died later. Wounded in the guts, he was. His intestines were punctured. When he was given water to drink, to cool him off, it came spurting out of the holes in his body. Then there was Obil. His eyes were blown clean out of his head. When they landed on the path they wriggled around and around for ages. He died too. And then there was that poor blighter—aah—whose entrails were shot out. His intestines and stomach were blasted right out of his body. Huwlael Tila, he had a bullet go into his throat and come out there. And Naway copped it here in the shoulder. It went right through him and out here. They say that the same 'arrow' went through them both. Mae-dop Wend's father had his hand shot. Cleaved in two it was. And Hoboga Waeniym lost an ear."

In most cases, relatives could do little except watch the wounded get better or die. One of the more fortunate ones, Pabol, recalled: "My wound healed itself, with no operation or anything—unlike poor Hiyt Duwaeb."

Others killed pigs in an attempt to facilitate their recovery. Tensgay remembered that "Hoboga Waeniym, he killed a pig in offering [to placate his ancestor spirits]. He was wounded here. He didn't die until recently." Makwes added, "Those wounded who feared they might die decided to kill and eat some of their pigs. They ate them to give themselves strength to fortify themselves in their weakness. There were few offerings to ancestor spirits. I didn't hear of any."

Relatives operated on some poor souls to try and remove bullets. Makwes said, "We operated on Kal Waendiyaem. We cut him with flint blades to remove the 'arrow.' The thing we removed was black with holes in it. It was round. We took it from his shoulder here. It was small and round and pitted with holes. It just went into his flesh, not into any organ or bone."

Following the shoot-out, there was a funeral the like of which the Wola had never before witnessed. Makwes, who helped collect up the dead, recalled: "There was no moon at the time.* 'Tomorrow, the day after,' we thought, 'we'll collect up the corpses.' We sat terrified indoors with our doors securely fastened. Some hadn't returned. Some hadn't returned from the forest but sat cowering under rock outcrops. We collected those who had fallen nearby, but farther away we left them. We got them that day and spent the night with the corpses in with us because we feared that those whites would return to eat them. Then next day, when we had collected all of the corpses we could, we lashed them to poles in the clearing at Sezinda. It was full of poles with corpses tied to them. Like pigs at a pig kill! We were surrounded by corpses, there was no room left. We gathered them up one after the other. Some relatives of the dead carried their corpses off to their homes to mourn and bury. In sorrow, in mourning, many of us killed pigs [as part of the mortuary exchange following death]. And we slaughtered the pigs of those killed too."

Enjap recalled, "After we had collected up the corpses, they formed a pile that reached up the trunk of a casuarina tree to the first branches, to where it forked out."

After a few days of mourning, they disposed of the corpses. Ongat remembered: "I helped lash the bodies to poles. We mourned over them a few days, and then we put them in raised exposed graves. We didn't bury them in the earth. We built platforms at a rock face. Some relatives carried corpses off elsewhere to mourn and bury. Those left at Sezinda we laid out at the rock face [bordering the path]."

Not all those killed received a proper funeral. Pabol said, "There was Henep Obaynol. He was completely blasted to pieces. We couldn't pick

* Editors' note. Actually, according to the *Nautical Almanac* of 1935, the moon was in its third quarter. The full moon followed on May 18.

up his corpse; he was in bits. We collected up what we could of his body and deposited it in a crevice of the rock face. The others we lashed to poles and mourned properly before laying out."

One body was not found at all until much later. Ongat told about it: "There was this man from the Wola [of the Nembi Valley] region who had come up to share in the harvest of the pandanus nuts with friends— remember the pandanus trees were ripening at the time. When he arrived at their place he couldn't find anyone [for they had gone off to see the patrol], and he set off in search of them. He was in the forest there, off the path, when the shooting started. He was hit, but nobody knew about it. Sometime later his relatives came searching for him. The friends he had come to visit had no idea of his whereabouts. They hadn't even known that he had come to visit them. The lost man's relatives searched for him and found his corpse—absolutely rotten it was and stinking—where he had fallen."

Meanwhile Hides, O'Malley, and the patrol went on. After leaving Sezinda, Naenk says, they "spent the night at Shobera. Then they went on to Mungtay. And then Meruwt, where they say they killed many more men. They didn't kill any more of us around here."

The last those living in the "Wen" valley heard about the patrol concerned this second shoot-out at Meruwt (Pembi Andaa, see Chapter 7) where they heard, with some gratification, that one of the patrol members was killed. Ongat and Tensgay related what they had heard: "At Meruwt —ooof—there was more violence. Someone there shot one of the patrol through his laplap cloth with a bone-tipped arrow. He hit a black-skinned member. They [the patrol members] buried him, people say, in the soil inside their house and covered over the spot with ash and charcoal like a fireplace. The people of Meruwt saw it when they left. The man who shot him, Haebuw Momborlom [Mombilal Nal], he's still alive. After that, where the patrol went, search me."

The passage of the patrol through the valley of the Waga led to the coining of oaths still used today by speakers as expletives to emphasize a point. Kabiyn and Enjap explained: "[People said] they were *towmow hundbiy*, pale-skinned ghosts. And since that time, you know, up there [towards Margarima] they've used *towmow hundbiy* as an oath they swear. But down here [in the upper Nembi Valley] we say *Sezinda* to affirm a pledge. Since that killing occurred at Sezinda, the word has become a strong oath that we swear when we are angry."

7. ACROSS THE NEMBI PLATEAU

ROBERT CRITTENDEN

After spending the night on the ceremonial ground at Shobera, the patrol was on its way at first light the following morning, May 12. It was a beautiful day. Hides and O'Malley admired the extensive and sophisticated system of drains and hedges that ranged across the valley. In contrast to the hooting, derisive crowds of the day before, they were accompanied by a following of apparently curious and friendly natives who came down from the farmsteads in the surrounding countryside.

"All were unarmed," Hides wrote, "and those not carrying presents of food were walking uprightly with their arms folded. It was all so pleasant; women and children could be seen in the green potato fields, the little boys ran with the party. How we wished it would continue always. There was no yodeling now, no derisive laughter to follow stumbling police and carriers: all the people were genuinely friendly, courteous and respectful" (PR: 78).

The local people, however, for all their curiosity, were apprehensive. They had heard the news of the battle at the Korpe defile the day before, and although that was the concern of another group of people and not their affair,* it was not very reassuring. Moreover, it was difficult to read the intentions of these strange beings. Some informants remember trying to offer Hides and O'Malley bananas or sugarcane as they marched along. The white men appeared to ignore them. Disconcerted at this apparent refusal of friendly relations, the Wola tossed the food in the patrol's path

---

*According to Sobey Sowey, the people of Kasebi and Shobera thought the fight was started by a man named Kel Melam aiming his drawn bow at the patrol (interview Nov. 19, 1985).

and stood back to watch what would happen. They were reassured to see the carriers and police scramble to pick it up and put it in their net bags.

The day was warm. The carriers were gorged with pork from the previous afternoon, and the police had satisfied their vengeance for the attack at Korpe by shooting up the women in the pig house. Surrounded now by apparently friendly people offering food as they walked along, a mood of reconciliation came over the patrol. While they were resting at one point, Hides overheard Sergeant Orai addressing the police and carriers: "You must forget the fight. You must remember that this is not your mother's country, that it belongs to these people; and you must not forget to treat these people as you were treated yourselves when the Government first came to your village" (PW: 124).

Hides, apparently unaware of the full irony of the situation was deeply moved: "It was the finest thing I have ever heard from a native," he wrote, "and it showed the great feeling of brotherhood that has come into the minds of these Papuans. Australians should learn more about this colony of theirs, for they can stand in front of the world today and show the results of their administration of a subject race" (PW: 124).

Kasebi

As they continued along, Hides remarked that the appearance of the people was changing. The finely woven wigs worn by men from Tari down through the Waga Valley were now giving way to shapeless mops of unkempt hair. The patrol was entering the country of the Nembi.

As noted in Chapter 5, Nembi country lay astride the confluence of all the major trade routes between the highlands and the Samberigi Valley and thus was situated at the focal point in the competition for pearlshell. The Nembi were skillful traders and aggressive warriors renowned for their bellicosity and fearlessness. Interclan hostility and distrust were central parts of their lives, and the various Nembi groups were almost continually fighting with each other.

As the patrol began to cross the Nembi Plateau, its journey, even in the course of a single day, would pass through a succession of mutually suspicious clan groups linked by uneasy and unstable alliances. Wading through the midst of this social minefield, Hides and O'Malley were to find the Nembi among the most difficult people they had to deal with.

For the moment, however, things were going well. The patrol traveled for the first part of the morning through the lands of the people of Shobera and those of their adjacent friends and allies. Farther down the valley the people of the Injip group of clans waited in some trepidation. The

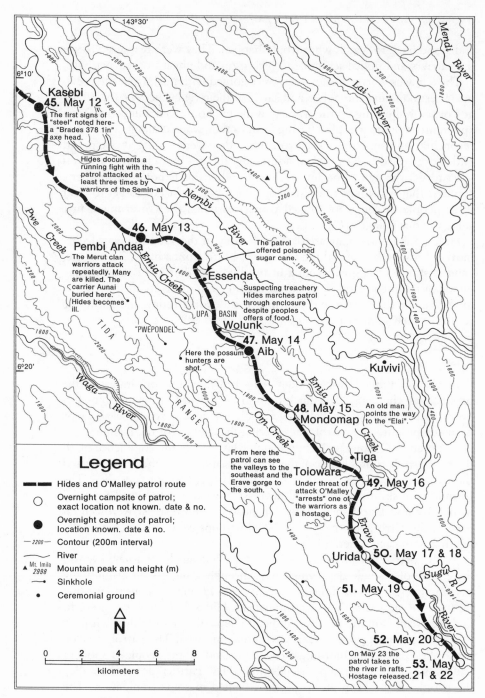

Mendi River

Lai River

6°10'

Kasebi
45. May 12
The first signs of "steel" noted here— a "Brades 378 1in" axe head.

Hides documents a running fight with the patrol attacked at least three times by warriors of the Semin-al

Nembi River

Pwe Creek

Emia Creek

46. May 13
Pembi Andaa
The Merut clan warriors attack repeatedly. Many are killed. The carrier Aunai buried here. Hides becomes ill.

Essenda

The patrol offered poisoned sugar cane.

Suspecting treachery Hides marches patrol through enclosure despite peoples offers of food.

UPA BASIN
"PWEPONDEL"
Wolunk

6°20'

T I D A

47. May 14
Aib
Here the possum hunters are shot.

Waga River

R A N G E

Emia

Kuvivi

48. May 15
Mondomap
An old man points the way to the "Elai".

Emia Creek

Om Creek

From here the patrol can see the valleys to the southeast and the Erave gorge to the south.

Tiga

Toiowara
49. May 16
Under threat of attack O'Malley "arrests" one of the warriors as a hostage.

Erave

Legend

━━━ Hides and O'Malley patrol route

○ Overnight campsite of patrol; exact location not known. date & no.

● Overnight campsite of patrol; location known. date & no.

—2200— Contour (200m interval)

⎯ River

▲ Mt. Imila 2998 Mountain peak and height (m)

⟍ Sinkhole

• Ceremonial ground

△
N

0   2   4   6   8
kilometers

Urida **50. May 17 & 18**

Sugu Ri

51. May 19

52. May 20

On May 23 the patrol takes to the river in rafts. Hostage released.

53. May 21 & 22

Map 10. Across the Nembi Plateau to the Erave River Valley (May 12–22).

previous day the Injip had been startled and frightened by the sounds of rifle fire from the direction of Sezinda. No one could tell what the sounds were. Then they heard the shrill yodeling cries of warning come echoing from the ridges and hilltops down the valley as the message was passed that something terrible was coming towards them. The Injjip in this region were the enemies of the people at Sezinda, but they recognized the voice of a Sezinda man named Hobera calling from a pinnacle where he was perched that the "Kutubu ol"—the feared cannibals and sorcerers of the lowlands—were coming to kill them all. Various versions of this news were shouted from hill to hill until the Injip warriors did not know what to believe. They were badly frightened. Sobey Sowey remembers they heard that sugarcane and bananas had been thrown back by the strangers at the people who had offered it to them—a bad omen signifying an arrogant refusal of friendship.

Like the Wola, some people speculated that the pale creatures were ghosts (*tomo*) come back from the land of the dead to find their relatives. The black men accompanying the two ghosts collected up the food. Others connected the strangers with the Nembi version of *mbingi* and the light-skinned and dark-skinned brothers. According to this version, in the distant past when the sweet potato first came into the area, light-skinned and dark-skinned people lived together. One day there was a terrible natural disaster: the sky fell down, the earth quaked, the forests burned, and the hills slipped into the valleys. One light-skinned man and one dark-skinned man escaped the disaster, and they both shared the work of planting a new sweet potato garden. They then parted, but the dark-skinned man returned and ate all the sweet potatoes himself. When the light-skinned man came back and discovered this, he was so incensed that he stormed off in anger. Perhaps, some Nembi speculated, this strange group of beings approaching them now, stealing food and killing people, might be that light-skinned man angrily returning.

As the patrol drew nearer, the Injip collected great bundles of sugarcane and bananas (foods which not only signified ordinary hospitality but also had ritual importance in ceremonies for appeasement of spirits and ancestral ghosts) and gathered uneasily at Kasebi ceremonial ground to await them. To be on the safe side, they also strung their bows in case the strange beings did not prove friendly.

When Hides and O'Malley arrived a little later, at midmorning, they were gratified to find that the people at Kasebi were "friendly men who brought plenty of food." Besides the usual bananas and sweet potatoes, the patrol was given neat parcels of wood salt, a delicacy traded in from the Enga country (*PW*: 124) and quantities of cured ginger grown locally. Eaten together in small quantities, with the ginger dipped in salt cupped in the hand, the astringent mixture is a favored stimulant in the area. In fact, two neighboring groups are known to this day as *sembi nak*, "the wild ginger men," for the abundance of this plant (*Zingiber officinale*) in their area. The people seemed so hospitable that Hides decided to stop there for the rest of the day and stay the night.

The patrol had traveled that day along a well-worn track down the western side of what Hides called the "Wen" plateau (the gentle slopes of the western rim of the Nipa Basin). The *hauma* at Kasebi is a small ceremonial ground of the Injip group of clans, about 1 km north of their main center at Mungte. Standing at Kasebi and looking southeast, Hides and O'Malley and their men could see the country at the northern end of the Nembi Plateau. While the patrol had pitched camp on the ceremonial ground, a large crowd of men came to watch the carriers and police erect the tent flies and wonder at all the paraphernalia of the white men. That afternoon, the local people began to bring their sick and injured to Hides for treatment.* One old man who seemed to have some influence led Hides to a man whose spine had been "broken" in a recent fight. By gestures he indicated that he expected Hides to cure him. "I did not know what to do," Hides wrote. " 'Give him quinine,' suggested O'Malley. 'It's as good as anything we can do' " (PW: 125). However, Hides thought this case called for something more dramatic. So he straightened the man's back as best he could and bound him up with a splint. To his astonishment, the man (who had hobbled in bent over, supported on two sticks) now walked away unaided. Hides tried to caution him to take it easy lest he injure himself further, but he was too excited to listen. As he walked away, Hides hoped he wouldn't die before the patrol had left the district. No one remembers this incident in Kasebi today.

A little later the old man approached him again carrying a bundle wrapped in barkcloth and leaves. He carefully unwrapped it to reveal a magnificent pearlshell dyed with red ochre. This was the first whole shell Hides had seen since he left the coast. The reverence with which the man treated it and the expression on his face as he looked at the two patrol officers told them plainly that he was asking whether they had brought any such beautiful things with them. It was a hopeful gesture and an invitation to enter a trading, and thus friendly, relationship. Sadly, Hides had

---

* In the absence of informants' comments, it is difficult to assess why the people of Kasebi did this. Possibly they had heard rumors of the medical efforts of government patrols in the lower Erave, Mubi, or Samberigi valleys, but this is very far away. More likely, Nembi thinking here was similar to that of the Huli in believing that powerful spirit beings could cure (as well as cause) illness. Many of their rituals (including the important *kaebal* and *yegil* ceremonies) were addressed to ancestral spirits and sky people to ensure good health, growth and fertility, and productivity of the soil. It may have been perfectly natural for those in ill health to be brought with suitable ceremonial oblations to a powerful spirit to be cured.

to decline, for the patrol carried no shell. The old man, however, was un-convinced, and eventually Hides had once again to empty out the metal medicine chest to show he had nothing hidden there. Although keenly disappointed, the old man invited Hides and his men to settle permanently at Kasebi. Hides found it awkward to refuse politely this generous offer, but finally managed to communicate that they had to return to their women far away to the south.

While at Kasebi Hides noted another significant finding in his field diary: "We saw the first sign of steel this day. It was a 'Brades' 378, no. 1 ax head, worn to about half its original size. It was a great thrill, for it told us we were coming back again to parts where European influence could be seen" (PW: 126).

The Nembi Plateau

The following day Hides and O'Malley looked out over the region they were to travel that day:

"The grass country and cultivations still extended before us. To the northward, six or seven miles away, was a great mountain precipice of rock that rose between nine and ten thousand feet, and formed the northern walls of the Wen [Nembi] Valley. The glistening ribbon of the Wen [Nembi] River itself flowing slowly over wide, cultivated flats, could be seen thousands of feet below us from where we stood on the grass table-land. . . . The entire length of the floor of the valley . . . was green with potato vines. The numerous little farmhouses that could be seen and the roads and drains running everywhere across the carpet of green were a marvelous sight." (PW: 128)

Hides was again seeing things larger than life. The escarpments he de-scribes are nowhere more than 300 m in height. He was correct, however, in describing the valley as heavily populated. Considering the unpredictable receptions they had been given over the previous few days, Hides and O'Malley wanted to avoid going down into the valley, preferring to stay on the rolling basins and tablelands of the Nembi Plateau, where the population seemed less dense and the topography offered better cover.

The Nembi Plateau is flanked on the north and east by the valley of the Nembi River, which rises in the Nipa Basin and flows southeast to the Erave. To the west the plateau is bordered by the Tida range, which separates it from the valley of the Waga River and the Papuan lowlands. Within these boundaries, and elevated 200–300 m above the valley floor, the Nembi Plateau is not really a plateau at all but a series of intercon-nected broad basins and hollows separated by parallel hogback limestone ridges that trend from northwest to southeast and are strung together by intermittent streams. In places this country provides some of the most rugged and fantastic landscapes in the world. The rivers seem at first to follow the lie of the land, but then vanish suddenly beneath the ground and then, as abruptly, reappear out of the rock some kilometers away. It is in the patchy grasslands of the plateau valleys and basins where the vol- canic soil is relatively deep and more fertile that Nembi clansmen build their homesteads. The population densities here are among the highest in Papua New Guinea (Crittenden 1982). The ridges and rivers that cross this broken terrain shape the geography of clan enmity and alliance. The Pwe, Emia, and Om creeks, which drain the plateau intermittently from the northwest to the southeast, divide it into a number of regions. The Pwe flows south through a densely populated valley, disappears under- ground, and emerges again in another small but moderately fertile valley (see Map 10). These two valleys house perhaps the strongest of the Nembi alliances, with the Pwe Pond El of the lower Pwe Valley not having known defeat in living memory.

The Emia Creek flows parallel to the Pwe a few kilometers to the east. Its headwater streams, emerging on the northwest of the plateau below the rim of the Nipa Basin, dissect the large, open, saucerlike basin in- habited by the powerful Semin-al alliance of clans and also the Merut and Werut-Marop clans a few kilometers southeast of Kasebi. The Emia continues southeast four or five kilometers, before sinking beneath the foot of bare limestone cliffs. It reemerges again lower down to the south into a former lake bed, the Upa Basin. Here the ceremonial grounds of Mui-*hauma* and Upa-*hauma* provide a focus for the warriors of five other clans (the Murupa, the Puit, the Pelen, the Albalapa, and the Palom), while another two *hauma*, Essenda-*hauma* and Ulin-*hauma*, are perched high on the escarpment that separates the basin from the Nembi Valley to the west.

South of the lower Pwe Creek basin and west of the lower Emia, the Om Creek has scoured a small and isolated valley. Here in extremely precipi- tous cockpit karst of the lower Nembi Plateau another ten clans* make their gardens in the thin soils of an inhospitable country and build their houses on rocks and crags.

The northern end of the Nembi Plateau, including the Injip area around Kasebi, is (and was, unknown to Hides) a culturally and economically transitional zone in several respects. It is believed that in ancient times the region was originally populated by groups migrating down the Waga

---

* These are the Heropa-Yandolopa, the Maey-Muit, the Petum-Wogia, the Werrin-Petum, the Poreleb-lb, the Kari-Engi, the Olorop, the Angaspa, the Nei, and the Enduspar clans.

and Nembi valleys from the Enga heartland in the highlands.* Later, descendants of these people at the southernmost extent of this movement (which reached the Erave Valley and the Mubi River lowlands) turned and began to migrate back up the Nembi Valley again. The ceremonial ground at Kasebi is astride the meeting point of these continuing southward and northward movements. Thus the majority of clans north of Kasebi describe their origins to the north and are principally allied with people in that direction, while clans to the south point to the lower Waga Valley, the Mubi River lowlands, and the Erave Valley as their place of origin. Trade connections and hostilities are also aligned to some degree along this division. Clans to the south of the Injip had extensive connections with the groups farther to the south and were deeply involved in the trade in pearlshell. Groups to the north of the Injip had few such connections and consequently their access to the shell trade was limited. The Injip were on good terms with neither group.

To the southeast of Kasebi, in the region the patrol was shortly to traverse, was the extremely powerful Semin-al alliance of clans, and between them and the Injip there is a longstanding and fierce enmity. The present-day Semin-al is composed of some thirteen clans and a myriad of subclans dovetailed throughout the clan territories, each centered upon its own ceremonial grounds. This situation is the result of a complex history, and the configuration of clans today is not the same as it was in 1935. Endemic warfare in the past meant that some clans and subclans disappeared while others rose in importance. This, plus the breaking and forming of new alliances and the rising and falling fortunes of Big Men, kept the balance of political alignment continually shifting. Movements of individuals, whether to seek refuge, to support allies in warfare, to stay for extended visits with affinal or matrilateral kin, or simply to seek better gardening land, meant that people's places of residence and group affiliations could change considerably over their lifetimes and were confusing even to their contemporaries.† These historical and cultural conditions make it difficult

---

* The evidence for this comes from linguistic materials (see Franklin and Franklin 1978: 72; Franklin 1968: 90; Crittenden 1982: 98–103) as well as local tradition, and genealogical and network analysis.

† To further complicate matters, individuals among the Semin-al distinguish among themselves by using a clan or subclan name as a suffix. This suffix can vary depending upon who is referring to whom and their respective places of residence. Thus the suffix can represent either a man's natal patrilineal clan, his mother's natal clan or subclan, or the mans's place of residence if living with his wife's people. Individuals may therefore be known by different names to different people or at different times in their lives, and this, in addition to the use of alternative names associated with the taboo relationships of marriage ties, makes it extremely difficult to identify particular individuals with certainty when discussing events of 50 years ago. Thus, to take one example, in the course of tracing the identity of one man, Pobe Toa, I found some informants who said he was from Holop subclan of the Semin-al and

today to identify with certainty the exact groups the patrol encountered in 1935. At the same time it points up the problem faced by the patrol itself of passing through a social landscape that was constantly in the process of change.

Mombilal Nial and the Raiding Party

One consequence of this complex social and historical situation on the Nembi Plateau was in fact already in motion as the patrol moved out of Kasebi, though they were unaware of it. In May 1935 a youngish man of forceful personality named Mombilal Nial, who normally lived with his mother's people, the Merut, in the region south of the Semin-al, was paying an extended visit to his father's kin at Sezinda. He had relatives among both the Injip and the Semin-al, and he could, by being careful, safely travel from Merut to Sezinda across these two intervening warring alliances. In any case, Mombilal Nial was in Sezinda during the clash at the Korpe defile and was upset and angered over the shooting of his relatives. He wanted vengeance and began traveling along tracks parallel to the patrol route, attempting to incite every group he met to attack them. Nial's was only one voice among many, however, and the people of Shobera and Kasebi decided that the better part of wisdom (especially after what happened at the defile) was to extend hospitality. Undeterred, Mombilal Nial continued on to the Semin-al, where his activities may well have contributed significantly to what happened to the patrol that day.

As the patrol was departing from Kasebi, the old man who had invited them to stay the night before came up to Hides and explained by signs that the next people down the road (that is, the Injip's enemies, the Semin-al) were hostile and that he should be cautious. Hides seems to have interpreted this as warning of a specific plot to attack the patrol. He patted his rifle and indicated that the patrol could take care of itself.

They set off southeastward along a track over the Nembi Plateau. Despite the abundance of food in the past two days, everyone was thin and worn from nearly five months of traveling. One carrier, a Goaribari named Aunai, was too weak to walk and was being carried lashed to a pole like a pig. Hides believed that the weakened condition of patrol members was obvious to the surrounding population and feared it made them look like an easy target to attack.* They passed without incident through two deserted Injip ceremonial grounds and shortly afterwards arrived at

---

others who remembered him as of the Arop of the Merut. It proved impossible to straighten out.

*As a point of interest, no informant in this region ever mentioned thinking the patrol was in a debilitated condition. Most remembered being frightened of it.

a third, where they were met by a crowd of about "two hundred" men. Although these men were still Injip, they appeared to Hides and O'Malley as an entirely new group. All were unarmed and seated on the ground, and a spokesman mimed assurances that they did not wish to fight. However, their silent demeanor and apparent desire for the patrol to be quickly on its way made Hides suspicious. He requested guides to accompany the patrol and show them the track. There was a hurried consultation among the warriors, for the ceremonial ground was at the very border of the enemy territory of the Semin-al, into which they normally did not venture.

Presently, three men agreed to go and led the patrol off. However, they only escorted it out of the ceremonial ground and a hundred meters or so down the track before turning back. Shortly afterwards the patrol heard loud yodeling break out from warriors out of sight in the scrub on either side of them. The Injip were calling out to confirm that the ghosts, *tomo*, or whatever the strange beings might be, were moving on. But Hides and his men, who associated yodeling with impending attack, heard it with a foreboding chill. They proceeded cautiously, watching for ambush.

In the meantime, the warriors of Semin-al, who knew from the yodeling of the past two days that something was up among the Injip, were also keeping a sharp watch. Continual mistrust of their neighbors kept these Nembi warriors constantly on the alert. As women cultivated sweet potato, the men watched over them, and when the men worked the gardens themselves, their weapons were never far from hand. From rises in the terrain men peered across the gullies into the surrounding cane grass for movement along the hidden trails connecting the hamlets and ceremonial grounds. It was on this kind of watch that warriors of the Semin-al first saw the movement of the line of men coming down the track from the direction of their enemies to the north. Sumbual Jun of the Injip remembers that the Semin-al, thinking this was a raiding party, quickly gathered a force and maneuvered around behind it to spring a trap.

The patrol was struggling along a wide but deeply cut path in slippery red clay. On either side the path was enclosed with dense stands of tall cane grass high as a man's head. The burden of bearing the weakened carrier Aunai was exhausting even though six men had been assigned to the task. After moving about 1.5 km beyond the boundaries of Injip, Hides halted the patrol at a grassy knoll to rest, a little to the southwest of the present-day ceremonial ground at Hont. Three tracks led into the clearing: one came from the northwest from the upper Pwe Creek and the Enjua and Obua alliance of clans. From the northeast came the track the patrol had been following, and to the south this track continued through the territory of the Semin-al.

Suddenly a terrific din of yodeling broke out, and a mass of men armed

with bows and "battle axes" appeared rushing upon the patrol from behind, along the track they had just followed. When Hides saw them they
were less than sixty yards away (PR: 80).* He grabbed his rifle and began
shooting into them as they rushed into the clearing. "As they did not stop,
I shouted to O'Malley to protect himself with the police that were with
him and ran down to stand with the sergeant and his four police. When I
reached the sergeant, the natives were upon him at close quarters. Armed
Constable Budua lost his head and started swinging his rifle at a man who
was attacking him with a bone-tipped assegai. He called to me for help,
and I saw him struggling on the ground with his assailant. Two other
natives were going to the assistance of Budua's assailant, and, running
towards the helpless constable, I shot one of his attackers and pulled the
other off him, allowing the latter to run off. The attack was now over; it
had lasted less than a minute. On the tracks held by our assailants I saw
four dead men" (PR: 81).†

Looking back towards where O'Malley stood with the carriers, Hides
saw a large body of warriors coming from behind to attack them. He
called O'Malley and the rest to come down, and they immediately started
moving again.

Here again, in Hides's account of this (and subsequent) battles, he makes
the puzzling mention of native warriors carrying "assegais," short stabbing spears used by Zulu warriors in Africa. No similar weapon is used in
the highlands of New Guinea, so it is difficult to know what he is talking
about. Perhaps some warriors carried an arrow in their hand ready to fit
to a bow string quickly, or even for use for jabbing in close combat. Many
of the Nembi arrows were tipped with broad blades of bamboo or had
long points shaped from human leg or arm bones.

The patrol continued to follow the track through the cultivations. They
paused only long enough to take enough food for the day. About half an
hour later, still hurrying along, Hides, who was in the lead, broke through
a hedge around a cultivation and found himself confronted with a large
group of bowmen wearing headdresses of cassowary feathers and accompanied by other men carrying painted shields and the "short stabbing

---

* In his testimony at the inquiry Hides shortened this distance to 30 yards.
† Budua's account of the incident, given at the inquiry in Kikori runs as follows: "One
man I fire cartridge miss. I fired again and missed. He came at me with a spear and tried to
spear me. I hit the spear with my rifle and knocked it away. He came at me again and caught
me by the hair. We struggled and we fell. I was underneath, he on top. He pulled out his
Kosilo [what Hides called a "battle ax"] and try to break my head. I held it. I turned him
over in the struggle and got on top. I called out to Taubada, I fright. Taubada came. I did not
see Taubada shoot a man then. I saw the body nearby afterwards. I got up when Mr. Hides
came and let the man go. Mr. Hides told me to let him go. Mr. Hides no shoot that man, I
no shoot that man, we let him go. The man that Mr. Hides shot—his body was near me like
this when I got up (indicates three yards)" (IQ, Budua's testimony).

spears." There was no cover for himself or the two police with him and the foremost native had his bow drawn on them not 35 m away. It is not clear whether the men actually started to advance, but Hides thought they were about to and opened fire. "The rush had to be stopped," he reported, "[or] we would have been at close quarters with these men in no time" (PR: 81).

Fearful that some of his men would be injured or the patrol trapped, Hides now temporarily abandoned any attempt to make friendly contact and was ready to shoot first and ask questions later. Two of the warriors fell, and the rest broke and made off. Hides was convinced they were the same group that had attacked the patrol earlier. About half a kilometer farther on, as the patrol was threading its way between some limestone pinnacles, the same warriors regrouped and confronted them again. "There was no mistaking their intention," Hides wrote in his report, "for every man was closing in on us. I therefore ordered O'Malley and the police to fire again. I saw two men fall, and then the attackers fell apart, some running to the right and some to the left" (PR: 82).

Some of these repeated attacks may well have resulted from Mombilal Nial's rallying the warriors of the Semin-al. Hides was astonished at the warriors' determination; they were quite unlike any Papuan fighters he had encountered before. By now, with all the yodeling and movement of armed men throughout the countryside, the situation seemed increasingly perilous. Aware that he and his men were advancing with their fingers constantly on the trigger, Hides later attempted to explain the situation in his book.

"I cannot describe the dangers and difficulties of the expedition at this stage. I thought at the time of the sea captain who had lost his vessel and who, upon being asked by the board of inquiry if he had anything to say, replied that he had had to decide in a few seconds a question that had taken the board weeks to consider. And so it was in this case. . . . After the last treacherous attack . . . from which we were extremely lucky to escape without casualties, I could not afford to give them any further opportunities. If four or five of our party were wounded . . . there was no one to carry them, and our food situation was precarious. . . . If they [trapped] us, I was certain none of the party would reach the coast alive" (PW: 130).

Today the Semin-al do not remember these repeated clashes clearly. The names of some of those who were killed are remembered, but the exact places and circumstances, and which Semin-al groups they belonged to, are forgotten.

Continuing along the path, the patrol came upon a young man with a bow and arrows. Hides had him disarmed and his bow and arrows broken. He tried to make him understand by signs that the patrol had come in peace and did not wish to fight. He then sent him off to convey the message to the warriors who could be heard yodeling all around in the high grass, hoping to get them to calm down.

The Stand at Pembi Andaa

Whether this message had an effect on the warriors of the Semin-al is unclear, for shortly thereafter, Hides and O'Malley and the patrol crossed the southern boundary of their territory and began to move through the hamlets and ceremonial grounds of the Merut. The Merut were enemies of the Semin-al alliance and at the time deeply involved in hostilities with them. The patrol was headed southeastwards through the scrub fallow land overlooking the Nembi Valley. Opposite them, near the southern borders of Merut territory, the Merut warriors had sent their women, children, and pigs for refuge from the fighting with the Semin-al.

It didn't take long for the Merut warriors, with all the yodeling and shooting over the Semin-al border, to locate the patrol heading right toward their families' places of refuge. Here again, the Nembi account of what happened next is unclear. Ebi Abeial remembered that many of the Merut men were rushing to where the women and children were hidden to defend them. According to him, the patrol police mistook the movement of these warriors for the buildup of an attack on the patrol. All the time other warriors were yelling at the patrol to leave the place and go to the Pwe Pond El (their enemies) and kill them. Still others were said to be calling out for sugarcane, bananas, and sweet potatoes to be brought to the patrol. Amidst this, no doubt, Mombilal Nial returned to his home territory and began urging his friends and relatives to attack. The picture is one of confusion, but the Merut were very determined, and some of them decided to go for attack.

Meanwhile the patrol had traveled about 1.5 km from where Hides had sent the youth off with the message of peace to the Semin-al. The officers had been hoping that things would begin to calm down. But, upon looking back, Hides saw: "armed men coming from all directions on the road behind us, all of them showing they had no intention of ceasing hostilities. They crowded along the road, and ran down side tracks, shouting and yodeling; and sometimes, when well out of range, a man would let fly an arrow as a taunt. . . . Their determination was discomfiting, so I decided to camp while we had yet time" (PW: 131).

Looking ahead, across a narrow ravine, Hides saw a defensible spot: a small "farmhouse" built on a flat space on top of a rise, partly surrounded by impenetrable cane grass. This was a place known locally as

Pembi Andaa. As the officers came up into the clearing, they found about twenty warriors waiting for them. They were fully armed but apparently not hostile. At another time this might have been an opportunity to make peaceful contact, but with the mass of shouting, yodeling warriors a short way down the track behind them, Hides felt that the situation was developing too fast. He and O'Malley greeted the men by the house but explained by signs that they could stay only if they put away their arms. They seemed to understand but made no move to comply. However, they soon left of their own accord. As the rest of the patrol straggled in, Hides quickly surveyed the situation.

Three tracks led into the area, one from the east, one from the west, and one from the north. The former two were deeply cut into the clay and practically roofed over by the cane grass along the edges. The other track went up over a rise to a space where they pitched the camp. Hides dispatched a carrier under police escort to get water and others to help carry in Aunai. The water party and the last of the carriers arrived back in camp at the same time with the report that massed warriors were closing in from two sides. Hides sent all the carriers into the farmhouse and told them not to move, got O'Malley to supervise setting up the officers' tent fly, and posted his most steady and trusted police to watch each of the three tracks into camp while replacements stood ready if any of them should be wounded. The rest of the police were stationed around the farmhouse in case the warriors should break through into the camp. If that happened, it would probably be the end for the patrol. Hides was depending on the impenetrable cane grass around the clearing, and the narrow entrances to the paths to render the place defensible.

The yodeling and shouting of hundreds of warriors came from all around them, and then the camp was attacked. "A number of men rushed the camp from three directions," Hides later reported to the inquiry; "[they had] bows and arrows in their hands [and were] firing at us as they came. While guarding one track, I narrowly escaped an arrow in the back from a track opposite me. I ordered the police to open fire and to prevent any man getting into camp. . . . The method adopted by the attackers was —after the first rush had been beaten off—they would steal up covered by [the] grass and tunnel-like tracks and fire point blank at us from ten or fifteen yards. They were shot in the very act of firing at us" (IQ: 5).

Given the nature of the pathways and the cane grass, it took only three men to effectively hold off the attackers, while Hides, O'Malley, and the rest of the police held positions around the farmhouse guarding the carriers. The three police guards at the "tunnel" entrances were now firing in earnest. The nature of the tracks made it possible for Merut warriors to come within 5–6 m of them to fire their arrows. The confusion and desperation of the situation was described at the inquest at Kikori by Sergeant Orai.

"The people began to come like sands. We put guards, Agoti one track, Dekadua one track, Koriki one track, all guards. An arrow came in amongst us [the one that almost hit Hides in the back]. Another man came and fired at us, and Dekadua shot him. Another track, another man came, Koriki shot him. Another man came behind him to take his place, and Koriki shot him too. Another man came up to Agoti with his bow pulled, and Agoti shot him. Another man came up to take the dead man's place, and Agoti shot him. I was looking after the carriers. I was not fighting. I said to the police, 'If any of you is killed, I will take your place.' Mr. Hides and Mr. O'Malley were with me and the carriers in the camp. Some of the natives got right up close to the camp—like this. If we and the white men were soft that day, we all dead men in that place. They came up by the tracks again and again, and the guards shot them in the track and they ran into the sirio [cane] grass and died there. I no see them. I see only five bodies on the tracks. They did not run away, they came [in order to] surround the fly and kill us. I went to Agoti and told him to be strong; I told him to shoot straight if they tried to shoot him. I said 'Be careful, be quick or you will be dead.' I went to Koriki and told him the same—this in the middle of the fight. . . . I went to Dekadua and told him the same. I went back to the fly and told the carriers not to move or they would be dead" (*IQ*: 13–14).

Hides, himself making the rounds of his guards, came upon Agoti "crouched by the side of the eastern track with his left shoulder forced into a niche in the clay, and many arrows were embedded in the clay all around him. As I crouched behind him, just after he had repulsed the first rush, I asked after the present temper of the attackers.

" 'These people do not know how to run,' Agoti said without taking his eyes off the track. 'What shall we do, Taubada? No plenty cartridge.'

"I told him to continue as he was doing. Agoti had the worst track to guard on that terrible afternoon, and I don't think any other constable could have stood the constant strain. This big silent Agoti, this brave unassuming Papuan; no reward would be too high for his conduct.

"Agoti—is he dead?' would be the continual query of the carriers. They had great faith in this constable" (*PW*: 134).

The fight began at about three in the afternoon and lasted until sundown. Hides estimated that the constables stopped about six charges. About an hour after the last rush had been repulsed, an old man appeared on a rise about 200 m away and, waving a fern branch, shouted something three times, then disappeared. This was undoubtedly the ceremonial fern used to soak up pig's blood as an offering to the ghosts and ancestors at the *kaebal* ritual (see p. 136). The old man was telling them to go away and leave the Merut in peace.

Quiet fell over the camp. After all the shooting, Hides saw only two dead warriors, and those were not more than 10 m from the tent fly, their bows and arrows still in their hands. Whatever other bodies there were lay out of sight down the tracks. Hides had hurricane lanterns, filled with nearly the last of their kerosene, hung on sticks in the middle of the eastern and western tracks, and he posted guards all night.

Among the Merut, the effect of the rifles had been devastating. Hides estimated six or seven might have been killed (*PR*: 85); the actual number was fourteen (not counting the eight shot previously among the Semin-al).* Many more were wounded. The bodies lay on the tracks where they fell. They were collected together the next day after the patrol moved on and were hurriedly placed without funeral on ledges of the limestone cliffs of nearby pinnacles, still in their feathers and all that they had been wearing, including any valuable pearlshell. The people of Merut and Semin-al were in a state of shock. Despite their familiarity with fighting, they had never experienced anything like this before. They held no ceremony, no period of keening over the dead. There were no mortuary payments of pearlshells and pigs to the clans of the mothers of the dead and no real thoughts of vengeance. On whom could one take revenge? Whether they were spirits or men, they were gone the next day.

Meanwhile, during the night, as the carriers slept and Hides and O'Malley were sitting by the fire, the sick carrier Aunai died. He was buried in the early dawn, and the spot concealed with ashes and leaves. That night also, Hides felt the first pangs of the severe dysentery that was to plague him for the rest of the patrol and almost take his life. The pain was so intense that he was unable to sleep. At dawn he struggled to his feet and gave the order for the patrol to move on. They proceeded cautiously, watchful for ambush. But a silence lay over the countryside, and they had advanced more than a kilometer through the grass mounds and hollows before the local people realized they were on the move.

Back at Pembi Andaa, while the Merut were collecting their dead, Mombilal Nial and his relatives were searching for the body of their clan brother Kear Koriap in the cane grass. Searching in the clearing of the farmhouse, they discovered the grave of Aunai, and uncovered him. Mombilal Nial claimed he himself had shot the dead carrier with an arrow during the

* Those of the Semin-al killed were Wangal Lawob, Shobal Sonk, Polonk Shom, and Pobe Ton (wounded and later died). Four others were wounded but recovered. Those killed among the Merut were Kear, Masawan, Pealupi, Unjtanda, Enja Kolep, Olshem, Melanek, Kalpael, Wnmowi, Tomp, Kont, Horobal, Moresink, and Ol.

fight, and the grave was quickly filled in again. This story spread throughout the region and established the renown of Mombilal Nial.

A Trying Day

As the patrol continued along the track, they began to be followed by groups of unarmed men who, silent and watchful, kept their distance. The track again led to the edge of the Nembi Valley, and they could see the river meandering through the cultivations below. In the background, to the northeast, was the precipitous limestone wall of the Nembi-Lai divide. Hides, suffering excruciating stomach pain, assessed the situation. Below them, the track led down through the dense population of the valley floor. Anxious to avoid further confrontations, Hides headed the patrol along a track skirting the southern margin of the valley where the population appeared somewhat less dense. However, this forced them to descend part way down the valley side (close to the present-day Tindom hill). A large group of armed warriors stood waiting for them at the edge of some gardens. These were the Mborl people, traditional enemies of the Merut and, like them, renowned as fierce warriors. Looking back, Hides saw the large crowd of Merut who had been following him sitting on a grassy hill (on their side of the boundary), watching to see what would happen. Despite their warlike readiness, however, the Mborl seemed willing to parley: in front of the massed warriors three old men were sitting silently on the ground. In the absence of informants who remember this incident, it is impossible to say whether the Mborl had heard anything of the fight at Pembi Andaa the day before or whether this influenced their present posture.

Hides halted the patrol and advanced by himself with two constables to explain by pantomime that the patrol came in peace, that they were hungry and wanted food, and that the people behind them had attacked them the day before. The warriors remained impassive, affecting an air of indifference, as though they did not understand. Like others before them, they too were uncertain how to respond. In a moment of inspiration, Hides gave a bushknife to one of the old men as a gesture of good will. This seemed to break the ice. The man turned to the others and gave an excited speech, which Hides thought seemed positively inclined towards the patrol. The other warriors remained unmoved, and before the old man could accommodate this response, Hides seized the opportunity to ask him if he would guide the patrol towards the south. After a moment's thought, the man jumped up and, taking constable Agoti by the hand, led off. About forty warriors—probably his followers and relatives—put down their weapons and accompanied them. As they started moving, Agoti turned to Hides and commented: "A big fight was sleeping here, Taubada, but the old man's belly has changed and it will not come now" (PW: 139).

Nevertheless, it was touch and go. The armed warriors, yodeling, rattling their arrows, and snapping their bow strings, followed behind, flanked them, and ran across the path in front. They continually encircled and pressed upon the patrol. In this nerve-racking situation, Hides kept the old man near and had him shout at the warriors to move back whenever they seemed to approach too close.

They walked south and southwestward back up the valley side onto a small cleared tableland separating the Nembi Valley and the northeastern portion of the Nembi Plateau from the southern plateau and Emia Creek. There they arrived at an archway built over the track. It was the boundary of the territory of the Palom, Pelen, Puit, and Murupa clans, enemies of the Mborl.* Their guide bid them farewell, and he and the yodeling warriors departed. Entering through the arch, the patrol continued alone.

After a time they encountered another group of men, who were unarmed but wary. They greeted the patrol in a friendly manner. They had not yet, in fact, heard of the battle with the Merut at Pembi Andaa the day before. As they became aware of the exhausted and half-starved condition of the carriers, however, their wariness turned to open arrogance and contempt. As the day wore on, their increasingly provocative and intimidating tone and their rattling of arrows and pressing in on the patrol became difficult to bear. One of the carriers, a man named Kaivamore, cracked under the strain and began to cry and wail that all was lost. This only made matters worse, Hides wrote, for: "The natives appeared to think we were all of the same calibre as this cowardly carrier. They laughed openly at him and soon commenced to jeer at us" (PR: 86; PW: 140).

The patrol was experiencing the difficulties of traveling in a weakened condition through a region where violence was common and every man a hardened fighter. These warriors were capable of enthusiastic friendship but were also contemptuous of the weak and quick to take advantage where they perceived vulnerability. They were continually testing the situation and were ready to act on any show of uncertainty with confrontation.

The debility of the members of the patrol and Hides's desire to avoid violence required that he exercise the greatest restraint at the provocative treatment of these naturally proud and independent warriors—and at the same time sense exactly when to be decisive and firm. It was here that

* The Palom, Pelen, Puit, and Murupa were allied to clans in the neighboring southern Nembi Valley, but fighting with the Mborl, Merut, and other clans on the Nembi Plateau and the Nembi Valley to the north.

Hides's courage, his intuitions about the people and the situation they were in, and his qualities as a leader were most severely tested. His patrol report conveys the tone of a man struggling between the temptations of exhausted passivity and the rigor of grim determination.

A young warrior named Chou attached himself to the patrol as a self-appointed guide. He led them through the ceremonial grounds of Essenda-*hauma* and Ulim-*hauma* of the Pelen and Palom clans and headed towards the Upa Basin. While they were going along, a young man standing with a group of warriors a little way off the track suddenly drew his bow and fired an arrow directly at O'Malley. This was probably intended more as a test of mettle than an actual attack, to see what the strangers would do. He missed (not necessarily intentionally), but Chou immediately made Hides sit down, forcing him, in effect, to signal he was not going to be put out by this provocation. Hides for his part was paralyzed with astonishment.

"What could I do? . . . They had made no further act of war. One could not shoot them down in cold blood. As O'Malley and I sat wondering what the next action would be, this same youth who had fired the arrow . . . came up and stood before us with his arms folded. Chou would look at him and then look at us. O'Malley . . . accused the youth of having fired the arrow, and the young man nodded and smiled as though to say: 'What are you going to do about it?' " (*PW*: 141).

Chou then indicated that he wanted to lead the patrol down to the valley flats. Hides refused, wishing to avoid that heavily populated area. Chou insisted, however; taking Hides by the hand, he led him and the patrol on. "There was nothing else to do but follow him," Hides wrote later, but he suspected Chou was up to something. "I was determined they would not trap us. One mistake on our part now, and no member of the party would reach the coast" (*PW*: 142).

He was in this frame of mind when Chou led them towards the Koryi-ripa ceremonial ground of Wolunk-*hauma* belonging to the Pwe Pond El alliance of clans. This *hauma* was built in a defensive position on a spur overlooking the gorge of the lower Emia Creek and was surrounded by a high palisade—a common feature in the region. Inside were seated about "three hundred men," all with "battle axes" in their belts. Chou and the others invited the patrol to come inside and sit down, offering sugarcane and bananas for refreshment. Nearby Hides saw freshly cut poles and vine rope laid aside for some immediate purpose. Believing these to be the accoutrements of capture, he sensed a trap. Conferring quickly with Sergeant Orai, he and O'Malley and four constables entered the stockade and stood guard while the rest of the police escorted the carrier line through and out the other side. The natives jumped up to urge the hungry men to sit down and eat but they passed on by, leaving their hosts discomfited.

When the whole patrol was safely out of the enclosure, Hides asked Chou to guide them on, but the latter laughed at him and angrily indicated that he would go no further. Other warriors in the group prevailed upon him to go, however, and he eventually came along. All the men in the stockade retrieved bows and arrows from somewhere and accompanied the patrol along flanking paths on each side of the route.

From Hides's point of view, the natives, especially Chou, were becoming increasingly treacherous. Chou seemed to be trying alternately to dominate, intimidate, mislead, and entrap the patrol. After leaving Wolunk stockade, Chou became conspicuously more truculent. In response to directives from the warriors flanking the patrol, he shoved his way among the carriers counting their weapons and demanding that Hides break the (unstrung) bows that some of them carried. Hides broke one to appease him, but Chou remained obstinate. Hides angrily threw him off the track and proceeded. Further on Chou demanded to be given an axe and attempted to wrest one from one of the carriers. It seemed clear to Hides that he was trying to provoke a fight. The bands of warriors were watching keenly from nearby. "Kick him away," O'Malley suggested. The police too were spoiling to punish him. However, Hides, wishing to avoid possible bloodshed, gave him the axe. But to save face for surrendering to this peremptory demand, he indicated to Chou that he expected to be supplied with food later on (*PW*: 144).

What was really happening here? Was the invitation at Wolunk-*hauma* an offer of hospitality that Hides mistakenly turned down, or was it really a trap as he suspected?* Who was the young guide Chou? What was he trying to accomplish in dealing so provocatively with the patrol in the way that he did? We do not know.

During the 1940's and 1950's, malaria moved into the lower Nembi Valley and the Emia Creek from the Erave Valley and started a chain of events —deaths from the disease itself, deaths from the fighting that followed upon those deaths, and subsequent out-migration of local people—that has left almost nobody in the lower Nembi area today who actually saw the patrol. As a result, no one today can remember who it was who led Hides and O'Malley to Wolunk-*hauma*. "Chou" is not even a name used on the plateau. The word *chu* (together with *fa*, *fu*, *pu*) is a gloss of the imperative verb "you go!" used in the sense of "piss off!" or "fuck off." Perhaps this is what the young warrior was saying to the patrol (Hides: "What is your name?" Answer: "Fuck off!").

---

* The purpose of the mysterious poles and vine rope that originally led Hides to suspect a trap remains obscure. Hides seems to have thought they were for trussing captives—or victims for a cannibal feast. Conceivably they could have had some such purpose (though the Nembi were never cannibals), but it is more likely they were nothing more than construction materials put aside for the repair or further construction of the stockade.

One can speculate that whether this man had brought the patrol to Wolunk-*hauma* to offer them hospitality or to entrap them, his failure to accomplish either of these objectives may have made him feel he lost face with his fellows. If this was so, some of his subsequent provocative behavior might be interpreted as an attempt to "pay back" the patrol or extract some compensatory acknowledgment that would restore his standing in the situation in front of his clansmen. But the fact remains we have no local accounts.

Most people have heard stories—especially about the killings in the Merut territory—and many can trace the patrol route through their territory, but there is no detailed memory of the majority of the events that Hides describes. Wolunk-*hauma* is now abandoned (though the site can still be distinguished through the cane grass on top of its spur), and its owners, the Koryiripa clan, are reduced to two households, both living with neighboring clans.

The Possum Hunters

Hides's way of dealing with the difficulties he and his men met with that day was to keep moving, while keeping close watch on every single native all the time. It was now getting late in the afternoon, and they still had to find a place to camp. Hides chose a spot that could be easily defended at the foot of a limestone pinnacle a few hundred meters from present-day Aib, overlooking the lower Emia gorge. The patrol had eaten almost nothing that day, and the carriers dropped with exhaustion on the ground. It had also been one of the longest day's treks for some time. Hides and O'Malley had made repeated requests for food to every group they had encountered, but the Nembi had simply ignored them or demanded an outrageous price for a very small amount, or offered food as an enticement to trap them. In all fairness, there may not have been much food available. The continual warfare among the Nembi and the repeated devastation of gardens frequently resulted in food shortages in the region in the 1930's. On the other hand, unlike the Huli and Wola, the people in the lower Nembi region were familiar with steel and prized it highly. Yet, inexplicably, they were not willing to trade for it. Although the natives came in large crowds to view the patrol as it set up its ragged tent flies, no one offered to sell them any food. Instead they continued to mock and deride the exhausted party. Chou came up to where the carriers lay sick and exhausted on the ground and shoved one inert body with his foot, provoking great laughter. The police were furious and spoiling to teach him a lesson, but Hides restrained them, sensing that the surrounding warriors were just waiting for an excuse to start something.

It is difficult to assess the feelings of the Nembi from our point in time. It is not unreasonable to suppose that, like the people higher up the valley, they simply did not know how to comprehend what was happening. Were these fearsome yet pathetic creatures *hundabi tomo* ("red spirits"), or were they ordinary men? The Nembi were probably much more uncertain and frightened than they let on, but they were also dealing with the situation as they normally dealt with situations of danger and uncertainty in their lives: by projecting an arrogant attitude and testing and provoking the opposition at every point to locate its vulnerability. Their real mixture of feelings is perhaps revealed in a curious incident remembered by Hides in his book.

"As I lay on my dirty canvas bed [that evening], I was suddenly aroused with a terrific din of screaming and laughter, and I saw hundreds of men and boys rushing in a frightened manner down the cultivation away from us. I thought that perhaps one of the police had assaulted an insolent native, and they were fleeing in fear; but I found on inquiring that the natives were just having a game. They all came back and stood calmly walking around us again, when one man without any reason whatever suddenly screamed and bolted from us, and the crowd, taking their cue from him all screamed and did likewise. It was their little game, pretending to be frightened of such a miserable little party as our own" (*PW*: 145–46).

While Hides interpreted this as mockery (and doubtless in part it was), one cannot help but be struck with the similarity of this game to that played by children around the world in coming to terms with something they fear but are beginning to realize will probably not hurt them. Papuan children (or middle-class kids in the West for that matter) can sometimes be seen approaching a dead snake or other fearsome object and then fleeing from it, repeating the performance again and again. Whatever mockery the Nembi may have intended by this behavior towards the patrol, it is difficult to believe that it did not express real feelings of fear and ambivalence at another level.

In any case, after a day of such difficulties and ill-treatment, Hides fully expected treachery that night. He had a lamp filled with the last of the kerosene and, hanging it on a pole to light the perimeter of the camp, posted a strong guard with instructions to shoot any intruders on sight. Not long after dark, his fears were justified.

"At about 8 P.M. there was an attack upon the camp, Dekadua meeting the rush from the point where he was on guard and shooting the foremost native: and fearing a second more determined rush in the darkness, I drew the guards in closer and gave them instructions that should this happen they were not to attempt to hold the natives themselves but to fall back and all form in front of the flies. Every member of the party stood to for the rest of the night" (*PW*: 146).

Unfortunately, in one of those ironies that make a travesty of our most considered judgments, Hides was mistaken. The hurricane lamp he left burning near the camp threw an eerie light that was reflected back from the limestone behind it. According to Nenja Aibpeling of Aib, who, when interviewed in 1986, was a blind and crippled old man dependent on a grandchild to lead him about, it was an unnatural light that no one in the valley had ever seen before. Two men, Ebobi Wa and his brother Palonk, had gone off into the forest the previous night to hunt for possums, taking advantage of the light of the waxing moon. They did not see the arrival of the patrol or the setting up of the camp at Aib. The first thing they saw as they returned late that evening was the twinkling light of the hurricane lamp below them in the clearing. It was like nothing they had seen before —was it the moon itself or part of it that had fallen from the sky? Cautiously they crept down towards it in the undergrowth to see what it was. Constable Dekadua was standing guard at the camp. Hearing rustling in the bushes and following the orders he had been given, he raised his rifle and fired. Ebobi Wa fell half into the bushes with his entrails spilling across the path. His brother fled in terror.

According to Nenja one shot was heard. O'Malley, in his testimony at the inquiry, also reported one shot. Dekadua in his testimony recalled the incident this way: "I guard. They came up. . . . Plenty, plenty they came and close in on us. They came up like (crawling on hands and knees with bows and arrows). All right, I no fire. They came close like this (a few yards), and I shot the first man. It was nearly dark, and I could not see well; they came up, and I fired again. I no see if I hit or miss. I fired four or five times" (*IQ*, Dekadua's testimony). Perhaps, given the stresses of the day, this is what he really believed happened, but only two men were actually approaching the camp. It was being in the wrong place at the wrong time that caused Ebobi's death.

The people of Aib retrieved Ebobi's body later that night, and his relatives began wailing in grief and calling out the news across the valley. "Howling and yodeling commenced," Hides noted. "It started in the farmhouses below and was taken up for what seemed miles around. [It] even came to us from the valley flats below in a maddening din. And it kept us up till daylight the following morning" (*PR*: 89).

Continuing Difficulties

All night the wailing and yodeling from the surrounding hamlets up and down the valley led Hides and O'Malley to believe that the natives were gathering from all parts of the region to attack them. To preclude this, they roused the carriers by starlight, packed their gear, and were on their way at dawn. Thick morning mists filled the limestone basins and helped conceal their movements.

At Aib the main path drops to the floor of the Emia gorge to the southeast and is overhung with cane grass—more a tunnel than a track—the perfect spot for an ambush. Hides viewed this with suspicion. He and O'Malley still wanted at all costs to avoid moving down into the narrow valley. They began searching for a track that would lead southwards up over the plateau away from the population. They traveled now through a landscape of small steep cultivated basins among cliffs and limestone pinnacles that loomed ghostly white in the morning mists.

As soon as day broke, the Nembi warriors found them. Hides recalled in his book: "The sun had not long risen when armed men began to appear all around us. . . . There were hundreds of these natives, old men and young men, and all of them armed with bows and shields. They encircled us continually, crossing our path in front and rear and yodeling all the time. Their yellow reed arrows, wet with dew, flashed in the morning sun. I was still trying hard to find a road that would lead us out of this dense population, for our position was becoming more and more dangerous; the whole party was incredibly weak, and we were forced to halt at short intervals for a rest" (PW: 148).

Indeed, Hides was very ill, much worse than the day before. His eyesight was affected, and he was so weak he had to remove his heavy patrol boots because he could no longer lift his feet to walk. He felt his strength ebbing away. "Never have I been through such a trying experience," he wrote, "and never have circumstances given me such a hopeless outlook" (PW: 147). If he sometimes seemed barely able to control the situation, he did not lose his intuition, courage, or determination.

To O'Malley he seemed heroic. In a revealing account quoted by Hides's biographer O'Malley described an incident from that day: "We came to a steep climb. As we neared the top, the leading constable stopped, then came back down the track informing us that just above the top of the rise was a village and that hundreds of people, all armed, were waiting there. Hides asked to sit down and rest, and after a short time he said, 'It's about time we got going.' He refused all help, drew himself to a standing position and marched at the front of the patrol to the village. With sign language he asked for food. Each of the people were carrying small bundles of sugarcane, and Hides extended knives to them in payment. With grins on their faces they handed over the sugarcane and then left the village. As the last man disappeared over the ridge, Hides, just before he collapsed, called out to the carriers, 'Do not eat the sugarcane unless you peel it.' It is difficult to control hungry men and some of the carriers munched into the cane and became violently ill. I said to Hides later, 'How did you know something was wrong with the sugarcane?' and his reply came back 'I suspected something—I did not like the grins on their faces.' I can still remember that walk of Hides . . . one could see the strain and the lines of pain in his face, but he was not going to show those savages that he was weak and ill" (Sinclair 1969: 158).

The morning wore on. The patrol moved slowly along still looking for a route away from the valley and stopping frequently to rest. The air was filled with yodeling and the sound of bows and arrows rattling against wooden shields. Nembi warriors were all around them.

Hides vividly describes the situation with these warriors in his book, claiming from time to time that they numbered over a thousand. Despite the undoubtedly beleaguered situation of the patrol, this was a considerable exaggeration. At Aib and along the tracks leading from it a thousand warriors could not possibly have gathered even if there were a thousand in the area. The Petum, Wogia, Mae-Mui, and Heroba-Yandalopa clans of the area could not muster more than a few hundred fully armed warriors at any one time. It is clear, however, when one stands where Hides must have stood that even one hundred would have seemed a very large number. The path is narrow. To the east lies the gorge of the Emia Creek and to the west the towering limestone pinnacles of the southern Nembi Plateau. A hundred excited Nembi warriors massed in these confines, running back and forth and yodeling, would have been a daunting sight indeed. Moreover, they were fierce and determined. They rushed the patrol on two occasions as it was trying to find its way across the rugged countryside and had to be driven back with rifle fire. Four Nembi warriors were killed.

The country here is laced with a confusing network of foot paths, and without a guide the patrol exhausted itself all morning following one after another wrong turn and then having to retrace its steps. Finally the police located a track leading south that wound steeply up and over the side of the valley. Ignoring the blandishments of a group of warriors trying to lure them into the valley, Hides led the patrol upwards between the pinnacles and cultivations towards the divide to the Om Creek basin. Not far below them on the valley track a crowd of warriors who had been lying in ambush broke cover yelling with rage and frustration. Safely out of reach, the patrol could see below to the southeast the Emia Creek snaking its way between cliffs of limestone before disappearing underground. They reached the timber above the sweet potato gardens and breasted the top of the ridge.

As they dropped into the coolness of the broad forested basin on the other side, it seemed to Hides that they were in a changed world. The yodeling warriors were left behind, and they found themselves among the quiet farmsteads of the Wogia-Pengerup and Angaspa people. They arrived at the Mondomap-*hauma* and there met an old man. Hides gave him an axe, and he invited the patrol to stay the night at the *hauma*, then left to gather people to bring food. The people were friendly and seemed not the least frightened of the patrol. "What a difference it was," Hides wrote, "the relief of getting away from native treachery and to be free of the yodeling—if only for a few hours—was indescribable" (*PW*: 151).

Today, again because of the toll malaria has taken on the region, no one remembers when Hides and O'Malley and their men came out of the trees from the northeast or who the old man was who befriended them. In the absence of informants, it is impossible to know what the people thought. It is quite possible, given their position on the trade route, that they had heard something of European patrols farther south. In any case, given the hostility of the warriors of the Emia, it seems remarkable that those of the Om should greet Hides and O'Malley and their men with such outgoing friendliness. To Hides the journey seemed full of such inexplicable contrasts.

Seated peacefully around the campfires among these friendly people, with police and carriers eating well, Hides's mood began to lift. He had a feeling they were not far from the goal of their journey and with the hostile warriors for the moment behind them there returned his old enthusiasm for exploration. "With plenty of food," he wrote, forgetting his illness, "good tents and plenty of equipment, we would not have minded wandering on indefinitely, and taking our time" (*PR*: 90).

This evening was an interlude in their trials. Much later, while Hides was writing his book, he pictured himself that evening looking affectionately over at his carriers and reflecting on their loyal character and the sacrifices they had made.

"Kemane, the bright and cheerful old Goaribari, loyal and courageous always, was scraping the ashes from cooked potatoes for O'Malley. . . . Kemane would hand O'Malley two potatoes and then hold up a third from the fire and look at (him). . . . O'Malley would tell him to eat that one.

" 'Thank you, thank you, Taubada,' Kemane would say in his English, and stuff the half-baked potato into his mouth. He was like a child, or a faithful dog that was happy because he saw his master happy.

"God help all of them, I thought. Nothing was too good for them; they had shown, as many others of their kind, just how big and good are some of the things in the heart of the Papuan. In crossing the limestone barrier, and in the weeks before it, they had given all their strength in their heroic work [when there were supplies to carry], and now it was our sacred duty to take every care of them" (*PW*: 151).

The next day the patrol climbed the eastern wall of the Om Basin and emerged into open country again. Below them 3–4 km away flowed the waters of a large river. The guides who had accompanied them pointed to it and said "Elai." This was the Erave River, which forms the upper reaches of the Purari. Hides knew instinctively that he had reached his goal. From this vantage point overlooking the Erave they could see the broad, heavily populated grassland valleys of the Mendi, Anga, Angura, and Kagua rivers, which converged upon it from the north and east. To the south the Erave River flowed into an immense gorge in the limestone barrier. Hides now weighed up their options: "To the eastwards, and then possibly to the southeastwards we were assured of food—even if the inhabitants were unfriendly and would not give; to the southeastwards was the hungry, uninhabited gorge . . . but this gorge might lead us quickly down to the Purari or Erewa [Erave] as it is called in its upper reaches. . . . We were all tired of unfriendly natives, and I had a growing fear the carriers would not last much longer. I decided we would go down into the gorge" (PR: 90).

The patrol descended into the Erave Valley alone, as their friendly guides were not on good terms with the people there. They passed through the country of the Angaspa at Tiga-*hauma*. Farther down were the Kari-Engi. These people, together with the Abrup and Kembeney of Urida still farther down the valley, had direct links with the Mubi River lowlands and Lake Kutubu to the west and southwest. Many of them spoke not only Nembi, but also Foi, the language of Lake Kutubu, and Kewa, the speech of the people across the Erave. Today their former gardens can be seen as mounds and ditches beneath the cane grass and secondary bush. Because of malaria, hepatitis and other diseases, very few people live in this part of the Erave Valley nowadays, in spite of its former importance on the trade routes of the region.

As the patrol descended into the valley, Hides noticed that the settlement pattern was changing. The scattered hamlets and farmsteads found in the highlands they had been traveling through in the last three weeks now gave way to villages reminiscent of those on the Papuan coast. They seemed to be coming back to more familiar country.

After the friendly reception given the patrol by the people in the Om Basin, that which they received from people of the Erave Valley was a disappointment. As had happened before, the people were wary of strangers who came from the territory of their enemies and so greeted them with reserve. Once again Hides's appeals for food were ignored, or people demanded outrageous prices for very little offered. Hides tried giving presents of steel to men he hoped might be influential on their behalf—but without result. He was frustrated at what he saw as the lack of common human sympathy in these people whom he believed could clearly see the patrol was in need. They were able to get no food from them.

The following day, as the patrol moved slowly southward along the Erave Valley local warriors once again tried to trick them into an ambush.* Hides, ill as he was, was by now thoroughly exasperated with this kind of treatment. So, recognizing some of those who had tried to ambush them standing in the next village they entered, Hides had the biggest and most striking-looking man arrested and handcuffed. "I considered I [was] justified in arresting [this man] not just for the reason of making him answer a charge of attempted murder, but to use him as a means of bringing enlightenment to his inhospitable people" (PR: 92).

Just how Hides meant to accomplish this is unclear. It was foolish to contemplate bringing this man all the way back to Kikori. But Hides evidently felt the need to do something to satisfy the patrol's frustration with the constant changeability, hostility, and lack of generosity of the local people. In effect, the man they arrested was less an example than a hostage.

The arrest was made without fuss. Hides made a speech to explain why he had taken the man and told the people they would now have to provide the patrol with food. He ordered the police to shoot two pigs (which he paid for), and the patrol moved out of the village in close order across the cultivations. By the end of the afternoon they were approaching the funnel of the gorge. Apparently no warriors followed them, though from the sullen demeanor of the villagers as they left, Hides and O'Malley believed that they had not seen the end of it.

Their situation was not good. There were cultivations visible across the river, but little food on the side they were traveling, and the country ahead appeared timbered and largely uninhabited. They had managed to gather about two days' supply of poor quality sweet potatoes by robbing some cultivations near the village. The remaining reserve of rice they had saved for crossing the limestone barrier (at the cost of almost starving the carriers) was woefully small. Hides himself continued to be very ill, and it was all he could do to keep moving. Indeed, over the last four campsites, the patrol seems not to have covered more than about 9–10 km. Hides could hardly eat anything, his pain was intense, and he could only sleep by taking liberal doses of chlorodyne. His main objective at this point was to reach the coast safely, to win through before they were massacred or died from starvation, exhaustion, and disease.

The following day Hides was too ill to travel. While they rested in camp, they were visited by a large group of insolent but unarmed natives. These men spoke to the prisoner for a while, and then one of them approached Sergeant Orai and inquired which way the patrol planned to travel the

---

* The following material is taken almost entirely from Hides's account. Past this point in the Erave Valley today there are very few inhabitants and no one who remembers the passage of the patrol.

next day. Orai cannily told them they planned to cross the river eastwards at a vine suspension bridge not far away.

The next day, the patrol was off at daybreak as fast as they could move heading south for the limestone country of the Erave Gorge. Behind them they heard the furious yodeling and calling by the natives who had been lying in ambush by the track to the bridge and who realized they had been tricked. Hides and O'Malley breathed easier as the patrol entered the limestone forest. No attacking force could effectively approach them there among the craters and fissures and the tangled vegetation. Ironically, the same kind of country that had nearly destroyed them just before they entered the highlands now served as their refuge.

They traveled slowly deeper into the gorge over the next two days until the path disappeared. The walls of limestone now towered overhead on each side of them. Police scouts reported extremely difficult country ahead of them with no food. Hides and O'Malley realized that the exhausted carriers (not to mention Hides himself) would probably never make it climbing the limestone, so they decided to try rafting down the river. Like Monckton at the headwaters of the Lakekamu, however, Hides realized that he was taking a big risk. The water was still a slow-moving stream, but the altitude was close to 1,500 m and Hides knew there had to be a sudden drop somewhere not far away. Still, if they could gain 9–10 km by traveling on the river, it would save many days trying to cut their way over the limestone.

For two days they worked to build the rafts. The carriers were too weak for this, and most of the work fell to the police. Hides and O'Malley had only a little rice to eat, while the police and carriers had to subsist on wild mushrooms and Goru palm foraged in the forest (PR: 95). It was not so surprising that the carriers now fell to quarreling among themselves and stealing one another's food. At this time Hides's orderly, Corporal Emesi, also came down with dysentery.

On the morning of May 23, Hides released their prisoner. He did not want to expose him to the risks they would face in the gorge. The man, no doubt astonished that he was not killed by his captors, urged Hides not to take the river, but to return with him to his people where he would insure that they received better treatment. Hides gave him a few presents and bid him farewell.

It is not certain exactly where the patrol put its rafts in the water, except that it was somewhere in the vicinity of the river crossing of one of the trade routes from the Lake Kutubu/Mubi area and the Kagua Valley near to Urida, a fragile vine bridge south of the confluence of the Sugu and the Erave.

The patrol set off on five rafts, including one small raft sent ahead to scout the route for rapids and falls. The trip was perilous. The walls of the gorge closed in on them, becoming steeper and more impassable, while the water alternately carried them smoothly or careened them madly around little limestone islands. After making about 9 km, they heard warning shots fired by the constables on the scout raft followed by the roar of falling water. Quickly working the other rafts to the eastern bank, most of them managed to scramble safely ashore. Only one crew had to swim for it while their raft was carried on by the current and splintered in the rapids below.

8. THROUGH KEWA COUNTRY

LISETTE JOSEPHIDES AND MARC SCHILTZ

The patrol had landed on the eastern bank of the southeasterly-flowing Erave. The carriers' hearts sank as they contemplated the climb over the limestone ridges along the sides of the gorge. Very ill himself, Hides was greatly concerned about their morale.

"No country has worried me as much as this terrible limestone gorge," he wrote. "I had no food to give my party, no knowledge of people or villages to which to lead them; I could only tell them that beyond this terrible country was the Purari, and that they had to make one more big effort. But if the carriers were much longer without hope, I knew only too surely that they would die" (*PW*: 166).

After spending a wet and miserable night on the rocks beside the river, they began the difficult climb up the limestone escarpment which rose 500–600 m above them (*PR*: 86). Emerging at the top into limestone forest, they encountered a local man out on a hunting expedition. Relieved to find someone who knew the country, Hides had him captured and handcuffed by the police to use as a guide.*

---

* The Kewa narratives that form the basis of this chapter were collected in December 1985 in the settlements of Yakopaita (Aka), Yalapala, Ayakoe (Uripi), Kalalo, Tiripi, and Raipala in Kagua District of the Southern Highlands Province. Informants came from a number of tribes in the area: Yala, Perepe, Amburupa, Tepenarirepa, Sumbulu, and Koiari, and one from Yanguri in Mt. Murray. The accounts are so closely contextualized within the history of local events—recorded in previous years—and sufficiently consistent with each other that we are confident of their general authenticity. Moreover, with some exceptions, they were obtained separately, without consultations between informants. And finally, most of our informants were old and trusted ones, whose hallmark was brevity and disinclination to speculate.

Open public discussions concerned with "finding the talk," or criticizing accounts given, made it possible to gauge the feelings of both the elderly and the vociferous younger men

The man led them eastwards to his hunting shelter near Maisapalu, a bushland belonging to the Tepenarirepa tribe. There he offered them a few sweet potatoes and mushrooms before they camped for the night. The following day he led them to a sweet potato garden nestled in a glen surrounded by limestone pinnacles. He indicated they could take what they wanted. Hides says he paid for the food but does not mention with what. The carriers were so hungry they went on to ransack another garden nearby. "When starving natives get in this frame of mind," Hides remarked, "they do not care what happens to them" (PR: 97). Patrol discipline appeared to be at the edge of breakdown.

For two days the captive guide led the patrol eastward through the cratered terrain of the limestone forest. They were all so weak that they had to stop every fifteen minutes to rest. At about 11 A.M. on May 26, the patrol emerged into grass country again, overlooking a magnificent cultivated tableland: "It extended away before us eastward and north-eastward, great rolling areas of grass country interspersed with steep pinnacles of limestone that resembled pyramids in a yellow desert. There were cultivations too, and smoke was rising from many points within view. We had come upon another large population" (PW: 170).

Still far from the familiar Purari lowlands, Hides and his men were about to encounter another group of highlanders, a people known today as the Kewa. In his report, Hides came to refer to them as the "Iumburave," but where he got this name is unclear. "Iumburave" is not the name of any tribe or local group in the area. Indeed, in 1935 the people of the vicinity did not have any overall name for themselves. They used the term "Kewa" to refer to neighboring people to the south and "Mirupa" to refer to the people to the north. Nowadays "Kewa" is used to denote the whole linguistic group of which they are a part, numbering some 50,000 people, most of whom live within the present administrative unit of the Kagua District of the Southern Highlands Province, an area largely to the north of the patrol's route. It was the southern Kewa tribes between the Sugu and Erave rivers whom the patrol was about to encounter.

---

concerning these events and their lasting effect. Regrettably, very few women participated in these discussions. Women tend to be in the garden working rather than sitting around the village. In any case, most women saw little of the patrol because they were made to hide when it appeared; and of those who had seen it, many have since married and gone to live at their husbands' villages. Our thanks to the following informants, who favored us with their time and experience: Siame of Amburupa tribe and Bolame of Koiari, the only women who had stories of the patrol; Agula, Ana, Michael, Pisa, Pupula, Roga, and Yembi, all Yala; Nopa, Yamba, and Yia, of Amburupa; Perapu, a Perepe; Rambe and Sigale, Koiari; Rorepa, a Sumbulu; Tueri from Yanguri; and Yapa of Tepenarirepa. Rimbu, our regular Yala informant, did his usual public relations work and guided us through it all, while Justin Yatu of Batri village and the University of Papua New Guinea, helped us with place names.

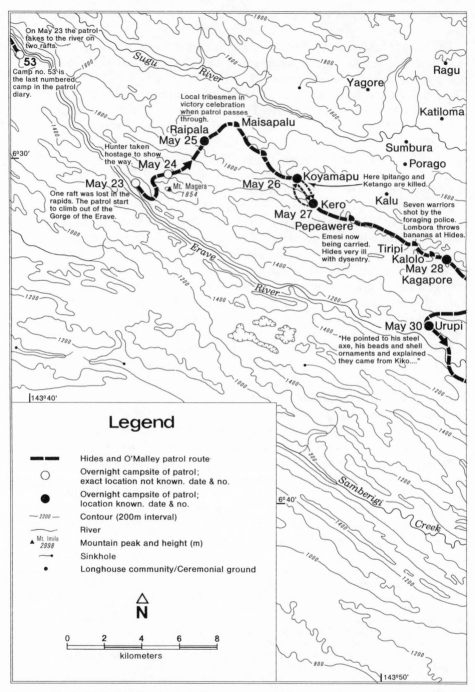

On May 23 the patrol takes to the river on two rafts.

53

Camp no. 53 is the last numbered camp in the patrol diary.

Sugu River

Local tribesmen in victory celebration when patrol passes through.

Maisapalu

Raipala
May 25

Hunter taken hostage to show the way.
May 24

May 23

One raft was lost in the rapids. The patrol start to climb out of the Gorge of the Erave.

Mt. Magera
1854

May 26

Koyamapu
Here Ipitango and Ketango are killed.

Kero

Kalu

Seven warriors shot by the foraging police. Lombora throws bananas at Hides.

May 27

Pepeawere

Emesi now being carried. Hides very ill with dysentry.

Tiripi

Kalolo
May 28

Kagapore

Erave River

Yagore

Ragu

Katiloma

Sumbura

Porago

May 30 Urupi

"He pointed to his steel axe, his beads and shell ornaments and explained they came from Kiko...."

Samberigi Creek

Legend

— — — Hides and O'Malley patrol route

○ Overnight campsite of patrol; exact location not known. date & no.

● Overnight campsite of patrol; location known. date & no.

— 2200 — Contour (200m interval)

River

▲ Mt. Imila 2898 Mountain peak and height (m)

Sinkhole

• Longhouse community/Ceremonial ground

△
N

0 2 4 6 8
kilometers

Map 11. In the land of the Kewa (May 23–June 4).

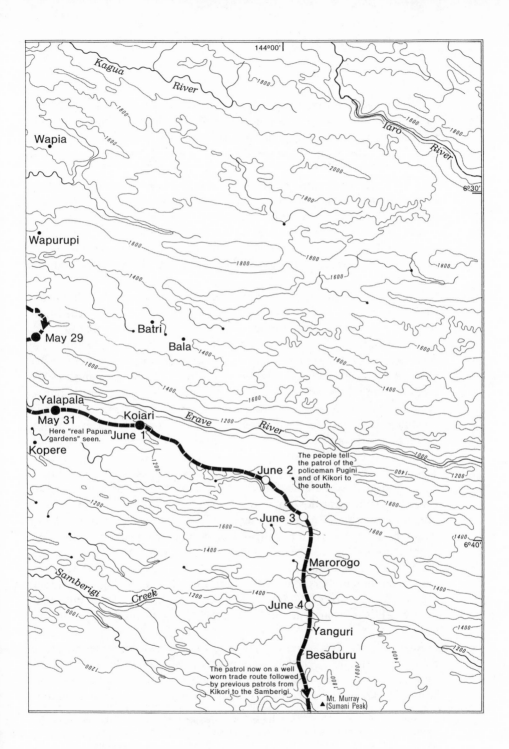

144°00'

Kagua

River

1800

Wapia

1600

1800

Iaro

River

1600

1800

1800

6°30'

2000

1800

Wapurupi

1800

1800

1600

1400

1600

1600

May 29

Batri

1400

Bala

1400

1600

1600

1400

Yalapala

May 31

Koiari

Erave

1200

River

1000

Here "real Papuan gardens" seen.

June 1

1200

Kopere

June 2

The people tell the patrol of the policeman Pugini and of Kikori to the south.

1400

1200

1600

June 3

1600

1600

1400

6°40'

Samberigi

1200

1400

Marorogo

1400

1200

Creek

1200

1400

June 4

Yanguri

1400

1200

1000

Besaburu

The patrol now on a well worn trade route followed by previous patrols from Kikori to the Samberigi.

1800

1200

Mt. Murray ▲ (Sumani Peak)

Trade Routes and Big Men

The rugged terrain of the southern Kewa area bears many resemblances to the Nembi Plateau. There were also striking cultural and linguistic continuities between the Kewa and the Nembi, Wola, and Huli whom the patrol had already encountered (Franklin 1968). However, the Kewa in this area knew little of these northern neighbors. Their trade and travel orientation was primarily to the south and the northwest (to Samberigi, Kikori, and Kutubu). No warning of the approaching patrol had come to them down the Erave. When the party appeared in Maisapalu, it was coming from the direction of the *Magera to*, a vine bridge crossing the Erave on the trade route from Lake Kutubu to the northwest. Because of this, Kewa informants still believe the patrol came from Lake Kutubu or Orokane.

The country between the Sugu and Erave rivers lay on the general pearl-shell route from the Gulf of Papua. In the 1930's, most trading expeditions from this area moved south to the "Sembo" people of the Samberigi Valley to obtain steel axes, bushknives, pearlshells, bailer shells, and cloth. They carried tobacco (*sogo*) and bars of salt (*aipa*) down the same route that Hides was to travel and usually returned through Hamoreke and Kopere, making a round trip of it. The salt they used was not made locally but received from the "Madi" (Mendi) people farther north. Traders from that locality presumably traveled south to trade with the Kewa even as the Kewa traveled south to trade with Samberigi. Most traders traveled only short distances, while the trade goods were relayed over far longer ones.[*]

Informants described the situation this way: "The people of Erave/ Kerabi (known as the Pole) went to Samberigi to trade with the Sembos, those of Tiripi went down to Erave to trade with the Pole, and those of Sumbura went to Tiripi. Thus there was no direct trade or barter (*dubu pawa*) between the Sugu people and the Sembos. It would have been unusual in those days to travel so far out of one's territory. The Kewa who went to Samberigi did not take their pigs there to barter, as they would have been too cumbersome on the road. But when some Big Men traders exchanged their axes acquired in Samberigi at the site of Sumbura market (which was a bartering place even then), they fetched big fat pigs for them."

Although the Kewa knew vaguely of the coast (Kikori) as the provenance of cloth and steel, they were not really sure how the Sembos came by these items. Indeed, the Samberigi people may have had a deliberate strategy of keeping the people to their north and the whites from the coast

---

[*] Some individuals did, however, travel longer distances. Diviners and dancers were often escorted to the Sugu on these trade routes. Some Yala clans claim that they originated in Samberigi, and affinal relations exist with both Samberigi and Kutubu peoples.

in as much ignorance of each other as possible in order not to lose control of the trade (see Chapter 5). As Ana, an old Kewa man of the Yala tribe remarked: "Those Sembos and Pole used to deceive us and mislead us all the time, but now that there are Yala people living in Samberigi, we are getting information about these things." *

Trade items were important for the Kewa. Indeed, without shells a man could scarcely participate in major exchanges or even marry. Steel axes were relatively plentiful among them as compared to the Nembi. When the patrol arrived with only a few axes left and no shell at all, the Kewa considered it rather ill-equipped with exchange items.

Trade, however, does not appear to have been the pivotal part of Kewa economy that it was for the Nembi and Samberigi people, nor did the Kewa control the long-distance trade between different tribes. Nevertheless, trade was politically significant because most of the Kewa traffic in axes and shells was dominated (as among other highlands peoples) by Big Men (*amoali*). These individuals were able to corner the market in steel to obtain pigs, which they used to support the elaborate ceremonial exchange activities involved in the competition for prestige.

Kewa Big Men seem to have been less powerful than their Melpa neighbors, who managed the elaborate *moka* exchanges in the Mt. Hagen area (Strathern 1971a, 1971b), but their influence was rooted in similar political strategies and cultural notions of social reproduction. By means of the ceremonial pig kills that they presented as a necessary part of a clan's reproductive cycle, they controlled the flow of wealth to which production was subordinated. The control of production at home provided the basis for their political influence abroad. Access to trade items enabled them to recruit more labor and increase their pig production, and their ability to dispose of large numbers of pigs meant that they could form the personal trade or exchange relationships that guaranteed the flow of long-distance trade items such as axes and shells into their group. The flow benefited the whole group, but it passed through the Big Man's hands; and Big Men strove to make this local control an aspect of their social role.

The Settlement Cycle

One of the most visible differences of the southern Kewa region from other highlands societies that Hides and O'Malley had passed through was

---

* Editors' note. Despite Ana's disclaimer, and despite Samberigi attempts to deceive the Kewa about the source of pearlshells, it is highly unlikely that the Kewa had heard nothing about patrols prior to the arrival of Hides and O'Malley. There had been eight patrols to the region just south of their borders since 1908. Some of these patrols were known to the Wiru people north of the Kewa, so Kewa must have known of them as well (see Appendix A and Clark [forthcoming]). Indeed, a number of Kewa statements in this chapter suggest they knew a fair amount about such patrols.

in the settlement pattern. Kewa not only lived in scattered settlements but also congregated in villages, often of considerable size. The most elaborate settlements, constructed in preparation for major pig-killing feasts, contained one or more low tubelike houses (*neada*) sometimes 100–150 m long. Often two such *neada* were built parallel to each other, leaving a broad strip of ceremonial ground in between. At the far end, standing partly between the two *neada*, would be the men's house (*tapada*), which was raised on stilts and was often itself of considerable length to accommodate men's ceremonial dancing. Behind these central structures were the women's houses and farther back, obscured by groves and discreet bushes, stood the spirit and cult houses.

In the 1930's, as today, the construction of these elaborate settlements usually heralded a major pig-killing feast. Frequently they represented concentrations of people of various groups who had been driven from their lands by fighting and had gathered for refuge for a while on the land of one ally. A pig kill on these occasions served many functions. It consolidated newly made alliances or initiated a process of group accretion that publicly emphasized group unity under an overarching tribal name. It appeased the spirits and elicited their assistance in ensuring the health of the community and the fertility of its gardens. It commemorated Big Men who had been killed in battle and compensated their relatives. It restored damaged relations with neighbors—and, in accomplishing all this, it publicly marked the ascendancy of the sponsoring group and its particular Big Man.*

In times of peace, when people did not need to live in large villages for military strength, the initiative for a pig kill might originate with two or more agnates who wished to make a name for themselves and decided to construct a new settlement on ancestral land. They would start building the *neada* and *tapada* and embark on various strategies to attract other households from nearby settlements to join in their endeavors. This was a complicated, long-term process, and the time lapse between the building of *neada* and the actual pig kill could be as long as ten years.

After the ceremonial pig kill the various participating households would usually disperse again, some returning to their original homesteads, some constructing new ones nearby or moving farther afield to support another group that was planning its own pig kill. Where this dispersal was not the

---

* Pig kills also played a crucial role in the definition of gender roles and the social evaluation of male and female. Women could not host pig kills in their names, since they were not carriers of the group name, but lived virilocally on their husbands', brothers', or fathers' land. Thus, pig kills eclipsed the role of women as forgers of social relations and contributed to cultural justification for their political subordination. The agnatic idiom further advanced this, by providing descent ideologies for groups that were in reality based on male solidarity (not true agnation), as against female organization.

result of warfare, it usually resulted from the desire to avoid the disputes and social tensions that overcrowding and close cohabitation in a large village entailed. Kewa preferred dispersal to confrontation and violence since clan brothers and allies were expected to uphold an ethos of amity and cooperation that distinguished in-group relations from out-group ones. Additionally, men dispersed because they wanted to kill their pigs in as many places over their lands as possible, rather than always on the same spot. Killing pigs consecrated the land on which it was done and was a public statement about the pig killer's link to that land. Scattering pig kills across the countryside therefore reflected a strategy whereby individuals or clans strengthened their claims to specific plots of land.

This pattern of residential flux has been termed "pulsating settlement" by Rappaport (1968), who described similar residential oscillations among the Maring of the Bismarck Range. The most permanent features of the Kewa landscape are named tracts of land. Within these, settlements wax and wane as households move around. New settlements are called by the name of the new site on which they are built. Small "kitchen gardens" (*yamanu*) with mixed crops soon appear around new houses. Major staple gardens (*modomapu*) are planted farther afield. These contain mounds for sweet potatoes interspersed with sugarcane, pitpit, and various greens, and may be replanted for several years without fallowing. Kewa also plant true swidden gardens (*emapu*) in bush fallow and abandon them after a single harvest. In some places they dig contour ditches to stop pig foraging. But compared with the complex grids characterizing Huli areas of cultivation, Kewa gardens present a more haphazard and untidy appearance.

The pulsations of Kewa settlement pattern had little to do with subsistence strategies for gaining access to hunting and gardening land. They were mainly political in motivation, related to the formation of military alliances and the support of ceremonial activities and Big Men. As in other places in the highlands, Kewa men held to a strong ideology of agnatic descent, while in reality the formation and composition of their groups was rather heterogeneous. "*Ruru*" is the only word the Kewa have for social groups. It is applied both to named patriclans and to what we render in English as "tribe": a congeries of named patriclans occupying a common territory, whose numbers fluctuated according to political and military conditions. A long association resulted in a clan's being assimilated into a tribe and adopting the tribal name. At the same time, depending on their political aims, two clans of the same tribe could play down their association with each other and claim to be of different *ruru*. In fact, both tribes and clans were faction-ridden internally. Personal reasons informed decisions about whom to side with in battle, with the frequent result that clansmen could be fighting on opposite sides of an altercation. War was part of social relations just as marriage, and there was no such thing as a permanent enemy or an unfailing friend.

Kewa society, like Nembi, represented a situation of shifting alliances. Warfare frequently drove defeated groups off their lands, and people had to adopt alternating strategies of aggression and allegiance to deal with political contingencies. In these circumstances, local group formation was more than simply a function of agnatic descent and shared interests of clans belonging to the same tribe. Residential groups that cooperated for ceremonial or military purposes usually consisted of a core faction of clan agnates but also included people from other clans or even other tribes. The effective political coherence of these groups depended largely on the leadership of their Big Men, who achieved their reputations through their persuasive oratory, their ambition and political deftness, and their preparedness and ability to shoulder the obligations and responsibilities that went with this role. Renown as a fierce warrior (*muduali*) was useful, but the real test of a Big Man was ability to keep his faction together by offering workable solutions to divisive problems. He had to wield power without seeming to hold it over his support group: for his control over them was fragile and depended, ultimately, on their trust in him. If he tried to coerce their obedience, he could easily lose their support.

Warfare

Warfare was endemic in the region. Though the victors often drove defeated groups off their lands, acquisition of territory was not the victors' goal. They were more concerned with the settling of old scores; their military objectives were to rout the enemy and neutralize them as a fighting force. Once a war had started in one place over some incident (pigs, sorcery, or women), it had a tendency to travel across the countryside from one group to another, taking in the tribes it found in its way, leaving refugees and devastation behind. Many times when informants talked of a particular war, they would say, "We don't know the cause of this war. It was brought into our territory by this and that tribe that came to take refuge with us. So we had to become involved in it. . . . It came from this direction, and we joined it because it came and we had no choice." As the fighting moved, it created new grievances and new reasons for extending hostilities; or clans would remember old grudges and take the opportunity to resolve them. Once started, wars developed an impetus that carried them, cyclone-like, into other territories of ever more tribes. Aggressors might pursue their enemies into hitherto neutral places of refuge, but if the enemy gathered new allies there and turned and defeated them, the war could change direction, with the former victors now in full flight.

For all this, Kewa wars did not result in large numbers of fatalities. Although they sometimes ambushed their enemies, in most wars there was ample warning of attack, and killing was not wanton or indiscriminate. Crisscrossing kinship ties between neighboring groups that both married and fought each other made for a web of loyalties between individuals in different groups that had to be observed on pain of supernatural retribution. Deaths were not taken lightly and were either avenged or settled by payment of compensation.

These details of Kewa warfare are important, since all accounts of the patrol indicate that when Hides and O'Malley and their patrol appeared in the Kewa country, they unknowingly arrived in the midst of a major war. Ana, a man of the Yala tribe, felt he had to go back many years to situate the complex circumstances, starting from when he was about fifteen and already fighting.

"The 'war over the pig's belly' started in Pepeawere, then came down to Tiripi, Porago, and Sumbura. Many tribes including the Koiari and the Tepenarirepa were fighting the Amburupa and gaining on them fast. The Perepe were sorry for the Amburupa's lone struggle, and offered them refuge in Sumbura. In one day the Koiari confederacy took Tiripi and harried Sumbura. The Yala living in Agema were not in the fray at the time, for their three Big Men advised them to keep out of it. Seeing the routing of the Amburupa and the Perepe, however, they disobeyed the Big Men and went to their aid.

"When Yanyali was killed by the Koiari, these Big Men were angry and in retaliation killed Koiari Rundu. A few months later the Yala stole a pig from the Tiarepa of Yagore. This was a bad move, because they had no allies at the time, and when the Tiarepa attacked them, they were joined by the Koiari and other tribes with a grudge against the Yala. Nobody was killed in this fight, but the Yala were overpowered and fled to Wapia in the east. War found them there too, when the Waluaparepa attacked Wapia. At first the Yala had the upper hand and took Ragu and Katiloma, chasing their enemy to Yagore. But from there they all banded together and defeated Wapia, so the Yala fled to Bala, near Batri.

"They stayed there with the Andai tribe for a few years, building a ceremonial longhouse and killing pigs. Then a war came to Batri. It was brought into Bala by the Yatupa and Enalu, who were pursued by the Waluaparepa, Kanarepa, and Meleperepa. Five Yala men were killed, and the rest fled to Kananda, a place without any residences, and stayed in makeshift sheds. Here they were trapped by the Meleperepa and Perepe, and many people died. The Yala retreated further to Kopere, south of the Erave River, where they stayed for some months until a Tepenarirepa man from Wata, named Maisa, responding to the pleas of his Yala wife, es-

corted them home with him on his way back from a trip south where he
had been recruiting dancers for his impending longhouse pig kill. They
settled in Koyamapu and assisted in the Tepenarirepa pig kill. Maisa then
helped them to avenge their earlier defeat by the people of Pepeawere by
rallying together the Sumbulu, Yala, Kamarepa, Koiari, and Tepenarirepa
tribes. Pepeawere was laid waste then, and its inhabitants chased out.

"Soon, however, there was more trouble. A Tepenarirepa man died,
and his clan believed that the Eno had brought this about through one of
the spirits they had recently acquired. At about that time an Eno woman
married to a Tepenarirepa man named Perosi fell sick. Perosi asked his
father-in-law, Kalua, to build a spirit house and kill pigs for her. Kalua
did so, but while he was carrying the killed pigs to his son-in-law, the
Tepenarirepa, mindful of the earlier death, ambushed and slew him on
the road. The Eno then recruited the help of the Urupa and the Pamarepa
and attacked the Tepenarirepa and their allies. The Tepenarirepa alliance
had just scored a victory following the slaying of Rakia, the Pamarepa Big
Man, and were celebrating when the patrol suddenly appeared. The war
continued after the patrol left, until Wata was vanquished and the Yala
once again fled to Wapia."

This complex situation formed the backdrop to the arrival of Hides and
O'Malley. As we shall see, it not only shaped the events the patrol encountered but also informed the Kewa's understanding of the patrol's behavior,
which some came to see as vengeance for the sacking of Pepeawere.

The Koyamapu Incident

Unaware of the local hostilities, Hides and O'Malley and their handcuffed guide led their party from the edge of the forest across the grassland
toward the first cultivations they could see. They waved and called to
some women digging potatoes as they approached the first garden, but
the women fled as soon as they looked up. Bolame, a Koiari woman, now
about sixty, was a girl of ten when the patrol arrived.

She recalled, "We were in our garden at a site called Kambe.* Some
policemen came out of the bush first, followed by the carriers with more
policemen bringing up the rear. The white men (*kadipi*) were in the middle. A man of the Sumbulu tribe called Degema was with them, handcuffed. He had been caught while hunting possums in the bush, and he
was carrying a net bag full of them. As the policemen approached us, we
cried out in fear and trembled all over. We had never seen such creatures

---

* Kambe is over the southern rim of the plateau where a path enters the Magera bush and
leads down to the vine bridge on the Erave.

before and thought they must be *remo* (ghosts). The first thing we noticed was their strange smell, which we now know as the smell of soap. One of the white men seemed strong, he walked straight and had a strong voice, while the other one did not look well and appeared to have difficulty walking. With sign language the policemen indicated that they were thirsty and wanted to help themselves to our sugarcane. They then asked us the way to the settlement. Still trembling with fear we took them to Maisapalu. My father who stood at his pig house some distance away saw them approaching and shouted to us to bolt, lest the *remo* should carry us off."

The patrol followed the women slowly. Presently they came in sight of a large village hidden in a grove of bananas. "The yodeling and singing of hundreds of natives came to our ears. It was a wide road we were following. It led us up to a high arch of wooden stakes at the door of which stood a single man, covered with a shield and with his bow drawn full upon us. Without halting, I waved his weapon away and indicated we had not come to fight. He stood until we were within twenty yards of him, then he lowered his weapon and fled. I tried to get our prisoner to call out, but he just looked sulky and would say nothing, appearing to harbor a grudge for the indignity he had suffered [of being handcuffed]. Perhaps he thought it was his turn to laugh now" (*PW*: 170).

They passed through the archway (actually a part of the village fortifications—the bowman who fled had been the sentry there) and found themselves surrounded by about 200 men in the middle of the victory celebration of the killing of their enemy, the Pamarepa Big Man Rakia. In a flash all of them had their bows up and drawn with arrows fitted, and they stood behind "grotesquely painted shields of wood."

"They were the fiercest savages I had ever seen," Hides remarked, "all of them were silent, watching us with unflinching eyes. It was a tense moment; the drop of an arm could have brought death and destruction to the lot of us, for we were too tired to dodge arrows now, or fire quickly in defense. It could easily have been a massacre" (*PW*: 171).

Hides held up his arm to them in a friendly gesture, turning his hand from side to side to indicate they did not want to be molested. Then he released his prisoner as a gesture of good will and signed he wanted peace and something to eat. The Koiari and their allies relaxed, laid down their weapons, and invited Hides and his men to rest in the shade while plying them with sugarcane and bananas. The captive vanished, not to be seen again.

The patrol found itself in a village of over 30 dwellings, including several longhouses reminiscent of Papuan Coast structures that Hides was familiar with. This community, Raipala, was at that time very large by Kewa standards, with a population of several hundred. A large number of war refugees from several allied tribes were temporarily settled there—as were others at the communities of Wata and Koyamapu farther down the track located on lands belonging to the Tepenarirepa tribe.

Alert to the distinctiveness of new peoples, Hides observed: "The people were new, too. They were big, black Papuans who wore bands of cowrie across the forehead and large head-dresses of cassowary feathers. Many of them had boar tusks and cylindrical-shaped pieces of quartz through the nasal septum. Nearly every man carried an article of steel. . . . These big, black Papuans called themselves the Iumburave. They had the finest shields of primitive manufacture I have ever seen. . . . I should take these men to be the finest fighters in Papua" (*PW*: 171).

Although the Kewa do not really differ in appearance from other Papuan peoples of the Southern Highlands, they may well have appeared unusually black to Hides on this occasion because they had blackened themselves ceremonially for war. Hides does not much seem to have noticed he arrived on a ceremonial occasion. His interest was drawn instead to the steel axes the men were carrying. Many carried the "Brades" brand, indicating the Kewa had trade links with the Gulf of Papua. Others were marked with an American brand, the "Charleston Steel Works," and the owners indicated they had obtained them from white men from the northeast. Hides surmised one of the Leahy brothers' patrols had passed somewhere not too far away.

After resting at the village and being refreshed with gifts of bananas and sugarcane, the patrol moved on, escorted by crowds of friendly warriors along a wide track to the southeast that led between several longhouse villages. Toward late afternoon they arrived at the village of Koyamapu on the shoulder of a limestone pinnacle at an altitude of 1,646 m. The crowds of men who had accompanied them pointed to their axes and explained excitedly to the villagers (so Hides made out) that they (Hides and O'Malley) were the ones who had sent them these items from the south. "All were greatly pleased with our presence," Hides remarked, "and did all they could do to show they were friendly" (*PW*: 172).

For their part, the Kewa observed Hides and O'Malley in detail. One was tall, the other short, one weak with a feeble voice, the other strong with a powerful one; one had his eyes half-closed and lay much of the time on a cot (Hides's illness had begun to affect his eyes) with his shirt off while the other was standing with his shirt on. Some people thought that the weaker one who could hardly walk was a woman. Most Kewa suspected everyone in the patrol were *remo* (ghosts), others felt that the *karea repa* (carrier line) were beings more like themselves. A number of informants perceived the rank distinctions between members of the patrol. The "red men" (the officers) were clearly distinguished from all others because they carried nothing but their binoculars and flasks. They also ate "*remo* food": little white seeds (rice). The Papuan policemen were distinguished from the carriers because they carried only their guns, whereas the carriers were weighed down with everything else. Pupula, who helped the patrol set up camp, noted that these distinctions were preserved in their sleeping arrangements. "They put up three shelters: for two they simply fetched posts which the police secured in the soil to fix the flysheets on. These were for the officers and police. The third was a 'real thatch house' for the carriers and also served as a kitchen."

Many people, according to Pupula, were alarmed by the patrol's appearance, their peculiar smell, and their clothes, and so made themselves scarce. Others were fascinated and desired to see more. The authority/obedience relations between patrol members were clearly marked, and the ceremony of raising the Australian flag at the campsite with police presenting arms, described in detail, inspired the Kewa with fear and awe.*

Those who responded to the stranger's request for food received razors, matches, and knives in return. Hides was short of steel and would not part with it readily at this point, but both he and the people of Koyamapu described the situation as one of friendship and good will.

Before settling down for the evening, Hides and O'Malley looked over the country to the southwest. Some 6–8 km away they could see the end of the grass country and the edge of the timber of the limestone barrier again. "The people told us that beyond this now dwindling barrier there was a large river, and that on that river were men who stood on logs and paddled themselves along with sticks. They were telling us of the Purari and the canoe people [there]!" (*PW*: 173).

Very early the following morning, May 27, the patrol broke camp and, "with a crowd of friendly followers," descended to a "large waterless grass basin . . . [whose] southern walls were formed by the limestone barrier" (*PR*: 98). Halfway across this basin, however, according to Hides's account, they met a new people, and he did not like them.

"The people of this last section were not friendly to us, and refused us food while they held weapons in their hands. I had no alternative but to take the food; we could not be suffered to starve now when everyone was so weak. But while the police were digging potatoes in the cultivations, numbers of [the natives] encircled us. We could not see them in the long grass, but we knew where they were by the continual din of yodeling they kept up.

"One native stood on a limestone pinnacle two to three hundred yards

* Editors' note. This detail about raising the flag while the police presented arms (also giving matches and razors in trade) is likely to be a conflation of Kewa experience from later patrols. The Strickland-Purari patrol did not do this.

away, and judging by his yodeling I could see that he was directing the advance of the men around us, and that they were hostile; for the yodel is the 'kill call' of these people,* and in every attack upon us, large forces of men have always appeared to rush us directed by systematic yodeling. This native, therefore, was a menace, so I fired at the limestone rock at his feet. He scurried away, and although he continued to yodel out of sight, and also the others around us, we were able to move away from the last of the cultivations without being molested. We camped out on the grassland near an old park of casuarina trees that was surrounded by wild bananas" (PR: 98–99).

Such is Hides's account. If we try to follow it on the map, however, a number of questions arise. The patrol was headed southwest into the region around the ruins of Pepeawere village (laid waste in the "war over the pig's belly" not long before). This area was uninhabited at the time, the next closest people being the inhabitants of the community of Tiripi some distance away. Who then were the "unfriendly people" the patrol allegedly encountered?

Our informants' narratives of the patrol's movements described a rather different series of events than does Hides. According to these accounts, when the patrol left Koyamapu, it did not proceed southwest to meet another, unfriendly group. Instead, after descending a little way into the grass basin beyond a place called Kero, several police and one white man turned around and *came back* to the outskirts of Koyamapu, where they proceeded to kill a number of pigs and two men before returning to Kero to camp the night. The story was recounted by six men (Pisa, Agula, Roga, Pupula, Ana, Sigale) and one woman (Bolame).

"When the guides, who were on their way back to the village, left the party at Kero and turned back towards Koyamapu, they assumed the patrol would go on to Tiripi, as they had directed them. Back in Wata and Koyamapu, the warriors resumed their rejoicing over the killing of their enemy Rakia, which the patrol had interrupted. They did this with yodeling that ended with hoots of 'uuuu!'

"The guides then became aware that one white man and three police had turned back and appeared to be pursuing them, so they shouted to the people in the settlements to run and hide. Meteke, one of the guides, was shot at as he ran, but he fell to the ground and crawled away unhurt. The other guides did likewise, so they escaped. We would all have been killed if they hadn't warned us. Parents were afraid that the crying of their young children would give them away and considered killing them.

*As among the Huli, Nembi, and Wola, Kewa yodeling may be a "kill call," but it is also the normal way people communicate over long distances. The sound itself does not necessarily have blood-curdling, treacherous, or murderous qualities.

"Ipitango [a local Big Man] climbed a limestone pinnacle just above his pig house when he heard the commotion. This was just outside Koya-mapu. He saw the returning patrol shoot so many of his pigs that in the end he could not bear it and shouted to them to stop: 'You *remo*, aren't you satisfied with one or two pigs? Must you kill *all* my pigs?' so they shot Ipitango himself in the head, and he fell down dead.

"They then proceeded into Koyamapu. Sigale, a little boy at the time, was staying with a man named Ketango when he heard the cry that the *remo* were on the attack. He was so terrified that he scampered away without warning Ketango, who was in his house cooking. When Ketango realized the danger, he tried to run, but a war wound on his leg slowed him down. They shot at him but didn't kill him, and he ran back at them crying. So he was battered to death with sticks and bayonets.

"They carried the killed pigs back to Kero, where they cut them up and cooked them in saucepans. They camped there and the following day proceeded to Tiripi. After they had gone, we went to Kero and found the pigs' heads and entrails lying in ditches, so we cooked and ate them."

Although informants had not seen who had done the shooting, they heard it and later saw the bodies. The cartridge cases were found and treasured as neck decorations for many years. The wounds on Ipitango and Ketango were described in detail. Ipitango had a small, clean bullet wound in his forehead and a larger one in the back of his head where the bullet passed out. Ketango was battered and had stab wounds in his but-tocks. He was of a Tepenarirepa clan, whereas Ipitango was a Yala man (six of his male grandchildren now live in Kalu). He was a Big Man pre-paring to make a reparation payment. Hence there was a large number of pigs gathered on his premises (100–200 according to informants), which would normally have been farmed out in care of partners and affines.

The two accounts correspond reasonably well, though they represent diametrically different understandings of what happened. Hides took the Kewa yodeling as a call for attack; the Kewa say it was a warning to others that the patrol was returning in pursuit of them. Hides says his police were taking produce from cultivations; the Kewa say they were killing pigs. For Hides the man on the pinnacle was a menace orchestrating an attack on the patrol out by the grass basin. He fired at his feet to frighten him away. To the Kewa, Ipitango was protesting the slaughter of his pigs near the village and was shot between the eyes and killed.

If this is so, the question is, why did these patrol members turn back to kill Ipitango's pigs—and Ipitango himself, together with Ketango? Our informants could give few explanations for this. One story alleges that there was an agent provocateur among Hides's police, a man from Perepe named Walali, who instigated the shootings in revenge for the destruction

214 THROUGH KEWA COUNTRY

of Pepeawere; we will look at this story later. A more straightforward explanation was given by Bolame, who speculated the patrol mistakenly thought it was under attack:

"When . . . they broke camp and moved towards Pepeawere, we Koiari and our allies thought we had seen the last of them. So we resumed our jubilations over the killing of the enemy Rakia. Hearing the cries of 'iiiii' and 'uuuuuu,' the patrol must have thought it was about to be attacked, for it turned back towards Wata* and killed Ipitango and many of his pigs, and later also killed Ketango."

However, the Kewa themselves were not satisfied with this explanation, for they repeatedly stressed that they neither displayed nor entertained aggressive intentions toward the patrol, but went out of their way to show friendship.

According to Hides, the patrol was in need of food for the journey across the limestone barrier. It is possible that, seeing no cultivations in the "grass basin" ahead (the devastated ground around Pepeawere), he turned back to provision the patrol from the gardens of the Koyamapu people he had just left. Perhaps the sight of Ipitango's pigs was too much for the famished police who, craving meat, simply turned back to kill some of them. What Hides himself was doing there is unclear. In any case, given they were stealing food, Hides had good reason to expect attack. He was unable to see the village or its inhabitants from the place where he stood because of the high grass. When the yodeling commenced, it seemed to him he was hearing warriors closing in. When Ipitango appeared on the pinnacle yelling about his pigs, Hides thought he was directing the attack and shot at him. According to the Kewa, Ipitango did not "scurry away"; he was hit between the eyes and killed instantly. Similarly, when Ketango ran towards the police in sheer terror and confusion, he also was killed. If this is true, then Hides's story is deceptive.

What then was going on here? Why should Hides forcibly take food from friendly people who had treated him hospitably? And why would he make it appear in his report that those he treated in this way were an unfriendly group farther down the track?

Both he and O'Malley had been shaken by their experience on the Nembi Plateau and by now, sick and exhausted, were very easily alarmed by the sound of yodeling. The police, for their part, had become all too ready to deal with locals violently. Hides believed that by shooting at Ipitango he was preempting an attack. On the Nembi Plateau this would have been understandable, for there the patrol was often surrounded with

* That is, in the direction of Koyamapu. Wata was on the other side of Koyamapu from where the patrol was standing.

shouting warriors. In this part of the Kewa country, however, even by his own account, the people had not been acting provocatively toward the patrol and had expressed no aggressive intentions. It would appear that at this point Hides's judgment was becoming confused, and he was close to losing control of his police. This is further suggested by the events of the following day.

The Kagapore/Kananda Incident

The next morning, May 28, the patrol arrived at a small garden at the foot of the limestone barrier. Several women bolted as soon as they caught sight of the strangers, but an old man approached and was friendly. Through signs he communicated to them that the track over the limestone barrier lay to the southwest and then invited them to stay where they were for the night. Presently another 40 men came up, unarmed except for steel axes, and afterwards, while the patrol was erecting shelters, others arrived bringing small amounts of potatoes and bananas. Hides was very sick and lay exhausted on the ground.

"I sat up to receive these presents (of food), only to be told, however, that we could not have them unless we gave an axe in exchange. One axe for a handful of food!

"It was too much; we only had a few axes left, and, as we needed them badly, such an exchange was impossible. I told them so. But they shook their heads and indicated there would be no food without axes. One man holding a small cluster of bananas I beckoned forward. To him I tried to explain that we were all sick people; that we wanted food for strength and to carry us over the barrier; and I indicated that he ought to give us food freely because they had plenty and we had none" (PR: 100).

Hides seems to have felt that he was appealing to common compassion and humanitarian feeling.* The force of this moral imperative, however, did not impress itself on the man. He threw the bananas at Hides and made off.

Hides then appealed to the old man they had encountered first, offering him an axe and asking if he could dig for sweet potatoes in the garden below. Hides reports that he was too sick to understand the situation properly and so had O'Malley detail the sergeant, five constables, and eight carriers to go with the old man. Should they be attacked, the sergeant was to try to scare the assailants off by firing into the air.

Rifle fire was heard only twenty minutes after they left. O'Malley started

---

* In PW these exhortations seem to be addressed to the people of Koyamapu, who neither refused food nor demanded payment.

off to investigate, but Hides stopped him as he believed he was too weak for the exertion. When the police returned fifteen minutes later, the sergeant reported that they had been "treacherously attacked while digging potatoes as they had been directed by the old man; that after firing a volley in the air, he had been compelled to stop the rush by firing directly at the assailants; and that some men had been shot" (PR: 100). In his deposition to the resident magistrate in Kikori a few weeks later, Sergeant Orai told the story as follows.

"Mr. Hides said, 'Take Agoti, Dekadua, Budua, and Koriki.' One ax we took and some carriers. Mr. Hides said: 'Go and look for food. If the people come with bows and arrows don't shoot them, fire above their heads first.'

"I went and found potatoes and one man (a native) said: 'Don't dig them, they are old, come and dig here.' I went there with him, and he said 'No, not here, come over here and dig.' I went there, and he said, 'No, not here, come down here and dig.' I started to dig where he showed me, and he went away.

"I said to the police 'Look out, he might be doing something and the people come.' Presently, I looked and saw we were surrounded by armed men on every side. No. 1 arrow came, and I told the police to fire in the air. More arrows came, and I fired again in the air. I said to Agoti, 'Try again in the air.' Two more arrows came close, and I said 'Enough.' One man came close and was going to fire, and I gave orders to Agoti to shoot him. Others came like that, and we shot them. Agoti shot three, Tabu shot two, Dekadua shot one. One man very strong; Budua tried to shoot him, and he no fright; he sidestepped and was missed. I call to Budua, 'You shoot him straight, you will be dead.' Budua put in another cartridge and fired. Cartridge no good, no fire. Budua called out 'Sergeant, close up I am done'; I ran to him and shot the man dead. When I did this, they opened up a bit, and I said 'Quick. Let us get back.' I shouted to Budoa to shoot a pig running nearby. We got some potatoes and the pig. I guarded the rear because all the men (warriors) were still there.

"Up at the camp Taubada [Hides] fired for me to hear. He was calling us. I said, 'Hurry.' I reported to Taubada and told him all. I told him that we were nearly all dead at that time down there. I reported to him that I had tried to stop shooting them, I tried four times in the air, and they no stop, therefore I tell police to shoot straight. Mr. Hides said, 'True you fire in air first?' I said, 'Yes, true, Taubada.' I told Taubada we shoot seven (IQ: 4).

Although he did not know for sure what had happened, Hides supported his sergeant of police in his patrol report: "I know the people, and

I know Sergeant Orai as a fair, cool, and courageous man, and I accept his word unreservedly" (*PR*: 100).

From our informants we got the following composite story. The patrol came down towards Tiripi from the Puawimala bush between Tiripi and Pepeawere and made camp at a place called Kagapore. Wapana, an Amburupa man, met them when he went to his garden and shouted back the message to those as far as Kananda: "*Remo epapia*" ("the ghosts are coming"). Using sign language, these strangers gave them to understand that they wanted food. The cry was again relayed to Kananda, and people from Amburupa, Tangerepe, Perepe, and Kambia tribes, as well as others, came bringing bananas, leaf tobacco, greens, and sweet potatoes. Lombora, another Amburupa man, brought a bunch of bananas on which he made paring movements, indicating that he wanted a knife. When the white man remonstrated with him, he threw the bananas at his chest and bolted. Yia Uliando, an Amburupa informant, continued the story in detail.

"The white man in the shirt [O'Malley] spoke to the police. I don't know what he said, but his voice was strong, the police stood to attention, and we locals were afraid. Some ran off to the Yawi stream, some to Kalidipa, and others ran around in circles in sheer terror. The police fired a few shots over our heads, and we ran off in all directions. I tripped over a stone and hurt myself; Maita fell on top of me. I ran down to Kananda where the Batri road starts and climbed a little knoll and looked down. I saw the police going down the little track to Paware. The people of Wapurupi had heard that the patrol was asking for food and dispensing medicine, so they were coming up this road with their vegetables and their sick. They hadn't heard that the police were now chasing us. Sokolopa's three sons Aguluma, Ala, and Kuluma came first with Lapa. All four were shot dead by the police as they came up the Paware road. The police then went back towards Kananda where they killed Walape, who was Lombora's brother, and Epo, who was his son. They also killed Rala. Yapea, the brother of Lapa, was hit as he ran* and had his apron and testicles shot off, but he survived, as did Liano and Kapisi, who were wounded."

All the casualties were Amburupa men. When asked why the police should have started shooting, Yia, who was about sixteen at the time, said he did not know, perhaps they were as afraid as the locals were, but he stressed that those killed had not been armed.†

* Both Yapea and Lapa were brothers of Nopa, one of our informants.
† The necessity for sifting through a mixed variety of accounts of this incident can be seen from the fact that another informant claimed Aguluma and his brothers *were* armed, having just returned from fighting in Kambia. This informant, Amburupa Yamba, also said that Epo and the others were shot first and that he saw the white man shoot them. The rest

Yia's account suggests that Hides did not grasp the impact of ordinary patrol behavior on the local people. The routine procedure of detailing police to some duty was a frightening spectacle to a people who had never seen firearms, were not familiar with the authority/obedience relationship exemplified, and did not grasp the meaning of what was unfolding before their eyes. They could see its dramatic aspects only: the quality of command in the white man's voice and the trained policemen snapping to attention. All this followed an event where the strange "red man" had been displeased by one of their kinsmen. They did not understand what this ritual meant but judged that it purported them no good. Just before this, Lombora had acted towards Hides in a manner reminiscent of the insolent behavior of the Wola native at Huwguwn a few weeks before (see Chapter 5). He demanded a high return for a small offering and, when it was not forthcoming, threw the food at the patrol officer.

Here there was plenty of room for misunderstanding of intentions. Lombora had plucked up courage to try to find out what kind of being Hides was and establish a friendly relation by offering an exchange of food for a knife. Hides thought he was demanding an axe as an exorbitant price for the food and refused. But to the Kewa, where refusal of reciprocity is the characteristic of an enemy, a witch, or a spirit, Hides's action carried implications of malevolence and danger. Lombora fearfully threw the bananas at Hides to indicate that *he* wasn't refusing and made off to safety. What really happened after Hides and O'Malley detailed the police to get food is not totally clear, for neither officer apparently accompanied them, but the result was a number of Kewa killed by police (out of sight of their officers) under questionable circumstances. It seems that in this encounter Hides's ability to assess the situation deserted him. He should have suspected by now that the police would shoot people when they got the chance, and he should never have let them out of his sight. What is clear is that Hides was obsessed with worry over the safety of his men. He had two overwhelming fears: first, that if anyone was wounded and had to be carried, it would greatly reduce their chances of getting through and, second, that any lack of firmness or resolution on the part of the patrol would suggest weakness to their adversaries, who would then attack.

---

of the Amburupa rejected this account in the strongest terms as untrue. A Perepe informant, Perapu Ropa, claimed that the Amburupa had killed two policemen in Kalalo; that one was buried there, while the other was seen walking past with an arrow sticking out of his head. Sigale, a Koiari man, also told us that the Amburupa had killed "one or two policemen," but he knew this only from hearsay. According to Nopa Pondo, another Amburupa, there was no killing of policemen by his people. Some non-Amburupa informants speculated that the Amburupa kept back some information from us because they did not want to be blamed for giving provocation for the attack. It is unclear what the origin of these stories could be, since according to the official report, all of the constabulary returned alive to Kikori though Hides's orderly, Corporal Emesi, died of illness soon thereafter.

The behavior of the patrol in the Kewa country was not only disastrous, but also puzzling. The forcible taking of food from the friendly people at Koyamapu and the killing of Ipitango were out of character for Hides. Why the police should have opened fire on the people at Kananda who, according to the Kewa, were nonbelligerent is equally difficult to explain. At this historical remove, the story is anything but clear.

What is clear is that when Hides and O'Malley arrived in the Kewa country, the patrol had been traveling continuously for almost six months, and everyone was exhausted, starving, and ill. In this state, Hides had already concluded that the Kewa were "the fiercest savages I have ever seen," though this was based primarily on what he had seen of their cere-monial dress and wooden shields at the victory celebration at Raipala. His state of mind at Koyamapu may perhaps be gauged from a further fan-tasy that follows his description of shooting at Ipitango on the limestone pinnacle.

"I [imagined] these big black Papuans, with boar tusks . . . through their noses, killing and burning and driving the weaker people before them, just as possibly they did the light-skinned Tarifuroro, hundreds—perhaps thousands—of years ago. Their fierce murdering tactics would be terrible, for they would show no mercy on the lives of the weak" (PW: 176).

This overwrought statement was entirely a product of Hides's imagi-nation, for by his own account, until Ipitango shouted from the pinnacle, none of the local people had done anything threatening towards the patrol. It seems to reflect a sense of violence and danger out of proportion to the reality of the situation, fueled by his anxiety about the safety of his party, and it was affecting his judgment.*

It is apparent that Hides had an uneasy conscience about the two inci-dents in the Kewa country, for in his patrol report he fudges his account to make it appear that the incident at Koyamapu occurred with a different people in an uninhabited region around Pepeawere. In his book he omits the account of the police killings at Kananda entirely, skipping three days' travel, so it looks as though the patrol moved directly from Pepeawere to the Erave River. The events in Koyamapu and Kagapore/Kananda† un-doubtedly mark the lowest point of the patrol. It seems likely that these incidents were cruel blunders, and Hides knew it. But he wanted to cover them up.

That night the patrol slept at the camp in Kagapore. They were not

---

* Editors' note. We cannot ignore another possibility: that Hides was aware of making a serious blunder and that this speculation, written after his report, was intended in part to provide a greater appearance of justification for his action.

† Kagapore was the settlement; Kananda and the road toward it were where the killings occurred.

disturbed. After suffering so much damage, the local people kept away. The following morning the patrol made an excursion into the Rala bush and slept there, then turned southwest to Urupi, where they made camp on May 30. After that they passed out of the southern Kewa country. Our informants knew that they then went on to Erave and camped on the present site of the Catholic mission.

Local Explanations: Walali as Agent Provocateur

One of the most interesting aspects of our investigation into the Strickland-Purari patrol was the appearance, in several informants' accounts, of a man named Walali, who was said to have been instrumental in the killings of Ipitango and Ketango at Koyamapu and also of the Amburupa men at Kagapore/Kananda. He was mentioned by nine informants out of seventeen, and most others had heard of him though they were not always sure how he fitted into their stories. The most complete accounts picture Walali as one of the constabulary accompanying the patrol. According to Pisa he was the son of a man named Yenge of Perepe clan and, as a boy, had gone to stay with his father's sister in Samberigi (an area then on the edge of government influence). While still young he followed a government patrol to Kikori Station and was brought up there by local officials. Eventually he became a policeman and accompanied the Strickland-Purari patrol back to the Kewa country. There, although he spoke no Kewa to anyone, he was recognized by people in Yalapala by a scar between his eyes.

When the patrol arrived at Koyamapu, according to this account, Walali learned that his clan, Perepe, had been defeated in battle and driven from their lands around Pepeawere by the Yala and Tepenarirepa. As a "returned kinsman" (as ghosts are returned kinsmen) it was Walali's duty to avenge them. When the people of Koyamapu (mostly Yala and Tepenarirepa enemies of Perepe) resumed their victory celebrations the next morning, Walali told the white man that the war cries of the villagers were directed at the patrol and that they would be killed if they spent the night there. It was this treachery that was alleged to be responsible for the deaths. According to Agula, Walali translated Ipitango's pleas to spare his pigs into a threat to attack those who were butchering them so that the white man shot him. Though none of our informants actually saw who killed Ipitango and Ketango, Sigale insisted that it was Walali who had stuck his bayonet into Ketango because of the enmity over Pepeawere.

Six informants also mention Walali as being involved in the incident at Kagapore/Kananda among the Amburupa people the next day. The Amburupa were allies of the Yala and Tepenarirepa against Perepe. Pisa said

that Walali was still out to avenge the Perepe by causing mischief between
the patrol and the Amburupa. Thus, he said, when Lombora tried to make
the white man understand that he wanted a knife for his bananas, Walali
told the white man that Lombora wanted to kill him with his axe. The
white man then slapped Lombora across the face and went inside his tent.
Lombora bolted, but Walali shot and killed his brother and his eldest
son, both of whom were standing there. Pisa himself did not see this but
claimed that other witnesses had told him. He believed that Walali was
acting with the permission of the white men, who told him he could settle
any scores he wanted.

Walali then killed the other five men in Kananda and later planted
cordylines at Urupi to stand for the men he had killed.* It was the custom
in those days to give the leaf of the red cordyline to the relatives of the
person avenged, and this is what Walali did for the Perepe at Urupi. Much
later Pisa heard that some Yala man had killed Walali and his brother in
Samberigi, thus avenging the Kewa deaths. Walali was also said to have
been the first to tell the Kewa that the patrol were not *remo* (ghosts) but
gavman (the government), and in Tiripi and Kalalo he is said to have translated the message that the patrol wished to dispense medicine—though
this can be seen as treachery, since when the people arrived they were
shot.

This account of Walali was intriguing and in tune with traditional practices in war and payback. But while it injected the episode with cultural
significance, its historical accuracy was unconvincing from the start. Of
five informants (Pisa, Agula, Bolame, Pupula, and Ana) who gave accounts
of the Koyamapu incident, only two (Pisa and Agula) mentioned Walali
spontaneously. The others admitted when asked that they had heard of
him but could say little about his part in the episode. Other people (particularly Amburupa) denied that such a person as Walali ever existed. It
eventually became clear that while many people knew something of the
story, they had all heard of Walali only well after the patrol had passed
through the country; they had not been aware of him at the time it was
there. By most accounts, it seems to have been the Perepe themselves who
first circulated the story—perhaps hoping to bank on the reputation that
such a powerful (if fictional) kinsman would provide. According to the
patrol report, however, there was no one named Walali on the patrol, nor
did the party include anyone who spoke Kewa or who came from the area
from which Walali was supposed to have come.

How did the stories of Walali originate? Walali appears to be a composite figure put together over the years from stories of the activities of
patrol police that circulated around the Kewa area just before and after

* In some accounts the cordyline leaves are replaced by pig tethers or wild pitpit (*ambu*).

the Second World War (see Appendix A). What is important for the Kewa
is that the story of Walali made their experience with the Strickland-Purari
patrol culturally meaningful. Whether as folk hero or trickster figure,
Walali made this violent episode comprehensible to them and involved
them as actors in events rather than just as victims. In a sense, the strange
white people became important only as they empowered Walali to strike
a few blows for the Perepe in the "war over the pig's belly."

Hindsights

The Kewa were impressed that the patrol had appeared as if out of the
blue. They had had no hint of the existence of these creatures from their
parents or ancestors, who normally passed on all there was to be known.
According to Sigale, an old Koiari man, "We didn't know where these
creatures came from; we wondered if they had come from the sky, from
under the ground, or from inside the water. We thought they might be
remo, but we had never seen remo before; they are not normally visible.
We were very scared of them and thought that eventually many of them
would come back and finish us all off. Yet at the same time we liked the
good things they had brought with them, such as matches and knives."

The Kewa found no easy way to incorporate these strange beings into
their cosmology. Most of the time, informants referred to the patrol as
"the remo line." As ghosts of the dead, remo were known by their actions;
they did not normally appear to living people in broad daylight. At night,
people who passed a burial site or an open space might feel something
brushing against them and interpret it as remo. More often, one saw remo
in dreams where they appeared to warn the sleeper of some impending
evil. Unlike Nembi and Wola ghosts of the dead, Kewa remo were not
evil or malevolent spirits, though they did have to be placated. The Kewa
normally only feared remo of the recently dead—and only for a couple of
weeks. If, for example, a young mother died, her husband and his relatives
would do all they could to cajole her children not to cry lest they cause the
mother's ghost to think they were neglected and so come to carry them
off. After this time, the remo is unlikely to interfere directly in the affairs
of the living and would eventually be consigned to the larger category of
ancestral shades, rimbu, which are honored collectively by the Kewa.

Occasionally Kewa also referred to patrol members as rarineli.* These

---

*Also known as kolodoali, kaliapoali, or bukin. Besides remo, people also referred to the
patrol as amali and kapona (two forms of grass said to have appeared at the same time as
the patrol) or kandipi (literally, "red man"), which now means "European" (cf. Huli, Wola,
Nembi hundipi). Amali sounds so much like "O'Malley" as to suggest an etymology there.
For a fuller discussion of the complex origins and use of the word kapona in this general
area of the highlands, see Clark (forthcoming).

are malicious sprites who have never been human and are not bound by moral laws. They can assume any shape and delight in tricking human beings—being especially fond of taking the form of beautiful maidens who ensnare young men.

Despite the reference to the patrol as "the *remo* line" (or *rarineli*), the Kewa were not necessarily convinced by that interpretation. Nevertheless, many took precautions against known *remo* propensities for stealing and kidnapping by burying valuable possessions and advising young women (who were believed to be in particular danger of being carried off) to run and hide. One young girl was actually hidden by her mother in the hollow of a tree until her father came to tell her that the *remo* had gone.

The uncertainty as to whether the patrol members were really ghosts is reflected in the disputed accounts of how the bodies of Ipitango and Ketango were disposed of. One informant said the bodies were smeared with tree oil (*wambala*) and buried in swampy ground, and their names could not be spoken for a long time. Kewa customarily avoid speaking the names of the dead, but they practice swamp burial only in cases when the victim is believed to have been put to death by a *remo*, which they fear might return to the village burial ground and cause further mischief. Another informant denied that an important man like Ipitango would have suffered the indignity of a swamp burial but conceded that his body was kept in the men's house for only two days (instead of the usual four or five) and was watched over only by old men. All the young men were sent to stay in the bush and in caves in order to be safe from *remo*.

Whether the dead were buried in a swamp or not, their mode of disposal did not follow the usual practice. Kewa mortuary rites and attendant practices are based on the manner of death and herald the action to be taken in retaliation. The respect felt for a killed person was expressed in warlike sentiments of revenge, not only because the individual is treasured as a kinsperson but because his unavenged spirit (*remo*) is feared. But if ancestral ghosts (*remo*) take a life, there could be no question of vengeance. When this happens, mortuary ceremonies are muted, and the dead are disposed of quickly in the hope that the ancestors will be placated. In this case the Kewa were not sure whether the patrol were *remo* or not. Hence the contrasting claims over the types of rites, for the incident could not be satisfactorily fitted into their beliefs. In any case, perfunctory funerals are customary when no action is proposed to follow the killing. Pomp and ceremony in these circumstances where the deceased's clansmen could do nothing to take revenge would merely reveal their helplessness and expose them to ridicule.

How then did the patrol fit into local Kewa cosmology, appearing as it did so rudely on a set unprepared for it? Not very easily. The Kewa were never fully comfortable with consigning the patrol to the realm of *remo*. The subsequently fabricated accounts of Walali represent an attempt to fit the patrol into the *human* moral order and in this way find a more satisfactory place for it in the local scheme of things.

Throughout our discussions with informants nearly 50 years later, one of their recurring questions was that of responsibility, retribution, and God's justice. Was it right, was it Christian, to have killed these people? Who was responsible for these killings? Would they meet those killed again in the afterlife? While the older men tended to narrate the events without passing moral judgment or comment, the younger men (who had not been born at the time) expressed open resentment at the killings. They granted that Lombora at Kagapore may have given some provocation but not enough to result in the shootings. They claimed vehemently that the Kewa were unarmed and that they did not attack the patrol. The overwhelming feeling was that they had been killed for nothing, and the *kapona* (government officers) were to blame. These younger men were products of a changed world and could dispense with the story of Walali. In rejecting his part in the killings, they rendered the incident as one in which their fathers were passive victims in events they did not comprehend.

A number of informants ended their accounts of the patrol by describing another event that happened a few months later. One day there was a loud buzzing noise whose source and direction they could not identify. Some said it was a hornbill (*sau*) flying in the sky, while others believed it to be the *ruru* frog from the forest floor, which cries only during rainy periods.

The Yala, by then defeated at Wata and sojourning in refuge in Wapia, suspected this strange noise was the *remo* returning. The *remo* had killed members of only the Yala, Tepenarirepa, and Amburupa tribes, so if they were returning now, it must be to finish them off. If the sound was coming from inside the ground, these three tribes had better go elsewhere to fight, for whatever it was would grab their legs and pull them under. *Remo* were believed to have their homes underground, so the implication here was quite plain.

The sound they had heard was undoubtedly an aircraft. Several months after Hides had passed through the region, Ivan Champion flew over on a cloudy day, reconnoitering the route for the Bamu-Purari patrol of 1936.*

---

* Much later, in 1943, a large number of Australian and American warplanes passed over on their way from bases in northern Australia to bomb Japanese positions on the north coast —and this time they were seen. Yala Roga was in the Wapia spirit house just after killing pigs when they came. "First people thought they were birds, but then some people said that they had houses inside for the *remo* who had killed so many of them on the earlier occasion, and they wondered with trepidation what might be in store for them this time."

Lower Pwe Basin in the Southern Nembi Plateau. Extensive cultivations lie among the pinnacles and dolines of one of the most heavily populated areas in Papua New Guinea, through which the Strickland-Purari patrol passed. (Photo: M. J. J. Bik, CSIRO, 1961)

Gardens and ceremonial ground in the lower Pwe Basin. The ceremonial ground (*hauma*) is behind the guesthouse constructed in lowland style for Lake Kutubu visitors. A long, low, highland-style guesthouse runs down the side. (Photo: M. J. J. Bik, CSIRO, 1961)

Nembi Plateau today, looking south over Emia Creek. This densely populated and extremely rugged karst landscape is the view Hides would have seen as he walked over the divide into the Emia Valley. (Photo: Crittenden, 1981)

The Emia Valley below Aib where Ebobi Wa was killed. "Howling and yodeling commenced," Hides noted as the people in the valley called out the news of Ebobi's death and wailed their grief. "It started in the farmhouses below and was taken up for what seemed miles around." (Photo: Crittenden, 1981)

Dense limestone pinnacles of the southern Nembi Plateau ("broken bottle country"). The house in the foreground gives some sense of scale; these pinnacles are 45–60m high. (Photo: M. J. J. Bik, CSIRO, 1961)

A trench cut deep into the soft volcanic ash of the Nembi Plateau serves as a path into a homestead and ceremonial ground. Protected by two fences and dense cane grass on either side, this gives an idea of the approach to Pembi Andaa, where the patrol held off repeated attacks by Merut warriors. (Photo: Crittenden, 1981)

Typical Sugu valley settlement at time of a ceremonial exchange of pigs, much
as Maisapalu would have looked at the time the Strickland-Purari patrol arrived.
(Photo: Josephides, 1979)

"Hides with Black Papuans of the Iumbarave," apparently taken near Kagapore before the shootings. Hides was very ill at this time and wears a grim expression. According to Yamba Pabala, the man on the left is Webo (Epo) Lombura, who was shot by Hides's police shortly afterwards. The young boy on the extreme right is a younger clan brother named Walawe. (Photo: O'Malley, in *PW*, facing p. x)

Southern Kewa warrior with the underarm shield common in the area. Hides commented: "A typical member of the Iumberave. I should take these men to be the finest fighters in Papua." (Photo: O'Malley, in *PW*, facing p. 168)

A mortuary structure in the Kewa country. This elaborate form of burial, common throughout the Southern Highlands at the time of contact, was not afforded to Ipitango and others killed by the patrol. (Photo: Hides, in *PW*, facing p. 154)

Pupula, an important eyewitness of the patrol, and his wife. (Photo: Josephides, 1979)

The Wharf at Ogamobu Plantation on the Kikori River in the early 1930's. Here Hides, O'Malley, and their exhausted patrol arrived on June 18, 1935. (Photo: Mrs. G. Allen-Innes Collection, Mitchell Library, Sydney; File A2118)

The house at Ogamobu Plantation. Here Hides and O'Malley ate the first breakfast of bacon and eggs they had had in six months. (Photo: Small Picture Collection, Australian School of Pacific Administration Donated Collection, Mitchell Library; FM2/641-648, Plate 8 ACC 2079)

The government station at Kikori in 1928, with its entire population. Armed constabulary flank the government officers. Constabulary wives sit in front. To the left are government staff and other government employees. (Photo: Small Picture Collection, Australian School of Pacific Administration Donated Collection, Mitchell Library; FM3/844, Plate A27 ACC 2216)

The "Route of the Strickland Purari Patrol" drawn by D. Macpherson for *The Sphere*, a London picture magazine (Sept. 14, 1935, p. 391). The caption reads: "The route taken by Mr. J. G. Hides when they penetrated recently the uncharted mountains of Eastern New Guinea and found, walled off from the world by 7000 foot high limestone cliffs, an intensively cultivated valley with no villages, but well-built dwellings inhabited by the Tari Furora—a strange light-skinned race of short stature possessing high cheekbones, finely moulded features, and mops of fuzzy hair."

The map is wildly inaccurate, showing the Hegigio/Kikori flowing into the Erave and the patrol route running deep into the Mandated Territory, then doubling back on itself to return to the coast. The "Tari Furora" and "Waga Furari" are shown as isolated high valleys enclosed by sheer mountain walls. Though not much as geography, it is a splendid representation of Hides's patrol in the popular imagination: the hero's journey to the lost world. (Photo: Evan R. Gill Collection, Mitchell Library, F988.4)

9. RETURN TO KIKORI

EDWARD L. SCHIEFFELIN AND ROBERT CRITTENDEN

After leaving Kagapore on May 29, the patrol crept up the spurs of the limestone barrier. Looking back over the country they had crossed, they could see the cultivations of the Kewa stretching away to the north and east. "People like sand," remarked one of the constables once again; "People like sand!" There was no population like this to be seen in the villages of the Papuan coast.[*]

For the next three days they struggled on over uninhabited dog-toothed limestone ridges. What they ate is unclear—very probably they had food taken from Kewa gardens, but most of the small supply of rice had been soaked and ruined when the patrol had rafted down the Erave more than a week before. Eventually, the trail gave out, and they had to proceed through the forest by compass bearing. However, Hides's health was beginning to improve, and he discovered he was able to keep down a little solid food. Slowly, his strength began to return. On the fourth day they found a faint track and, following it, emerged from the forest into a newly made garden. "Real *Papuan* gardens!" Hides exclaimed. "With taro, sugarcane, and potato vines growing around the stumps of fallen trees" (*PW*: 177). It was a forest swidden planting and marked the return, after nearly three months, to the kind of country and people—"the real Papua"—with which Hides and his men were familiar. The grasslands with their contour drains, stake-fenced fields, and hordes of yodeling warriors were finally behind them. They were in the home country now.

A large crowd of wary bowmen appeared and advanced cautiously upon

[*] In the absence of field research from this area, we must rely on *PW* and *PR* for information for this chapter.

them, but perceiving Hides's friendly wave put down their weapons and prepared a very welcome feast.

"The gardens were soon filled with scores of men," Hides wrote. "They made us all sit down; they lit fires, and they cooked the best food that could be obtained. Nothing was too good for us, and the friendly smile that every man gave us seemed to tell us they knew well what we had all been through. They would not take presents, but we were so moved by their kindness that I made the first man we had met accept two axes" (*PR*: 101–2).

Later in the afternoon they crossed the Erave (called Erewa locally) by means of a stout vine suspension bridge and camped in a garden. Crowds of people appeared, and everyone was in a jubilant mood that evening. The contrast to their receptions in the highlands was striking.

"No people could have treated us more kindly," Hides wrote. "They built our shelters, made our fires, and brought more food than we could eat or carry. There was no need for guards now. . . . We rested in peace and in all possible comfort with these people."

With a rush of feeling he added: "It all made me conscious of what Papua meant, and of the other officers who had gone before us. They had wandered over these parts, among these people, and had left them, not with a fear of the government but with a respect and welcome which we were now enjoying" (*PW*: 178).

For the next few days the patrol received a warm and generous welcome wherever they went. Hides guessed that the country they were now traveling through had been visited by government patrols before.* On June 2 a man came up to him and shouted: "Pugini, Pugini, Polisimani!"† Rec-

---

*Josephides and Schiltz found one informant from this area, who gave a different story. According to Tueri Pamenda, when the patrol arrived, his clansmen armed themselves in order to avenge their dead killed by a previous patrol. Tueri was told by his father that at the time they had tried to steal some bushknives from the patrol and subsequently some of them were killed. Tueri said that when the Strickland-Purari patrol came through, the white man told them to put up their weapons and bring some food, which they did and were paid with salt. But when they demanded more salt the patrol, seeing their weapons, became afraid and started shooting. Five men were killed, Tueri asserted, and three wounded. Tueri was ten at the time and claimed to have seen this with his own eyes. But Josephides and Schiltz could find no one who could corroborate his story—and Hides certainly gives no hint of it. Also the patrol was not carrying salt as trade. Tueri may have been referring to earlier patrols. During Faithorn and Champion's patrol in this region in 1929, one man was shot by police in an altercation over stolen knives and blankets. Patrols led by Beaver (1911) and Flint and Saunders (1922) also involved shootings (see Appendix A).

†Pugini was a widely known figure in the region. Born near the Sirebi River, he knew the language of the people of the Samberigi area. He joined the constabulary early on and accompanied Flint and Saunders on their extensive exploration of the Samberigi and Kerabi villages in 1922 where he was useful as an interpreter. He returned again with Saunders in 1924 and with Faithorn and Champion in 1929. During these patrols he formed friendships with local men of influence whom he met along the way and who also accompanied the

ognizing the Papuan term for the constabulary (*polisimani*), Hides was delighted: "It was the first civilized word we had heard since leaving the Strickland over five months ago."

This native took it upon himself to guide the patrol like a master of ceremonies: "[He pointed] out the places of interest as he led us across the valley and up the southern slopes. . . . He was an entertaining sort of person, never tiring of talking and explaining by gesture. Here had been a good garden. The taro had been like this! But on the other side—well— he turned his hand to dismiss the thought. . . . If there was a bad bridge, he apologized for its condition; and all the people of note who came to meet us were introduced to O'Malley and myself.

" 'It's like a vice regal entry,' said O'Malley" (*PW*: 183).

Hides was certain they had passed within the reach of coastal patrols when he noted an old gentleman wearing a pendant made from the lid of an old corned beef tin.

There was much good food that night. The party was beginning to get stronger from the abundance of food pressed upon them in the last few days. The men were still weak, but their spirits soared. Only Corporal Emesi remained ill. "The poor man's nerves were completely gone," Hides wrote. "He still thinks we are in the grasslands and that he can hear yodeling. Over and over he would repeat 'My lamp is going out' " (*PW*: 184).

Now that they were in the area known to administration patrols, Hides had a good idea where he was and began to think about which route he should follow to the coast, still a considerable distance to the south. He decided against an original plan to follow the Erave/Purari to its mouth:

"The route that had been taken by Faithorn and Champion [in 1929] down the Erewa through Hathor Gorge did not appeal to me in the party's present condition, for we were all still very weak, and we had no food or tents; so though I realized the Zambrigi (Samberigi) route down through the Iehi Chasm was dangerous in the wet season, I decided to take it. There was no food at all on the Erewa route until reaching the flat country below the gorge, whereas through the Zambrigi we passed through populations" (*PW*: 185).

Two days later, the patrol reached the head of the Samberigi Valley. By now they were accompanied by substantial crowds of friendly people,

---

patrols as guides and interpreters. Subsequently, Pugini retired at the rank of lance corporal and, in 1935, was living in his home area near the Sirebi River. He apparently parlayed his extensive travel experience and personal connections gained during his patroling years into a lucrative trading position. His reputation and influence in the area was such that Hides got the impression that he controlled the trade route from the Samberigi Valley north to the Erave (cf. Wagner 1979b: 140–65).

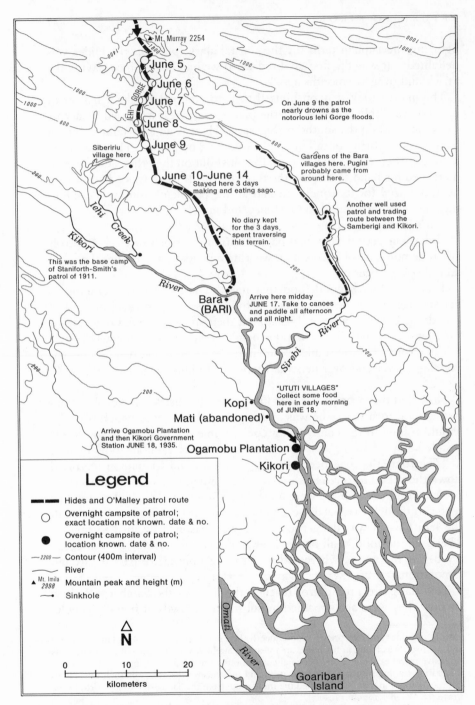

Map 12. Over Mt. Murray and through the Iehi Gorge to Kikori Station (June 5–18).

some of whom helped carry Emesi and a weakened carrier who could not walk. Everywhere they went they were greeted with cries of "Pugini, Pugini, Polisimani!" These people remained with them as they traveled southward along the old patrol route through the Samberigi Valley up to the flanks of Mt. Murray.

Descending the other side on the following morning, they entered the upper reaches of the lowland tropical forest. Not long afterwards they came upon an old campsite of a white man littered with a few rusted tins, the detritus, as they later learned, of a prospector who had passed through the area three months before. They were getting very close to home, but had to endure one last harrowing moment. On the night of June 9 they were trapped by a flash flood in the narrow chasm of the Iehi Gorge southwest of Mt. Murray. The rushing water rose nearly to their waists in the darkness, then subsided before it was high enough to carry any of them away. All managed to emerge from the chasm in the morning.

When they arrived at Bara village on the Kikori River, Hides was greeted by the headman: "We thought you finish, Taubada. . . . Long time you leave Daru. We wait, wait. Kikori government wait too; but all people say you finish this time. But you come" (PW: 196).

The next day, June 18, the patrol straggled into the first European settlement, Ogomobu Plantation on the banks of the Kikori River, and shortly afterwards into Kikori Station itself. Hides and O'Malley were barefoot, filthy, and dressed in rags. Both looked half-starved and were completely exhausted, but they were grinning like children that they and their men were safely returned.

Kikori Station was in the charge of Resident Magistrate W. R. Humphries, a tough, experienced man whom Hides admired and after whom he had named a mountain range near the Papuan Plateau. Upon the arrival of the patrol Humphries and his wife administered to their needs. Corporal Emesi and the weakened Orokolo carrier whom they had been carrying for nearly two weeks were taken to the infirmary for medical treatment. The carrier recovered, but Emesi died that night.

He was buried the next day in the falling rain. Hides accompanied Sergeant Orai and some other constables as they carried the body to the gravesite. They placed Emesi's wooden comb, his looking glass, and his sheath knife together with him in the grave.

" 'It is government work,' said Dekadua.

" 'True,' replied Orai" (PW: 201).

Reflecting on what the patrol had accomplished, Hides wrote: "O'Malley and myself [have] now completed the work [of exploration] in Papua. We had discovered the platform of the Kikori westward of Hagen, and the beautiful valley of the Tari Furoro and its light-skinned men; and as we had marched farther to the eastward, we had traced the three river systems of the Purari that drained this tableland; and we had crossed and re-crossed the terrible limestone barrier that formed its southern walls" (*PW*: 184).

"And now that the patrol is ended, I think of it as it might have been had the natives chosen to spare us: that they did not, and that a lot of them sought to kill us, and that we had on occasion to fight for our lives and so kill some of them, is a circumstance that I shall never cease to regret" (*PR*: 108).

10. AFTERMATH AND REFLECTIONS

EDWARD L. SCHIEFFELIN AND ROBERT CRITTENDEN

The journey was over.* "The two officers," wrote Resident Magistrate Humphries, "seemed to be bordering on a state of nervous breakdown" (*IQ*: letter to Government Secretary, Port Moresby, July 3, 1935). Hides was deeply worried over the bloodshed caused by his patrol. He knew there would have to be an accounting and he wanted to forestall the rumors that were sure to fly when word of the patrol got out. On June 19, the day after they arrived at Kikori Station, Hides asked Humphries to carry out a formal inquiry. Considering the wretched state Hides and O'Malley were in, Humphries wanted to wait until they had had a chance to recover, but Hides insisted it be held immediately. Actually, by holding the inquiry right away, he probably improved his chances of getting a sympathetic hearing: the two men still bore the marks of their ordeal and, in the short time since their return, there had been little opportunity to recount the events of the patrol, let alone reflect upon them. The inquiry, held June 19–26, was completed before anyone in the outside world even knew they were back. Statements were taken from the officers, a number of the police, and several carriers. Humphries listened and asked clarifying questions but did not probe inconsistencies or lacunae in the account or seriously cross-examine the witnesses.

According to the evidence presented, the patrol had opened fire on the natives on at least nine occasions: five in which it actually repulsed attacks and four in order to prevent incipient attacks at close quarters. At least 32 men had been killed by rifle fire—though it was noted that the full casual-

---

* The historical information for the first section of this chapter is largely drawn from Sinclair 1969.

ties, particularly in the battle on May 13 with the Merut at Pembi Andaa, were unknown. (With these, and other casualties Hides did not know about, the number was actually about 54.) A total of 133 rounds of .303 ammunition had been fired, leaving 297 rounds remaining when the patrol returned. No member of the patrol had been killed or seriously wounded in the skirmishes.

Commenting on the incidents where the patrol had fired "preventatively," Humphries noted the enormous difficulties and dangers that would have beset the party had it been forced to carry wounded. He concluded: "If I am right, and I am writing in the light of nearly a quarter century's experience in this country, the act of firing on the natives on these four occasions reduced the inevitable bloodshed to a minimum" (*IQ*: Humphries to Government Secretary, July 3, 1935). This was to become the basic government position on the shootings during the patrol. When the report arrived in Port Moresby, it was duly noted and filed. No details of the numbers killed were ever released to the press.

Hides and O'Malley arrived in Port Moresby about July 20. As stories of their discoveries began to circulate, there was tremendous excitement. The finding of a large and unsuspected population deep in the mountains of the Papuan interior was an event of major significance. Sir Hubert Murray was extremely pleased and sent a telegram to the Prime Minister's Department in Australia: "Very difficult expedition carried out with complete success in spite of extreme hardship reflects greatest credit on all concerned" (quoted in Sinclair 1969: 172).

Later he wrote in the introduction to Hides's book: "Mr. Hides and Mr. O'Malley have carried out a really remarkable piece of work; work which demanded an unusual amount of pluck and endurance on the part of all, and on the part of the leaders, a rare power of inspiring courage and enthusiasm in men who, like themselves, were half dead with hunger and fatigue" (*PW*: xii).

The achievements and discoveries of the Strickland-Purari patrol soon received international publicity. They caused a tremendous stir in Australia and throughout the Commonwealth. Hubert Murray received congratulations from England and from colonial officials in other parts of the empire.

This denouement stands in ironic contrast to the aftermath of Staniforth Smith's patrol of 24 years before (Chapter 1). Both patrols involved mistakes of judgment, suffered from starvation and incredible hardship, and resulted in a number of native deaths (though Smith's were among his carriers, not people he encountered). Neither patrol could afterwards give an adequate account of exactly where it had been. History, however, has treated them quite differently—largely for political reasons. Smith's patrol had been an attempt to challenge Murray's prestige as part of an effort to unseat him as lieutenant governor. Hides's patrol was mounted by Murray and was a showpiece of the final years of his regime. Naturally Sir Hubert condemned the one as a bungled disaster while hailing the other as an outstanding success. The Australian colonial office and the world press followed suit.

But apart from Murray's sensitivity about his political image, the Strickland-Purari patrol really had made some very important discoveries. In finding a large interior population, perhaps comparable to that discovered by the Leahy brothers in the Mandated Territory, Hides and O'Malley had changed the picture of Papua overnight. No one knew what exciting potential this apparently rich and populated interior might hold. Shortly afterward, when Lake Kutubu was discovered,* Hubert Murray lost no time in opening a patrol post there, supplied by flying boat, to serve as a staging base for the exploration and consolidation of the highlands. It was as if the landscape and population of Papua had suddenly increased by a third.

Reflections on the Patrol

While Murray was very pleased with the discoveries of the Strickland-Purari patrol and praised it highly, he was privately distressed at the amount of violence it had involved. "It is regrettable there were so many casualties," he wrote to the Minister in Charge of Territories. "I cannot remember a previous occasion on which so many lost their lives, but I also cannot remember an occasion upon which so many desperate attacks were made by so great a number of natives, and over so many days" (*IQ*: letter of August 12, 1935).

Indeed, the killing of more than 30 people by a single patrol had not been seen in Papua since the punitive expeditions under the administrations of MacGregor and LeHunt back at the turn of the century.[†] Subsequent patrols into the Tari Basin and the Waga and Nembi valleys a few years later encountered difficulties from time to time, but they never experienced the level of persistent harassment and bloodshed involved in the

---

* Lake Kutubu, the largest body of water in Papua New Guinea, was discovered from the air during one of the flights made to check the route of the Strickland-Purari patrol. Because of an intervening mountain range, the lake remained hidden from the patrol as it passed through the nearby Wola and Nembi country.

† It is probable that native casualties of clashes with patrols were underreported once Murray took office, but they could not have been large compared to those of earlier times: W. Armit reported killing 54 Papuans on patrol in 1900; A. Elliot killed 40 in 1901; and A. Walsh 32 in 1902 (Griffin, Nelson, and Firth, 1979: 18). LeHunt himself led the punitive expedition against the Goaribari in retaliation for the murder and cannibalism of Rev. Chalmers in 1901, which resulted in over 100 Papuan deaths (see Chapter 1).

Strickland-Purari patrol. In fact, violence and treachery were unusual in most situations of first contact in Papua. What, then, was unusual about this expedition?

The question became more puzzling within a year. In 1936 Ivan Champion and C. T. J. Adamson led the last major exploratory expedition in Papua from the mouth of the Bamu River into the Southern Highlands and then down the Purari to the sea. They traveled north and south of Hides and O'Malley's route, through similar regions populated by similar peoples, yet without experiencing any violence or causing any casualties at all (see Sinclair 1988). For this reason (and others that were less laudable) it was inevitable that Hides would receive some criticism over his conduct of the Strickland-Purari patrol. That he was not infallible is clear from the story. But the situation was not a simple one.

Perhaps the single most significant factor affecting the Strickland-Purari patrol was that, unlike subsequent patrols through the area, Hides and O'Malley had to operate for the last month of their journey under conditions of near starvation. In part, this was the result of two crucial miscalculations. The first was that Hides abandoned half his supplies in the Etoro country before he ever entered the highlands (Chapter 2). At the time, this was a calculated risk, to avoid an ambush of his carriers as they relayed the rice through the depths of the tropical forest. Hides expected on the basis of his experience that he would be able to trade for food from local populations he hoped to encounter farther down the line. It is a simple exercise to estimate what difference it would have made if the patrol had not abandoned half its rice. Had they lived entirely off full rations of rice, the patrol could have made it about as far as Songura in the upper Waga Valley. Traveling at half ration and supplementing with whatever little food they could obtain along the way, they could have made it most of the way through the Nembi country, perhaps even as far as the Erave River before running out of rice. This would have brought them through the worst of the journey without undue privation, to the threshold of the less hostile Kewa country.

The hunger of the patrol was aggravated by their physical exhaustion. When Hides and O'Malley arrived in the Huli country, they and their men were worn out from three months of hard travel. Their situation may be compared to that of Champion and Adamson on the Bamu-Purari patrol a year later. Champion and Adamson arrived on the southern portion of the Papuan Plateau after three months of hard travel in about the same condition that Hides arrived in the highlands: exhausted and with their men beginning to show symptoms of beriberi.[*] The local plateau population

---

[*] Champion figured that, in order to relay their supplies 150 km through the forest, his carriers had had to walk over 900 km in the three months they were on their way to the Papuan Plateau (Champion 1940: 204).

(the Bosavi people) was sparse, and, like the Etoro and Onabasulu, they preferred to hide in the forest rather than confront the patrol. Though timid, they were familiar with steel and eventually proved eager to trade pigs and garden produce for it. Under these circumstances, Champion was able to rest his patrol for two weeks at the hamlet of Ewelo and allow his men to recuperate. Hides and O'Malley did not have this luxury. They emerged in the highlands to find themselves amidst a heavy population of assertive and warlike people unfamiliar with steel and unwilling to accept it as trade. The standoffish attitude of the Hulis and their reluctance to sell any food meant that the patrol had to keep moving.

Once in the highlands the Strickland-Purari patrol had so little rice that it became almost entirely dependent on the local people for food. This was not the first time Hides had faced this kind of situation, but his difficulty in obtaining supplies for his men in this case was unusual. The most common explanation for Hides's difficulty points up his second miscalculation: the patrol was not carrying mother-of-pearl shell. Indeed some informants among the Wola and Nembi, recalling the lack of this item, thought the patrol had brought no trade goods at all. The lack of pearlshell in turn exacerbated the effects of other factors.

For example, in the Huli region people lived in dispersed farmsteads; many who visited the patrol's camps came from some distance away. They did not own the gardens in the immediate vicinity of the camp and could not sell food from them even if they had wished to. Further on, the Nembi frequently suffered chronic food shortages because gardens were often destroyed in their constant fighting; they may not have had much food to eat themselves. In some places one gets the impression that the people did not sell food to the patrol because they feared it and wanted it to go away. Elsewhere, when the patrol was manifesting clear signs of exhaustion, illness, and starvation, the warriors may have refused to sell them food in hopes of weakening them further.

It is also possible (though the evidence is equivocal) that some regions were experiencing a bad crop year. Most informants deny there were food shortages when the patrol passed through, and Hides repeatedly mentions the luxuriant growth of sweet potato vines in the gardens he saw throughout his journey. On the other hand the year 1934 may have been a time of drought at least in some places. The Fox brothers reported in the diary of their trip that it rarely rained in the Tari Basin in November 1934 and that most of the streams they crossed were dry. If there was a dry spell in the Tari Basin in late 1934 and early 1935, it may well have extended throughout the area. Sweet potato crops are more readily harmed by flooding rains than drought, but very dry spells can have a significant effect. The Southern Highlands from the Tari Basin southeastward across the Waga and Nembi valleys is a complex series of altitude-related ecological microenvironments in which some areas may experience severe frosts or droughts (or excessive rainfall) in a given year while others nearby do not. One valley may have food shortages while another nearby has enough. Interestingly, sweet potato plants sometimes produce abundant leaves when damaged by drought or excessive rain, but bear few tubers (Anders 1983). If Hides was passing through such an area, it would have been easy to mistake such growth for evidence of plenty. In the final analysis, however, the complexity of the ecological situation and the poverty of historical data make it almost impossible to determine the degree to which any given area traversed by the patrol may have been experiencing food shortage.

Be that as it may, had Hides and O'Malley been carrying pearlshell it is likely that they would have been able to override most of these difficulties and obtain the supplies they needed. Again the experience of Champion and Adamson's patrol is instructive. In November 1936, while crossing from the Augu to the Mendi Valley, they camped near the southern end of the Nipa Basin not far from the Korpe defile. Like Hides and O'Malley they had difficulty obtaining food in this area—at first.

"We asked for food, but they brought none. [An] old man pointed out that it took a lot of work to make gardens and that there wasn't much food. Even a new tomahawk had no effect. . . . [Next day] when we wanted to buy more food with steel goods they would not listen. So we brought out mother-of-pearl. . . . They [suddenly] got very excited. Some of them ran down the slope and in a few minutes the valley resounded with calls." Men came hurrying in to see the shell. They clasped it to their breasts, passed shells from hand to hand. Adamson marked out a square on the ground with sticks and told them that the square had to be filled with food as the price of one shell. In half an hour men came in with bags of sweet potato (Champion 1940: 243–44).

Champion found, however, that though avid for shell the people still brought less than he had asked for and demanded more than he wanted to give. His patrol had plenty of rice, however, and he did not have to worry about refusing to buy food that he thought was too high priced. Patrol officers were to complain until well into the 1960's about the difficulty of obtaining food from these warrior traders (Mendi PR 1, 1950–51; Mendi PR 4, 1952–53).*

* It is worth mentioning that hard bargaining was not a quality restricted to the Wola and Nembi but was characteristic of many peoples along the trade route. In 1922 Flint and Saunders patrolling through the Samberigi Valley remarked: "Our only complaint against the people is their meanness. They have never brought more than two or three bananas to the camp at one time. In exchange they asked for tomahawks [axes] or knives" (Kikori PR 13, 1921–22). A year later Saunders noted: "The people brought in a few handfuls of potatoes and still demanded an axe in payment, in spite of the fact that this must be the third patrol to the district, and that they must have some ideas of value now, so it is not ignorance this

The absence of pearlshell had a further consequence for the Strickland-Purari patrol: without it, Hides and O'Malley had very limited means of forming a common ground for friendly relations with the local tribesmen, which undoubtedly contributed to their embattled passage through the highlands. No subsequent patrol experienced that degree of harassment. In part this may be because the warriors had learned about firearms from Hides and O'Malley's police and so were reluctant to enter an armed confrontation with later patrols. But that is not the whole story.

Hides and O'Malley were attacked for several different reasons. At least twice the patrol was mistaken for an enemy raiding party. At other times hostility may have resulted from resentment over police and carriers filching from gardens. However, unlike any subsequent patrols, Hides and O'Malley and their men were hungry and weak. Treachery was unusual (on first contact), O'Malley later explained, "but here it was different; here were sick and starving men. [We] were just bait for the taking. . . . These people realized the position we were in and although they had plenty of food, they did not give it to us; . . . they waited for us to drop" (Sinclair, personal correspondence). The Huli, Wola, and Nembi were hardened to violence and scornful of weakness. They were used to responding aggressively to something they feared if they thought they could get away with it. The weakened physical condition of the patrol seriously compromised its ability to project the appearance of men who could handle themselves competently in the face of force. It invited harassment by warriors seeking to locate its vulnerable points. There is no contradiction between informants' recollections that they were terrified of the patrol and the conviction of Hides and O'Malley that the tribesmen perceived their weakness and deliberately attempted to prey upon it.

The results were predictable. As the patrol became more and more exhausted, it tempted the surrounding warriors to greater harassment. Increasingly beleaguered, Hides and O'Malley found it difficult not to see danger and treachery at every turn. This situation evidently reached its tragic culmination in the Kewa country, after the worst danger of harassment by local warriors had passed, but the signs of it were already evident on the Nembi Plateau. A careful reading of Hides's report suggests that when the patrol arrived at Aib in the Emia Creek area, it received a more friendly reception than Hides realized, but Hides posted guards and the result was the shooting of Ebobi Wa, the possum hunter who had crept up to investigate the "moon" of lantern light that night.

This can be compared with a similar incident four years later during a patrol camped at the Benaria River south of Tari. The officer reported: "At

time. Without exception I think they are the meanest people I have ever had anything to do with" (Kikori PR 17, 1923–24).

10:15 P.M. the guard A.C. Bego gave an alarm and said he saw two armed men sneaking around the tent. But we saw no one." No shots were fired, and the next morning "we learned that two small boys, seeing the bright light near the tent, which they likened to the moon, had crept up to see what it was" (Lake Kutubu PR 6 1939–40). Unlike Hides and O'Malley, however, this patrol was strong and well-fed, and it had not been surrounded and threatened all the previous day by hostile warriors. Hides had been so pressed that, despite a relatively nonhostile reception at Aib, he expected to be treacherously attacked that night and set the guards with orders to shoot any intruders on sight.

Hides knew that Wola and Nembi warriors pressed the patrol as hard as they did because they believed it was vulnerable. He also realized that they did not know the "wooden sticks" (rifles) carried by the police were deadly weapons and that the patrol was well able to defend itself. Therefore, throughout the journey he attempted to warn advancing warriors to stay back by firing a volley over their heads. Though it may be argued that shooting harmlessly over people's heads is no deterrent once they discover that no one has been hurt, almost every time Hides fired a warning shot during the patrol, it succeeded in frightening the warriors from immediate attack. But it was not enough to stop their harassing behavior. In later years it became standard practice for patrol officers to instruct truculent and threatening groups of warriors with a more dramatic demonstration of firearms by killing a pig or by shooting through several war shields or thicknesses of timber. Though this was usually done in camp after friendly relations with the local people had been established, sometimes it had to be done at the moment of necessity. In May 1939 Adamson and Atkinson were patrolling through the Emia Valley (parallel to the Nembi) when arrows were fired at them from a group of about 60 excited, yelling warriors in front of a village. Adamson quickly sent the carriers to a safe position and deployed the police. Then he approached some older men who seemed friendly. "[I] put a rifle bullet through the biggest piece of fence timber I could find," he remarked laconically. "They all examined it, and a young boy raced off [with it] to the [warriors] where I could see it being passed hand to hand. The [warlike demonstrations] ceased after this" (Lake Kutubu PR 9, 1938–39).* One wonders if the Strickland-Purari patrol might have suffered less harassment if Hides had thought of something like this.

---

* Eventually the Nembi got accustomed to these demonstrations (without losing any respect for the power of the rifle) and tried to turn them to their own ends. A postwar patrol camped among the Merut on the Nembi Plateau also gave a demonstration of the power of a rifle on a line of stacked warshields. The patrol officer reported that instead of giving the "requisite signs of wonder and respect, the Merut warriors . . . whooped with joy and invited the patrol to join in a fight against the neighboring enemy clan" (Mendi PR 5, 1953–54).

Patrol Leadership

Without pearlshell to ease the way, the success of the Strickland-Purari patrol depended heavily on the quality and character of its leadership. That Jack Hides was a courageous and resourceful leader who could inspire profound loyalty in his men and move them to extraordinary efforts is clear from the record. But the focus here is on another issue. Much of the conduct and success of any patrol depended on the nature of the officers' relations with the Papuans involved—whether they were the new people he encountered or his own carriers and police.

While on patrol, the usual style for patrol officers was to maintain a certain rank distance from police and carriers modeled on the relation of a military officer to his men. Within this framework the degree of actual warmth, mutual respect, informality, and friendship across ranks was worked out in the nuances of daily interaction between the officers and men. It was partly recognition of this factor that led Sir Hubert Murray to emphasize the importance of character in his officers.

Compared to most Australians in Papua at the time, Hides would have been labeled a "liberal." Although brought up largely in a narrow colonial milieu, his restless imagination was inspired by Papua's unexplored wilderness and exotic peoples. He loved Papua deeply. His writings are remarkable for their ability to communicate an intimate feeling for Papuan life, to evoke a sympathetic interest in its character and concerns. He genuinely liked Papuans and wrote with appreciation of Papuan men of courageous, generous, and straightforward character whom he met, whether members of the constabulary or warriors from the interior arrested for cannibalism and murder. By all accounts, Papuans for their part liked and admired Hides. Among themselves they referred to him affectionately as "Jack-a-Hide" rather than the more distanced (and, from the white community's point of view, more appropriate) term, Taubada.

Nevertheless, Hides clearly shared Murray's view of the inferiority of traditional Papuan culture (though he did think it had value), and he felt a liberal colonialist's paternalistic concern towards Papuans themselves. Like many of Murray's outside men, he believed in the essential moral and civilizing mission of the Australian colonial administration to the people of Papua.

Hides paid attention to skin color in his writings and sometimes seemed to correlate it with levels of cultural advancement. In an intriguing passage in *Papuan Wonderland* he reflects upon "the light-skinned people of the Tari Furoro" (the Huli), picturing them as representatives of an enlightened culture once dominant over a wider region to the southeast, but now being driven back by darker others, forced to retreat.

"The finely woven wigs of human hair [throughout the Wola and Nembi country]; the beautiful axes of stone; the extraordinary method of advanced cultivation; all, I am sure, originated with the intelligent and artistic people of the Tari Furoro. Possibly at one time they inhabited the whole of this gigantic tableland [the Waga Valley and Nembi Plateau] . . . and possibly the big Black Papuans [the Wola, Nembi, and Kewa], better fighters and a more virile type, entered somewhere from the east, to drive them continually back westwards across their roads and cultivations until today we can only find them in their sanctuary up against Mt. Jubilee, the Victor Emmanuel Range, and the great forbidding limestone barrier that all form the sides of their Papuan Wonderland. Whence came these pretty, light-skinned men is something that is not for me to answer" (PW: 154).

Like others of Hides's speculations, this picture was largely imaginary. The Huli are not noticeably lighter-skinned than other highlanders, are not relatively more artistic, and are certainly not inferior fighters. However, in this passage are gathered in a single romanticized image all the contrasts—light- vs. dark-skinned, "civilized" vs. barbaric, artistic vs. warlike, superior vs. inferior—that formed the terms of racist discourse which preoccupied colonial Australians in Port Moresby. Here, however, it was the Huli that played the white man's role in the colonial Australians' worst fantasy: a light-skinned community increasingly beleaguered by threatening blacks (see Chapter 1).

Hides was clearly familiar with the racist discourse of his community. His racial attitudes, however, seem to have been complex. In various places in his writings we find a mixture of admiration and blatant stereotype in his descriptions of Papuans under his command. In his description of the battle of Pembi Andaa, for example, where the carriers were crowded for shelter in a native house while the police held off a large body of Merut warriors, Hides describes Constable Agoti courageously holding off a body of warriors with his rifle while arrows struck the ground all around him: "Agoti had the worst track to guard that afternoon, and I don't think any other constable could have stood the strain. This big silent Agoti; this brave unassuming Papuan: no reward could be too high for his conduct."

Almost in the next line, however, he switches to a comic image: "I saw Kaivamore [already known to the reader as a feckless, thieving carrier] stick his terror-stricken face out of the house to ask at random: 'What about us when the police are dead?' And Sergeant Orai told him he could take the bows of the dead and 'break his way' to the coast. Kaivamore started to howl at this, and to ask himself why he had left his mother, his wives, and his peaceful palms of the Orokolo coast, [until finally] some carrier rudely pulled him back into the house" (PW: 134–35).

Here the policemen Agoti and Orai are pictured as courageous and responsible men, embodying Empire virtues of loyalty, steadfastness, and sense of duty, faithful native troops, while Kaivamore, yanked out of sight wailing with cowardice, appears like a black caricature from a 1920's musical comedy. Both of these images were familiar enough racial stereotypes among empire colonialists. But, judging by Hides's overall writings and behavior, his racial attitudes appear to have been relatively tempered by the ease with which he had been able to communicate with Papuans. Since childhood, he had spoken fluent Motu and some Koiari, the languages of the people in the vicinity of Port Moresby. He sensed a common humanity with Papuans, and he had a restless curiosity to better understand the lives, motivations, and feelings of these people, whom most of his contemporaries merely despised.

Hides was, however, more of a romantic than an ethnographer. Though he wrote striking descriptions of Papuan life, he saw Papuan culture in terms of the contrasts that were most striking to his own imagination. Given colonial stereotypes of bush Papuans as ruthless killers and cannibals, it intrigued him that they were also sensitive human beings who appreciated beauty and cared deeply for one another.* He abhorred the violence in Papuan life, but he was attracted to the exuberant strength and energy he sensed beneath it. It was this underlying vitality that he felt was the wellspring of Papuan potential for the future, if under Australian guidance it could be turned to more useful and constructive purposes. It was to this task that he saw his career contributing: bringing law and order to native life so that it could have the security to advance from its chaotic state to that of proper civilization. "When [this] will come," he wrote, "I do not know. But this I do know: that the Papuan, taken quickly after the civilizing effect, will stand up to the [revolutionary change] and will become just as good an industrialist as he is today a cannibal, a fighter, and a likable gentleman when you get to know him" (Hides 1935: 170).

The Papuan Police

As a patrol officer who had spent his boyhood among his father's constabulary at the Port Moresby jail, Hides had a special place in his heart

---

* Hides often felt himself moved by this realization. Sitting in camp one evening after arresting some men for brutal tribal killings, he heard the sounds of massed singing coming from nearby villages across the ravine: "I listened enthralled; my mind seemed to leave physical discomfort for the moment and to draw a picture of those savages across the distance. I did not see them as practiced murderers, but rather as human beings who were living their own lives as Nature had taught them. And the music . . . made me forget all about cannibalism . . . and made me think only of the strength and beauty of the life of the savage" (Hides 1935: 147). As noted in Chapter 2, such sentiments are in part what Rosaldo (1989) has termed "imperialist nostalgia," the mourning of the passing of traditional society, even when one has oneself contributed to that passing. This was a popular theme in late colonialist romantic literature.

for the Papuan police. Like many officers he had immense respect for their courage, bushcraft, and ability to size up the attitudes of new peoples they encountered. Like other officers, he delegated responsibility to them for carrying out important tasks and sought their opinion and advice during critical moments on patrol.

The amount of discretion allowed police with regard to the discharge of firearms on patrol was a matter for the judgment of the individual officer. It was always a tricky business. Ivan Champion, for example, seems to have distanced himself as an officer from the police and carriers of his patrols. He knew that policemen from the Northern Division (now Oro Province) boasted in their home villages of the numbers of people they killed while on patrol. Determined not to have any unauthorized shooting under his command, he held his police under threat of instant dismissal from the force (including the stripping of their uniforms in the field and reduction to carrier status) if they fired their rifles without a direct order from himself or his accompanying officer (Sinclair 1988: 174; see also Nelson 1982: 53). This restriction applied even if arrows were being fired at the patrol.

Hides was not so restrictive. He had had experience with constables who "exceeded orders" and fired upon local people when they shouldn't have, but like other officers in the Papuan Service he felt he could trust men he knew well to know when it was appropriate to fire. It was for this reason that he handpicked the constabulary for the Strickland-Purari patrol. These police were undoubtedly good men. However, it is evident that over the course of the journey they developed their own fund of anger and resentment at the provocations and niggardly treatment they felt they received from highland populations. On a number of occasions it was the police who were first to open fire upon local warriors from the patrol—without orders from Hides and usually out of his sight. Hides had given them this discretion and defended their actions in reporting the incidents, but the issue remains clouded because, as we now know, his trust was misplaced. On two or three other occasions, police constables simply shot people out of anger and spite. There is no evidence that Hides knew of these shootings, but the discretion he had given his police and the particular difficulty of this journey opened the way for the partial or clandestine breakdown in discipline that plagued the patrol.* Arguably, if Hides and O'Malley had adopted the kind of measures practiced by Champion, there might have been less loss of life.

---

* It was not particularly unusual for members of the armed constabulary to take illegal liberties with the property, persons, and even lives of local people if they were out of sight of their officers and thought they could get away with it—as informants who remember the early days of patrolling in the highlands will affirm (see Kituai 1988; Connolly and Anderson 1987). That was precisely what Champion's orders prohibiting the unauthorized discharge of firearms by police was designed to prevent.

Hides and the Highlanders

Jack Hides had always found it natural and easy to form good relations with Papuans he knew on the coast, and he was confident he could do the same with Papuans he met anywhere. Handling first-contact situations required a certain skill. An officer patrolling into new country had to project a calm, confident, and reassuring manner in the presence of excited, frightened, and wary people—and be able to stand his ground with restraint in the face of hostile demonstrations. Jack Hides had these qualities. He knew that the people he met had never seen Europeans before, that they sometimes thought he and his men were not beings of this world.

Unfortunately, he seems not always to have been able to apply this insight usefully. He liked Papuans and seems to have extended himself to them with a certain personal warmth. But he expected, assuming the patrol had done nothing provocative or threatening, that once the immediate shock of surprise and fear had been allayed and some gifts perhaps distributed, the local people would relax and offer hospitality and friendly treatment in return. If, despite all this, warriors refused his friendly overtures and gifts; if they first seemed friendly and later turned hostile; if they tried to direct the patrol along impossible paths or lead it into ambush, Hides didn't always seem to have the circumspection to see that these might be a frightened people's attempts to keep Strange Beings away from their lands and families. Rather, he often took it as treachery and deceit—a betrayal of his offers of friendship. It was as if, in extending personal warmth to new peoples in the process of peaceful contact, there was too little distance between his professional activity and his romantic imagination: between the procedure for making peaceful contact and the personal warmth and outgoingness that he naturally extended in the effort. As a result, he often responded with anger and resentment to what he saw as native perfidy rather than with gestures aimed at calming and reassuring excited, fearful, and uncertain people.

Hides found it particularly difficult to understand what he saw as a miserly response of the highlanders to his requests for food. Given the general hospitality and generosity he was used to among coastal Papuans,* he was comparatively unprepared for the treatment he received at the hands of the highlanders, the implications of which he found insulting and worrisome. "We have got no potatoes and no pig," he wrote in the Wola country, "though it is obvious to these natives that we are weak and half-starved" (PR: 70). He could understand neither their reluctance to give

---

* Hides felt the coastal Papuan cultures with which he was familiar were more generous and hospitable by nature. Their hospitality, however, may well have been a result of long familiarity with government patrols and their expectations.

food to the patrol nor the high price demanded for what little sweet potato was offered for trade.

On top of this, the patrol received strikingly different receptions from one group to another. The fragmented political organization and constant warfare between neighboring alliances inclined Nembi and Wola to be suspicious of any unknown parties approaching from adjacent territories, especially if it was from the direction of their enemies. But these social and political implications of the patrol's movement do not seem to have occurred to Hides.

All of these difficulties became aggravated as the patrol became increasingly dependent upon the local people for its food. The fact of the matter is that to some degree Hides's expectations were misplaced. His experience and knowledge of Papuans of the coast were not a sufficient basis for understanding these new people in the highlands and did not prepare him well for his reception there. At first he didn't realize this and thought he understood more of what the highlanders meant than he actually did.

The newly contacted people, for their part, didn't know what the patrol was or where it came from—except, as they guessed, that it was from beyond the peripheries of their world: the land of the dead, *dama* spirits, cannibal sorcerers from Lake Kutubu, sky people, ancestral ghosts. Most felt initial astonishment and fear toward the patrol, followed by curiosity and occasionally avarice, though they acted in different ways. All felt the patrol was a potentially dangerous unknown, to be approached warily. The Etoro and Onabasulu of the Papuan Plateau fled into the forest after a brief confrontation and left the patrol largely alone. Among the Huli, the local politics of influence played a significant part. Established leaders tried to head the *dama* away from their domains, while an ambitious younger man apparently hoped to form a traditional alliance with the *dama* to gain power for his own ends. A common response from all the peoples the patrol encountered was that they followed it, partly out of curiosity, sometimes trying to offer it gifts of food, at other times probing for its vulnerabilities to see what it would do, or perhaps harassing it simply to keep it moving along out of their territory. Occasionally they attempted outright attack. This harassment continued through the Wola country and was especially severe among the Nembi, who pressed harder as they perceived the patrol to be increasingly debilitated and weak. Hides's response was always to keep moving, to avoid areas of heavy population, to fire warning shots if warriors approached too close, and to shoot the warriors themselves if they attacked or seemed about to in a dangerous situation.

The refusal to sell food likewise seemed to have several sources. The Etoro and Onabasulu feared that accepting gifts from supernatural strangers would bring about some kind of world disaster. Some Huli (mostly leaders) felt the same—that the strange objects offered would be somehow harmful. Whether or not they were short of food, the Wola and the Nembi, like many peoples along the trade route, were experienced hard bargainers and charged high prices even among themselves. But they may also have inflated the price because the patrol seemed desperate and vulnerable and they thought they could get away with it. They did this to later patrols also (see Lake Kutubu PR 9, 1938–39). In any case, nothing the patrol was carrying was perceived as sufficiently valuable for them to go out of their way to trade for.

The Kewa, on the other hand, were friendly and generous to the patrol with gifts of food: they were wary lest these beings prove to be ghosts of the dead, but curious and excited to be visited by beings who were connected with the origins of axes. The shooting of Kewa people would appear to be a tragic mistake resulting from Hides's misperceptions of the situation due to his severe illness, his exaggerated expectations of native treachery and attack, the desperate condition of the patrol, and the vengeful, frustrated anger of his police. In a sense, the Kewa paid for the sins of the Wola and Nembi.

Fame and After

While Hides and O'Malley were still in Port Moresby writing up their report, news of the Strickland-Purari patrol arrived in Australia. The discovery of an unknown land of carefully cultivated valleys hidden in the interior fastness of the Papuan mountains—peopled by allegedly light-skinned men wearing flower-bedecked wigs—naturally intrigued the popular imagination. The newspapers lost no time in picturing this as a new Arcadia and lighting it with a blaze of publicity.

"Mystery Men of Papua!" read the *Sydney Morning Herald* on July 24, 1935; "Mr. Jack Hides' Discovery. Valley peopled by race of new natives. Fertile soil tilled with wooden spades."

According to the *Edinburgh Evening News*: "(July 23) An exploring party just returned from the New Guinea hinterland reports the discovery of a vast mountain-locked plateau inhabited by simple agricultural and agreeable people with light brown skins and large mops of hair adorned with daisies. . . . That such a Utopian pre-civilization should still exist in any part of the world is a matter of more than passing interest. . . . For us who live in the frenetic turmoil of a world dedicated to progress and enlightenment, it is almost impossible to envisage the simple existence of these happy arcadians."

Such headlines continued for weeks: "Island of Secrets! Wonderlands That Still Await Discovery! Yodelling Men Attack Worn-Out Party! Riddles of Wildest Papua! Driven Mad by Jungle Strain! Are There New Racial Types in Papua? Shots Amid Forest Peace! Fierce Fight in Papua! Central New Guinea Gives Up Its Secrets!"—the reading public couldn't get enough of it (Sinclair 1969: 174–75).

When Hides and O'Malley arrived in Australia for three months' leave, they discovered they were celebrities. Crowds met them as their ship pulled up to the dock. They were hailed as heroes and barraged with requests for lectures and interviews; they were besieged by the press. As the excitement continued through the following weeks, O'Malley tired of the attention and gradually withdrew from the limelight. Hides, however, was dazzled by it. He was a good speaker and a natural storyteller and was always in demand for public lectures. From the podium, he held his audiences spellbound with his tale of tropical forests and highland valleys. Though Hides minimized the violence of the patrol in his lectures, and emphasized the exploration, the story of two white men and an intrepid band of carriers and police pushing their way through the wilderness, beset by starvation and savage warriors, was an epic of courage and endurance that kept audiences continually enthralled. The newspapers compared him favorably with Scott of the Antarctic, Lawrence of Arabia, and Stanley of Africa. For a civilization still sunk in the Great Depression and threatened with the gathering forces of war, it was heartening to know there were still wonderful discoveries to be made in the world and men of grit and inspiration like Hides who could seek them out.

It was not only the Sydney newspapers and lecture audiences that romanticized Hides and O'Malley's expedition. Hides contributed to the process himself. During his hectic schedule of appearances in Australia, he was hard at work editing his patrol report into the book *Papuan Wonderland*. With some pruning of events here, some heightening of the drama there, a paragraph or two of philosophical reflection in appropriate places, he molded the overall effect of the narrative more cleanly to the genre of romantic adventure story that he thought it represented.*

In the process, Hides couldn't resist mythologizing himself a bit. He downplayed his feelings of exasperation at the people he encountered and presented himself as rather more high-minded than he actually had been

---

* Thus, for example, in *PW* Hides took the description of A.C. Budua swinging his rifle at an attacker in a skirmish with the Semin-al (Chapter 7) and incorporated it into his story of the battle at Korpe Defile a few days earlier (Chapter 6). The switch seems primarily literary in motivation, to better dramatize the close quarters of the Korpe battle. The skirmish with the Semin-al from which the incident was taken was dropped from the book, but Hides evidently didn't want to lose this vivid bit of action. The most serious alterations of the historical record in the book are the omission of the account of the police shootings of the Kewa at Kagapore and the foreshortening of the march from Koyamapu to the limestone barrier.

on patrol. In a favorite image that appears several times in the book, Hides pictured himself standing on some high promontory gazing out over newly discovered country and reflecting on its beauty, thinking of other great Outside Men who had gone before him to such regions as these or envisioning a future when the tropical forest would be tamed and planted in grain. In *Papuan Wonderland* (no less than in the newspapers) Jack Hides, patrol officer, becomes Jack Hides, Hero of the Quest.

Meanwhile, in this blaze of celebrity there were a few sour notes. Mick Leahy, the famous prospector-explorer of the Mandated Territory, raised the claim, after reading Hides's report, that he and district officer James Taylor had first discovered the regions Hides and O'Malley passed through during an earlier exploratory expedition in 1934. Hubert Murray did not believe this, but it was difficult to substantiate the claim when even Hides and O'Malley didn't know exactly where they had been. Hides was no cartographer. He had carried with him only a compass and an aneroid barometer. With these inadequate instruments and the preoccupation of leading his party through continual harassment by unfriendly warriors, it was not surprising his map was crude and approximate. In fact, Hides's original sketch suggested that his route was about 50 km north of where it actually went (Sinclair 1969: 180). The situation was clearly unsatisfactory, and so Murray arranged for Hides, Ivan Champion, and James Taylor to fly over the region to get a better idea of the general topography and see if they could improve the map of where the patrol had been. Murray also hoped to garner the medal of the Royal Geographical Society for Hides when he went on leave to England that year. (In this, however, he was to be unsuccessful; the Society was much more wary in accepting the maps of Papuan expeditions since their experience with the claims of Staniforth Smith—see Chapter 1).

The publicity that continued to surround Jack Hides began to concern Murray. It was not good for the morale of the Papuan Service to have one man singled out for undue celebrity when many others could equally well have undertaken the expedition—or had already done similar exemplary work and remained unsung. According to Hides's biographer, a number of officers openly resented the attention Hides was getting. Some accused him of deliberately seeking the limelight with his writing and lecturing activities. Others said that theirs had always been a "silent service." The great patrols had always been carried out with no fuss and no publicity, and Hides was transgressing this grand tradition.* Others perceptively noted, however, that the publicity surrounding the Strickland-Purari patrol had

---

* This allegation was not true. Many patrol officers and administrators wrote books about their experience in Papua, including MacGregor, Austen, Monckton, H. L. Griffin, Beaver, Humphries, Champion and Karius, and Hubert Murray himself.

finally put Papua on the map by drawing world attention to this otherwise neglected corner of empire. But by now the amount of publicity Hides had received was becoming a source of embarrassment to the Papuan Administration.

This was the general climate of feeling in Port Moresby to which Hides returned in January 1936. Hides was a sensitive man, and he was deeply wounded by the cool reception given to him by many officers he knew and respected in the Papuan Service. He became moody and depressed (Sinclair 1969: 185). Following the completion of the aerial reconnaissance, Hides was posted to Misima as assistant resident magistrate to his old friend Alex Rentoul. On the way there, Hides learned that the administration had passed a regulation prohibiting officers of the Papuan Service from privately publishing any information or knowledge gained about the country gathered in the course of their official duties (see Sinclair 1988: 196). Hides felt this regulation had been aimed specifically at him. He plunged deeper into depression and began drinking so heavily that after a few weeks Rentoul sent him in for medical attention. He was given three months' sick leave in Australia.

In the next few months, although he recovered his physical health, Hides's spirits remained very low. Despite praise heaped by reviewers upon *Papuan Wonderland*, which came out at this time, he remained unhappy and resentful about his treatment by the administration. When his leave drew to an end, he resigned from the Papuan Service.

Hides's resignation did not end his career as an explorer. While he was in Australia, he was approached by a group of investors who wanted to engage him to search for gold in the interior regions he had just explored. Upon his resignation, Hides accepted the offer and eventually led an expedition into the mountains at the headwaters of the Strickland River. This expedition, though radio-equipped, proceeding as planned, and resupplied at appropriate points by air, met with disaster when David Lyall, Hides's companion and the mineral expert for the journey, fell ill. As Lyall's condition worsened, the radio gave out, and the aircraft could not find them. Hides abandoned the bulk of his food and trade goods and turned back to make a dash for the coast. On the journey many of his carriers came down with beriberi in the Strickland Gorge, and five of them died. Hides himself became so weak he could hardly stand. They arrived on the coast ill and completely exhausted. Lyall died a few days later of a perforated stomach ulcer. Hides was devastated by the loss of his companion, who had become a close friend. Shortly afterwards he learned that the gold lease his party had been investigating on the Strickland was worthless. The entire expedition had been for nothing. He returned to Australia in poor health, deeply depressed and drinking again (Sinclair 1969: 254).

In June 1938, his health still not recovered from the effects of hardship now exacerbated by alcohol, he contracted a severe case of pneumonia; three days later he was dead. He was just short of 32 years old.

His companion of the Strickland-Purari patrol, Jim O'Malley, continued to serve as an officer in the Papuan Service and as an officer in the Australia New Guinea Administrative Unit (ANGAU)* during the Second World War; he eventually retired at the rank of District Officer in Madang and moved to Sydney, Australia. O'Malley died there at the age of 63 in 1975, the same year Papua New Guinea became an independent nation.

If *Papuan Wonderland* can be said to be the heroic account of the Strickland-Purari patrol, this volume might be termed the ironic one. If Jack Hides's mistakes and miscalculations were responsible for getting the patrol into its difficulties, it also has to be said that Jack Hides deserves the credit for getting it out. Given the tremendous hardship, illness, and danger experienced by the patrol in the latter part of its journey, it is remarkable that it got back from the highlands to the coast at all. It was Hides's unflinching determination (supported by O'Malley) that pushed it along kilometer by kilometer, day after day, maintaining sufficient discipline to keep everyone together, despite an outlook that was extremely discouraging, until finally they made it through to Kikori.

It was not just the patrol's discoveries, but also this heroic struggle that gave the story the proportions of epic. Champion and Adamson's Bamu-Purari patrol of 1936, which covered similar territory without making a mistake, losing a man, or firing a shot in anger, was a brilliantly carried out expedition. However, it attracted little attention. Part of this subdued reception was due to the restrictions placed on publicity by the colonial administration after its experience with Hides and part to the fact that Champion's discoveries revealed no new surprises in the Papuan interior. But neither did his patrol involve a dramatic struggle against starvation and calamity. Hides's expedition, on the other hand, was the stuff of romance, a story of discovery through suffering and struggle against terrible odds, a moral achievement as well as a great expedition. Because of this lasting appeal to the Western imagination, it is the dangerous Quest courageously accomplished that has become Hides's legacy to story and history, rather than the near disaster barely survived.

On First Contact: Adventure Story as Interpretive Framework

The account given here of the Strickland-Purari patrol is an ethnographic and historical reconstruction of the expedition, organized around

---

*A unified military government of Papua and the Mandated Territory of New Guinea set up during the confrontation with the Japanese during World War II.

the theme of cultural first encounter. Throughout we have tried to elucidate the structure of the events, not just in terms of the cultural orientations and social-historical circumstances each side brought to them, but also by uncovering the particular structure of interaction that lay beneath them and gave them their actual historical form. It seems appropriate, as we conclude, to review the way the argument is constructed, elucidate the questions and conceptual issues that have guided it, and point to some of the insights it reveals.

The argument here is presented in the form of an adventure story: the narrative follows a set of protagonists who must overcome various obstacles in a series of suspenseful, action-oriented occurrences in order to achieve their final goal. We have told it this way in part to convey the excitement and drama of the geographic and anthropological discovery process. But the story also entails constructing an analysis and interpretation of the material itself, which emerges in the way the story is told, in its narrative strategy, rather than in adherence to an explicit theoretical framework.*

The narrative constructs the account in two ways: first, through the juxtaposition of voices; and second, through the exposition of a complex series of events that uncovers the underlying forces and processes that brought them about.

On the visible surface, the story is told in several voices: the writings of Jack Hides (with gleanings from Jim O'Malley, the police, and the carriers), the reminiscences of Papuans who encountered them, and the more distanced commentaries and explications of their ethnographers. The gaps between these stories represent not only their differences in point of view, but also the rough edges of what we can know—the fragmentary and selective nature of the available material that results from the losses to time, the limitations of each participant's experience of the events, and the inevitable incompleteness of ethnographic fieldwork. As the account proceeds, the voices of the protagonists and commentators become positioned in relation to each other (and to the story itself), and the events unfold as multiply perceived.

It is in the continuities of the narrative, amidst the multiple voices, that the hand of the editors can be perceived. The direction of the narrative action closely follows the continuities of the Australian (European) experience of the patrol—rather than the more disjointed experience of the

---

*As others have pointed out, this has always been more or less true of all ethnographic literature that takes the form of analytical or interpretive ("thick") description (Marcus and Cushman 1982; Marcus and Fischer 1986), but it is only recently that anthropologists have become critically aware of the degree to which text construction and literary genre inform (or become) interpretation and analysis (Clifford and Marcus 1986; Rosaldo 1989).

Papuans it encountered. Although the quality of the Papuan experience comes through in the various local accounts and the division of the narrative into separate ethnographic pieces, it is not the same as if the story were presented as a collection of punctuate encounters, each embodied in a separate local Papuan history. The line-of-the-journey narrative links these local events together in a way that was not apparent to the Papuans who experienced them at the time. As an adventure story it remains a European one.

Other continuities contribute to consistency of emphasis and tone. The importance of issues of power and knowledge in the encounter between Papuans and Europeans emerges naturally from the material, but the agenda of keeping them in focus was inspired by the writings of Michel Foucault (1979, 1980). Throughout, we have tried to maintain an attitude of disinterested sympathy towards all those in the encounter so that the ambiguities that each of them faced in the situation may emerge clearly.

The personal stories, historical accounts, and ethnographic materials presented here refract against each other even more than they are complementary, so that the juxtaposition of voices particularly exposes the incommensurability between highlands and colonial cultures and sets out the ethnographic and theoretical issues to be addressed as structures of differences. (Indeed, the degree to which this story takes place as a series of mutually uncomprehending monologues with relatively thin structures of coordination is fairly striking.) As a result, a series of important questions and analytical concerns are raised which become central to the development of the account.

The most obvious of these are questions of ethnography and situation. What exactly were the different cultural orientations, values, attitudes, and agendas that each side brought to the encounter and in which each grounded perceptions of and reactions to the Other? How were they historically situated?

For colonial Australians there was, behind everything, the desire to seek ever more natural resources, labor, markets, and opportunities for wealth —and to do this they followed the model of British imperial expansion and establishment of political and economic hegemony over technologically less advanced peoples. The process was given a certain rationale (and was to some degree restrained) by the notion that it was the duty (as well as the right) of the white race to bring law and order and Christianity to primitive tribal societies. In the Papua of the 1930's, these forces and ideas underlay the struggle between Hubert Murray and the commercial interests, the colonial attitudes towards Papuans, the appeal of adventure and exploration in the hinterland, and the exacting tradition of the Papuan Service.

Highland Papuans, on the other hand, inhabited a limited universe in which the visible geographical boundaries were conceptually close to their cosmological ones, and most of them had difficulty imagining that anyone lived beyond them. In these societies resolutely egalitarian and individualistic men competed for prestige and a modicum of political stability through participation in complex cycles of ceremonial exchange. Out of this was generated their driving obsession with pigs and pearlshell, their tightfisted trading practices, and their constant internal rivalries and endemic warfare.

This structure of difference immediately affected the nature of the encounter. Hides and O'Malley's experience in the Papuan Service meant that they expected to meet new peoples as they journeyed into unvisited regions—but they wrongly assumed these people would be essentially similar to those they already knew on the coast. The Papuans of the Southern Highlands, for their part, assumed the visitors from beyond their cosmological peripheries were spirits, ancestral ghosts, or other powerful beings. At first sight, it might seem there was a certain convenient fit between the attitudes of the patrol officers, who regarded themselves as members of a superior civilization, and the Papuans, who regarded them as supernatural beings. But the situation didn't turn out to be this simple. For one thing, while Papuans regarded spirit beings as unusually powerful, they also believed them to be essentially similar to themselves—and thus open to the same weaknesses, manipulation, threats, and blandishments.*

In addition, the confrontation between the highlanders and the patrol was mediated through contrasting forms of social and political organization. The patrol was a tightly organized, hierarchical group modeled on a military tradition and a caste society. It entailed a division of labor and responsibility and responded to a chain of command. Subordinates obeyed the decisions and directives of their officers, and the whole could act (most of the time) as a relatively disciplined and organized unit. The egalitarian highlanders, by contrast, individualistic and politically fragmented as they were, could not easily come to a consensus about what concerted action to take towards the patrol. Some were for fighting it; others wanted to seek advantage from it; many apparently simply accompanied it out of excitement or curiosity. Later in the journey, the warriors, though initially amazed and afraid, quickly perceived that, whatever these creatures were, they were in a weakened condition, and they began to probe them

---

* In fact, much of the power of spirits in the Southern Highlands comes from the fact that they are invisible, and it is in part because their nefarious operations cannot be seen that they are so difficult to counter. It is likely that highlands peoples assumed they had better leverage on the patrol than over most collections of spirits because it was in plain sight and its operations could be observed.

for vulnerability. Yet for the patrol, even during the most hostile native demonstrations and despite its own physical weakness, the organization of police and carrier lines was evidently tight enough so that the warriors did not often feel confident in making an open assault even when they greatly outnumbered the patrol.

In the midst of the various incommensurabilities between the protagonists, the action of the adventure story pushes for an elucidation of what happened that privileges social forces over structures of difference and the particularities of historical events over general questions of ethnography. This opposite interpretive direction treats structures of difference as contexts that condition the events and the forces in the action and provide the arena in which they play themselves out. The narrative lays out the action through which these events are brought about. Contexts and protagonists become engaged, and a particular course of historical action develops, through which many things become changed.

This becomes evident first in the way ethnography becomes involved in the unpredictable, purely historical contingencies of a situation: those breaks of fortune to be found in particular decisions made, the presence or absence of significant individuals, the particular point in the growing season or the cycle of warfare, the political situation in Port Moresby or in the Waga Valley. It seems to have been the untimely appearance of Aibali, the medium, that prevented the establishment of friendly contact with the Etoro at Sarado longhouse (Chapter 3) on the Papuan Plateau. This arguably set the stage for the killing of Heyosi and for Hides's abandonment of half his supplies in the Etoro country. The state of hostilities between the Merut and the Semin-al led the Merut to mistake the patrol for a raiding party and resulted in the battle of Pembi Andaa. Finally Hides's illness made the expedition yet more vulnerable to Nembi harassment and clouded Hides's judgment in the Kewa country. These and many other similar sorts of situations formed the particular contingencies the patrol and the highlanders had to deal with, each according to their own best lights, in their encounters.

Beneath this level of contingent events, the narrative action unfolds a glimpse of the engagement of the particular social processes internal to each group which generated some of the responses of the patrol and particular highlanders to the situation. Some mature highland leaders (like Puya and Kamburu) were concerned with averting danger to their families and property and tried to head the patrol into uninhabited country. Excited younger men couldn't resist being provocative, or (as with Pakadya/Mambu and possibly Chou) attempting to align themselves with the patrol in order to manipulate it and perhaps gain some local political advantage. Hides and O'Malley, for their part, were concerned to establish friendly relations with the local people and to avoid provoking conflict. Later these priorities had to be tempered by the need to get food. The behavior of the patrol was also affected by an internal struggle to maintain authority and discipline as carriers became increasingly hungry and police increasingly angry and vengeful towards the local populace. Hides worried that his own insistent restraint in the face of apparently outrageous local stinginess and provocation would be taken by the police as a sign of fear and weakness and that he might lose control over them.* The police, for their part, found ways to take revenge on the local people when they were out of sight of their superiors. These conflicts arising in the situation, and the tensions to which they gave rise, were intrinsic to the social processes of each group and provided much of the motivation for the specific actions each undertook.

Finally and most important, through all of this, the adventure narrative lays out an inexorable account of the accumulating experience of the patrol with the highlanders, the increasing toll of its hardships, and the maturing consequences of ill-fated decisions. The result is both the transformation of the patrol's behavior in the situation and an alteration among the relevant ethnographic factors that affected its encounters as it went along.

In the early part of its journey, when the patrol arrived in the highlands, it presented a relatively confident, well-organized, and friendly aspect to the Huli, consistent with the guidelines laid down by Hubert Murray. The Huli, taken by surprise, frightened, and uncertain as to how to handle the situation, presented themselves as wary, standoffish warriors who tried to manipulate the patrol in various ways to neutralize (or utilize) its powerful presence in their midst. When the patrol arrived in the Kewa country, however, it had been through nearly a month of starvation and hostility among the Wola and Nembi and was expecting to deal with more of the same. The Kewa, self-confident from recent success in war and apparently curious and excited by the arrival of the patrol, presented a relatively open and hospitable aspect to their visitors. They were confronted with an exhausted, beleaguered group of men, reduced to garden thievery, whose leaders, sapped by illness and hunger, were now primarily focused on survival while a vengeful police contingent were spoiling to take out their resentment on the local people.

This transformation in the relative positioning of the patrol in relation

---

* In fact, after the patrol returned and Hides had received considerable publicity, some of his enemies in the Papuan Service spread a rumor that Hides had permitted some of the excessive killing by the patrol in order to maintain credibility with the police. We do not think there is any evidence for this, but it is also unlikely that Hides would have reported it if it were true.

to the highlanders demonstrates the degree to which the encounter was more than a matter of structures of difference. The relevant ethnographic surfaces that presented themselves in the confrontation of the patrol's encounters during the journey were continually changing in relation to the events of the encounters themselves. The story thus provides a perspective on first encounters that does not easily emerge from accounts in which historically the explorers always remain in control of the situation or in which the events are seen too simply in terms of fixed ethnographic contrasts and relations of domination.

It is in fact partly because the Strickland-Purari patrol had such a difficult time and so many things went wrong that it is so instructive as an example of the process of exploration and first contact. When things run smoothly, it is often harder to see important subtleties and subplots of the process going on beneath the government officer's projection of supreme competence.

Patrols in the Papuan Service always tried to assume the upper hand in dealing with the Papuans wherever they went, by never allowing Papuans to think a patrol was vulnerable. Patrols were better armed than local Papuans, had more disciplined organization, and were under the command of experienced leaders drawn from a powerful, complex society bent on expanding its hegemony. Their purposes, methods, and goals were precisely spelled out. Patrols that followed Hides and O'Malley in later years always carried sufficient food and the right trade to ensure that they would never be in a position of dependency in relation to the people they encountered. This situation of power and dependency was inverted for Hides and represented an anomalous situation for the highlanders he met. The beings they feared were clearly hungry and weak; it was a situation calculated to bring out the most arrogant and abrasive aspects of the local warriors. At the same time, the patrol was still powerfully armed, and this could potentially bring out the worst in the officers or police. Although it is a tribute to Hides's leadership that the patrol was able to maintain restraint as well as it did, the situation reveals how the stresses (as well as strengths) inherent in the organization of administration patrols affected their behavior and illustrates the kinds of ambiguities local highlanders felt they faced (and that they also projected) in their own attempts to gain control of the situation and deal with the intruders into their domain.

The strengths of the adventure story, as we have discussed it, lie in its making explicit a series of historical actions, revealing their internal dynamics, contexts and subplots, showing where the points of tension are and how they develop, and demonstrating the process by which a series of events progresses to a denouement. It is not as effective at commenting on all this. We here reach the limitations of the adventure story as a form of analysis. Given the kind of action-in-context narrative that it is, it does not lend itself easily to reflection upon its own complexity and construction. Unlike a theoretical piece, it cannot readily encompass a commentary upon its own argument without at the same time destroying itself as an adventure (or, at any rate, none of us are skillful enough writers to know how to do this). Thus we have devoted this chapter and the following one to the issue of providing reflective commentary.

11. THE HISTORICAL IMPACT: SOUTHERN HIGHLANDS EPILOGUE

EDWARD L. SCHIEFFELIN, ROBERT CRITTENDEN, AND THE CONTRIBUTORS

The encounters between the Strickland-Purari patrol and the peoples of the southern highlands strike a Westerner as memorably violent and dramatic. However, highland Papuan peoples normally had a liberal share of violence and drama in their own lives, and we have to ask whether the events of first contact actually had some lasting effect on their perceptions of themselves or on their understanding of their subsequent history. This cannot be assessed by looking at the complexities of the encounter alone. To locate the full cultural and historical significance of the encounter we have to look at what happened afterward. We need to know whether the people understood their world or the subsequent events in their lives differently in the light of their experience with the patrol and determine the degree to which any such understandings motivated or influenced their subsequent historical activity. In this chapter, we will look at what happened to the people along Hides and O'Malley's route in the years after the passage of the patrol and find what reverberations followed their first encounter with Europeans.

Exploration and Administration After 1935

After Hides and O'Malley, the next Europeans to enter the southern highlands region were Ivan Champion and C. T. J. Adamson in 1936. In one of the multiple ironies that pervade this story, the day after Hubert Murray assigned Jack Hides and Jim O'Malley the task of carrying out the Strickland-Purari patrol, the other great explorer of Papua, Ivan Champion, applied for the same job, and Murray had to turn him down. After Hides and O'Malley returned, Champion approached Murray again. This

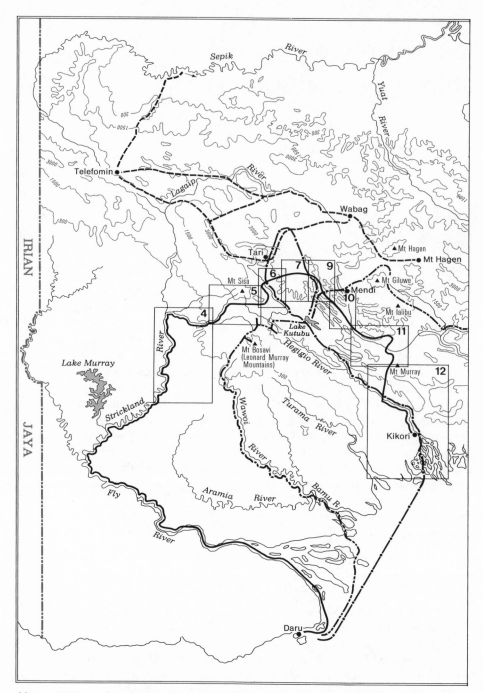

Map 13. Major exploratory patrols of 1935–39. (Sector maps of the Strickland-Purari patrol are shown and numbered as in the text.)

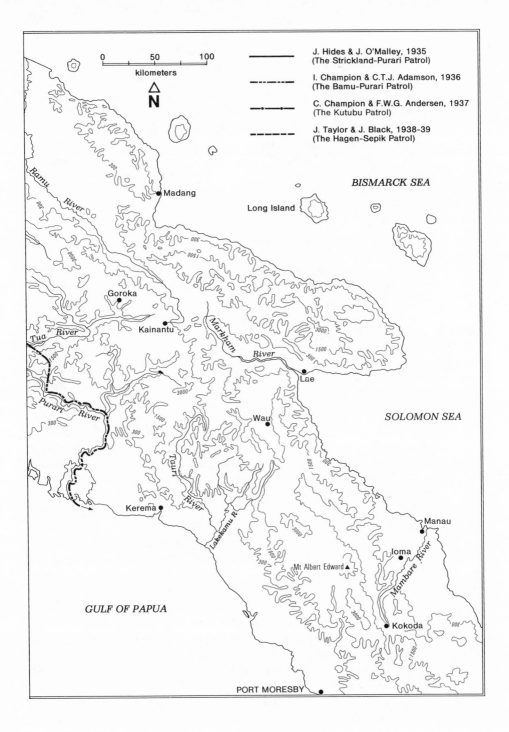

time he proposed to lead a patrol through the unexplored country south
and north of the Strickland-Purari route. The Bamu-Purari patrol was
to be the final major exploratory expedition into the interior country of
Papua.

On April 25, 1936, Champion and Adamson set off from the mouth
of the Bamu River. Their mandate was to ascend the Bamu, cross the
southern edge of the Papuan Plateau and move eastward to the newly discovered Lake Kutubu. From the lake they were to head north, crossing
Hides and O'Malley's route in the Waga Valley, and then turn eastward
to the northern headwaters of the Purari. From there they were to follow
the river back to the coast.

Some lessons had been learned from Hides's experience. Champion was
allowed to reconnoiter his route from the air before embarking, but he,
too, had to stage his supplies forward as Hides and O'Malley had done,
and he, too, was out of communication for the entire eight-month journey.
Unlike Hides, Champion was a self-taught surveyor with a passion for
knowing where he was at all times. He carried a sextant and a radio that
could pick up a time signal from San Francisco with which to figure his
exact position every day (Sinclair 1969: 214). Adamson had been a prospector before joining the Papuan Service and was expected to accurately
assess the gold-bearing prospects of the area through which they passed.
Last, and perhaps most important, Champion and Adamson carried plenty
of mother-of-pearl shell.

Recruitment of carriers proved to be difficult. Stories of the hardships
and dangers of Hides's journey had spread throughout the coastal Papuan
villages, and no one wanted to accompany another such expedition. Champion and Adamson finally had to fill their carrier ranks with 30 volunteers
from the prisoners in the Port Moresby jail.

The two officers led their men up the Bamu and Wawoi rivers and
climbed Mt. Bosavi from its western flank. When they reached the Papuan
Plateau, the local people avoided them, and the patrol had only brief encounters with them. Turning eastward, Champion and Adamson and their
men managed with difficulty to cross the Hegigio/Kikori River, which
was in full flood, and marched to Lake Kutubu. They briefly explored
the region around the lake and, after becoming acquainted with some of
its people, headed northeast across the limestone barrier along the trade
route through the Augu and Waga valleys. Emerging into the highlands on
the Nembi Plateau near Kasebi, they crossed Hides and O'Malley's track
and headed northeast over the Lai River into the Mendi Valley. A little
past Mt. Giluwe (Hides's "Minaret Mountain") they turned southeast and
then went down the Kaugel and Nebilyer valleys along the northern borders of the Purari watershed. They then traveled around the northeastern

shoulders of Mt. Karimui until they arrived at the Purari River. The entire expedition took eight months, covered nearly 1,500 km, and, despite some privation, was accomplished without any significant hostile encounters or the loss of a single human life.

Within a year Hubert Murray established a patrol post at Lake Kutubu to serve as the staging point for the intensive exploration and consolidation of the highlands. It was supplied by Catalina flying boat, which flew directly from Port Moresby. Over the next few years, government patrols fanned out from Lake Kutubu, examining the surrounding lowland areas, and then moved up into the Nembi and Waga valleys, northwest into the Huli country, and southeast to the Kewa. This work had just scratched the surface of the task at hand, however, when the Second World War broke out and Kutubu Patrol Post was closed down for fear of Japanese attack.

The patrol post wasn't opened again until 1949. In the intervening nine years the old order in Papua and the Mandated Territory came to an end. Hubert Murray died in 1940 (at the age of 78) while undertaking an administrative tour of inspection. With advent of World War II and the threat of Japanese invasion, the governments of both Papua and the Mandated Territory were taken over by the Australian military, and the two territories were governed under a unified administration. The upheavals of the war threw the old plantation and business economy into disarray, and many long-established colonial families left the territory permanently for Australia.

Toward the close of the war, as the American army moved to recapture and consolidate the northern coast, Papuans and New Guineans were astounded at the massive numbers of men and the mountains of food and equipment that moved through their country. It gave them their first real vision of the unbelievable wealth and power of an outside world they hardly knew existed. Moreover, traditional colonial race relations were undermined as Papuans experienced working and fighting (seemingly as equals) alongside black and white American soldiers. To them this was the revelation of a new dispensation, and it held out the promise that they too could have a part in it.

Meanwhile, deep in the interior mountains of the southern highlands, though people sometimes heard the rumble of bombers in the distance, the upheavals of war and politics affected their remote communities hardly at all. It was not until 1949 that the administration of the unified Territory of Papua and New Guinea reopened the patrol post at Lake Kutubu to resume the task of exploration. The post was staffed by a new generation of patrol officers. Many of those who served in the southern highlands in the 1950's and early 1960's were young Australians who had been inspired to join the government service by reading *Papuan Wonderland* and other writings of Jack Hides. Most had been born in Australia and trained in the recently created Australian School of Pacific Administration, rather than being personally chosen by the lieutenant governor from among the colonial families of Papua.

Exploration and consolidation were pushed forward rapidly throughout the territory in the 1950's and 1960's. The remaining areas of uncontacted peoples were brought under administration control by about 1968. Airstrips were constructed, schools and medical facilities built, and various development projects introduced and tried out. Under the insistent prodding of the United Nations and an increasing liberal sentiment in Australia, Papuans and New Guineans were introduced to the rudiments of Western-style local government and began moving in the direction of national independence. In 1975 Papua New Guinea became an independent nation.

Legacy of the Strickland-Purari Patrol

While developments moved at a dizzying pace in Port Moresby and in the major centers of economic development in the central and western highlands, in the southern highlands, still an area of uncertain potential and difficult access, events moved much more slowly.

THE GREAT PAPUAN PLATEAU (EDWARD L. SCHIEFFELIN)

The passage of the Strickland-Purari patrol through Etoro and Onabasulu country is still remembered in a few stories told by older men among the Onabasulu and Bosavi people. It is difficult, however, to assess the impact of those events for subsequent historical developments in the region. Part of the problem stems from the severe depopulation of the Etoro and Onabasulu people by epidemics in the 1950's, which killed many of those who had seen the patrol. But it is also true that the people of the region had largely avoided the patrol, and except for the armed confrontation at the Etoro longhouse and the old Onabasulu woman captured briefly at Ogesiye, nobody actually encountered Hides or O'Malley face-to-face. At the same time, the Onabasulu and Etoro were never able to figure out what the patrol was or make it fit into any convincing cultural explanation. So, once it had passed on and local consternation had died down, they readily turned to other matters of more pressing local import, involving traditional hostilities with their neighbors. Their history, however, was already slipping out of their hands.

About eighteen months later, Champion and Adamson appeared on the southern portion of the plateau, moving up the Wawoi River into the territory of the Bosavi (Kaluli) people. Their carriers were sick with beriberi, and the patrol stayed at a deserted longhouse for two weeks eating fresh vegetables from local gardens to allow them to recover. The Bosavi people were extremely frightened of the patrol and for the most part stayed in the forest out of sight.* Although they were familiar with steel and extremely anxious to get it, few of them actually came out to trade with the patrol for it. Interestingly enough, none of my Bosavi informants thought that Champion and Adamson were spirits, nor did they draw a connection between the Bamu-Purari and the Strickland-Purari patrols, though these patrols crossed the plateau within eighteen months of each other and along tracks not more than 10 km apart. Instead, informants stressed that the patrols had come from different directions—one west, the other south —and hence were associated with different (peripheral) places of origin. Hides and O'Malley approached from downstream of the Rentoul, the direction in which human souls travel after they die, a place of spirits and the dead; Champion and Adamson approached from the direction of Helebe, the mysterious source of steel. They were not comparable.

Bosavis who saw the Bamu-Purari patrol recall this encounter as a quasi-mythical event of fearsome and wonderful character: the Coming of Helebe. They feel it to be a qualitatively different experience from that of the arrival of subsequent patrols in the 1950's. Most stories about "Helebe" today emphasize the quantity of axes and pearlshells the patrol is said to have distributed. Old men talk glowingly of the size and quality of these items, the like of which, they claim, they have not seen since. A few others now regard "Helebe" as marking the end (or the beginning of the end) of the old order of things.

When the patrol post was opened at Lake Kutubu across the Hegigio, the first priority for the administration was consolidation of the highlands peoples who, with their heavier populations, seemed to offer greater potential for development. This, plus the intervention of the Second World War, meant that the next patrol did not visit the Papuan Plateau until sixteen years later, in 1952.

In the meantime, life continued on the plateau much as before, with its disputes, prestations, alliances, and battles. Several Bosavi communities became embroiled in a dispute with the Etoro that culminated in a massive raid in which an Etoro force descended on a Bosavi longhouse, burned it to the ground, and massacred most of the community of 26 people. The raiders managed to escape to strongly defensible positions in the mountains and remained so wary that the Bosavis were unable to get revenge and had to leave the situation at a stand-off. To the east, the Onabasulu and Namabolo continued to raid each other across the Hegigio.

In 1952 and 1953 the government sent three extensive exploratory pa-

* Champion later characterized them as the most timid people he ever encountered (personal communication).

trols into the plateau area from Lake Kutubu to examine natural resources and establish friendly contact with the people. As with the previous patrols, the people's response was fearful and wary. Most fled their
dwellings to hide in the forest. A few young men, eager for adventure
and fascinated by the cloth and steel given to the carriers, boldly attached
themselves to the patrol as guides and message bearers. But for the rest
it was only with the greatest difficulty that the government officers and
police could round the people up and communicate their peaceful intentions. The situation was further complicated by the fact these early patrols
were accompanied by numbers of Namabolo guides and interpreters, traditional enemies of some of the people on the plateau and not above using
the patrol to accomplish their own agenda. One canny Namabolo leader
informed a patrol officer that the Onabasulu had recently killed one of
his kinsmen (neglecting, however, to add that he had already taken revenge and now feared reprisal). The officer decided to investigate and led
a patrol into Onabasulu country. The Onabasulu, seeing their traditional
enemies leading a patrol into their territory, fled terror-stricken into the
forest. The police managed to round up a few of them, and the government officer delivered a stern lecture on violence and murder. A few pigs
were then expropriated and given to the Namabolo in compensation for
the death of which they had complained. With this gesture, the traditional
fighting between the Onabasulu and the Namabolo came to an end.

The other outstanding enmity was resolved soon afterwards, though
not by government intervention. During 1952 an outbreak of measles and
mumps moved into the Fasu country from Erave. Despite precautions by
patrol officers, the epidemic crossed the Hegigio and broke out among the
Onabasulu and Etoro in 1953 shortly after the above-mentioned establishment of peace. The effect was devastating. The Etoro alone lost nearly
50 percent of their population (Kelly 1977), and the Onabasulu suffered
almost as badly. The Etoro, still living in unresolved tension with the Bosavis over the massacre of the longhouse community, came to believe this
plague had been sent by Bosavi witchcraft as a form of revenge. Unable to
stand the losses any longer, they sued for peace. The Bosavis were agreeable, and the two tribes were able to settle the matter by a dramatically
staged exchange of compensation.

Beginning in 1958, the administration began to patrol the plateau region
regularly about once every two years, censusing the population, dispensing
medical care (the disease yaws was eliminated from the region), ensuring
that latrines were dug, the dead buried (rather than placed on exposure
platforms), and house sites kept clean and tidy. Execution of witches was
prohibited, as was the use of violence as a means of conducting disputes.
As the "pax Australiana" became established, it became clear to the people

of the plateau that their lives were irrevocably altered, but they had no clear idea what new form it was going to take. Disputes and enmities left hanging by the prohibition on violence continued to rankle unresolved. Whatever the new form of their lives, it was to begin with frustrated hopes, growing pains, false euphorias, fits and starts.

During the 1950's and 1960's mission activity had been following close upon the administration opening of new areas in the highlands. Traditional Papuan New Guinean cultures with their body nakedness, exotic, "primitive" customs, and frequent violence were the evangelist's very image of Satan's country. The armies of Christ had been on the offensive on the island of New Guinea from the end of the nineteenth century. In 1964 the advance columns arrived on the Papuan Plateau. Two missionaries from the Unevangelised Fields Mission walked in to the Bosavi country from Lake Kutubu, leading a party of Papuan evangelists and workmen to build an airstrip and mission station.

The clearing and construction of the airstrip was an undertaking on a scale vastly grander than anything the people of the tropical forest had ever thought of before. It excited their imagination. Even more, it seemed to bear the promise that something wonderful was coming to them, a promise of a wholly new and different future. A kind of millennial excitement filled the air as a workforce of over a hundred men assembled from most of the Bosavi and Onabasulu communities. Many of the people who arrived on the work site shared longstanding grievances and enmities. However, the euphoria pervading the project was so high that men sought out their enemies of their own accord all over the workforce and made peace with them. Nothing like this had ever happened before; it was an extraordinary watershed event. After that, informants told me, people no longer feared to visit places where they had no relatives or to walk the paths between villages unarmed, nor did they feel ill at ease any longer in a crowd of strangers.

Midway through the work, an event occurred that seemed to confirm their wildest fantasies. As hundreds of tribesmen watched from the edges of the half-cleared airstrip, an aircraft swooped low overhead; axes and bushknives, bolts of cloth, beads and paint, sacks of rice and cartons of tinned fish rained down from the sky. A mission supply drop. The Bosavis watched in amazement. If this represented the promise of the new age, the future looked very bright indeed. It was more wealth than any of them had ever seen in one place at one time before.

Nothing quite as dramatic as this ever happened again. After the airstrip was completed, a small trade store was established there, but it was perpetually out of stock. A Papuan pastor looked after the station buildings; no missionary was to arrive to head the mission for another six years.

The outside world remained mysterious, and the promise of some sort of new way of life remained elusive.

In the late 1960's the administration began to push economic development as the key to the future. Government officers were urged to introduce cash crops to their constituencies, and patrol officers passing through the plateau region attempted to set up coffee blocks and show people how to cultivate peanuts and chilies. The projects all failed due to their inappropriateness for the area or lack of sustained supervision. Even had the crops succeeded, it is difficult to know what could have been done with them since there were no roads to ship them out. The fact of the matter was that the plateau area is difficult to administer, let alone develop. It is five days' walk from Lake Kutubu, and two days from the present patrol post at Komo. A patrol requires about two months to adequately cover the communities of this region, which contains only about 2,400 people. Consequently patrols never visited the plateau very frequently, and in 1968 the government ceased patrolling the area altogether. The resulting vacuum of political and ideological leadership was filled by the mission and the pastors of the evangelical church.

In 1970 an Australian missionary and his wife arrived to open a school and clinic at the mission station and to coordinate the effort of evangelism across the plateau. The standard and style for evangelization, however, were set not by the missionaries but by an extremely energetic evangelical convert pastor from the Huli people who was established at a centrally located Onabasulu village. Largely under his influence (and that of his protégés, who rapidly spread throughout the villages) the people of the plateau embarked on an extended period of religious ferment. A vigorous pace of religious observance was set, with services held twice a day.

All this evangelical activity gave the impression that Christianity was the wave of the future. The pastors themselves were the evidence of its advantages. They and their wives wore European-style clothes, owned pots and pans, did little work in the gardens, and received a small salary from the mission on a regular basis. They were linked with and supported by the larger, more privileged system of the outside world. The people of the plateau understandably drew the conclusion that the church was the major road to comparative wealth and status for Papuans, not only on the plateau, but in the outside world as well.

Evangelical excitement spread widely through the communities of the Papuan Plateau throughout the middle 1970's. Pastors continually urged their congregations to give up the "old ways" and turn to the "new." All traditional ceremonies and prestations were given up and replaced with Christian celebrations. Some communities abandoned living in longhouses and moved to single-family dwellings; men abandoned traditional dress for shorts and T-shirts. All of this activity and ferment was spurred on by the continually goaded awareness that Judgment Day was just around the corner. It was not until the end of the 1970's that it began to look as if Judgment Day was not going to arrive so soon as had been expected, and the evangelical fervor began to cool off.

In the meantime, other events had been coming to fruition that were to have considerable impact on the plateau. After Papua New Guinea became an independent nation in 1975, development planners gave special attention to speeding the development of the Southern Highlands. The provincial government allocated K20,000 for the construction of a new airstrip in Bosavi, larger and more centrally located than the one built by the mission in 1964. By this time a fair number of Bosavi and Onabasulu men could speak some English and had had some experience with work or school outside of the area. Construction began in early 1980 using hand tools and local labor. Unlike the construction of the mission strip in 1964, this effort did not have a millennial flavor. Nevertheless, the enormous amount of work involved, the relatively vast amount of money it brought into the region, and the increased government presence in the form of agricultural extension and local development workers sent to the region have seemed to offer an alternative road to advancement.

With the completion of the airstrip in 1984, the flow of money onto the plateau again dropped to the barest trickle. Christian evangelism is considerably muted compared to the 1970's. Today (1989) at the new airstrip a few men and women, prisoners at the makeshift jail, can be seen cutting the grass under the supervision of a local Bosavi man hired by the government as station caretaker. Nearby smoke rises slowly from the house of the agricultural extension officer, a Huli man who, with the help of a few Bosavi youths, is experimenting with the potential of cardamom as a cash crop in the region. This venture seems to have a reasonable chance of success since cardamom grows naturally in the tropical forest, requires very little care, and when harvested carries a high enough value-for-weight to be airlifted out of the region and still make a profit. There are still no roads in the area.

A group of enterprising young men from several communities have come together with a prominent local medical orderly and Christian leader to build a school, a trade store, and a medical clinic near the new airstrip in order to provide these services (now only available at the mission) closer to home.

From the perspective of the ethnographer, the very remoteness of the plateau region and the lack of access roads has been a blessing in disguise. There is no town for young men to hang around in, no group of restless disgruntled outsiders to cause trouble, and (so far) no access to alcohol. Low population density means there is little competition for local resources, and while there are occasional disputes between individuals and groups, traditional enmities of the days before contact have not been carried over into the present scheme of things. Despite the evident boredom and lack of opportunity in the region, the absence of other more exciting but destructive elements has meant that the traditional communities have remained socially intact and are not experiencing the increasing problems of crime and unrest found in larger, more prosperous centers of the Southern Highlands. If things continue to go this way and cardamom proves to be a successful cash crop, in a few years the region might experience a modest prosperity.

THE HULI (BRYANT ALLEN AND STEPHEN FRANKEL)

It is ironic that most Huli living in the late 1930's remained unaware of the Strickland-Purari patrol, while many everyday Australians sat enthralled at Hides's lectures and gazed at his photographs of "Besoso" and "Mambu" and other "light-skinned men of the Tari Furoro." A much greater number of Huli had been affected by the Fox brothers' passing through the Tari Basin than by Hides and O'Malley's movements across the lower Tagari Valley. Since the establishment of the Tari airstrip in 1951, the Huli have come to realize that Europeans are not *dama* but men, albeit wealthy and powerful ones. But between 1935 and 1951 they assumed the "red skins" were *dama* (see Chapter 4), powerful spirits or deities who can cause sickness or misfortune among humans, control the weather, and affect the productivity of gardens and pigs. They are considered capricious and often malevolent by the Huli. Humans can attempt to influence *dama* by various forms of ritual activity (*gamu*) ranging from simple spells to complex rites involving large numbers of people. A common form involved the sacrificing of a pig as an offering to the *dama* who was suspected of causing the misfortune or illness or who, it was thought, might assist humans in a particular endeavor (Glasse 1965; Frankel 1986).

When the Fox brothers moved down the Koroba Valley toward the Tagari River in 1934 they were approaching Huli country along an important route to the major shrine (*kebanda*) at Gelote, the place where the Huli believe the world was created. Passing close to Gelote, they continued in the direction of another major ritual center at Bepenete, an important focus for the *dindi gamu* rite (see Chapter 4 and Map 2). To the people of the region it appeared as if they had emerged from one of these two major ritual sites. Panguma Lomoko explained to Allen in 1986: "An important place is over there, a *kebanda* known as Bepenete. That was the direction they came from. They came from there to here and killed many men. So we said, 'The *dama* have emerged from the *kebanda* now.' So we killed many pigs and ate them. If we had not done this, we would have all died, or so we believed then. After they had come from there to here and killed many men, and gone up into the mountain Ambua and disappeared, we killed many pigs."*

From that time on, Huli believe that the depredations of the *dama* have increased. Hubi Hondonogo of Bepenete explained to Frankel that before that time (1934) the *dama* had remained confined to the precincts of the sacred sites, particularly Gelote. "These *dama* emerged in my time. When you whites were ready to come to our land, these demons preceded you. They consumed people voraciously. They show us many roads that lead to death. Men are few, demons are many. When I was a boy, they emerged. All this sacrificing pigs to *dama* began then. In my father's time, they did not sacrifice for this profusion of *damas*. They sacrificed for the spirits of their ancestors. In those days life was good. Since the *damas* emerged, life has become hard for us" (Frankel 1986).

The belief, inspired partly by the Fox brothers' expedition, that the *damas* escaped into the world about the time the white man appeared, has been linked with the perception of world decline provided in the lore of *dindi gamu*. Many Hulis believe that their world took a major downturn at that time, and this understanding deeply affects their view of their history up to the present. A number of portents and disasters seemed to occur in the years immediately following that early, momentous event.

In January 1936, an aircraft appeared through the Tari Gap and flew partway across the Tagari Valley. This was the flight carrying Ivan Champion, Jack Hides, James Taylor, and F. E. Williams, scouting the territory for future patrols. Many Huli who saw it were terrified and thought it was another manifestation of the *dama* they had recently seen on the ground.

About eighteen months later, the pace of unusual events increased. In September 1937 a patrol led by Claude Champion appeared from the north and traversed southward across the Tari Basin.† Six months later another patrol came in from the east, led by Ivan Champion, and moved north

---

* The wounds suffered by those killed during the time the *damas* marched across the valley were described to Allen by Hauwi Yuinako at Linapini in 1986: "Hamurumamake was killed in Yangali territory. When they shot him he was thrown back across a ditch about 5 m. He had a large hole in his chest. He had a net bag tied across his chest in our fashion. The knot of the net bag was driven into the hole in his chest and out through a bigger hole in his back. We could not understand what had made a hole like this. They [older men] just said the *damas* killed him."

†Claude Champion left Lake Kutubu and followed the Waga River north across the northern part of the Nembi Plateau to the Andabare Valley (now located in Enga Province). He then turned west and south and entered the Tari Basin from the north, crossing Huli territory in less than a week, passing close to Paijaka, Hoiebia, Wabia, and Benaria before returning to Lake Kutubu.

almost as far as the sacred shrine at Bepenete.* Three months after that
Jim Taylor and John Black appeared from near the Benaria Valley, leading
200 carriers and police on a patrol seeking to link Mt. Hagen with the
headwaters of the Sepik. They established a base camp at Hoiebia, building large bush houses and receiving air drops of supplies. Although Taylor
and Black were not involved in any violent incidents, armed police and
carriers from their expedition were responsible for killing an unknown
number of Huli while scouting or foraging for food away from the main
body of the patrol.† Further patrols returned briefly in May and December of 1939 (when Ivan Champion made a circuit of the Tari Basin) and
again in 1940 when Adamson returned some Huli laborers who had been
working at Lake Kutubu. At this point the Second World War intervened,
and the Lake Kutubu outpost was closed. The Hulis did not see Europeans
again for eleven years.‡

     This period of crisis in Huli cultural history was exacerbated by a num-
ber of other disasters. Between 1935 and 1937 there appears to have been
a famine brought about by a period of excessive rainfall. Then in 1941
a prolonged drought resulted in widespread bushfires and crop failures.
Frosts over parts of the Tari Basin made the situation worse. In 1943
an epidemic of bacillary dysentery, originating from Allied soldiers near
Goroka almost 300 km to the east, spread rapidly throughout the densely
settled parts of the highlands. Exactly when it reached Tari is uncertain,
but it is said to have caused numerous deaths besides those brought about
by the famine. The situation was not helped by the simultaneous outbreak
of porcine anthrax, which devastated the Huli herds of pigs.

     To alleviate these disasters, the Hulis sacrificed more pigs to the *dama*
at Bepenete. Then a new millenarian cult (called by Huli *mara gamu*) was
introduced to the area by the Waka Enga people to the northeast. The
ritual promised to reverse their misfortunes, allay their uncertainties, and
restore the productivity of gardens and pigs. Some even thought it would
bring back *mbingi*, the legendary fall of soil from the sky believed to have
restored Huli prosperity generations before (see Chapter 4). Cult leaders

     * Neither of the Champions nor Huli witnesses who remember them reported any violent
incidents.
     † Taylor's patrol also had other repercussions. When word reached Port Moresby that a
patrol from the Mandated Territory was operating in the Tari area, Hubert Murray convened
a conference with officials of the Mandated Territory to settle once and for all the location
of the boundaries between that territory and Papua. It was determined that the Tari Basin,
together with the Waga and Nembi valleys were included in Papua and should henceforth
be explored only by Papuan Administration Officers operating out of Lake Kutubu.
     ‡ Editors' note. Actually they were visited once by a patrol led by Danny Leahy, who came
in during the war to rebuild the airstrip at Hoiebia and recruit a few men for the police
(Ashton 1979; see also Crittenden 1982: 231).

told the Hulis to break their bows, to inter their dead (rather than raise the bodies on platforms), and to end traditional separation of the sexes, instructions that Hulis were later to identify with "the path of the Europeans." When *mara gamu* failed to bring the benefits it promised, it was abandoned, and Hulis returned to traditional custom. The uncertainties of the times, however, were already resulting in a period of increased unrest and intensified fighting.

At this point, in the early 1950's, the Australians returned to establish a patrol post and construct an airstrip at what is now Tari. Government officials were followed almost immediately by missionaries of four different denominations, who divided up the Huli region between themselves and began to proselytize. The Huli observed these developments with interest and trepidation. With their society in a more than usually disordered state, they were alert to any traditional or novel methods that might alleviate their political and ecological problems.

The Huli saw some hidden purpose in the alterations the Australians began to make in the local landscape. Their major sacred sites were hidden in groves of hoop pines (*Araucaria cunninghamii*), and the actual shrines were commonly approached along broad avenues through the trees. Hulis noted that the Europeans were now building similar roads all over the Tari Basin. Also significant was European interest in the hoop pines themselves, which they began to cut to make their houses. In the Huli view, the pines had been planted by the founding ancestors and did not belong to humankind. The appropriation of these trees by Australians suggested their relationship in some way to the founding ancestors. As one man explained to Frankel: "We thought the whites were the owners of these trees. We hadn't planted them. They had the right tools to cut them, chain saws and sawmills, but we couldn't cut them. They weren't ours." The buildings of the government station, missions, and churches in the Tari area are largely constructed of wood from the Huli sacred sites.

Mission Christianity quickly began to exert a powerful influence over Huli thought and religious observance. The Huli, however, understood their Christianity in the larger context of *dindi gamu* lore. According to an important tradition, a number of generations ago a major *dindi gamu* rite was performed at Bepenete. One of the requirements of the ritual was for a little blood to be drawn from the finger of a "red-skinned" boy from the Duna country. This youngster was called Bayebaye, which means "perfect" and refers to the hoped-for fertility of people, crops, and pigs and the condition of social harmony. Unfortunately, in the enthusiasm of the moment, the boy was killed rather than having his finger cut. His mother returned in mourning to her home in Duna keening a curse on

Huli crops, fertility, and social order.* The disastrous killing of Bayebaye and the legacy of increasing decline it is believed to have brought in its wake have weighed heavily on the Huli ever since.

As Hulis became familiar with mission teaching, they perceived parallels between the death of Bayebaye and the crucifixion of Christ. Many Hulis now use the names Bayebaye and Jesus interchangeably. The fate of the former is associated with that of the latter, and Christianity has become linked with the assumptions of *dindi gamu* lore. Hulis were also attracted to Christianity through its promise to protect them from the *damas*, but they have found that it is not without a price: they must also give up a great deal of traditional protective and strengthening ritual that (to them) has nothing to do with the *damas* and is not religious in character. Waiting for *mbingi* has tended to be replaced with expectation of Judgment Day.

Today life in Huli land is a feisty bustle of development projects and local government politics. Helicopters rattle overhead, carrying equipment and workers to oil rigs in the hinterland. Despite all this activity, however, work is scarce, and young men who have completed high school find few opportunities. They hang around in the towns or return to the hamlets, where they become involved in local politics and the fierce competition for development funds. Once again, rivalries between competing clans and factions, now exacerbated by alcohol, have resulted in renewed tribal fighting. Government offices in Tari were burned to the ground in 1986 by angry losers in the local political elections. So, amid economic growth, the introduction of modern medical care, and the increasing availability of modern commercial facilities, Huli society continues its traditionally turbulent course. Although the stakes are different, the various factions and individuals continue vigorously, and sometimes violently, to jockey for advantage against each other. To the young, hungry for a place in the sun and impatient with the lack of opportunity and the restraints and traditions of their elders, it seems the life they think they are entitled to is always just beyond their grasp. To traditionalists it appears that the depredations of the *damas* and the legacy of Bayebaye and *dindi gamu* continue to cast their shadow over Huli life.

As one old ritual expert and traditionalist, Yaluduma-Dai of Gelote,

---

* Her mourning lament, according to tradition, ran as follows: "I, Bayebaye's mother, am leaving you here. I will take the propitious path. But you will find famine. You will have to slaughter your herds. You will fornicate. You will grovel for food. You will forage for rubbish. She will tell you that she is your mother, but you will take her anyway. She will tell you she is your sister, but you will take her anyway. He will tell you he is your father, but you will kill him anyway. He will tell you he is your brother, but you will kill him anyway. You will find famine. You will be able to think of nothing but where to find food. There will be plagues and you will find death" (Frankel 1986: 23).

observed: "[Nowadays] young men mature too soon. They refuse to work the land, dig ditches, or look after pigs. They just roam around fighting, stealing, fornicating, and will not listen to their fathers. People take what is not theirs, they help themselves to others' belongings and wives. This is the time for us to die. It is now the afternoon. There is not much left to us now. The world is dry. . . . Before it was new ground, but now the earth is old and worn out" (Frankel 1986: 24).

THE WOLA AND THE NEMBI (ROBERT CRITTENDEN)

Two years after the Strickland-Purari patrol passed down the Waga Valley and across the Nembi Plateau, the first exploratory patrols began to appear from Lake Kutubu. Meanwhile, other changes taking place in distant regions of the highlands were beginning to affect the wider regional economic system of which the Wola and the Nembi were a part. These changes began as reverberations of administration presence even when the nearest outposts were a considerable distance away.

It was the enormous demand for pearlshell in the highlands that had given the people of the lower Nembi Valley their particular strategic advantage at the junction of the trade routes running from Samberigi to Lake Kutubu and the Mendi and Lai river valleys. In the mid 1930's, however, the opening of patrol stations and mining enterprises at Mt. Hagen in the distant Wahgi Valley provided a more convenient and abundant source of pearlshell for their highlands customers than that available over the trade route. In 1937, the same thing happened in the lowlands when the government brought pearlshell to Lake Kutubu. While at first the Nembi were delighted to have these new sources of wealth, they soon found that their position on the trade routes had been outflanked and their strategic advantage was lost. At the same time the growing supply of shells brought about an inflation that undermined their value. These changes, however, were realized only gradually as administration patrols systematically explored and consolidated the Southern Highlands.

Nembi and Wola who saw the early patrols were impressed with the officers' apparently limitless wealth and the grand style they projected in command over armed police and lines of carriers. By and large they received the patrols warily and showed a healthy respect for their firepower —undoubtedly a result of their experience with Hides and O'Malley.* In

* In a radio interview in 1980 Claude Champion described the following encounter with Wola near Sezinda during a patrol from Lake Kutubu to Tari: "At one of the places on the Wela [Waga] where [Hides] had had a terrific fight, killing a lot of people, the men greeted us with bows and arrows; but they made signs that they didn't want any 'boong, boonging.' We put our rifles down and eventually the natives put their bows and arrows down and we gave them some shell" (Nelson, 1982: 121).

fact, patrol officers frequently found traces of the passage of the Strickland-Purari patrol. Adamson and Timperley, passing a few kilometers from where Hides had shot his way out of the Korpe defile, were shown the skull of one of the casualties of that conflict placed upon three sticks in the form of a shrine (Lake Kutubu PR 3, 1938–39). No local hostility or resentment was expressed towards them, however. Later they encountered people wearing shell cases and cartridge clips as ornaments. Ivan Champion, leading a patrol through the lower Emia Valley earlier that same year, noted that the local people "took great pains to explain they went about unarmed and had no intention of attacking us" (Lake Kutubu PR 1, 1938–39). Attacks later made on patrols near Kuvivi and in the Sugu Valley were attempts to rob them of their trade goods rather than acts motivated by resentment and vengeance for the deaths caused by Hides and his police. As noted earlier, patrol officers made a point of demonstrating their rifles to people in the villages by shooting a pig or putting a bullet through a stack of shields so that local warriors could see how they defended themselves.

Hides's difficulties with the Nembi and Wola have often been attributed to the fact that he did not carry shell with which to trade. Later patrols, however, though well supplied with this commodity, didn't always have an easier time of it. The Nembi and Wola, despite their avidity for pearlshell, still drove extremely hard bargains in their trade, at least from a European point of view. Champion's experience on the first patrol after Hides and O'Malley to enter the lower Emia Valley paralleled Hides's at Huwguwn: "We tried to buy food with shell. One man took the swag and said he would fill it with potatoes. We saw him digging in the garden, and then he brought it back with about 15 pounds and demanded a shell. I offered him a small piece of shell, but he became arrogant, so I picked up the bag and emptied his potatoes on him. It had a good effect. The others laughed at him and he went away so I threw the small piece of shell after him as he had left his potatoes" (Lake Kutubu PR 1, 1938–39).*

On a later occasion it took Adamson and Atkinson two hours of haggling to purchase a pig for an axe and four pearlshells (Lake Kutubu PR 9, 1938–39).† Even years later, in the 1950's, some patrols considered they

---

* Even seasoned anthropologists have had their difficulties with these people. F. E. Williams, stationed at Augu for field work in 1938, remarked: "If in some future life I have the opportunity of choosing a scientific profession, it will have to do with stones or vegetables, them as which will stay and work with me just as long as I want them, and not pester me afterwards: and if things go wrong, there will be no serious consequences to be feared if one smashes them with a hammer or spade—not of the sort that would follow if one strangled an informant with a pair of calipers or stabbed him to death with a lead pencil, as I have so often been tempted to do" (Papua Annual Report 1938–39: 40–41).

† By comparison prices at Lake Kutubu in the period 1937–40 were up to three shells for a pig and up to two for a copra sack of sweet potatoes (Papua Annual Report 1939–40).

could not afford to trade with the Nembi at all (Mendi PR 1, 1950–51). In view of these difficulties, all patrols considered it necessary to carry significant quantities of rice.

In the hiatus during the Second World War while the Kutubu patrol post was closed, a new source of trouble came upon the Nembi as malaria began to move up the Erave Valley. The increase in the number of deaths, which was interpreted as the result of sorcery, led to an escalation of tribal fighting as groups retaliated upon one another for their losses. The intensity of the fighting accelerated a process of slow migration already underway from the Erave Valley up into the Nembi area. The pressure of warfare and population movement sent waves of violence up the Nembi Valley and Plateau as people jostled for land, fought back, or were themselves felled by the new mosquito-born illness. By the time the administration returned to Lake Kutubu in 1949, the Nembi were more deeply involved in warfare than before. Their warrior confidence and traditional truculence had returned.

In 1952, during one of the early patrols back through the area, J. S. McCleod reported sourly: "The natives northeast of Lake Kutubu have never been noted for their cooperation. They are arrogant and have been continuously parsimonious with food and assistance to patrols. Mr. Champion has always reported adversely on the Nembi, Lai, Wage, and Mendi peoples. . . . To the northeast of Kutubu locals appear to be very anxious to be rid of [the government]" (Mendi PR 4, 1952–53).

Rather more perceptively, another officer, C. E. T. Terrell, remarked: "I interpret what has been regarded as arrogance by previous patrols as a natural independence of thought and action, and the attitude prevailing is 'If what I do doesn't suit you, well, that is your concern'" (Lake Kutubu PR 1, 1953–54).

The administration had, however, decided to make Wola and Nembi behavior very much its concern, and once it had established administrative centers at Mendi and Tari and nearby adjacent valleys, it opened the patrol post at Nipa in the Wola country to put a stop to tribal fighting. The tribesmen did not make the task easy. J. Jordan, the officer in charge at Nipa soon after it was opened in 1959, reported: "Attempts were made to get the people to meet the patrol, but the only result was that the patrol was given a rather juicy badinage of obscene comments by persons sitting on nearby ridges" (Nipa PR 2, 1959–60).*

Besides jeering insults, the Wola and Nembi threw stones and released

---

* These were undoubtedly similar to the insults reported by another officer in a nearby area: "'We will skin your penis'; 'Go drink your mother's menstrual fluid'; and 'Our axe will drink your urine'. This latter threat apparently refers to the killing blow used in this area when the attacker strikes his victim through the back to the kidney" (Mendi PR 4, 1961–62).

arrows at patrols. This struggle came to a head in 1960 when patrol officer Doug Butler was knocked down in a scuffle and his leg deliberately broken by a Nembi warrior who smashed it with a rock. The administration was furious. Four large patrols were organized and sent to converge on the Nembi Valley from four different directions. The officers in charge showed little respect for pigs and property of uncooperative tribesmen. This unprecedented show of force finally succeeded in intimidating the Nembi and bringing about their compliance. The following year an officer visiting the area reported: "Everyone went out of their way to ensure that nothing occurred which might possibly arouse the patrol to action; . . . at Semin a deputation led by the [village headman] approached me and wanted assurance that we would not take any action against them because it was raining and the census had to be postponed" (Mendi PR 17, 1962–63).

Once Australian law and order was established in the region, the administration built a road up the Nembi Valley and made a few attempts to bring economic development to the Wola and Nembi through the introduction of cash crops. Traffic in pearlshell along the trade routes had by now ceased to be important. So the Nembi and Wola began looking to money and "bisnis" as the new route to economic advantage (Crittenden 1987). The results, however, were disappointing. The Nembi and Wola were hindered by the marginal agricultural potential of their lands. Coffee was introduced to the Nembi Plateau in 1965, and chilies in 1971, but acreage given to these crops was never large nor very productive. Moreover, such projects only made economic sense if the land where they were produced was close to the road. This and other factors set in motion another migration of population, as people moved their homesteads to be nearer the roads. Ultimately, however, the administration itself could not make up its mind about the economic future of the region.

For the people, the primary motivation for economic activity continued to be the seeking of prestige and renown through competitive ceremonial exchange. After the cessation of warfare, previous clan enmities were contested within the exchange system. These rivalries, exacerbated by competition for land and the lack of opportunity for obtaining cash, became increasingly fierce. In 1974 fighting broke out again between clan alliances over the ownership of cattle for a new cattle project. Several cows were killed, and a number of clansmen ended up in the Nipa jail. Purely economic considerations were not what was at stake, however. Contrary to original administration expectations, the Wola and Nembi never saw these projects as developmental, profit-making ventures but rather as traditional attempts to gain renown and political advantage in the continuing rivalries between local clans and Big Men, using new means and objects of exchange. Where cows are kept on the Nembi Plateau, they are viewed as large pigs to be displayed and killed at pig-killing ceremonies for the glory of the clans that owned them.

After Papua New Guinea achieved independence in 1975, the various conflicting forces that had been slowly gathering since the time of contact came to a head. Prior to contact, the pattern of traditional Wola and Nembi clan alliances was complex and ever shifting. Clans rose and fell in political prominence through the manipulations of Big Men in ceremonial exchange and the vicissitudes of fighting. All this resulted in considerable mobility. People gathered to the support of one alliance or another were driven off their lands by fighting or themselves drove another group away. People who had lost their lands always hoped to regain them at some future time when they had recouped their strength or managed to gain some powerful allies. Dispersal of the group or dispossession of its lands was thus regarded as a temporary setback in the constantly shifting scheme of political fortune. When the administration officers pacified the region in the 1960's, they artificially froze this ongoing process by recognizing the clan boundaries and lands occupied at the time of pacification as the permanent situation for the future. Beneath the surface of this formalized status quo, however, seethed traditional enmities, unsettled disputes, frustrated schemes, and above all, the unequal distribution of land in the more fertile areas of the region. To these pressures and grievances were added those of people who now wished to relocate closer to roads, missions, health centers, and other modern amenities. The situation was made still more volatile by the continuing in-migration of people from the Waga Valley.

Local political development sponsored by the administration unwittingly preserved preexisting political enmities when the traditional regional clan alliances were made to form the basis of new local government council wards. Elections in 1980 for provincial government revealed the continuing antagonism between these alliances when individuals only voted for those candidates from their own groups. The peace of the late 1960's and 1970's was shattered in 1981 when all of these tensions erupted into warfare in the Pwe Creek Basin; fighting has continued sporadically in the region ever since.

Today (1987) the Nembi, and to a lesser extent the Wola, find themselves pushed to the sidelines of the Western-based commercial economy. With poor agricultural land and little access to cash, they feel they have little to bargain with. Though they retain their feisty independent spirit, they are frustrated at their lack of access to money and economic development and have come to think of themselves as beleaguered and abandoned. Marginalized at the edge of the highlands, their traditional trading economy shattered, fighting among themselves for land and local political advantage, their backs to the lowland forests, they have come to believe they are the forgotten men of Papua.

KEWA AFTERMATH (LISETTE JOSEPHIDES AND MARC SCHILTZ)

Following their contact with the Strickland-Purari patrol, our informants claimed, the Kewa people living around Sumbura were not keen to show themselves openly to later patrols. If this was true for Sumbura, however, it was not the case for all Kewa.*

The region around the Kagua, Sugu, and Erave valleys was marked by extensive tribal fighting in the late 1930's. Following the Strickland-Purari patrol, in the period before World War II, three patrols out of Lake Kutubu passed through these regions, and a fourth passed nearby.† All remarked on the hostility of the local people—toward each other as well as toward patrols. On the last patrol, in June 1938, a patrol officer in the Kagua Valley was forced to shoot and kill a man who drew a bow on him. Later, during the war, ANGAU patrols apparently also traveled through this region, as they were widely reported by trading parties to later government officers (Lake Kutubu PR 8, 1952–53).

The first patrol to reenter the Kewa area after the Second World War originated at Mendi. It traversed the Sugu Valley and camped at Tiripi not far from Koyamapu (Mendi PR 4, 1952–53). This was followed not long afterwards by a patrol led by E. D. Wren from Lake Kutubu, which visited Kurusa and Arawa, two villages close to the left bank of the Erave that Hides had passed through (Lake Kutubu PR 11, 1953–54). B. B. Corrigan traveled down the Sugu twice in 1956 (Erave PR 3, 1955–56, and PR 3a and PR 3b, 1956–57). Shyness, if not hostility, however, continued towards these patrols. At this time the Kewa, like the Nembi and other highland peoples, were stubbornly embroiled in tribal fighting, and patrol officers were forced to act with considerable firmness to compel them to stop. This activity did not quickly win Kewa trust, though the men understood and respected the use of force, being warriors themselves. The struggle to end

---

*Among the peoples of the Sugu and Kagua valleys to the north, there is every probability that they knew of government patrols through the Samberigi and Erave valleys before the arrival of Hides and O'Malley (indeed Faithorn and Champion had crossed the Erave in that vicinity in 1929 [Kikori PR 19, 1928–29]). People from these four valleys had extensive trading relations with each other, and such news would have spread by word of mouth, especially when someone was killed. A man from Tembikene village (in Pagia, Wiru District) was shot by Faithorn and Champion's police at Koaire just north of the Erave River to the east of Batri in 1929.

†I. Champion and Adamson (Lake Kutubu PR 1, 1938–39); Adamson and Atkinson (Lake Kutubu PR 9, 1938–39); I. Champion and Timperley (Lake Kutubu PR 10, 1938–39); and Adamson and Bramell (Lake Kutubu PR 1, 1939–40).

tribal fighting lasted until the late 1950's. The Kewa tried many strategies, including avoidance and noncompliance, to evade government control.

In 1957 a patrol officer attributed a poor turnout for census to resentment following the arrest of local leaders of a tribal fight in nearby Turire in the previous year (Kagua PR 2, 1957–58). The officer had managed by shouting to rally some boys and men, whom he sent off to "fetch the women," but fear and suspicion resulted in only a meager turnout, especially of men between the ages of 30 and 40. The officer was evidently heavy-handed in his response, for he was subsequently criticized by his superior for conducting his patrol like "a Nazi village-sacking party" (Erave PR 1, 1957–58). In 1958 some men were arrested at Batri for not working on the road (Erave PR 5, 1957–58). Also in 1958 R. S. Bell reported that his patrol received a friendly reception (Erave PR 2, 1958–59), while a few months later G. J. Hogg's patrol (Erave PR 5, 1958–59) was avoided by the same people, who then kept out of the way of Butler's patrol (Kagua PR 2, 1957–58).

The firm tactics of some of these patrols left strong impressions on many of our informants who, now in their thirties, were little boys at the time. Some were more vociferous than their fathers in describing recollections of their communities' predicament when they were small. Michael, one of our assistants, pantomimed being manacled and pulled along: "Liklik rong mipela save Kalaboos tasol" (the slightest transgression landed us in prison).

When the "red men" once spent the night in Paipanda near Aka, the Kewa thought they had come to kill them, so they ran and hid. One patrol officer proposed that a school be established to instruct the *luluais* (government-appointed village leaders) in the rudiments of their duties (Erave PR 3, 1957–58). The sort of training received in the meantime was wryly and laconically described by Michael: "Becoming a *luluai* was no easy matter. First they would seize a man and beat him up thoroughly, then put him in a uniform and give him good food, soap, and loincloths. Then he would come back and tell us how good they had been to him, and urge us to obey the government."

One is reminded here of Ongka's description of the schizoid state induced in *luluais* in Mt. Hagen. These men would go into paroxysms, use their close kinspeople roughly, and abjure them not to speak in front of them for fear of death, for the white man had turned their stomachs back to front and made them mad (Ongka 1979: 12).

Michael also described the inducements of working on the Kagua airstrip: "While we worked on Kagua airstrip, there was a *kiap* [patrol officer] who would not deign to hand spades to the men, but threw them in their faces. If a man failed to catch one, he would simply get hold of him by the scruff of the neck, spin him round, and throw him down. He was one hell of a hard man."

The officer's behavior was recounted with a mixture of wonder, awe, incredulity, enormous amusement, contempt, and mild outrage. Another informant in his late thirties, Rimbu, described how censuses were taken: "We had to stand in line, the men in front with their wives and children behind them. We saw our fathers shaking with fear as they stood to be counted. When Michael ran away, they cuffed his father, for not keeping a better hold on him."

To see their fathers, onetime fearless warriors, used like naughty children and punished far more severely, could not fail to impress these young boys. The old warriors themselves spoke candidly of their changed condition. As Ana put it: "In the old days we were strong, aggressive people, who talked, fought, and lived hard, but now that the government has come among us, we are tame and peaceful."

Though at first Kewa hid from patrols, gradually they became more familiar with the new order. They embraced Christian missions enthusiastically, rapidly, and apparently irrevocably. Elected councillors replaced village constables. Radios appeared in villages, telling people of the new, wider world and spreading the knowledge of the pidgin lingua franca. Aid posts and schools were built. Finally, independence followed self-rule in 1975. In the process a new generation of men and women had come of age intent on getting a hold on the newly established order.

But have traditional Kewa usages really disappeared half a century after Hides and O'Malley's patrol? At first sight it appears that ceremonial exchanges and pig kills have increased and that village-based activities have not lost their importance. But a closer look at these activities reveals there are new objectives and strategies behind them. New sources of power and wealth now exist beyond the confines of the local community. They beckon to the young people brought up under the influence of mission ideologies and the cash economy. Young men sign on for contract labor on distant plantations, and villagers grow coffee at home. Some have opened trade stores, and others have bought trucks and run transportation services.

An important change has been the virtual collapse of Kewa traditional trade links with their southern neighbors—the Sembo middlemen who brought them steel tools and pearlshells from the Gulf of Papua and tree oil from Kutubu. As described in Chapter 8, established men with large households were in a privileged position for controlling trade in prestige items. Because of this, they were able to act as patrons for young men anxious to get married and start households of their own. But these young men now look north, to the commercial centers of Mt. Hagen and to the coastal plantations farther afield to earn money. They have direct access to the new sources of wealth and can liberate themselves from their economic dependence on local Big Men. Moreover, the opportunities now open for young men can sometimes also be enjoyed by women, and this is affecting gender relations considerably.

At the end of this investigation into "first contact" one question continued to puzzle us. Why had our old informants never spoken of the Strickland-Purari patrol during our earlier periods of fieldwork? Their accounts in 1985 revealed that it had been important to them. Clearly, the experience was not forgotten years later, nor were the difficult experiences of subsequent years when other patrol officers returned to impose government rule. Our informants reminisced that no one had thought of taking up arms to halt the patrol's progress. But, as later patrol reports attest, not all Kewa thought of putting their arms down altogether either.

In the intervening two decades, the Walali story (see Appendix A) was a conscious attempt to incorporate this event into the Kewa experiential world of humans and spirits. Later, however, this inaugural act of state dominance began to blur as people experienced more and more the impact of this new power on their everyday lives. The younger generation now looks somewhat askance at what they saw as their parents' inept handling of events—which were, however, beyond their understanding. At the same time young people feel that the older generation experienced in those old days something they could never match: a lifestyle in which "government" was not a power above and beyond the people.

For the Future (Edward L. Schieffelin)

The apparently bucolic future of the Papuan Plateau, the feisty competition for development funds and local political influence among the Huli, and the continuing combative rivalry for prestige through competitive exchange (or any other means) among the Wola and Nembi—in the late 1980's all this has become overshadowed by events which may radically alter not only the Southern Highlands, but the whole of Papua New Guinea itself.

After a series of geological investigations carried out since the early 1970's, British Petroleum and a consortium of other oil companies revealed in December 1987 a report of extensive deposits of oil and natural gas under the Southern Highlands Province. Test wells drilled along the highlands rim just north of the Papuan Plateau and in the limestone country just west of the Iwa Range near Hedinia in the Fasu country have shown considerable promise (*Papua New Guinea Times*, June 1988). Preliminary estimates suggest that earnings from this hydrocarbon field might increase the revenues of the Papua New Guinea government by as much as 60 percent. If this assessment turns out to be correct, the consequences for the cultures and peoples of the Southern Highlands are difficult to imagine.

Petroleum may be regarded as the pearlshell of industrial civilization. The avarice it evokes, the ruthlessness with which government bureaucrats and multinational corporations compete over it, and the political forces, rivalries, and skulduggery that are called into play in the process are the modern version of life in the Waga and Nembi valleys in the late 1930's. These corporate struggles carried on from lofty glass buildings, plotted with the aid of computers, organized through satellite links, and fought by warriors who arrive on executive-class flights—all take place far beyond the peripheries of the people who inhabit the regions concerned. The direction of their future will be decided in deals struck between bureaucrats in Port Moresby and executives in London, Sydney, and New York, by people they don't know about and will never see. It might as well be the spirit world.

The southern highlanders, however, remain a feisty and independent spirited people. They welcome these development projects with enthusiasm now—but could very well become troublesome if they later feel they are not getting what they are entitled to from them. Just how much trouble they might cause for a giant development scheme is suggested by the difficulties the Papua New Guinea government is already experiencing with a handful of rebels angry over a huge copper mine on the island of Bougainville. In May 1989, after years of protest over the pollution of their rivers by the mine, resentment at high-handed treatment by company representatives, and growing conviction that they had been misled and inadequately compensated for the loss of their ancestral lands, a group of tribesmen shot a couple of company employees with arrows and took off into the tropical forest. Since then, according to the *Wall Street Journal*:

Armed with bows and arrows, shotgun shells hand-loaded with fishing sinkers, and stolen dynamite . . . about 100 villagers on the island of Bougainville have made the price of copper futures dance by shutting down one of the world's biggest copper mines—this country's largest employer and money-earner—for nearly eight months, at a cost to the government of nearly $1000 a minute in lost revenue. . . .
The results so far: at least 40 people have been killed, some 3000 mine workers are idle, about 4000 villagers are living in refugee tent camps, and thousands of non-Bougainvillean settlers on the island have packed and fled. (January 8, 1990)

Papua New Guinea government troops and police have so far (1990) been unable to quell the disturbance, which has taken on the character of a sputtering guerrilla war, and as of this writing the mine remains closed.

Southern Highlanders have shown throughout their history that they are quite capable of behaving in a similar manner to the Bougainville rebels. If, after considerable development investment has been made in the region and a significant proportion of the PNG national revenue is at stake, the southern highlanders become restive with their cut of the pie, the outcome seems fairly clearly written on the wall. Next time, however, the government response may well be quicker and more sophisticated.

In the meantime, at a place southwest of Tari not far from where Hides and O'Malley stood in 1935, gazing for the first time at the cultivations of the Huli people, there is a geological structure containing the largest deposit of natural gas discovered in the country in recent years. It is perhaps an awkwardly appropriate irony that this formation, and its accompanying drilling machinery, have been named after Jack Hides.

The Reverberations of First Contact in Subsequent History

The experience of first contact was invariably a memorable one for Papuans. The dramatic and uncanny quality of the event and its potential challenge to their traditional assumptions and beliefs about the nature of the world raise the question of what kind of lasting impact it may have had on the Papuan societies that experienced it. Objectively, of course, first contact was the harbinger of the (often extensive) social, political, and economic changes that followed upon the ending of tribal autonomy under administration control. However, we are interested in a different issue: To what extent did the experience of first contact itself affect the world view of the Papuans who encountered the patrol, influence their understanding of their subsequent history, or affect their self-perception?

One of the most sophisticated treatments of this question in the literature is Marshall Sahlins's (1981) analysis of the historical impact of Captain Cook's arrival in Hawaii in 1778. Focusing on the early contact process, or "structure of the conjuncture" as he termed it, Sahlins emphasized that people understand the events of such encounters in terms of their indigenous cosmological ideas, political assumptions, and ritual practices. These ideas and assumptions themselves gain new force and meaning through the very historical events they assimilate and then shape the perception and construction of subsequent events. In his structural/ historical study of Hawaii, Sahlins noted that Hawaiian tradition placed the origins of the gods and the chiefly lines at a mythical place (Kahiki) located beyond the horizon over the sea. Thus the arrival of powerful Europeans from across the sea carried powerful political and religious implications.

Captain James Cook happened to arrive in Hawaii at the commencement of a major festival honoring the yearly ascendancy of the indigenous god Lono. The Hawaiians took Cook to be Lono and treated him like a god. Cook, for his part, unwittingly recapitulated many of the moves expected of Lono on that occasion and allowed himself to be honored in rituals directed to that deity. Even his death conformed to the Hawaiian archetype: he was killed in a fight just after the end of the Lono festival at the point when a more warlike god (Ku) began his ascendancy.[*] Even though Hawaiians eventually realized that Cook was human, their responses to him as a god had powerfully recommitted them to their traditional assumptions about the power of beings from across the sea. These assumptions now became revalued and focused on Europeans, and this deeply influenced the behavior of the Hawaiian chiefs toward European visitors, setting in motion social and political processes that significantly shaped the transformation of Hawaiian society over the next 50 years.

The question for us is whether the experience of first contact in the Southern Highlands of Papua New Guinea was the source of similar profound cultural revaluations. Like Hawaiians, Papuans tended to identify the government officers and men who arrived in their regions with known spiritual or mythical beings who lived beyond the periphery of their worlds, and they geared their responses accordingly. What happened afterward, however, suggests that there are more complexities in the process of cultural revaluation of history than Sahlins was aware of or are revealed in the Hawaiian case alone.

Of all the groups the Strickland-Purari patrol encountered, the most profound effects of first contact for subsequent revaluation of self and history are exemplified among the Huli. Here, however, it was not the arrival of Hides and O'Malley but that of the Fox brothers that had the major impact. The Fox brothers' first appearance among the Huli near the Origin Place at Gelote and their passage across the Tari Basin by way of the sacred site at Bepenete were seen as the release of capricious *dama* spirits from Gelote into the world and were thought to have resulted in the plague of troubles that subsequently descended upon the Huli (Hides and O'Malley were themselves seen as such *damas*). These ideas were incorporated within the perspective of overall world decline already given in traditional *dindi gamu* lore, which in part aimed to restore prosperity by bringing back *mbingi*. *Dindi gamu* lore continued to shape Huli perspectives on events throughout the time of increasing contact, government consolidation, and expansion of missionary efforts. Although missionary efforts eventually succeeded in destroying the *dindi gamu* ritual complex, they have not deeply affected the *dindi gamu* outlook on life—which continues to contribute nostalgia and dissatisfaction to the Huli understanding

---

[*] Cook was not in fact the first European to contact Hawaii, but the events of his visit-as-a-god had the appropriate profound and memorable effects.

of their situation even to the present and imparts a millenial flavor to their hopes for the future.

The cultural revaluations and historical reverberations of Huli first-contact experience were dramatic. What is interesting, however, is that the first-contact situation among many of the other people Hides and O'Malley encountered seems to have had hardly any historical reverberations at all. First contact and its aftermath for them looks not so much like a "structure of conjuncture" as "a structure of *mis*juncture." If we look at the reasons for this, they suggest that a positive dynamic is involved in the failure of cultural assimilation of experience and that the social disorganization of knowledge may be involved to some extent with any historical process in a nonliterate culture. This involves a number of complexities in the early contact process that Sahlins does not explore.

One set of complexities has to do with the processes involved when historical activities and cultural structures do not easily articulate with one another. If we focus on the cultural aspects, it is clear that while a people's cultural views shape their perceptions of historical situations, the events of first contact may not always fit as easily into every people's key cosmological understandings as they did for the Huli or the Hawaiians. In other words, how resonant the events of first contact are likely to be for a people's post-contact history and self-perception depends to some degree on the centrality and importance of the cultural or cosmological ideas in terms of which they are understood.

The situation may be illustrated by the example of the Bosavi encounter with the Bamu-Purari patrol. We recall that the Bosavis regarded Champion and Adamson as beings from "Helebe," the mysterious source of steel axes in the south. They principally remember the patrol for how frightened they were of it and for the large number of steel axes and pearlshells it distributed. But the significance of the story seems to go little further than that. They do not link it with the passage of Hides and O'Malley through the Onabasulu country nearby only a year before. Indeed, even though Bosavis now realize that "Helebe" was the first government patrol into their area, they do not associate it with the later patrols that explored and consolidated the region from Lake Kutubu. Rather, they tend to recall the arrival of Helebe as a separate, dramatic, but rather isolated event, a harbinger of things to come, perhaps, but not a precipitating force. The point is that little in the story seems to have revalued later thinking or action in regard to Europeans or the arrival of other large distributions of wealth (the first mission airdrop, the money for the second airstrip). This seems to be partly because, while the sacred sites and *damas* were central to Huli cosmology, ritual activity, and understanding of themselves, the notion of Helebe was relatively peripheral to Bosavi worldview and social concern.*

The Bosavi encounter with Helebe suggested few implications for new understandings of further historical developments or changing worldview because Helebe itself played so little part in their ordinary lives. Nor did subsequent historical events accomplish a significant revaluation in the idea of Helebe itself in Bosavi cosmology. The Bamu-Purari patrol was the only patrol that ever approached the Bosavi region from the south, the direction of Helebe. If subsequent patrols had continued to come from this direction and had continued to be associated with Helebe, the idea of Helebe might gradually have come to assume more importance in Bosavi thinking. Such historically inspired changes in their worldview might then have more readily affected their understanding of events of their post-contact history. (For an example of this for the Wiru people near Pangia, see Clark, forthcoming.)

If we shift our focus to the historical aspects of the first-contact situation, we note that, even when the first contact events are assimilated by central ideas in the worldview, the eventual outcome of the situation is subject to uncertainties of historical contingency. That is, although a people's central cosmological ideas may be involved in framing their perceptions of the experience, it may also happen that subsequent historical events are so constituted that they disrupt or displace this understanding, or reframe it under another set of ideas. This may bring about a new revaluation of the original contact experience or reduce its relevance to later historical perception.

This seems to be in part what happened among the Etoro and Onabasulu. These people thought the Strickland-Purari patrol represented Spirit Beings approaching from the direction of the Road of the Dead or returning to the Origin Place at Malaiya, both places of central importance in their cosmological landscape. Some feared that contact with these beings or acceptance of their gifts would precipitate a world catastrophe. The Etoro in the first instance tried to avert this disaster by confronting the patrol and, when that failed, by avoiding it altogether. The Onabasulu of Ogesiya, on the other hand, believed the Beings had been drawn to the

---

* The point that the historical importance of an unusual event depends to a significant degree on the importance and centrality of the cultural ideas in terms of which it is grasped may be illustrated by the following hypothetical situation in our own tradition: A man who is desperately ill sees an apparition of a woman who lays her hand upon him. Shortly afterwards he recovers his health. If he is nonreligious and thinks the apparition is his mother who died when he was a child, he has a ghost story perhaps worth reporting in the *National Enquirer*. If he is Roman Catholic and sees her as the Virgin Mary, his experience falls within the purview of a major religious tradition; his recovery may be counted as a Christian miracle and given a much more fundamental significance and public attention.

area following the trail of their wayward "children" (axes and bushknives) and tried to return these items so that the patrol would leave before disaster struck. The patrol, however, far from reclaiming its "children," seemed inexplicably bent in spreading more of them around. At the same time, the Etoro and Onabasulu attempted to neutralize the impact of the patrol by their own activity. During its presence in the area, no one came out to greet it, no gifts were accepted, no food was offered or shared, and hence no obligations or connections were left outstanding. There was little left that might (at least from the Etoro/Onabasulu point of view) positively impel a connection between this set of events and any later ones.

The next patrol to approach the region came from the south, the direction of the Bosavi country, and was seen (by the Onabasulu) to embody quite a different problem: it was accompanied by their traditional enemies the Namabolo (Fasu), bent on obtaining restitution for a death. This kind of threat was anything but exotic, and the Onabasulu fled for fear of being killed by their enemies or "taken away" by their enemies' strange allies from the government. This reaction had little to do with their previous experience with Hides and O'Malley, and no continuity was established between the two experiences. Later patrols (also from a southerly direction) established peaceful relations, and the Onabasulu, during the early contact period, came to view the government as principally concerned with the forbidding of violence.

Another factor determining whether the experience of first contact changed local self-perception or gave particular direction to Papuan understanding of subsequent historical developments was whether or not the arrival of the newcomers engaged any important scenario of traditional action that incorporated them in the local cosmological framework.

In the Hawaii example, and among the Huli, early contact events were associated with cultural ideas that involved important ritual activities. The arrival of the newcomers required people to *do* something, and the explorers became the subjects of committed ritual action (rituals performed to Lono, pigs sacrificed to *damas*) rather than simply regarded as subjects of amazement and speculation. It was precisely through this ritual action that both Hulis and Hawaiians committed themselves to a particular version of what the events meant and set the direction of their thinking for the course of their subsequent history.

On the Papuan Plateau, by contrast, there were no significant rituals associated with such important features of the cosmological geography as the downstream direction of the Road of the Dead (for the Etoro) or the Onabasulu origin place at Malaiya.* Consequently when the patrol passed

* There were, in fact, some secret traditional rites performed at Malaiya from time to time by the custodians of the site, but they were done infrequently and only in the presence

through the area, it engaged no significant ritual scenario that would positively commit the local people to one understanding of the events over another. The tribesmen's attempt to return all axes and bushknives was, as we have seen, an improvised response that ultimately drew a blank. In the end, they didn't know what to think of the patrol.

These examples might be taken to imply that the assimilating scenarios must take the form of *ritual* activity, but there was no necessity for this. In other places in the highlands the same cosmological assimilation of the newcomers seems to have been accomplished simply by trading with pearlshell. Among the people of the Waghi Valley in the 1930's trade in pearlshells was so bound up with people's sense of self and the constitution of social relationships that trade in them by itself humanized the Leahy brothers and drew them into the Waghi world (M. Strathern 1988). The same might have been the case for the Strickland-Purari expedition had Hides been carrying pearlshell.

Another set of factors affecting the impact of first contact on subsequent history involves the perception of temporal continuity between events and the way memories are preserved in the local sociology of knowledge. One of the reasons peoples of the Papuan Plateau see such a discontinuity between first contact and subsequent government patrols is undoubtedly due to the long hiatus that occurred between them. After first contact, the Bosavi and Onabasulu did not see another government patrol for 16 and 18 years, respectively, whereas for the Etoro it was 29 years (1964), fully a generation: long enough for the initial experience to have faded into story. By comparison, the Huli received visits from patrols every two or three years following first contact, keeping the experience alive and relevant and developing its cosmological implications and ideas. Today the Onabasulu speak of their experience with the Strickland-Purari patrol as a frightening, uncanny event but not as a watershed one. The period of important changes for their perception started with the second patrol to their area in 1953.*

and knowledge of a very small number of persons. Since their nature was secret, they could have no widespread influence on social perception.

* This does not mean that Europeans find no place in traditional Onabasulu cosmology. Many people in 1984 still associated places beyond the periphery (such as Port Moresby and Australia) with the abode of the spirits, and despite conversion to Christianity, many still tended to associate Europeans with the "light-skinned children" of the mythological woman Guni (see Chapter 3). During a period of heightened evangelical fervor in the late 1970's, Onabasulu Christian converts opened a net bag said to contain sacred objects originating at Malaiya—remnants of things Guni's children had taken away in the Origin Time. The bag was found to contain a wooden spoon, one or two small coins, a pen, and a piece of wood from a gun stock. It would be intriguing to know the origin of these objects. Some may have been gathered from the detritus of the Strickland-Purari (or some later) patrol; others were perhaps passed in as curios over the trade routes or even found beside the Hegigio, washed

Finally, the impact of the experience of first contact on a people's understandings of their lives depends on the integrity of the social distribution
of knowledge. This complicates our Etoro/Onabasulu example somewhat.
Clearly if a people's perception of a set of events is to continue to affect
their understanding of their circumstances or of themselves, the community of people who know about it or shared the experience and/or for
whom it is salient must remain to some degree intact. If, through various circumstances, the group suffers serious social disruption, becomes
geographically dispersed, or is severely depopulated, the salience of their
shared experience becomes questionable at the same time as the social
distribution of their knowledge becomes disorganized.

Some groups around the world for whom shared historical and cultural
tradition is an important aspect of their sense of identity surmount this
problem by putting considerable effort into preserving the knowledge of
their history as a matter of preserving ethnic identity. Other peoples do
not. Among the people on the Papuan Plateau (and probably throughout
Papua New Guinea), the sense of shared history takes the form of a sense
of shared overlapping biography—the life you have shared with other
people who are significant to you. Such historical knowledge focuses on
events in the establishment and maintenance of relationships with particular others, not on group identity. Under these circumstances (to overstate
the case somewhat), if people become dispersed and lose contact with each
other, shared historical experience becomes fragmented into individualistic biographies scattered around the countryside. While events are not
forgotten by the individuals involved, they no longer operate as a body of
experience that marks the people as a group and hence they lose a great
deal of salience for social life.

Both the Onabasulu and the Etoro have suffered significant depopulation due to epidemics in the early 1950's, and the remnants of their
populations have had to regroup in smaller, more mixed communities. The
result has been a social fragmentation of the memory of the past and a reduced salience of such remembered events as first contact as referring to a
collective condition. Among the Etoro there was apparently no one living
in 1970 who remembered anything in detail about the Strickland-Purari
patrol (Kelly 1977: 26), and there were only a few among the Onabasulu
in 1976. The social disorganization of the memory of this event pro-

---

up from the overturned rafts of Staniforth Smith's 1911 expedition. Whatever their origin,
these objects were examined by the Christians and then summarily thrown away. Despite
this gesture, however, Onabasulu (as of 1989) are still extremely reluctant to show Europeans
the site of Malaiya. There is a residual fear that something might happen if "light-skinned"
people returned to the Origin Place. These ideas have faded since Hides and O'Malley's day,
but apparently have not become significantly revalued among the older generation.

vides another reason why the Etoro and Onabasulu experience with the Strickland-Purari patrol has not had a more profound impact on their later perspective on their history or themselves.

The continuing significance of the first-contact experience of the Wola, Nembi, and Kewa is more difficult to assess than for the groups discussed above. In some places, such as the lower Nembi and Emia valleys, socially shared knowledge of those events has been lost or dispersed due to the widespread demographic turnover in the region from epidemic disease, migration, and warfare. We know from later patrol reports that the Nembi from regions that Strickland-Purari patrol had passed through showed a healthy respect for firearms but gave subsequent officers no indication of resentment over people killed earlier by Hides and his men. The Wola re-member the battle of Korpe defile in a curse. But what lasting influence the encounter with the Strickland-Purari patrol may have had on how these people see themselves—or how they perceive their present historical/cos-mological continuity with the past in the light of it—we do not have the information to say.

In the final analysis, the experience of the Strickland-Purari patrol does not seem, *by itself*, to have had much lasting impact on the world view of most of the Papuans it encountered. However, it could arguably be said to have had one on the Euro-Australian civilization from which it origi-nated. *Papuan Wonderland* and Hides's other books sold about 20,000 copies altogether—probably a greater number than Papuan individuals who actually saw the patrol—and were fairly widely read in England and America (Sinclair 1969: 260). Hides's story of the patrol retains a respect-able place in the mythographic literature of exploration and adventure. The images of hardy explorers, tropical forests, cannibal warriors, and lost mountain valleys fits comfortably into a familiar genre of real and imaginative writing. Hides had been a patrol officer in part because he could not get this sort of story out of his blood. Neither could his young readers. His books inspired a generation of young Australians to sign up for service as patrol officers in the colonial territories after World War II.

Beneath the adventurous surfaces of the story, *Papuan Wonderland* reso-nated with favorite images and scenarios of the time and the amour propre of Western culture generally. Hides's wonder and excitement over the dis-covery of the highlands populations evoked Western nostalgia for an un-spoiled primeval world beyond the peripheries of civilization (cf. Rosaldo 1989). His general sympathy for Papuans (despite frustration and exas-peration with them) suggested an appealing nobility of character and a responsible legitimacy for the mission of bringing Western civilization to the hinterland. His battles with the Wola and Nembi suggested the suf-fering and sacrifice necessary to bring this about—as well as confirming

colonial stereotypes of Papuans as dangerous savages requiring government control (a message that was harder to draw from Champion and
Adamson's experience, since they had always remained in firm control
of their situation). All of this, in turn, drew its appeal from a still more
fundamental level. Through vicissitudes and narrow escapes, Hides (and
O'Malley as well) played out a scenario that is ever deeply enchanting to
the Western imagination: the Quest of the Hero. From this perspective,
the patrol is a version of an archetypal drama: the story of discovery and
achievement through journey into the unknown, the affirmation of manly
character through overcoming of formidable obstacles, the goal achieved
or the treasure won through courageous struggle. Hides was himself captivated by these images, acted them out with creative energy for most of
his career, and ultimately fell victim to them.

It was Hides's tragedy that his romanticism ultimately betrayed him.
The tension between his romanticism and the expediencies that he was
forced to play out on his patrol exemplifies the problems posed by the
Hero Quest as political practice. It was a tension that Hides felt keenly and
that made it difficult for him to accept emotionally and to understand fully
some of the situations he had to confront. As Hero he started out with
the best of intentions but found himself increasingly faced with frustration and a sense of betrayal when the targets of his romantic embracement
did not embrace back. The Papuan Others repeatedly refused to play the
role he assigned to them, stubbornly retained their own agenda, and did
not always share his assumption of the possibility of friendly openness or
expectation of reciprocal good will. More pragmatic patrol officers with
less imagination didn't expect as much.

But if the Heroic Quest was problematic as political practice, it was
splendid as romanticization of European colonial expansion. Cast in this
imagery, the development of the colonial enterprise became not the extension of further tentacles of commercial and political grip, but high
adventure. This is what drew young men to Papua after reading Jack
Hides. It worked because the Quest is not the property of the colonial
enterprise or imperialist nostalgia. It resonates as a far more universal
scenario of human aspiration. Thus, although Jack Hides served a thoroughly unappealing colonial regime, for those who read his stories, and
who feel a similar restlessness, his curiosity and imagination, his desire
for different landscapes and fascination with their people, his idealism
and determination strike a powerful chord. These are also central motives
in ethnographic research. The difference lies largely (at least we hope) in
the agenda they are made to serve.* In this light, Hides himself—with his

---

* The editors like to believe that ethnography—whatever else its theoretical or descriptive
purposes and however much it exists in a world where, as Foucault points out, all knowledge

adventurous spirit, his desire to see beyond the frontier, his excitement at his discoveries, and his determination to bring his men safely through the difficulties he had in part caused—stands as an imperfect but curiously appealing figure.

It is a final irony that the Quest, which, psychologically interpreted, generally represents the affirmative journey of the self to self-realization, maturity, empowerment, and freedom, should in a colonial context be the vehicle for subjugation. Hides was perfectly aware of what his job entailed but believed, like Murray (and as sung by Kipling), that it was for the good—good for the colonialists and also good for the Papuans themselves. Considering the chronic violence, insecurity, hunger, and misery that at least some of the Papuan groups he passed through continually inflicted on themselves, one may be tempted to believe he was not wholly wrong. On the other hand, people frequently prefer the misery they inflict upon themselves to that (even if less extreme) inflicted upon them by others. Not all Papuans did, though they usually had no choice. Still, in this case, it is best to consult the people themselves. And, as we should know by now, their answers most often reflect a situation more complex than we expected.

---

is bound up with regimes of power—tends (on balance) to advocacy for its subjects rather than control.

APPENDIXES

Appendix A: THE ORIGINS OF THE STORY OF WALALI

EDWARD L. SCHIEFFELIN AND ROBERT CRITTENDEN

The appearance of the imaginary figure of Walali in Kewa stories of the Strickland-Purari patrol is intriguing. While the motivation for making use of such a figure can be found in political contingencies (clan Perepe's desire to claim it had evened the score for a disastrous military defeat) or intellectual needs (to explain a series of incomprehensible events), the question remains, if Walali never actually existed, how did this figure originate? What is its historical basis? As Josephides and Schiltz indicate in Chapter 8, this is probably a confabulation from a number of stories about patrol police circulating in and around the Kewa area in the period just before and after the Second World War. In what follows we will explore some of the possible sources.

To begin with, it should be noted that members of the Papuan Armed Constabulary who accompanied government patrols in the early days often made a greater impression on the local people than the government officers themselves. Government officers tended to remain aloof, so that it was primarily through the police that the people experienced the force of the government presence. But more importantly, members of the constabulary often provided the only familiar social relationships that local people felt they had with the governmental structure of authority. European officers were shifted from one station to another every couple of years while the police tended to remain at one place for greater lengths of time. Thus, over time, as various patrols passed through an area, the local people might not see the same government officer twice but could become quite familiar with individual policemen who showed up in their villages again and again. As this happened, stories of the more outstanding or notorious of these characters would circulate, combine, elaborate, and become part of the lore and legend of government presence throughout a region. Hides encountered just such a sphere of reputation when he was greeted as he entered the Samberigi Valley with the name of Lance Corporal Pugini, a retired constable from Kikori Station.

It was out of such miscellaneous material that the story of Walali seems to have been constructed. A few materials are available to suggest how.

Until the Strickland-Purari patrol passed through the southern Kewa country, the closest approach of government patrols had been into the Samberigi Valley a day's walk to the south over extremely difficult country (though only about 15–20 km as the crow flies). First contacted in 1908, this region had subsequently been visited by seven government patrols.* As early as 1911 police on the patrol led by Wilfred Beaver and Henry Ryan shot two local men for harassing and thieving from the carriers. Illness and exhaustion struck the carriers as they were returning; one died, and four others had to be carried back to Kikori. In 1925 the patrol led by Alex Rentoul into the Samberigi Valley also experienced sickness among carriers and police, one of whom had to be taken in a litter back to the station. In 1929 during the patrol led by Faithorn and Claude Champion, one of the police shot and killed a native man in an altercation over stolen blankets and axes just north of the Erave River to the northeast of Batri. This individual was actually not a local man but a visitor from the Wiru people in the Pangia area one or two days' walk to the north, who had come on a trading expedition (Clark, forthcoming and personal communication). These and other events would have provided the basis for many stories about government patrols and police that circulated among the people adjacent to the southern Kewa in the late 1930's, and the Kewa had undoubtedly heard some of them. These stories would have formed some of the informational background the Kewa brought to bear in attempting to understand the meaning of their experience with the Strickland-Purari patrol.

Closer to Kewa country itself, Crittenden collected an interesting variant

* In all probability, the MacKay and Little expedition that ascended the Purari River in 1908–9 got as far as the Kerabi Valley just to the east of Samberigi (MacKay and Little 1911; Bell 1911). This would make them the first Europeans to enter the general region just south of the Kewa. First contact with Samberigi was made by Staniforth Smith in 1911 (Papua Annual Report 1911: 165–71). He was followed by Wilfred Beaver's relief expedition, also in 1911 (ibid., 176–87). The next patrol into the area was led by Flint and Saunders in 1922 (Kikori PR 13, 1921–22). Woodward and Saunders came through again in 1923 (Kikori PR 15, 1922–23), followed by another patrol by Saunders in 1924 (Kikori PR 17, 1923–24). Alex Rentoul led a patrol into the region the following year to assess the practicality of setting up a police post in the Samberigi Valley (Kikori PR 14, 1924–25). Finally, in 1929 Faithorn and Champion briefly crossed the Erave and glimpsed the southern Kewa country (Kikori PR 19, 1928–29). The next patrol in this area was Hides and O'Malley ten years later.

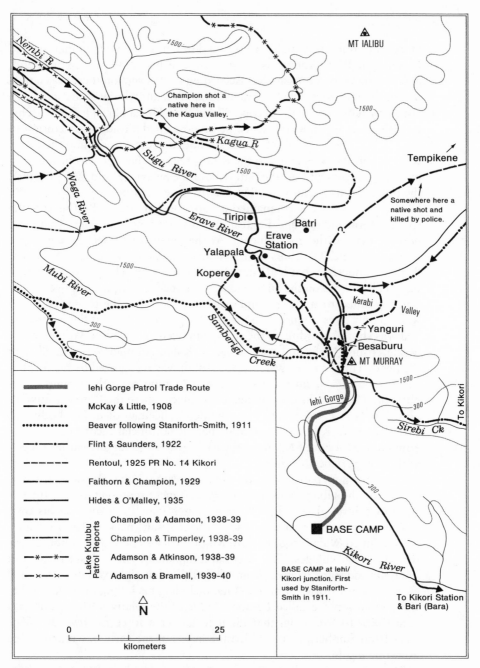

MT IALIBU

Champion shot a
native here in
the Kagua Valley.

Tempikene

Somewhere here a
native shot and
killed by police.

Tiripi
Batri
Erave
Station
Yalapala
Kopere

Kerabi
Valley

Yanguri
Besaburu
MT MURRAY

Iehi Gorge

Sirebi Ck

To Kikori

	Iehi Gorge Patrol Trade Route
	McKay & Little, 1908
	Beaver following Staniforth-Smith, 1911
	Flint & Saunders, 1922
	Rentoul, 1925 PR No. 14 Kikori
	Faithorn & Champion, 1929
	Hides & O'Malley, 1935
	Champion & Adamson, 1938-39
	Champion & Timperley, 1938-39
	Adamson & Atkinson, 1938-39
	Adamson & Bramell, 1939-40

Lake Kutubu
Patrol Reports

△
N

0   25
kilometers

BASE CAMP

BASE CAMP at Iehi/
Kikori junction. First
used by Staniforth-
Smith in 1911.

Kikori River

To Kikori Station
& Bari (Bara)

Map 14. A sketch map showing patrols and events in the Erave area that may have contributed to the Walali legend.

of a story about a "Walali" from two different informants (a man named Mambopoi, better known as Sikisi because he has six fingers on one hand, and Perapu Ropa of Yalapala). According to this version there was a man named Walali from Pole (an Erave-Yalapala man) who was abducted as a child to Kikori before the Second World War. He had been living with his father's sister in Samberigi when he accompanied a trading expedition to Bara village. He stepped into a Bara canoe to effect a trade, and the canoe was cast off. He was taken to the Kikori region where he was brought up by the "government." At the outbreak of the Second World War he joined the police or army and was wounded in the left buttock.

After the war he accompanied a patrol to Samberigi. By this time he spoke Motu, pidgin, and English and was no longer the old Walali but now a "man of the government." At the village of Kopere he cut a tree with a steel axe. The chips were sent around, and some came to Yalapala. People wondered what had cut the wood that way. The patrol came to a place called Wata on the Sugu and then camped at Tiripi. The government officer wanted to trade salt and beads for food, but the people of Tiripi wanted only axes. Lombora, a man of Tiripi, threw food at the white man and was shot. According to the story, a policeman was shot with an arrow in the ensuing fight and was buried at Kaba. Another was wounded in the head. Three natives were killed. Walali was recognized by his brother Yamo from a scar on his nose and was limping from the wound in his buttock. The patrol then camped at the place where the Catholic mission now stands at Erave where the wounded policeman died. His body was then carried to Kikori for burial. (There is no official record of any government patrol out of Kikori in the early 1950's—or at any earlier time—with an experience like this.)

When the next patrol came through the region, Yamo (Walali's brother) was made the village constable (the government representative in the village) of a little place called Pandebi. Later Walali returned on his own to Yalapala in order to take trade (tobacco, salt) back to Kikori. Yamo accompanied Walali to go back to Kikori. They slept in a bush house near the Samberigi villages. They were accompanied by five or six men from Yalapala and some relatives from Samberigi. That night Walali entertained everyone with stories of his exploits, including his killing of some Samberigi men at a place called Besaburu. One of the relatives from Samberigi crept back to Samberigi that night to gather a force for revenge. Warriors from Samberigi surrounded the house in the early dawn and killed everyone inside.

The similarity of this story to the one collected by Josephides and Schiltz is striking, but there are also important differences. In this account, Walali didn't become a policeman until after the Second World War, and the incidents of violence in the Tiripi area are presented as happening after that time. Indeed, the episode of Lombora demanding an axe and throwing food at the white man are so similar to what happened on Hides's patrol that it is tempting to believe that this incident was added to this later story based on the Kewa's earlier experience with Hides. (Lombora, however, was not one of those killed by the Strickland-Purari patrol.) In the same way, it is tempting to see the story of a dying policeman being carried back to Kikori as based upon stories of one of the sick policemen of Rentoul's 1925 patrol or Hides's orderly Emesi being carried back to Kikori.

In the same way, the story of Walali's death has resonances with historical facts. Although there is no record of a killing of a policeman in the Samberigi Valley in the 1950's, men from Besaburu were involved in the shoot-out with Beaver and Ryan's patrol in 1911. Beaver reported that while his patrol was ascending Mt. Murray, the people of Tugi and Besaburu (villages) continually stole axes from the carriers' belts. At least fifteen knives and axes were forcibly taken. When the patrol camped in a spot near to Besaburu, Beaver ordered Ryan to fire a shot to scare off the natives. Shots then rang out to the rear and although police were supposed to be shooting in the air, Beaver was told that two native men had been wounded (Papua Annual Report 1911: 179–80). It would appear that, in the Walali story, this incident is attributed to Walali and so provides the motivation for killing him. Thus, it serves as an imaginary payback for those remembered shootings—just as the story of Walali was itself the story of an imaginary payback for the killing of Perepe people.

Be all this as it may, the point is that there have clearly been various stories of a policeman named Walali circulating in the Samberigi/south Kewa region since the Second World War, and even the best of them seem to have some accretions borrowed from other sources. It is not hard to see how Perepe men might appropriate this story through multiple tellings in hindsight (and with a few changes) to support a claim of having evened the score for pre-war defeats.

A final suggestive link comes from Hides's book itself. On page ix of *Papuan Wonderland* there is a photograph of several Kewa warriors Hides calls "Black Papuans of the Iumberave." According to Yamba Pabala of Tiripi, the man on the left of the picture is Webo (Epo) Lombora, one of the men shot by Hides in the Tiripi/Kagapore area. The young boy on the extreme right of the photograph was identified as a younger (clan) brother named Walawe. In the account given to Josephides and Schiltz, this boy was one of those killed by Hides's police. However, Mukoro Kero, a man from Samberigi who used to work as a carpenter for the administration, said that in the 1950's, after the establishment of the Erave government station, a young man named Walawe enrolled as a policeman from the region.* Could this be the same man as in Hides's photograph, the younger brother of Epo supposedly killed by Hides's police? In any case, "Wala" is a common name stem in the Kewa region. Could stories about a policeman named Walawe be confused with stories about a policeman named Walali, both of them linked with killings by the Strickland-Purari patrol and projected by hindsight to before the Second World War? This is the kind of confabulated historification we are dealing with.

* Other confabulations enter here, as Mukoro Kero also said that Walawe was also known as "Pugini" (a common Samberigi name) but was distinct from the prewar Lance Corporal Pugini. Another informant, Keawi Wama, medical post orderly for Tiripi village in the Kewa country, said that Walawe had yet another name: "Kapona," the name of a policeman accompanying several prewar patrols out of Lake Kutubu to the Kewa country, and now a general term for Europeans among the Kewa and Wiru (see also Clark, forthcoming). Many ideas concerning the government, white men, power, and police are evidently being condensed together here.

Appendix B: A CARRIER'S STORY

ROBERT CRITTENDEN AND EDWARD SCHIEFFELIN

The voices of the men who served as carriers for the Strickland-Purari patrol are conspicuously missing from most of this story of the patrol. Apart from those whose experience is recorded through Hides's quotations or in the transcript of the inquiry, we have been able to find only one other account—that of Akiei Kaupi, which we reproduce here in its entirety.*

Akiei Kaupi was born in Mati village in the Gulf District and was recruited as a carrier by Jack Hides in December 1934. He accompanied the patrol for the whole of its journey. He was a member of the "Bara" people upstream of the Kikori Station, speakers of the Kairi language. He also knew Police Motu.† The "Bara" people, it will be recalled (Chapter 5), held an important position on the trade route between the Gulf of Papua and the Samberigi Valley. It appears from his story that Akiei had relatives or acquaintances on the northern flanks of Mt. Murray and would certainly have known of the Samberigi people (or "Okane" as Bara called them) beyond that mountain.

Jack Hides came from Samarai and collected me at Mati village. After signing on at Kikori, we went across to Daru. From Daru we went up the Fly River,

---

* This narrative is taken from a longer autobiographical interview conducted with Akiei Kaupi in 1960 by Nigel Gore (and designed to collect linguistic information rather than oral history) and translated by Robert Petterson, both of the Summer Institute of Linguistics. Their permission to include this translation in this appendix is gratefully acknowledged.

† Police Motu, used as the common language between white administration officers, the police, and coastal Papuans, was a pidgin developed from the Motu language of the people near Port Moresby. The Motuans were traditionally great traders who plied their sailing lakatois up and down the Papuan coast for hundreds of miles. Prior to contact they had already developed a pidgin version of their language, called Hiri Motu, which was then borrowed by the administration to communicate with its subjects.

and then on up to the headwaters of the Strickland, where we left the boat. After coming ashore we went on by foot into *Gunika* territory.* As we were setting off from one point the *Gunikas* arrived. There was a gun battle. We went on fighting as we went, till the food ran out. Then we started eating leaves.

In that fashion we came to a cold place, where the water was icy. One Orokolo man died there [Hakea, who died near the Tari Gap; see Chapter 4]. He was killed by the coldness of the water. We dug a grave inside a tent and buried him. At daybreak we just took the tent down [May 3]. Jack Hides said, "Let's make an effort to reach a better place and get out of the cold." And so, moving quickly, we went on to a better place. When we got to a better, warmer place we built a house, where we slept. We then set off, sleeping in various *Gunika* villages until we arrived at the headwaters of the Kikori.

We crossed the headwaters of the Kikori† and left the *Gunikas* at that village, at the village situated at the back of Lake Kutubu. From there we came along till we reached the headwaters of the Purari, where we made a raft, and came down until we reached a bad place. We unloaded on the other side of the Kikori [actually the Erave], and some *Gunikas* led us on down to the place at the back of Okane [Samberigi]. Jack Hides said, "This trail comes out at the mouth of the Purari. I don't want to go that way." And so we turned back to Okane [Samberigi] village and slept at the Yanguri's village, at Pasapuru [Besaburu]—that was the name of the village. We slept there three days.‡

From there we set off and climbed up over a high mountain, Pasapuru [Besabaru/Mt. Murray], and came down the other side, past Sokore, and slept down there. From there we set off and arrived at Yehi [Iehi] creek, which we crossed, and came along until we reached Parima's sons' place at the mouth of the Kenu [the Bara villages]. Then from Parima's village we came along as far as Keputuku and slept at Kaitoni's sons' place.

Then Jack Hides took a canoe that afternoon and came down to Kikori, arriving about 12 o'clock that night. But the rest of us slept at Keputuku, and then took a canoe down the next morning, arriving at Kikori at 4 o'clock in the afternoon.

This account told for the linguist's tape recorder is probably a very abbreviated version of the story Akiei would have performed for an audience of his friends and relatives gathered in his longhouse. Nevertheless, what is striking to a Westerner is the absence of any mention of the major struggles through the Waga Valley and the Nembi country that loom so large in Hides's report. It is tempting to speculate that this is because the experience was so awful and terrifying that Akiei didn't want (or wasn't able) to remember it. However, conventions of Papuan story construction may

* *Gunika* is a Police Motu term describing Papuans who inhabited areas outside the sphere of government control or influence. It has a rather pejorative meaning, akin to "wild-man" or the tok pisin "bus kanaka."

†Akiei may be referring to the Waga River which the patrol crossed near Huwguwn (Chapter 5). The headwaters of the Kikori (or Tagari) was crossed several days before they reached the Tari Gap.

‡ This does not tally with Hides's patrol report, which records they only spent the night of June 6 at Besaburu. However, the report does indicate the patrol camped from June 10 to 14 at an abandoned village site near a sago patch a few miles west of the mouth of the Iehi chasm. They used the time to rest and make sago. Perhaps it is this which Akiei recalls.

also be a part of the picture—especially in an account like this where the narrative structure is stripped to its bare bones. Akiei's account follows a program fairly typical of Papuan narratives (see Schieffelin and Kurita 1988), where the story is organized around a succession of named places (where things happened) rather than around a series of events. Here the narrative sequence moves quickly from Samarai (Island) to Mati village to Kikori Station to Daru to the Fly River to the Strickland headwaters (all known, or at least named, places) and then heads into unnamed (and unknown) "*Gunika* territory." The narrative of the *Gunika* experience is anchored structurally by two geographical locations: the "cold place" and the "headwaters of the Kikori" (more likely the Waga River). From there it skips without comment directly to the next known location, the Purari. The intervening territory, being geographically without "places," is also left narratively without incidents. Once past the Purari, however, and once again in territory familiar to Akiei, the story continues by way of villages of people he knows.

This is not to say that Akiei could not have told anything of what happened between the "Kikori" and the Purari if he had been requested—only that in producing the barest essentials of the account, the local conventions of storytelling, given the absence of named geographical locations, did not lead him to do so. It would have been fascinating to be seated around the fire in the longhouse when he told this story in full measure to his relatives.

REFERENCE MATTER

REFERENCES

References are divided into three categories: Patrol Reports and Annual Reports; Other Archival Documents; and General Works.

PATROL REPORTS AND ANNUAL REPORTS

Patrol reports dated before 1945 are held in the Commonwealth Archives, Canberra, CSR A518 Item C251/3/1 part 1 and part 2. Those dated 1945 and after are held at Mendi, Provincial Headquarters of the Southern Highlands Province, District Affairs Archives. Annual reports for Papua and New Guinea are held in the Papua New Guinea National Archives, Port Moresby, and in the Menzies Library, Australian National University, Canberra.

British New Guinea Annual Report 1892–1893.
Daru Patrol Report 4, 1937–38. C. Champion with F. W. G. Andersen.
Erave Patrol Report 3, 1955–56. B. Corrigan.
Erave Patrol Report 3a, 1956–57. B. Corrigan and R. Andrews.
Erave Patrol Report 3b, 1956–57. B. Corrigan and R. Andrews.
Erave Patrol Report 1, 1957–58. B. Corrigan.
Erave Patrol Report 3, 1957–58. B. Jinks.
Erave Patrol Report 5, 1957–58. G. J. Hogg and G. P. Jensen-Muir.
Erave Patrol Report 2, 1958–59. R. S. Bell.
Erave Patrol Report 5, 1958–59. G. J. Hogg.
Kagua Patrol Report 2, 1957–58. D. N. Butler.
Kikori Patrol Report 13, 1921–22. L. Flint and H. M. Saunders.
Kikori Patrol Report 15, 1922–23. H. M. Saunders and R. A. Woodward.
Kikori Patrol Report 17, 1923–24. H. M. Saunders.
Kikori Patrol Report 14, 1924–25. A. C. Rentoul.
Kikori Patrol Report 19, 1928–29. C. Champion and B. W. Faithorn.
Kikori Patrol Report 22, 1928–29. L. Austen.
Kikori Patrol Report 5, 1930–31. L. Austen.
Lake Kutubu Patrol Report 1, 1937–38. I. Champion with C. T. J. Adamson.

Lake Kutubu Patrol Report 1, 1938–39. I. Champion with C. T. J. Adamson.
Lake Kutubu Patrol Report 3, 1938–39. C. T. J. Adamson and A. Timperley.
Lake Kutubu Patrol Report 9, 1938–39. C. T. J. Adamson and K. C. Atkinson.
Lake Kutubu Patrol Report 10, 1938–39. I. Champion with A. Timperley.
Lake Kutubu Patrol Report 1, 1939–40. C. T. J. Adamson and A. Bramell.
Lake Kutubu Patrol Report 6, 1939–40. I. Champion and A. Timperley.
Lake Kutubu Patrol Report 1, 1950–51. D. J. Clancy (carried out in conjunction with Mendi PR 1, 1950–51).
Lake Kutubu Patrol Report 8, 1952–53. B. R. Heagney.
Lake Kutubu Patrol Report 1, 1953–54. C. E. T. Terrell.
Lake Kutubu Patrol Report 11, 1953–54. E. D. Wren.
Mendi Patrol Report 1, 1950–51. S. S. Smith (carried out in conjunction with Lake Kutubu PR 1, 1950–51).
Mendi Patrol Report 4, 1952–53. B. R. Heagney (includes letter by J. S. McCleod commenting on Champion's prewar patrols).
Mendi Patrol Report 5, 1953–54. J. A. Frew.
Mendi Patrol Report 4, 1961–62. A. C. Jefferies.
Mendi Patrol Report 17, 1962–63. F. E. Haviland.
Nipa Patrol Report 2, 1959–60. J. Jordan.
Papua Annual Report 1911.
Papua Annual Report 1912.
Papua Annual Report 1913 (an appendix to this report is Kikori–Bamu River PR, 1913, by Henry Ryan).
Papua Annual Report 1922–23.
Papua Annual Report 1929–30.
Papua Annual Report 1938–39.
Papua Annual Report 1939–40 (an appendix to this report is Lake Kutubu PR 10, 1938–39).

OTHER ARCHIVAL DOCUMENTS

Australian Broadcasting Commission. 1973. Talking with Jack Fox: 50 Years in PNG. Typescript of radio interview with Jack Fox (held in PNG Collection, University of Papua New Guinea, AP 995.2 F792).
Champion, I. 1936. Report of an exploratory flight by I. Champion, ARM, over the northern parts of the Western and Delta Divisions between latitudes 5° 50'S and 7°10'S and longitudes 144°E and 142°E. Typescript. PNG Archives, Port Moresby.
Fox, Jack. No date. Interview with Jack Fox, a series of tapes of recorded interview (Held in PNG Collection, University of Papua New Guinea, File AC 242).
Fox, Jack. No date. Ms. of diary of exploratory patrol with Tom Fox (held in PNG Collection, University of Papua New Guinea, File AL101, Box A101).
Hides, J. G., F. E. Williams, L. Lett, J. Taylor, and I. Champion. Typescript dated Feb.–Mar. 1936. Report of an aerial reconnaissance in Papua, 1936 (held in Archives of Royal Geographical Society, London).
Pacific Islands Monthly (various issues 1935–37).
Royal Greenwich Observatory, U.K. 1935. Nautical Almanac.
Territory of Papua. 1931. "Circular Instructions."
Territory of Papua. 1920. "Information for the Guidance of Newly Joined Patrol Officers."

GENERAL WORKS

Allen, B., and A. Wood. 1980. "Legendary Volcanic Eruptions and the Huli, Papua New Guinea," *Journal of the Polynesian Society* 89(3): 341–47.

Anders, M. 1983. "Screening and Breeding Sweet Potatoes (*Ipomoea batatas [L] Lam*) in the Southern Highlands Province, Papua New Guinea." Paper presented at PNG First Food and Crop Conference, Goroka, Eastern Highlands Province, Nov. 1983.

Ashton, C. 1979. "The Leahy Family." In J. Griffin, ed., *Papua New Guinea Portraits: The Expatriate Experience*. Canberra: Australian National University Press, pp. 169–94.

Austen, L. 1935. "The Delta Division of Papua." *Australian Geographer* 2(4): 20–27.

Beckett, J. 1977. "The Torres Straits Islanders and the Pearling Industry: A Case of Internal Colonialism." *Aboriginal History* 1(1): 77–103.

Bell, L. L. 1911. "Exploring in Papua." *Victorian Geographical Journal* 28: 31–63.

Black, R. H. 1954. "A Malaria Survey of the People Living on the Minj River in the Western Highlands of New Guinea." *Medical Journal of Australia*, Nov. 13, 1954, pp. 782–80.

Blong, R. 1982. *The Time of Darkness: Local Legends and Volcanic Reality in Papua New Guinea*. Canberra: Australian National University Press.

Brookfield, H. C. 1972. "Intensification and Disintensification in Pacific Agriculture: A Theoretical Approach." *Pacific Viewpoint* 13(1): 30–48.

———. 1973. "Full Circle in Chimbu: A Study of Trends and Cycles." In H. C. Brookfield, ed., *The Pacific in Transition*. Canberra: Australian National University Press, pp. 127–60.

Brookfield, H. C., and J. P. White. 1968. "Revolution or Evolution in the Prehistory of the New Guinea Highlands: A Seminar Report." *Ethnology* 7: 43–52.

Campbell, J. 1945. *The Hero with a Thousand Faces*. New York: Viking Press.

Champion, I. F. 1932. *Across New Guinea from the Fly to the Sepik*. London: Constable.

———. 1940. "The Bamu-Purari Patrol, 1936." *Geographical Journal* 96(4): 190–206 and 96(5): 243–57.

Chinnery, E. W. P. 1934. "The Central Ranges of the Mandated Territory of New Guinea from Mount Chapman to Mount Hagen." *Geographical Journal* 84(5): 398–412.

Clark, J. Forthcoming. "Sons of the Female Spirit: Men of Steel." *Ethnology*.

Clifford, J., and G. E. Marcus, eds. 1986. *Writing Culture: The Poetics and Politics of Ethnography*. Berkeley: University of California Press.

Connolly, R., and R. Anderson. 1983. *First Contact* (film). Sydney: Australian Broadcasting Commission.

———. 1987. *First Contact*. New York: Viking.

Crittenden, R. 1982. "Sustenance, Seasonality, and Social Cycles on the Nembi Plateau, Papua New Guinea." Ph.D. diss., Australian National University.

———. 1987. "Aspects of Economic Development on the Nembi Plateau, Papua New Guinea." *Journal of the Polynesian Society* 96(3): 335–59.

Ernst, T. 1984. "Onabasulu Local Organization." Ph.D. diss., University of Michigan.

Feil, D. K. 1988. *The Evolution of Highland Papua New Guinea Societies*. Cambridge: Cambridge University Press.

Feld, S. 1982. *Sound and Sentiment: Birds, Weeping, Poetics, and Song in Kaluli Expression.* Philadelphia: University of Pennsylvania Press.

Foucault, M. 1979. *Discipline and Punish: The Birth of the Prison.* Harmondsworth: Penguin.

————. 1980. *History of Sexuality*, vol. 1. New York: Vintage Books.

Frankel, S. J. 1981. "The Huli Response to Illness." Ph.D. diss., Cambridge University.

————. 1986. *The Huli Response to Illness.* Cambridge: Cambridge University Press.

Franklin, K. 1968. *The Dialects of Kewa.* Pacific Linguistics, Series B, Monograph No. 10. Canberra: Dept. of Linguistics. Research School of Pacific Studies, Australian National University.

Franklin, K. J., and J. Franklin (assisted by Yapua Kirapeasi). 1978. *A Kewa Dictionary with Supplementary Grammatical and Anthropological Materials.* Pacific Linguistic Series C, Monograph No. 53. Canberra: Dept. of Linguistics, Research School of Pacific Studies, Australian National University.

Gash, N., and J. Whitaker. 1975. *A Pictorial History of New Guinea.* Brisbane: Jacaranda Press.

Glasse, R. M. 1959. "Revenge and Redress Among the Huli: A Preliminary Account." *Mankind* 5(7): 273–89.

————. 1965. "The Huli of the Southern Highlands." In P. Lawrence and M. J. Meggitt, eds. *Gods, Ghosts, and Men in Melanesia.* Melbourne: Melbourne University Press, pp. 27–49.

————. 1968. *Huli of Papua: A Cognatic Descent System.* The Hague: Mouton & Co.

Griffin, J., H. Nelson, and S. Firth. 1979. *Papua New Guinea: A Political History.* Richmond, Victoria: Heinemann Educational.

Hastings, P. 1969. *New Guinea: Problems and Prospects.* Melbourne: Cheshire, for the Australian Institute for International Affairs.

Hides, J. G. 1935. *Through Wildest Papua.* London: Blackie and Son.

Hobsbawm, E., and T. Ranger. 1983. *Invention of Tradition.* Cambridge: Cambridge University Press.

Hope, P. 1979. *Long Ago Is Far Away: Accounts of the Early Exploration and Settlement of the Papuan Gulf Area.* Canberra: Australian National University Press.

Hughes, I. 1977. *New Guinea Stone Age Trade: The Geography and Ecology of Traffic in the Interior.* Terra Australis 3, Dept. of Prehistory, Research School of Pacific Studies, Australian National University.

————. 1978. "Good Money and Bad: Inflation and Devaluation in the Colonial Process." *Mankind* 11: 308–18.

Inglis, A. 1974. *Not a White Woman Safe: Sexual Anxiety and Politics in Port Moresby, 1920–1934.* Canberra: Australian National University Press.

Josephides, L. 1985. *The Production of Inequality.* London and New York: Tavistock.

Joyce, R. B. 1971. *Sir William MacGregor.* Melbourne: Oxford University Press.

Jukes, J. B. 1847. *Narrative of the Surveying Voyage of H.M.S. Fly, Commanded by Captain F. P. Blackwood. . . .* 2 vols. London: Boone.

Kelly, R. 1974. "Etoro Social Structure: A Study in Structural Contradiction." Ph.D. diss., University of Michigan.

————. 1977. *Etoro Social Structure: A Study in Structural Contradiction*. Ann Arbor: University of Michigan Press.

Kituai, A. 1988. "Innovation and Intrusion: Villagers and Policemen in Papua New Guinea." *Journal of Pacific History* 23(2): 156–66.

Langlas, C. 1974. "Foi Land Use, Prestige, Economics, and Residence : A Processual Analysis." Ph.D. diss., University of Hawaii.

Lawrence, P. 1964. *Road Bilong Cargo: A Study of the Cargo Movement in the Southern Madang District, New Guinea*. Manchester: University of Manchester Press.

Leahy, M. 1936. "The Central Highlands of New Guinea." *Geographical Journal* 87(3): 229–62.

Leahy, M., and M. Crain. 1937. *The Land That Time Forgot*. London: Hurst and Blackett.

Leroy, J. D. 1979. "Competitive Exchange in Kewa." *Journal of the Polynesian Society* 88(1): 9–35.

Lett, L. 1935. *Knights Errant of Papua*. Edinburgh: Blackwood.

Lindenbaum, S. 1976. "Kuru Sorcery." In R. W. Hornabrook, ed., *Essays on Kuru*. PNG Institute of Human Biology, Monograph Series No. 3. Faringdon, Berkshire: E. W. Classey Ltd.

MacKay, D., and W. Little. 1911. "The MacKay-Little Expedition in Southern New Guinea." *Geographical Journal* 38(5): 483–87.

Marcus, G., and R. Cushman. 1982. "Ethnographies as Texts." *Annual Review of Anthropology* 11: 25–69.

Marcus, G., and M. Fischer. 1986. *Anthropology as Cultural Critique: An Experimental Moment in the Human Sciences*. Chicago: University of Chicago Press.

Meggitt, M. J. 1956. "The Valleys of the Upper Waga and Lai Rivers, Western Highlands, New Guinea." *Oceania* 27: 90–135.

————. 1958. "The Enga of the New Guinea Highlands: Some Preliminary Observations." *Oceania* 28: 253–330.

————. 1973. "The Sun and the Shakers." *Oceania* 44(1): 1–37; (2): 109–26.

————. 1974. " 'Pigs are our hearts.' " *Oceania* 44(3): 165–203.

————. 1981. "Sorcery and Social Change Among the Mae Enga of Papua New Guinea." *Social Analysis* 8: 28–41.

Monckton, C. A. W. 1921. *Some Experiences of a New Guinea Resident Magistrate*. London: John Lane, the Bodley Head.

————. 1922. *Last Days in New Guinea: Being Further Experiences of a New Guinea Magistrate*. London: John Lane, the Bodley Head.

Murray, J. H. P. 1912. *Papua or British New Guinea*. New York: Charles Scribner's Sons.

Nelson, H. 1982. *Taim Bilong Masta: The Australian Involvement with Papua New Guinea*. Sydney: Australian Broadcasting Commission.

Nihill, M. 1987. "Roads of Presence: Social Relatedness and Exchange in Anganen Social Structure." Ph.D. diss., University of Adelaide.

Ongka, 1979. *Ongka: A Self-Account by a New Guinea Bigman*. A. J. Strathern, ed. London: Duckworth.

Peters, W., S. H. Christian, and J. L. Jameson. 1958. "Malaria in the Highlands of Papua New Guinea." *Medical Journal of Australia*. Sept. 27, 1958, pp. 409–16.

Radford, R. 1987. *Highlanders and Foreigners in the Upper Ramu: The Kainantu Area 1919–1942*. Melbourne: Melbourne University Press.

Rappaport, R. 1968. *Pigs for the Ancestors*. New Haven, Conn.: Yale University Press.

Rosaldo, R. 1989. *Culture and Truth: The Remaking of Social Analysis*. Boston: Beacon Press.

Ryan, D. 1961. "Gift Exchange in the Mendi Valley." Ph.D. diss., University of Sydney.

Sahlins, M. 1981. *Historical Metaphors and Mythical Realities: Structure in the Early History of the Sandwich Islands Kingdom*. Association for the Study of Anthropology in Oceania, Special Publication No. 1. Ann Arbor: University of Michigan Press.

Sartre, J. P., 1966. *Being and Nothingness: A Phenomenological Essay on Ontology*. Trans. and with an introduction by Hazel F. Barnes. New York: Washington Square Press.

Saunders, H. M. 1924. "A Patrol in Papua." *Queensland Geographical Journal* 39: 22–37.

Schieffelin, E. L. 1975. "Felling the Trees on Top of the Crop." *Oceania* 46(1): 25–39.

———. 1976. *The Sorrow of the Lonely and the Burning of the Dancers*. New York: St. Martin's Press.

———. 1980. "Reciprocity and the Construction of Reality on the Papuan Plateau." *Man*. 15: 502–17.

———. 1982. "The *Bau a* Ceremonial Hunting Lodge." In G. Herdt, ed., *Rituals of Manhood: Male Initiation in Papua New Guinea*. Berkeley: University of California Press, pp. 155–200.

Schieffelin, E. L., and H. Kurita. 1988. "The Phantom Patrol: Reconciling Native Narratives and Colonial Documents in Reconstructing the History of Exploration in Papua New Guinea." *Journal of Pacific History* 23(1): 52–69.

Schwimmer, E. 1987. "Gramsci, History, and the Culture Economy." In J. Clammer, ed., *Beyond the New Economic Anthropology*. Basingstoke: Macmillan, pp. 78–120.

Sillitoe, P. 1978. "Ceremonial Exchange and Trade: Two Contexts in Which Objects Change Hands in the Highlands of Papua New Guinea." *Mankind* 11: 265–75.

———. 1979a. *Give and Take: Exchange Among the Wola*. Canberra: Australian National University Press.

———. 1979b. "Man-Eating Women: Fears of Sexual Pollution in the Papua New Guinea Highlands." *Journal of the Polynesian Society* 86(1): 77–97.

Sinclair, J. P. 1969. *The Outside Man: Jack Hides of Papua*. Melbourne: Lansdowne.

———. 1988. *Last Frontiers: The Explorations of Ivan Champion of Papua, A Record of Geographical Exploration in Australia's Territory of Papua Between 1926 and 1946*. Queensland: Pacific Press.

Souter, G. 1963. *New Guinea: The Last Unknown*. Sydney: Angus and Robertson.

Strathern, A. J. 1971a. *The Rope of Moka: Big Men and Ceremonial Exchange in Mt. Hagen, New Guinea*. Cambridge: Cambridge University Press.

———. 1971b. "Cargo and Inflation in Mt. Hagen." *Oceania* 41(4): 255–65.

———. 1978. "Tambu and Kina: 'Profit,' Exploitation, and Reciprocity in Two New Guinea Exchange Systems." *Mankind* 11(3): 253–64.

———. 1979. "It's His Own Affair: A Note on the Individual and the Group in New Guinea Highlands Society." *Canberra Anthropology* 2(1): 98–113.

Strathern, M. 1988. "The Decomposition of an Event." Paper delivered at the session on Memory and Exchange, American Anthropological Association, Phoenix, Ariz., November.

Stuart, I. 1970. *Port Moresby: Yesterday and Today*. Sydney: Pacific Publications.

Trompf, G. 1977. "Bilalaf." In G. Trompf, ed., *Prophets of Melanesia: Six Essays*. Port Moresby: Institute of Papua New Guinea, pp. 20–107.

Wagner, R. 1979a. *Habu: The Innovation of Meaning in Daribi Religion*. Chicago: University of Chicago Press.

————. 1979b. "The Talk of Koriki: A Daribi Contact Cult." *Social Research* 46(1): 140–65.

Watson, 1977. "Pigs, Fodder, and the Jones Effect in Post-Ipomoean New Guinea." *Ethnology* 16: 57–70.

Williams, F. E. 1936. *Papuans of the Trans-Fly, Territory of Papua*. Anthropology Report No. 15. Oxford: Clarendon Press.

————. 1939. "Report on the Grasslanders: Augu-Waga-Wela." Appendix to Papua Annual Report 1938–39, pp. 39–67.

————. 1940. "The Natives of Lake Kutubu" *Oceania* 11: 121–57, 259–94, 374–401; and 12: 49–74, 134–54.

Willis, I. 1969. "An Epic Journey: The Journey of Michael Leahy and Michael Dwyer Across New Guinea in 1930." Master's thesis, University of Papua New Guinea.

Wood, M. 1983. "Kamula Social Structure and Ritual." Ph.D. diss., Macquarie University.

Worsley, P. 1957. *The Trumpet Shall Sound: A Study of Cargo Cults in Melanesia*. London: Macgibbon and Kee.

INDEX

In this index "f" after a number indicates a separate reference on the next page, and "ff" indicates separate references on the next two pages. A continuous discussion over two or more pages is indicated by a span of numbers. *Passim* is used for a cluster of references in close but not consecutive sequence.

Abiamp (axe factory), 132
Adamson, C. T. J.: and assessment of Hides, 45; and Bamu-Purari patrol, 234, 236, 238, 257, 260, 285, 291
Aez Saendaep; 159–62 *passim*
Agoti (constable), 56–57, 157, 182, 184, 216, 240–41
Agriculture, subsistence, *see under* Bosavi; Huli; Kewa; Nembi; Onabasulu; Papuans; Wola
Agula (Kewa informant), 199n, 212, 220f
Aib (patrol camp), 188, 237
Aibali (Etoro spirit medium), 74ff, 253
Aircraft: flights over Southern Highlands, 148, 224, 233n, 269; and reconnaissance of Bamu-Purari patrol, 148, 224; and reconnaissance of Strickland-Purari patrol, 233n, 247f, 260, 269
Akiei Kaupi (carrier), 301ff
Amburupa Yamba (Kewa informant), 217n
Ana (Kewa informant), 199n, 203, 207, 212, 221, 280
Ancestor spirits, *see under* Bosavi; Etoro; Huli; Nembi; Onabasulu; Wola
Andabare Valley, 269n
Andersen, F. W. G., 121
Anderson, R.: *First Contact* (book and film), 4n, 43n
Andidame (patrol camp), 121

Anga, *see* Kukukuku
Anthrax, 270
Armed Constabulary: on Strickland-Purari patrol, 2, 54, 56–57, 69–72, 74, 86, 106, 109–10, 115–17, 124, 151, 156–57, 163–65, 181–83, 215–20; as informants and historical sources, 8, 231–32; and patrol duty, 13, 25, 28–29, 47, 49, 69–72, 211, 241–42, 273; established, 28; discipline of, 47, 242, 254; on Erave-Purari patrol, 47, 226n, 278n, 296; firearms, 54, 116; seen as spirits, 104, 150; stealing food, 139–40, 145–46, 163–65, 215–20; on Hagen-Sepik patrol, 270; relationship to local people, 295–96. *See also individual constables by name*
Atkinson, K. C., 238
Augu Valley, 131, 236, 260
Aunai (carrier), 176f, 183
Austen, Leo, 42–43, 51, 53, 247n
Australian School of Pacific Administration, 262
Australian Territory of Papua, *see* Papua
Aworra River, 39
Axes, *see* Steel axes; Stone axes and adzes
Ayakali Yambilida, 89n, 112–21 *passim*

Baen (Wola arrow sheaths), 149
Bailer shell, *see under* Trade goods

Library of Congress Cataloging-in-Publication Data
Schieffelin, Edward L., 1938–
    Like people you see in a dream : first contact in six Papuan
societies / Edward L. Schieffelin and Robert Crittenden ; with
contributions by Bryant Allen . . . [et al.].
        p.   cm.
    Includes bibliographical references and index.
    ISBN 0-8047-1662-5 (cloth : alk. paper)
    ISBN 0-8047-1899-7 (pbk : alk. paper)
        1. Papuans—History.   2. Papuans—Social life and customs.
3. Purari River (Gulf Province, Papua New Guinea)—Discovery and
exploration.   4. Purari River (Gulf Province, Papua New Guinea)—
History.   I. Crittenden, Robert.   II. Title.
DU740.S34   1991
995.3—dc20   90-41760
                                                            CIP

Please remember that this is a library book,
and that it belongs only temporarily to each
person who uses it. Be considerate. Do
not write in this, or any, library book.

DATE DUE

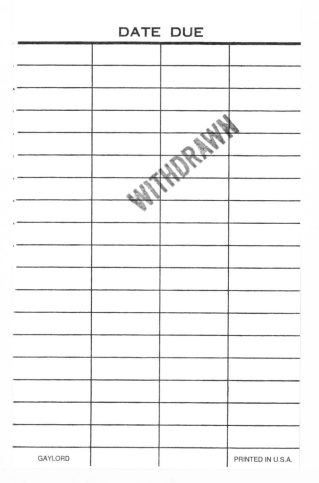

GAYLORD   PRINTED IN U.S.A.